THE MANY-FACED ARGUMENT

THE MANY-FACED ARGUMENT

Recent Studies on the Ontological Argument for the Existence of God

EDITED BY

JOHN HICK and ARTHUR C. McGILL

THE MACMILLAN COMPANY, *New York*

For permission to reprint from copyrighted material acknowledgment is made to:

The John Knox Press and The SCM Press, Ltd., for Karl Barth's *Anselm: Fides Quaerens Intellectum*, translated by Ian Robertson (London: SCM Press, and Richmond, Va.: John Knox Press, 1960); Librairie Philosophique J. Vrin, Paris, for A. Beckaert's "Une Justification Platonicienne," A. Forest's "L'Argument dans la Philosophie reflexive," and A. Hayen's "St. Anselme et St. Thomas," here translated by Arthur C. McGill, from *Spicilegium Beccense* (1959); Aschendorffsche Verlagsbuchhandlung, West Germany, for "Zur Theologie Anselms im Prosologion" by Father Anselm Stoltz, originally published by Winfriedbundes in *Catholica* (1933), and here translated by Arthur C. McGill; George Allen & Unwin, Ltd. (London), and The Macmillan Company (New York), for Bertrand Russell's *Logic and Knowledge*, edited by Robert C. Marsh (1956); *Mind* for Jerome Shaffer's "Existence, Predication and the Ontological Argument" (July 1962), Gilbert Ryle's "Mr. Collingwood and the Ontological Argument" (April 1935) and "Back to the Ontological Argument" (January 1937), and E. E. Harris' "Mr. Ryle and the Ontological Argument" (October 1936); Prentice-Hall, Inc., for Norman Malcolm's *Knowledge and Certainty* (1963); *Union Seminary Quarterly Review* for Charles Hartshorne's "What did Anselm Discover" (Vol. XVII, 1962); The Open Court Publishing Co., La Salle, Illinois, for Charles Hartshorne's *Logic of Perfection*.

Library of Congress Catalog Card Number: 67-12340

FIRST PRINTING

The Macmillan Company, New York
Collier-Macmillan Canada Ltd., Toronto, Ontario

Printed in the United States of America

CONTENTS

Part II. The Argument in Recent Philosophy

Preface

RECENT decades have seen a great and growing interest in the ontological argument for the existence of God, and a considerable twentieth-century literature has grown up around it. This interest, however, arises from very diverse points of view—historical, theological and philosophical—between which there has so far been little interplay. One of the purposes of this volume is to bring together writings of these different kinds, so that workers in each discipline may have contributions from the other fields readily available.

There has been an intense and many-sided investigation of the meaning of the argument for the man who first proposed it, Anselm of Canterbury. We provide both a survey and a sampling of this discussion in Part I of the present volume. Arthur C. McGill is chiefly responsible for the selection and translation of this material.

The argument has perennially fascinated the philosophical mind, and not least in the present century. The essays in Part II indicate the major recent developments in this area, and for the selection of these, John Hick is mainly responsible.

It is not possible within the limits of a single volume, of course, to do justice to all the important literature on this subject. We have chosen the following essays, first because of their intrinsic importance, but also to reflect the scope and variety of recent work. The bibliography at the end of this volume has been carefully selected, while surveying all the important lines of thought now being pursued on this subject. In connection with this bibliography, we are grateful for the help given us by William M. Frierson.

Note. References to the writings of Anselm first designate the title and chapter of the work, and then in parentheses give the volume, the page and the line where a particular passage occurs in the *Opera omnia S. Anselmi*, edited by Francis S. Schmitt (Thomas Nelson & Sons, 1946ff.).

PART I

The Argument in Anselm

I

Anselm of Canterbury

Proslogion

CHAPTERS II-IV[1]

In 1077, when he was prior of the Abbey of Bec in Normandy, Anselm wrote the *Monologion*, an extended meditation on the Christian understanding of God. He was dissatisfied with its logical complexity, however, and began to investigate whether everything which Christians believe about God's reality could be established by means of "a single *argumentum*," that is, by means of reasoning which develops the implications of a single premise.[2] After a period of much earnest and fruitless effort, the principle for which he was looking suddenly presented itself to him: God is "that than which a greater cannot be conceived."[3] As he said later, the meaning of this statement "is so forceful (*tantum vim*) that, by the very fact it is understood or conceived, the reality which it expresses is proved necessarily to exist in actuality *and* to be whatever we are bound to believe about the divine substance."[4] Probably in 1078 he wrote down his discovery as a meditation of twenty-six chapters.[5] He first entitled it *Fides quaerens intellectum*, then *Alloquium de ratione fidei*, and finally *Proslogion*.[6]

[1] St Anselm, *Opera omnia*, ed. by Dom F. S. Schmitt (I. 101-104). Translated by Arthur C. McGill.

[2] Anselm explains his project in the Preface to the *Proslogion* (I. 93.2-10). In his biography of Anselm, Eadmer makes the same point: "After this [the *Monologion*], it came into his mind to investigate whether that which is believed and preached concerning God could be proved (*probari*) by one, single, brief argument." *Life of St. Anselm* I. 19 (in R. W. Southern's translation, p. 29).

[3] *Prosl.* Preface (I. 93.10-19).

[4] *Reply* to Gaunilo, X (I. 138.30-139.3). Italics added.

[5] On the dating of Anselm's works, see Dom F. S. Schmitt, "Zur Chronologie der Werke des hl. Anselm," *Revue Bénédictine* XLIV (1932), pp. 322-350.

[6] On these names, see *Prosl.* Preface (I. 94.6-13) and *Epistle* 109 (III. 242.7-12).

Chapters II, III and IV are those concerned with God's existence. In the manuscripts each chapter constitutes a single paragraph. However, since Anselm shapes his writing with the utmost care for dialectics, the translator has taken the liberty of marking off each step of the reasoning as a separate paragraph and of roughly indicating its function with shoulder notes.

Chapter II. That God Truly Is

Opening Prayer O Lord, you who give understanding to faith, so far as you know it to be beneficial, give me to understand that you are just as we believe, and that you are what we believe.[7]

Starting Point We certainly believe that you are something than which nothing greater can be conceived.[8]

The Problem But is there any such nature, since "the fool has said in his heart: God is not"?[9]

Step 1 However, when this very same fool hears what I say, when he hears of "something than which nothing greater can be conceived," he certainly understands what he hears.

Step 2 What he understands stands in relation to his understanding (*esse in intellectu*), even if he does not understand that it exists.[10] For it is one thing for a thing to stand in

[7] If the clause "just as we believe" is taken in a parenthetical sense, so that the sentence reads, "give me to understand that you are (just as we believe), and that you are what we believe," then Anselm is making the familiar distinction between the fact of God's existence and the character of God's nature. However, if, as Anselm Stolz argues (see p. 200 n. 84), the clause "just as we believe" is taken in an adverbial sense, modifying the verb "is," then the statement makes no reference at all to the fact of God's existence. It simply distinguishes between understanding that God exists in the very special way which we believe (namely, as the self-existent one from whom everything else derives its being), and understanding that those attributes—the "what"—which our faith teaches belong to this very special way.

[8] On the terms of this key expression, see pp. 119ff.

[9] Vulgate Ps. 13:1; A.V. Ps. 14:1 and 53:1. Before Anselm, Augustine had used this Biblical text to raise the question of God's existence, in *On Free Will* II.ii.

[10] The meaning of Anselm's phrase *esse in intellectu* has been the subject of much discussion. I have found little evidence that the word *intellectus* ever suggested to Anselm, as it does to us, an organ (such as the mind) or a faculty (such as the intellect). It was chiefly the noun form of the verb *intelligere* and

relation to our understanding; it is another thing for us to understand that it really exists. For instance, when a painter imagines what he is about to paint, he has it in relation to his understanding. However, he does not yet understand that it exists, because he has not yet made it. After he paints it, then he both has it in relation to his understanding and understands that it exists. Therefore, even the fool is convinced that "something than which nothing greater can be conceived" at least stands in relation to his understanding, because when he hears of it he understands it, and whatever he understands stands in relation to his understanding.[11]

And certainly that than which a greater cannot be conceived cannot stand only in relation to the understanding. **Step 3**
For if it stands at least in relation to the understanding, it can be conceived to be also in reality, and this is something greater.[12]

---

signified the *act* of understanding. "To be *in intellectu*," therefore, does not mean "to be located in the intellect," inside the human head, as if this were a place, but to be located *in relation to* human thinking, to be present to the human act of understanding. Similarly, *esse in vise* does not mean "to be in the eyeball." See Adolf Kolping, *Anselms Proslogion-Beweis der Existenz Gottes* (Bonn, 1939), pp. 114f. When Anselm does want to speak of "place" with regard to mental activities, he uses the term *anima* (*Monol.* XXIII. I. 41.28f.; *De Concord.* III. 11, II. 274f.). To avoid the peculiar overtones of subjectivism and interiority which are today associated with the phrase "to be *in* the understanding" but which were completely foreign to Anselm, I have consistently translated *esse in intellectu* as "to stand in relation to the understanding." Anselm's remarks about this in *Reply* II (I. 132.10-21) seem to justify this translation. See p. 82.

[11] In making this shift in Step 2 from *intelligere* to *esse in intellectu*, Anselm is moving the focus from the human activity, as related to some mental object, to the presence of that mental object to the human activity, still without prejudicing the question of this object's actual existence one way or the other. Anselm is contending that we can think about something and analyze it, even before we have understood whether it actually exists or not, just like the painter with his as-yet-unpainted picture. For Anselm, then, the act of considering what would be characteristic of something than which nothing greater can be conceived does not require him or the fool to presume its real existence. Anselm also stresses this in *Reply* VIII (I. 137.6-10; translated on p. 19 f.).

[12] There is a problem in this sentence. Anselm writes that "if it is *vel in solo intellectu*, it can be conceived to be also (*et*) in reality." But if it stands in relation to the understanding "only" (*solo*), does not that exclude any possibility of its being conceived to stand outside the mind "also"? Does not this *solo* mean, "nowhere except in the understanding"? The word *vel* before the phrase *in solo intellectu* resolves this problem. For as an intensive particle, *vel* can be a synonym for *saltem*. In that case it would modify the phrase so that *solo* would no longer carry its full disjunctive force ("in relation to the understanding only and nowhere else"), and the phrase would then mean, "*at least* in relation to the understanding." *Vel* clearly carries this meaning in the last sentence of Step 2 above (I. 101.14f.), in *Reply* I (I. 131.1f., 131.6f.) and in *Reply* II (I. 132.22). See F. S. Schmitt in *Theologische Revue*, 1933, p. 222.

Therefore, if "that than which a greater cannot be conceived" only stood in relation to the understanding, then "that than which a greater cannot be conceived" would be something than which a greater can be conceived. But this is certainly impossible.

Conclusion — Therefore, something than which a greater cannot be conceived undoubtedly both stands in relation to the understanding and exists in reality.

Chapter III. That It Is Impossible To Conceive That God Is Not

First Part

The Thesis — This so truly is that it is impossible to think of it as not existing.

Step 1 — It can be conceived to be something such tnat we cannot conceive of it as not existing.

Step 2 — This is greater than something which we can conceive of as not existing.

Step 3 — Therefore, if that than which a greater cannot be conceived could be conceived not to be, we would have an impossible contradition: That than which a greater cannot be conceived would not be that than which a greater cannot be conceived.

Conclusion — Therefore, something than which a greater cannot be conceived so truly is that it is impossible even to conceive of it as not existing.

Second Part

The Thesis — This is you, O Lord our God. You so truly are that you cannot be thought not to be. And rightly so.

Reason 1 — For if some mind could conceive of something better than you, the creature would rise above its Creator and would judge its Creator, which would be completely absurd.

Reason 2 — Also, whatever else there is, except for you alone, can be conceived not to be.[13]

[13] Behind this statement lies the idea expressed in *Prosl.* XX (I. 115.23-25),

Therefore, you alone, of all things exist in the truest and greatest way (*verissime et maxime esse*), for nothing else so truly exists and therefore everything else has less being. **Conclusion**

Why, then, did the fool say in his heart: "God is not," since it is so obvious to the rational mind that you exist supremely above all things? Why, because he is stupid and foolish. **The Fool's Folly**

Chapter IV. How the Fool Said in His Heart What Cannot Be Conceived

How was the fool able to "say in his heart" what he was unable to conceive? Or how was it that he could not conceive what he said in his heart? For to "say in one's heart" and to "conceive" are the same thing. **The Problem**

However, if—or rather because—he really did conceive of it (since he said it in his heart) and yet did not really say it in his heart (since he was unable to conceive of it), then there must be more than one way for something to be said in one's heart, or to be conceived. **The Solution**

Indeed, a thing is conceived of in one way when the word signifying it is thought; in another way when the very thing itself is understood. **Step 1**

Accordingly, God can be conceived not to be in the first way, but not at all in the second.[14] Certainly no one **Step 2**

---

that in the case of a creature, which does not have the source of its being within itself, when it is thought about, there is nothing in it to prevent the mind from conceiving of its end and nonexistence. In *Reply* I (I. 131.31-132.3), Anselm explains this in a different way: "Whatever does not exist in its totality in any place or at any time, even if it does exist, it can be conceived not to exist." That is to say, there is a segment of reality which the mind can think about without having to acknowledge the existence of such a thing. But God does exist *semper et ubique totum*, so that there is nowhere for the mind to go to conceive of his nonexistence. Hence, Anselm's statement here in *Prosl.* III: except for you alone, O God (who exist from yourself and omnipresently), whatever else there is can be conceived not to exist.

[14] At this point in several later manuscripts the following sentences are added: "For no one who understands what fire and water are can think that the reality of fire is the reality of water. At the level of words, however, this confusion is possible." A comparison of the manuscripts clearly shows that this is a later interpolation.

who understands what God is can conceive that God is not. It is possible, however, for him to say this word in his heart, while giving it either no meaning at all or some alien meaning.

God is that than which a greater cannot be conceived. **Conclusion** Whoever understands this correctly at least understands that he exists in such a way that even for thought he cannot not exist. Therefore, whoever understands that God is so cannot even conceive that he is not.

My thanksgiving to you, good Lord, my thanksgiving **Closing Prayer** to you. For what I first believed through your giving I now so understand through your illumination that even if I did not want to believe that you are, I would be unable not to understand it.[15]

[15] In other places, Anselm makes just the reverse statement. Cf. *CurDeus homo?* I.1 (II. 48.19-21): "I consider myself to hold the faith of our redemption by the prevenient grace of God, so that even if I were not able to understand it in any way, nothing could shake the constancy [of my belief]."

II

Gaunilo and Anselm

Criticism and Reply[1]

A criticism of the proof, entitled *On Behalf of the Fool*, was sent to Anselm, prompting him to write a detailed *Reply*.[2] This criticism is attributed to Gaunilo (or Wenilo), a monk of the Convent of Marmoutier near Tours.[3]

Anselm's *Reply* poses something of a problem, since it is not a systematic treatment of either the original argument in the *Proslogion* or of Gaunilo's criticism. Rather, it has the character of a series of notes which Anselm put together without much attention to overall unity or development. Even the division of the *Reply* into ten chapters is a later publishing device, which gives a superficial impression of organization that is actually nonexistent.[4]

For this reason, it has been decided in the translation which fol-

[1] St. Anselm, *Opera Omnia*, ed. Dom F. S. Schmitt, I. 125-139. Translated by Arthur C. McGill. Here also, *esse in intellectu* is rendered "to stand in relation to the understanding."

[2] Of the nineteen extant manuscripts which contain Chapters II-IV of the *Proslogion*, nine also include this criticism and reply (I. 91).

[3] Two manuscripts used by Gerberon for his 1721 edition of Anselm's works identify Gaunilo as the author of this criticism. (See *Patrologia Latina*, vol. 158, col. 241, note 930.) Schmitt, however, indicates no such information in the manuscripts which he used for his edition (I. 125, notes on lines 1-2), and in his biography, Eadmer merely speaks of "a certain person (*quisdam*) who found fault with one of the arguments . . . and composed a writing against it." (*Life of St Anselm*, I. xix, p. 31.) If the author was a Gaunilo of Marmoutier, then he was probably Gaunilo, Count of Montigni, who was born about 1000, entered the convent in 1044 after some personal misfortunes, and lived there at least until 1083. This biographical information is reviewed by Barthélemy Hauréau, *Singularités historiques et littéraires* (Paris, 1861), pp. 201-205, and is derived from E. Martène, *Histoire de l'abbaye de Marmoutier*, vol. I, pp. 363-367, which was completed in 1707 but not published until 1874-1875.

[4] For various theories about the literary form of Anselm's *Reply*, see Adolf Kolping, *Anselms Proslogion-Beweis der Existenz Gottes*, pp. 100f.

lows not to offer the *Reply* as a continuous whole, but to place each unit of Anselm's discussion beside that passage by Gaunilo to which it is directed. In almost every case, Anselm's remarks make clear with which particular criticism they are concerned. The material is organized in the following way:

1. Gaunilo Para. 4: God cannot be conceived by man.
   A. *Reply* Intro. (I. 130.3-5).
   B. *Reply* I (I. 130.12-19).
   C. *Reply* II (I. 132.10-21).
   D. *Reply* I (I. 132.3-9).
   E. *Reply* VIII (I. 137.11-138.2).
   F. *Reply* IX (I. 138.4-19).

2. Gaunilo Para. 2: "That than which nothing greater can be conceived" is known in the same way as any false or dubious thing.
   A. *Reply* VI (I. 136.3-10, 17-21).
   B. *Reply* VI (I. 136.10-17).

3. Gaunilo Para. 2: Hearing "that than which nothing greater can be conceived" no more compels assent than hearing the word "God."
   Reply VII (I. 136.22-137.5).

4. Gaunilo Para. 3: The example of the unpainted picture is misleading.
   Reply VIII (I. 137.6-10).

5. Gaunilo Para. 5: Understanding something when it is named does not establish its existence.
   A. *Reply* II (I. 132.22-133.2).
   B. *Reply* I (I. 131.12-17).
   C. *Reply* I (I. 130.20-131.5).

6. Gaunilo Para. 6: The "Lost Island" criticism.
   Reply III (I. 133.3-9).

7. Gaunilo Para. 7: "That than which nothing greater can be conceived" can be conceived not to exist.
   A. *Reply* IX (I. 138.19-27).
   B. *Reply* III (I. 133.10-20).
   C. *Reply* I (I. 131.6-11).
   D. *Reply* I (I. 131.18-132.2).

8. Gaunilo Para. 7: It should be said that God's nonexistence cannot be "understood," not that it cannot be "conceived."
   Reply IV (I. 133.21-134.19).

9. Gaunilo Para. 1: Gaunilo's misstatement of the argument.
   Reply V (I. 134.24-136.2).

10. Gaunilo Para. 8: Conclusions.
Reply X (I. 138.28-139.12).

I.

Gaunilo argues that God's reality cannot stand in relation to the understanding of any man, much less in relation to that of the fool.

Gaunilo

PARA. 4 (I. 126.29-127.23)

It is said that there is "that which is greater than everything that can be conceived" and that this can be nothing else than God himself. When I hear that, however, I can as little conceive of it or have it in relation to my understanding, either according to its reality (*secundum rem*) or from some species or genus known to me, as I could conceive of or have in relation to my understanding God himself. And because I cannot conceive of God himself or have him in relation to my understanding, I am able to think that he does not exist. For I neither know the reality itself which is God, nor can I infer it from other similar things, since, as you yourself assert, his reality is such that it cannot be similar to anything.[5]

For if there is some man completely unknown to me, of whose existence I know nothing, and if nevertheless I should hear something about him, I can still think about him, even according to his reality, through that special or general notion by which I know what a man is or what men are. It might happen, of course, that the one who speaks to me is lying, and that the man about whom I am thinking does not exist. In that case, when I am thinking about him, I think of him on the basis of the true reality, not of this particular man, but of man in general.

Therefore, when I hear the words "God" or "something greater than everything," I cannot have that in relation to my conception or my understanding as I have this false, nonexistent man. While I can

5 Anselm asserts no such thing. On the contrary, he says (*Prosl.* XVII) that "You, O Lord God, have these attributes in yourself, in your ineffable mode, while you have given them to your creatures in their sensible mode." In *Monol.* XXXI Anselm explores in detail how creatures can be "more or less *like*" their Creator.

think of the latter on the basis of a true reality known to me [namely, of man in general], I cannot know the former at all, except on the basis of a word (*secundum vocem*). Solely on that basis, something true can rarely, if ever, be known. When "that which is greater than all things" is known as something true, it is not so much the words themselves which are known (although they are a true reality, that is, a sound of letters and syllables), as the signification of the words.

However [in the case of the fool who hears the argument], this is not known as if by someone who knows what is customarily signified by these words, by someone, that is, who knows it according to its reality, in a strictly true knowledge; but as if by someone who does not know it in its reality, and who thinks of it in one way only, according to the movement effected in his mind by hearing these words, and according to the meaning which he tries to fashion from the words heard. It would be astonishing if he ever hit upon the truth of its reality in this way.

It is firmly established, then, that when I hear and understand someone saying that there is "something greater than everything which can be conceived," I have this in my understanding not otherwise [than according to the words heard].

Anselm

A. REPLY INTRO. (I. 130.3-5)

Since the fool against whom I spoke in my little work does not refute me in these statements, but someone not a fool, who is a Catholic speaking on behalf of the fool, it is enough for me to reply to the Catholic.

B. REPLY I (I. 130.12-19)

I say: If "that than which a greater cannot be conceived" is neither understood nor conceived, and therefore does not stand in relation to the understanding or to conception, then certainly either God is not "that than which a greater cannot be conceived," or God is not understood or conceived and does not stand in relation to the understanding or to conception. I use your faith and conscience [as a Catholic] as a most compelling argument that this is false. Consequently, "that than which a greater cannot be conceived" is genuinely understood and conceived, and does stand in relation to the understanding and to conception. And, therefore, either the opinions by which you try to controvert me are not true, or what you infer from these opinions does not follow.

C. REPLY II (I. 132.10-21)

In my argument which you criticize, I said that when the fool hears "that than which a greater cannot be conceived" stated, he understands what he hears. To be sure, whoever does not understand when familiar words are spoken to him either has no understanding at all or a very obtuse one. I then said that if this expression is understood, it stands in relation to the understanding. But how can that stand in relation to no understanding which is demonstrated to exist necessarily in reality?

You say, however, that even if it stands in relation to the understanding, it still does not follow that it is really understood. Consider how to stand in relation to the understanding follows from the fact that it is understood. For just as that which is conceived is conceived by [the act of] conception; and that which is conceived by conception, just as it is conceived, so it stands in relation to conception—in the same way that which is understood is understood by [the act of] understanding; and what is understood by understanding, just as it is understood, so it stands in relation to understanding. What can be clearer?

D. REPLY I (I. 132.3-9)

Do you think that that about which these matters are understood can be partially conceived or understood, or can stand partially in relation to conception or to the understanding? If not, then it cannot be understood at all. If you say that this is not understood at all or does not stand in relation to the understanding because it is not understood *completely*, you should also say that the man who cannot look directly at the pure light of the sun does not see daylight, which is nothing else but the light of the sun. Certainly "that than which a greater cannot be conceived" is understood and does stand in relation to the understanding at least to this extent, that these matters concerning it are understood.

E. REPLY VIII (I. 137.11-138.3)

Further, you say with regard to "that than which a greater cannot be conceived" that when you hear of it, you cannot conceive of it through its own reality or through anything known to you by genus or species, and that you cannot have it in relation to your understanding because you can neither know it directly nor learn about it from other things similar to it. It is obvious, however, that the situation is quite otherwise.

Since everything less good is, insofar as it is good, similar to a greater good, it is evident to any rational mind that we can ascend from lesser goods to greater goods, and then, from those things through which we conceive of something greater, we can infer a great deal about "that than which nothing greater can be conceived." Who, for example, cannot at least conceive—even if he does not believe that what he is conceiving actually exists—that if there is something good which has both a beginning and an end, a good which has a beginning but no end is much better; and that better even than this is that which has neither beginning nor end, even if it were always passing from the past through the present to the future; and far better still—without regard to whether it actually exists—is that which in no way needs or is forced to be changed or be moved? Cannot such a thing be conceived? Can something greater than this be conceived? In this process, are we not taking those things through which we can conceive of something greater, and conceiving of that than which a greater cannot be conceived?[6]

This, therefore, is the source from which can be conceived "that than which a greater cannot be conceived." In this way the fool who does not accept sacred authority can easily be refuted, should he deny that "that than which a greater cannot be conceived" can be inferred from other things. If any Catholic would deny this, however, he should remember that "ever since the creation of the world, the invisible things of God, namely, his eternal power and deity, have been clearly perceived by the mind through those things which have been made" (Rom. 1:20).

[6] Here Anselm says that, by trying to think of the greatest good, a man only gains a *conception* of something than which nothing greater can be conceived. He does not establish the real existence of such a reality. In *Monol.* I-IV, however, Anselm uses this very procedure to prove the real existence of God.

F. REPLY IX (I. 138.4–19)

Even if it were true that the reality of "that than which a greater cannot be conceived" could not be conceived or understood, nevertheless it would not be false to say that [the expression] "that than which a greater cannot be conceived" can be conceived and can be understood. For example, nothing prevents "inexpressible" from being expressed, although the reality which is called inexpressible cannot itself be expressed.[7] In the same way "inconceivable" can be conceived, although that which is properly called inconceivable cannot be conceived. Therefore, when [the expression] "that than which nothing greater can be conceived" is spoken, what is heard can undoubtedly be conceived and understood, even if the reality itself than which a greater cannot be conceived cannot be conceived or understood. And even if anyone were so foolish as to say that "something than which a greater cannot be conceived" does not exist, he still would not be so impudent as to say that he could not understand or conceive what was said. Or, if such a person were found, his words should be discredited and he himself denounced.

Whoever denies that there exists something than which a greater cannot be conceived at least understands and conceives of the denial which he makes. But he cannot understand or conceive of this denial without understanding or conceiving of its parts, one of which is [the expression] "that than which a greater cannot be conceived." Therefore, whoever denies that this exists does understand and does conceive of "that than which a greater cannot be conceived."

2.

Gaunilo argues that if "that than which nothing greater can be conceived" is not known by some special kind of knowledge, then it is understood no differently from any other false or dubious thing.

Gaunilo

PARA. 2 (I. 125.14-126.4; 126.8-13)

It is said that this now stands in relation to my understanding for no other reason than that I understand what is said.

7 Anselm develops this same point in *Monol.* LXV.

But could I not be said to have in relation to my understanding all sorts of things that are false and do not exist in themselves in any way at all, since when someone speaks, I understand whatever he may say?

Certainly, with this exception: if that being's reality is so firmly established that it cannot be conceived in the same way as every false or dubious thing. In that case, however, I am not said to "conceive" (*cogitare*) of that which I have heard or to have it in relation to my "conception," but to "understand" (*intelligere*) it and to have it in relation to my "understanding." Only then would I not be able to conceive of this, except by understanding it, that is, except by comprehending rationally that it exists in reality. If this were so, however, there would be no difference between what comes earlier in time, which is to have a thing in relation to one's understanding, and what comes later, which is to understand that the thing exists—a difference seen in the example of the picture, which first stands in relation to the understanding of the painter and only later exists in the work. . . .

Finally, that this reality so exists that, as soon as it is conceived, it can be known only by means of a certain understanding of its indubitable existence—this must be proved to me by an incontestible argument. However, the one which we have been given—that this object now stands in relation to my understanding, since I understand what is heard—will not do. I believe that all sorts of uncertain or even false things can stand in relation to my understanding in this way, since I understand the words for them when they are spoken. This would be even more true if I, who still do not believe this argument, were deceived by such words and were to believe them, as often happens.

Anselm

A. REPLY VI (I. 136.3-10,17-21)

You raise the objection that anything false or dubious can be understood and can be in relation to the understanding in the same way as that about which I was speaking. I wonder what you see here against my desire to prove something doubtful. For this it was enough at first that I showed that this is understood and does stand in relation to the understanding in any way at all, since I later considered whether it only stands in relation to the understanding and so is false, or is also in reality and therefore true. Now if false and dubious things are understood and stand in relation to the understanding in such a way that, when they are spoken of, the one who hears of them understands the significance of what is said, that poses no obstacles to my assertion that ["that than which nothing greater can be conceived"] is understood and does stand in relation to the understanding. . . . Even if false things are understood in some way, and even if my definition applies not to all understanding but only to a certain kind, I ought not to be criticized for saying that "that than which a greater cannot be conceived" is understood and stands in relation to the understanding, even before it is certain that this exists in reality.

B. REPLY VI (I. 136.10–17)

Moreover, how can your two statements be reconciled, first, that if anyone says something false, you will "understand" him, whatever he might say; and secondly, that when something is heard which is not held in thought in the manner of something false, it is not "conceived" or grasped by "conception," but is "understood" and grasped by the "understanding"? For you say that you cannot think of this in any way except by an act of "understanding," that is, except by comprehending with true knowledge (*scientia*) that the thing itself exists.[8] How, I ask, can it be reconciled both that false things are "understood," and that to "understand" is to comprehend with true knowledge that a thing exists? Since this is no concern of mine, I leave it to you.

3.

Gaunilo argues that if "that than which nothing greater can be conceived" is not known by some special kind of knowledge, hearing of it no more compels the fool's assent than hearing the word "God."

Gaunilo

PARA. 2 (I. 126.4-7)

Furthermore, it can hardly be credible that when this something

[8] This distinction between "conceiving" and "understanding" is further elaborated in No. 8, p. 28 f.

["than which nothing greater can be conceived"] is spoken of and heard, it can be conceived not to exist in some other way than the way in which "God" can be conceived not to exist. But if both of these are conceived not to exist in the same way, why did you undertake all this argumentation against the one who denies or doubts that such a reality exists?

Anselm

REPLY VII (I. 136.22-137.5)

Next you assert that it can hardly be credible that, when "that than which a greater cannot be conceived" is spoken of and heard, it can be conceived not to exist in a way different from that in which "God" can be conceived not to exist. Even those who have achieved very little knowledge of controversy and argumentation could answer this criticism for me!

For is it reasonable for someone to deny the reality of what he does understand, simply because it is said to be something which he does not understand and therefore something which he should deny? Furthermore, if that which is partially understood is sometimes denied, and if that which is not understood at all is altogether denied, is it not easier to prove the reality of something doubtful from that which is partially understood than from that which is not understood at all? Therefore, it is not credible that someone should deny the reality of "that than which a greater cannot be conceived," of which he has heard and which he partially understands, simply because he denies the reality of "God," the meaning of which he does not know at all. Furthermore, if the former is denied because it is not perfectly understood, nevertheless is it not easier to prove the reality of that which is somewhat understood than the reality of that which is not understood at all? Therefore, in order to prove that God exists against the fool, I have not been irrational in using "that than which a greater cannot be conceived." For while he does not understand the word "God" at all, he has some understanding of this.

4.

Gaunilo argues that the example of the unpainted picture is misleading, because it confuses the conceiving of independently real objects with the conceiving of man-made objects.

Gaunilo

PARA. 3 (I. 126.14-28)

The example of the painter who now has before his understanding the picture which he is about to paint cannot sufficiently fit this argument.

Before it is painted, that picture is held in the artistic imagination of the painter, and what is in someone's artistic imagination is nothing but part of his understanding. For, as St. Augustine said, the carpenter who wants to build a chest through his labor first has this chest in his imagination. The productive principle here is not the chest which is made by his labor, but the chest which stands in his imagination. For what produces here is the soul of the craftsman, in which all such [man-made] things exist before they are produced. And what else is this principle in the productive soul of the artificer but his knowledge or understanding?[9]

However, except for these [man-made] things which are known to arise from the nature of the human mind, everything else which is heard or thought and which is perceived by the understanding to be true is in its reality one thing, while the understanding which grasps it is another.

Therefore, even if it is true that something exists than which nothing greater can be conceived, nevertheless when this is heard and understood, it is not like a not-yet-painted picture in the understanding of the painter [i.e., it is not a reality originating in the human mind].

Anselm

REPLY VIII (I. 137.6-10)

You laboriously prove that "that than which a greater cannot be conceived" is not like the unpainted picture in the mind of the painter. There is no cause for this criticism.

I did not use the merely conceived picture in order to claim that the object of my discussion was that same sort of thing. Rather I used

[9] In this paragraph, Gaunilo has given a condensed version of Augustine's description of human making in *The Gospel of John*, Tractate I.17.

it in order to show that something can stand in relation to the understanding even while it is understood not to exist.

5.

Gaunilo argues that understanding something when it is named does not establish its existence if its existence is denied or doubted.

Gaunilo

PARA. 5 (I. 127.25-128.13)

That this exists necessarily in reality is proved to me in this way: If this does not exist, whatever is in reality will be greater than it, in which case that which has just been proved at least to stand in relation to my understanding will not be greater than all things.

To this I reply. If it is said that this stands in relation to the understanding as something which cannot be conceived on the basis of the truth of any real thing, I do not deny that it does stand in relation to the understanding in this way. However, because it cannot possess real existence simply by standing in relation to the understanding, I certainly do not concede that it really exists—at least not until it is proved to me by an indubitable argument.

He who says that this exists because otherwise that which is greater than all would not be greater than all does not sufficiently attend to what is being said. I do not yet say—on the contrary, I deny or doubt—that this is greater than any real thing. I concede to it no other reality (if this can be called "reality") than of something which is absolutely unknown to the mind, but of which the mind tries to conceive on the basis of a word merely heard. Therefore, how is it proved to me that this "greater" exists in reality, simply because it is held to be greater than all things, when I deny or doubt that this is to be held at all? I deny or doubt it so completely, in fact, that in my view this "greater" does not stand in relation to my understanding or conceiving, except in the way in which many doubtful and uncertain things stand there.

It first must be made certain to me that this "greater" is actually somewhere; and only then, from the fact that it is greater than all things, will there be no doubt that it subsists in itself.

Anselm

A. REPLY II (I. 132.22-133.2)[10]

I said that, even if it only stood in relation to the understanding, it could at least be conceived to be also in reality, and that this is greater. Therefore, if it only stood in relation to the understanding, then "that than which a greater *cannot* be conceived" would be that than which a greater *can* be conceived. What, I ask, could be more logical? For if it only stood in relation to the understanding, could it not be conceived to be in reality also? And, if so, then does not anyone who conceives of this existing also in reality conceive of something greater than that which only stands in relation to the understanding? What, therefore, could be more logical than this: If "that than which a greater cannot be conceived" only stands in relation to the understanding, then it is that than which a greater can be conceived? But certainly that than which a greater *can* be conceived does not stand in relation to any understanding as "that than which a greater *cannot* be conceived."

Does it not therefore follow that if "that than which a greater cannot be conceived" exists in relation to *any* understanding, it does not only exist in relation to the understanding? For if it only existed in relation to the understanding, it would then be that than which a greater can be conceived, which is a contradiction.

B. REPLY I (131.12-17)

Let us nevertheless suppose that, even if it can be conceived, it does not exist. Now whatever can be conceived and is not, if it were, it would still not be "that than which a greater cannot be conceived." Therefore, if it were "that than which a greater cannot be conceived," it would not be that than which a greater cannot be conceived—which is utterly absurd. Therefore, if something than which a greater cannot be conceived can be conceived at all, then it is false to say that it does not exist. Much more is this so if it can be understood [and not just conceived] and can stand in relation to the understanding.

[10] Here and in the next passage, Anselm gives an expanded version of the argument in Step 3 of *Prosl.* II.

C. REPLY I (I. 130.20–131.5)

You think that because something than which a greater cannot be conceived is understood, it does not follow that this stands in relation to the understanding, nor that if it does stand in relation to the understanding, it therefore exists in reality.

I, however, say positively: If this can at least be conceived to be, it necessarily follows that it exists. For "that than which a greater cannot be conceived" cannot be conceived to be, except as without a beginning. However, whatever can be conceived to be and actually is not can be conceived to be through a beginning. Therefore, it is not the case that "that than which a greater cannot be conceived" can be conceived to exist and yet does not exist. Therefore, if it can be conceived to be, it necessarily is.[11]

6.

Gaunilo argues that if, in the case of God, "to be the best conceivable" entails "to exist," then we should also be able to demonstrate that the best-conceivable island must exist.

Gaunilo

PARA. 6 (I. 128.14-32)

Consider this example: Certain people say that somewhere in the ocean there is an island, which they call the "Lost Island" because of the difficulty or, rather, the impossibility of finding what does not exist. They say that it is more abundantly filled with inestimable riches and delights than the Isles of the Blessed, and that although it has no owner or inhabitant, it excels all the lands that men inhabit taken together in the unceasing abundance of its fertility.

When someone tells me that there is such an island, I easily understand what is being said, for there is nothing difficult here. Suppose, however, as a consequence of this, that he then goes on to say: You

[11] This argument represents a new form of the proof. It starts from what Anselm takes to be an epistemological fact, namely that when the mind conceives of something that does not exist, it may conceive of it as existing "through a beginning." But "that than which a greater cannot be conceived" cannot be conceived as existing through a beginning. Therefore, if it can be conceived, it cannot also be nonexistent.

cannot doubt that this island, more excellent than all lands, actually exists somewhere in reality, because it undoubtedly stands in relation to your understanding. Since it is more excellent, not simply to stand in relation to the understanding, but to be in reality as well, therefore this island must necessarily be in reality. Otherwise, any other land that exists in reality would be more excellent than this island, and this island, which you understand to be the most excellent of all lands. would then not be the most excellent.

If, I repeat, someone should wish by this argument to demonstrate to me that this island truly exists and is no longer to be doubted, I would think he were joking; or, if I accepted the argument, I do not know whom I would regard as the greater fool, me for accepting it or him for supposing that he had proved the existence of this island with any kind of certainty. He should first show that this excellent island exists as a genuine and undeniably real thing, and not leave it standing in relation to my understanding as a false or uncertain something.

Anselm

REPLY III (I. 133.3-9)

My reasoning, you claim, is as if someone should say that there is an island in the ocean, which surpasses the whole earth in its fertility, but which is called a "Lost Island" because of the difficulty, or even impossibility, of finding something that does not exist; and as if he should then argue that no one can doubt that it actually does exist because the words describing it are easily understood.

I can confidently say that if anyone discovers for me something existing either in fact or at least in thought, other than "that than which a greater cannot be conceived," and is able to apply the logic of my argument to it, I shall find that "Lost Island" for him and shall give it to him as something which he will never lose again.[12]

[12] Anselm apparently found this objection so weak that, instead of giving an extended and closely reasoned answer, he gently mocks Gaunilo. Without making any mention of God or of God's unique nature as a necessary being, he focuses exclusively on the island, and simply asserts that if his key phrase can be applied to this island, then this island does exist.

The point of this rebuke, which may not be immediately evident to modern readers, consists in the fact that such an application is obviously impossible. An island—even an ideal island—can only be a created thing, deriving its reality from beyond itself. In terms of the medieval understanding of "perfection," this would make the island radically imperfect. As Anselm says in *Monol.* XXVIII

7.

Gaunilo argues that since the existence of "that which is greater than all things" has not been proved, it can be conceived not to exist.

Gaunilo

PARA. 7 (I. 129.1-10)

When it is asserted to the fool [in *Prosl.* III] that this "greater than all things" is such that even to thought it cannot not be, and yet when this is proved to him on no other ground than that otherwise this "greater than all things" would not be greater than all things, he can give the same answer [as No. 5 above] and reply: When did *I* ever say that such a being, one that is "greater than all things," exists in reality, so that from this you could prove to me that it exists so fully in reality that it cannot be conceived not to be? First of all, it should be proved by some most certain argument that some superior reality, that is, a nature which is greater and better than everything that is, actually exists. From this we can then prove all the other qualities which must not be lacking from that which is greater and better than all things.

Anselm

A. REPLY IX (I. 138.19-27)

That which cannot possibly not be is obviously something that can

(I. 46.2f.), anything which must receive its reality from another "hardly *exists* at all," in any proper sense of the word.

Although Anselm does not consider it necessary to explain such an obvious point, this is made explicit by Bonaventure: "Against the objection of an island than which nothing better or greater can be conceived, we must say that there is no similarity [between this subject and this predicate]. For when I say 'a being than which nothing greater can be conceived,' there is no repugnance here between the subject and the predicate, so that this being can be conceived in a rational way. But when I say 'an island than which nothing greater can be conceived,' there is a repugnance between the subject and the predicate. For 'island' refers to a defective being, while the predicate designates the most perfect of beings. Therefore, since there is a direct opposition here, this island is conceived irrationally, and in thinking it the mind is divided against itself. It is no wonder, therefore, that we cannot infer that this island exists in reality. It is otherwise, however, in the case of 'being' or 'God,' since this is not repugnant to the predicate." (*De Myst. Trin.* Q. I, a. 1, *sol. opp.* 6, given by A. Daniels, *Geschichte der Gottesbeweise*, p. 40.)

be conceived and understood. He who conceives of this conceives of something greater than he who conceives of that which has the possibility of not being. Therefore, while he is conceiving of "that than which a greater cannot be conceived," if he conceives that it has the possibility of not being, he is obviously not conceiving of "that than which a greater cannot be conceived." However, the same thing cannot be both conceived and not conceived at the same time. Therefore, he who conceives of "that than which a greater cannot be conceived" is not conceiving of what can, but of what cannot possibly, not be. For that reason, what he is conceiving must necessarily exist, because whatever is able not to exist is not that of which he is conceiving.

B. REPLY III (I. 133.10-20)[13]

It is now obvious, however, that "that than which a greater cannot be conceived" cannot be conceived not to be, because it exists with the undoubted ground of truth itself. Otherwise, it would not exist at all.

Let us suppose that someone says that he does conceive that this does not exist. In my view, when he is conceiving in this way, he is either conceiving of "that than which a greater cannot be conceived," or he is not conceiving of it. If he is not conceiving of it, then it is not this which he thinks does not exist. On the other hand, if he is really conceiving of it, he at least conceives of something which cannot be conceived not to be. For if it could be conceived not to be, it could also be conceived to have a beginning and an end. But this is impossible [in the case of "that than which a greater cannot be conceived"]. Therefore, whoever really conceives of this conceives of something which cannot be conceived not to be. Whoever really conceives of it, then, does not in fact conceive that it is not. Otherwise, he would be conceiving of something which cannot be conceived. Therefore, "that than which a greater cannot be conceived" cannot be conceived not to be.

C. REPLY I (I. 131.6-11)

Further, if it can be conceived in any way at all, it is necessarily the

13 Because this passage immediately follows Anselm's remark about the "Lost Island," some commentators include it in his answer to that criticism. See, for instance, Karl Barth, *Anselm*, German p. 166, English p. 145. There is nothing in its contents, however, to associate it with the "Lost Island."

case that it exists. For while someone may deny or doubt the existence of something than which a greater cannot be conceived, he will not deny or doubt that, if it does exist, then in fact and for the understanding it is impossible for it not to be. Otherwise, it would not be that than which a greater cannot be conceived. As for things which can be conceived and yet do not exist, even if such things were to exist, in fact and for the understanding it is possible for them not to be. Therefore, if "that than which a greater cannot be conceived" can be conceived at all, it cannot not be.[14]

D. REPLY I (I. 131.18-132.2)[15]

Further still I say: Doubtless whatever does not exist in some place or at some time, even if it does exist in some other place or at some other time, can nevertheless be conceived to exist at no time and in no place, just as it does not exist at some time or in some place. For that which did not exist yesterday and does exist today can be conceived never to exist, just as it is understood not to have existed yesterday. And that which does not exist here but does exist elsewhere can be understood not to exist anywhere, just as it does not exist here. Similarly, if the individual parts of something are not

[14] In the first passage in this section (No. 7A), Anselm argues that conceiving of the nonexistence of "that than which a greater cannot be conceived" is a contradiction. In the second passage (7B) he shows that the mind cannot conceive of such a contradiction. Here in 7C he uses man's *subjective* inability to think of God's nonexistence as a datum to prove the *objective* impossibility of that nonexistence. He passes from the datum to the conclusion by means of his epistemological principle that whenever we conceive of something that does exist but might not exist, that thing always shows the possibility of its nonexistence to our minds. However, in the case of "that than which a greater cannot be conceived," we have something which our minds cannot possibly conceive of as not existing (7B) and which therefore does not show any possibility of its nonexistence to our minds. Anselm can now appeal to his epistemological principle and argue that, since in fact this does not show any possibility of its nonexistence to our minds (that is, since our minds really conceive of it as something which they cannot conceive of as nonexisting), there is objectively within it no possibility of its nonexistence.

[15] Here Anselm is not concerned with proving that "that than which nothing greater can be conceived" cannot be conceived not to exist. Instead, he argues that because this cannot be conceived not to exist, it therefore must exist *semper et ubique totum* ("always and everywhere in its totality"). He infers its onmipresence from its inability to be conceived not to exist. In *Monol.* XXII-XXIII he gives an extended discussion of what can be meant by saying that "the supreme nature exists always and everywhere in its totality" (I. 36.16f.).

where or when its other parts are, all its parts—and therefore the whole of it—can be conceived to be never and nowhere. For even if time is said to exist always and the world to exist everywhere, nevertheless the first does not exist always as a whole, nor the second everywhere as a whole. Just as the individual parts of time do not exist when the other parts do, they can be conceived to exist never. And just as the individual parts of the world do not exist where the other parts do, so they can be conceived to exist nowhere. What is composed of parts is capable of being dissolved by conception and of not existing. Therefore, whatever does not exist in its totality in any place or at any time, even if it does exist, can be conceived not to exist.

However, "that than which a greater cannot be conceived," if it exists, cannot be conceived not to exist, or else, if it exists, it is not that than which a greater cannot be conceived—which is inconsistent. Therefore, this never fails to exist in its totality in any place or at any time, but it exists always and everywhere in its totality.

8.

Gaunilo argues that it should be said that God's nonexistence cannot be "understood," not that it cannot be "conceived."

Gaunilo

PARA. 7 (I. 129.10-19)

When it is said that this supreme reality cannot be "conceived" (*cogitari*) not to be, it would probably be better to say that it cannot be "understood" (*intelligi*) not to be, or even that it cannot be "understood" to be capable of not being.

According to the proper meaning of this word "understand," false matters cannot be understood, although they can certainly be conceived, just as the fool conceived that God is not. I "know" (*scio*) most certainly that I am, but I also "know" nonetheless that I am capable of not being. I "understand" without any doubt that the greatest reality, which is God, both is and cannot not be. However, I do not know whether I can "conceive" of my not existing at the time when I "know" most certainly that I do exist. If I can do this, why can I not also "conceive" as not existing whatever else I "know" to exist with the same certainty [including God]? But if I cannot do this, then the impossibility of being conceived not to exist will not be the property of God alone.

Anselm

REPLY IV (I. 133.21-134.19)

Further still you say: While it is said that this greatest reality cannot be "conceived" not to be, it would probably be better to say that its nonexistence, or even the possibility of its nonexistence, cannot be "understood."

It is more correct, however, to say that this cannot be "conceived." For you yourself say that according to the proper meaning of this word nothing false can be "understood." Therefore, if I had said that this supreme reality itself could not be "understood" not to be, you would probably have made [three] objections: that nothing which is can be "understood" not to be, for the nonbeing of that which is is something false [and therefore not a proper object of "understanding"]; that the impossibility of being understood not to be is therefore not a property peculiar to God [but is characteristic of every object of "understanding"]; and finally, that *if* something which most certainly exists can be "understood" not to be, in the same way other certain things can also be "understood" not to be.

If one examines the matter closely, these objections cannot be made against "conceiving." For even if there is nothing existing which can be "understood" not to be, nevertheless *everything* can be "conceived" not to be, except that which is supremely. In fact all those things—and only those things—can be conceived not to be which have a beginning, or an end, or a combination of parts, and, as I have already said, which do not exist everywhere in their totality and always. [See No. 7D above.] But that alone cannot be conceived not to be in which conceiving discovers neither beginning nor end nor combination of parts, and which it finds existing always and everywhere in its totality.

You must realize, therefore, that even though you know with complete certainty that you exist, you can "conceive" of yourself as not existing. It surprises me that you say that you do not know this. For we do "conceive" of the nonexistence of many things which we "know" to exist, and we do "conceive" of the existence of many things which we "know" not to exist. We do this, not by making a real judgment, but by imagining that these things are as we conceive of them. In this sense, we can "conceive" that something is not when we "know" that it is, because at one and the same time we can "conceive" of the former and "know" the latter. In another sense, we cannot "conceive" that something is not when we "know" that it is, because we cannot conceive of something as both existing and not existing at the same time.

Therefore, if anyone distinguishes in this way between these two meanings of the word "conceive" [namely, conceiving by his own imaginative effort (meaning I), and conceiving within the limits of what he knows to be actual (meaning II)], he will understand that whenever something is "known" to be, it cannot be "conceived" not to be [in the sense of meaning II]; and yet that whatever is, except that than which a greater cannot be conceived, even if it is "known" to be, it can still be "conceived" not to be [in the sense of meaning I]. Therefore, it is the peculiar property of God that he cannot be "conceived" not to be [in the sense of meaning I], while many things, insofar as they exist, cannot be "conceived" not to be [in the sense of meaning II].

As to how it is said that God is conceived not to be [by the fool], I think that I have said enough about this in my little book [*Prosl.* IV].

9.

Gaunilo's misstatement of the argument.

Gaunilo

PARA. I (I. 125.6-13)

Against the one who denies or doubts that "that than which nothing greater can be conceived" really exists, it is argued that . . . because he understands this phrase, it is necessary that it not simply stand in relation to his understanding, but that it also exist in reality. Now this is proved because it is greater both to stand in relation to the understanding and to be in reality than only to stand in relation to the understanding. If this only stands in relation to the understanding, then whatever is also in reality will be greater than it, so that what is "greater than all things" will then be less than any real thing, and will not be greater than all things, which is a contradiction. That is why it is necessary that what is "greater than all things," which has been proved to stand in relation to the understanding, does not simply stand in relation to the understanding, but is also in reality, since otherwise it could not be greater than all things.

Anselm

REPLY V (I. 134.24-136.2)

You keep saying that, according to my statements, that which is "greater than all things" stands in relation to the understanding; if it stands in relation to the understanding, it is also in reality, for otherwise the "greater than all things" would not be greater than all things.

Now nowhere in all my writings is such a proof to be found. What is said to be "greater than all things" and what is said to be "that than which a greater cannot be conceived" do not have the same value in proving that what is so named exists in reality.

If anyone says that "that than which a greater cannot be conceived" does not exist in reality, or is capable of not existing, or even is capable of being conceived not to exist, he can easily be refuted. For what does not exist is capable of not existing. And what is capable of not existing is capable of being conceived not to exist. As for whatever can be conceived not to exist, if it does exist, it is not that than which a greater cannot be conceived; and it it does not exist but might exist, it would not be that than which a greater cannot be conceived. However, with regard to "that than which a greater cannot be conceived," we cannot say that even if it does exist, it is still not that than which a greater cannot be conceived; or that if it were to exist, it would not be that than which a greater cannot be conceived. Therefore, it is evident that neither does this not exist, nor is it capable of not existing, nor is it capable of being conceived not to exist. For otherwise, if it does exist, it is not what it is called, and if it were to exist, it would not be what it is called.

It seems, however, that this cannot be so easily proved of that which is said to be "greater than all things." The fact that what can be conceived not to exist is not greater than everything which does exist is less evident than the fact that it is not that than which a greater cannot be conceived. Nor is it beyond doubt that, if there is or might be something "greater than all things," it is or might be none other than "that than which a greater cannot be conceived." This is certain, however, in the case of that which is called "that than which a greater cannot be conceived."

Suppose someone says that there does exist something greater than all things that are, but that nevertheless this can be conceived not to be, and that a greater than it, even if not actually existing, can be conceived. In that case, can it be so obviously inferred that this something is not really greater than all things that are, as was so obviously established by my argument, and that it is therefore not that than which a greater cannot be conceived? In this case we would need some further argument than simply the statement that it is "greater than all things." In my argument, however, nothing else is needed except uttering the words, "that than which a greater cannot be conceived."

Therefore, if, in the case of that which is called "greater than all things," we cannot prove what "that than which a greater cannot be conceived" proves by and through itself, then you inaccurately accuse me of saying what I did not say, since it differs so much from what I did say. Even if there can be another argument, you should not have attacked mine for saying what can be proved.

Whether there is another argument can easily be judged by anyone who realizes that "that than which a greater cannot be conceived" does make proof possible. For "that than which a greater cannot be conceived" can never be understood except as that which alone is greater than all things. Therefore, just as "that than which a greater cannot be conceived" is understood and stands in relation to the understanding, and on that basis is asserted to be in reality, so also that which is called "greater than all things" is understood and stands in relation to the understanding, and on that basis its existence in reality is inferred by necessity.

You now see how correct you were to compare me with that fool who asserts that the "Lost Island" really exists solely because he understands the description of it![16]

[16] That is, you now see that my reasoning depends on the precise expression "that than which a greater cannot be conceived." If the phrase "that which is greater than all things" does not serve, much less does "the best-conceivable island."

10.

Conclusions.

Gaunilo

PARA. 8 (I. 129.20-25)

The other matters in this little book are discussed so truthfully and so brilliantly and magnificently, and they are so full of value, so full of the fragrance of the deep perfume of devout and holy feeling, that they should in no way be disparaged because of that which is argued at the beginning with true purpose, but less firmly. Rather, let that be argued more vigorously, and then the whole will be received with great respect and honor.

Anselm

REPLY X (I. 138.28-139.12)

I have now demonstrated, I believe, that in my earlier little book I have proved with sufficiently necesssary, and not with weak, reasoning that something than which a greater cannot be conceived really exists, and that this reasoning is not weakened by the force of any objection. The signification of this key expression is in itself so forceful that, by the very fact that it is understood or conceived, the reality which it expresses is proved by necessity to exist in fact, and to be whatever we are bound to believe about the divine substance. For about the divine substance we believe anything which to our thought it is absolutely better to be than not to be. For example, it is better to be eternal than not eternal, good than not good, or, rather, goodness itself than not goodness itself. Nothing, however, of this sort can fail to belong to "that than which a greater cannot be conceived." It is necessarily the case, therefore, that "that than which a greater cannot be conceived" is whatever should be believed about the divine essence.

I thank you for your kindness, both in your criticism and in your praise of my little work. For since you bestow so much praise on those parts which seem to you worthy of acceptance, it is quite evident that you criticize the parts which you find weak in a spirit of kindness and not of spite.

III

Arthur C. McGill

Recent Disscussions of Anselm's Argument

1. *The Historical Question*

In reviewing the recent literature on Anselm's argument, it is important to recognize that this historical work is a relatively recent phenomenon, in progress now for little more than a century; that it has been provoked by a very specific problem; and that its results must be judged accordingly.

Its main motive, although not its only one, has been dissatisfaction with the standard way of reading the argument. According to this standard view, Anselm's reasoning analyzes a purely mental concept and draws out the implications found there. It tries to establish God's existence, not from the visible things of nature or from a knowledge of the divine essence itself, but from an idea of God which we have in our understanding. Thinking of God as "that than which nothing greater can be conceived," Anselm's first step is to show that this idea can be thought by people. The unbelieving fool may deny that this idea corresponds to any real object, but even if he can do no more than understand the ordinary meaning of words, he will at least be able to think this idea when he hears these words which express it. Then Anselm poses the decisive question: Does this something which is being considered intellectually exist only in the fool's mind, or does it exist both in his mind and in reality also? Anselm answers that the former is logically impossible. If this something existed only in the fool's mind, he nevertheless could think of it as also existing in reality, which would be something greater. He would find himself in the intolerable position of conceiving of something greater than that than which nothing greater can be conceived. "This," Anselm concludes, "is certainly impossible. Therefore, something than which a greater cannot be conceived undoubtedly exists both in the mind and in reality."[1] Such is the standard interpretation, which sees the whole operation as moving exclusively at the level of ideas. To use Kant's term, it is an "ontological" argument. It analyzes a concept without once seeking contact with the data of sensory experience.[2]

When read in this way, however, the argument becomes susceptible of a criticism so sweeping and so thorough that very few men can be found today who would defend it in this form.[3] Since the recent historical investigations have largely accepted this criticism, we might note its seven major points.

1. Anselm's initial premise that the mind begins by thinking a legitimate idea is challenged. How do we know that this is an idea in any proper sense at all? Since it refers to nothing in our sensory experience, are we really able to "think" of something when we hear Anselm say, "that than which nothing greater can be conceived"? Or does the fact that this statement is in accord with our grammatical usage and seems to contain no inner contradictions obscure from us that nevertheless no clear concept is being expressed.[4]

2. Let it be granted that Anselm's phrase does convey an idea to us. This still may be what Descartes calls a "factitious" idea, wholly made up by our minds and unrelated to anything in reality. A merely thought idea gives the impression of floating in a vacuum, and the fact that some mind happens to think it is hardly a ground for us to take it seriously.[5]

3. Let it be granted that this is a valid idea. Still, how can Anselm expect that everyone will identify it with God? Those who worship

[1] *Prosl.* II (I. 102.1-3).

[2] *Critique of Pure Reason*, transl. by Norman Kemp Smith (London, 1929), p. 500.

[3] Among such defenders, however, must be included the editor of Anselm's collected works, F. S. Schmitt, "Der ontologische Gottesbeweise Anselms," *Theologische Revue* 32 (1933), pp. 217-223; and also D. M. Cappuyns, "L'argument de S. Anselme," *Recherches de théologie ancienne et médiévale* 6 (1934), pp. 323-327.

[4] Gaunilo, *On Behalf of the Fool* 4 (I. 127.10-14): "Something true can rarely, if ever, be known solely on the basis of hearing words." Kant, *op. cit.*, p. 501.

[5] Descartes, *Meditation* III. Kant, *op. cit.*, p. 501. Gaunilo, *op. cit.*, 2 (I. 125.15-17): "Couldn't I be said to have in my understanding all sorts of things that are false and do not exist in themselves in any way at all, since when someone speaks, I understand whatever he may say?" 5 (I. 128.1, 9-11): "It cannot possess real existence simply by being in the understanding. . . . In my view it is not in my understanding, except in the way in which doubtful and uncertain things are there."

fire or the world as God, and those like the fool who deny the existence of God altogether would certainly not accept this idea as an idea of God.[6] All that Anselm should say legitimately is what he states in *Proslogion* IV: "No one who understands what God is can conceive that God is not." He should not claim that anyone who hears his words automatically understands what God is.

4. Let it be granted that men might identify this idea with God. Certainly no Christian should ever do such a thing. The Christian believes that God's infinity and transcendence are such as to set him far beyond the grasp of all human concepts. Any proof that claims to begin with some "idea" of God, which it can readily communicate in a few words, shows by that very fact that it is not dealing with God at all.[7]

5. Let Anselm be granted his starting point, a genuine, thinkable, definable idea of God. The question must be raised whether he can use this idea as a basis for his argument. How can he prove God's existence from an idea of God which he himself has selected for this purpose? All that he has done, it would seem, is to adopt an idea that simply pre-empts the whole question of existence. God is such-and-such (e.g., perfect), and because such-and-suchness must include existence, therefore God exists. This is not to prove anything, but to move in a vicious circle, where the matter is settled by *fiat*. God is defined in terms of an idea that closes the question of existence even before it is ever opened.[8] We could just as well do this in the case of some hypothetical island, defining it as the best possible island, and arguing on that basis that any island that is the best possible must at least exist.[9] When we ask about the existence of something which we know only as an idea, we are really asking about the truth of that idea. And no logical analysis of the content of an idea can ever decide its truthfulness.

6. Let it be allowed that men have an idea of God and can argue

[6] Thomas Aquinas, *Summa contra Gentiles* I.11, *Nec oportet*. Gaunilo, *op. cit.*, 4 (I. 127.17-19): In the case of the fool, the key phrase "is not known as if by someone who knows what is customarily signified by these words . . . but as if by someone who does not know it in its reality."

[7] Gaunilo, *op. cit.*, 4 (I. 126.31-127.3): "I cannot conceive of God himself. . . . For I neither know the reality itself which is God, nor can I infer it from other similar things, since his reality is such that it cannot be similar to anything."

[8] F. Ueberweg, *Grundriss der Geschichte der Philosophie* vol. II, rev. by B. Geyer (Berlin, 1928), pp. 199f.: "Every deduction from a definition is only valid hypothetically, on the assumption that the subject of the definition is real." A definition, however, cannot be used to establish this assumption.

[9] Gaunilo, *op. cit.*, 6.

from it. Does this ever lead directly to the knowledge of his existence? Is existence a thinkable aspect of things, a property which can be grasped through an analysis of concepts? Or is existence only related to an act of judgment on our part, when we step beyond our concepts and, on the basis of sensory experience, affirm that something real stands in relation to them? This is the objection which Kant formulates so forcefully. He argues that the real existence of a thing does not affect our concept of it one way or another. Our idea of a possible but unreal hundred dollars is not one wit different from our idea of a hundred actual dollars that lie before us. This means that the term "is," or "exists," expresses a judgment by our minds and not some conceptual content. Therefore, since we must go beyond our concept of anything in order to be able to ascribe existence to it, no rational analysis of our idea of God will ever yield a knowledge of his existence. Every ontological proof is fallacious.[10] Anselm is asking the impossible when he directs us to think of his *quo maius cogitari non potest* as existing only in the mind, then to think of it as existing both in the mind and in reality, and finally to recognize that the second is "greater" than the first. Since, according to Kant, "to be in reality" adds nothing to our idea of a thing, our concept of this entity under these two conditions will be absolutely identical, and a comparison between them to determine a "greater" becomes impossible.

7. Let it be granted that we do have an idea of God and can think of his existence. All that Anselm's argument shows is not that God exists, but that our minds must think that he exists if they are to hold to this idea of him with logical consistency. But this is no way to become informed about what is objectively real.[11] In fact, even if God did not exist, it would still be the case that logically we would have to think of him as existing, as long as we identified him with this idea. What Anselm has done is simply to confuse the necessity of drawing an inference (logical necessity) with the necessity of objective existence (ontological necessity).[12]

This is the familiar criticism leveled against Anselm's argument—or rather, against his argument interpreted as the inference of God's existence from an idea of God. Anselm, it is maintained, gives no indication of why we should consider the idea itself as reliable (points

[10] Kant, *op. cit.*, pp. 504-506.

[11] Thomas Aquinas, *op. cit.*, I.11, *Nec oportet:* "From the fact that what is indicated by the name 'God' is conceived by the mind, it does not follow that God exists except in the mind."

[12] Kant, *op. cit.*, p. 501.

1-4 above), and even if it were valid as an idea, the objective fact of God's existence is not the sort of thing that can be inferred from its content (points 5-7). Until recently, interpreters usually responded to this criticism by trying to rewrite the argument so as to overcome these weaknesses.[13] But the historical investigators of our time have taken a different tack. Persuaded that this criticism is not only valid but also obvious, they have questioned the interpretation of the argument on which it is based. Does Anselm really offer us an "ontological" argument? If we examine in detail the intellectual world of the eleventh century, the whole scope of his writing and the precise language and purpose of the *Proslogion*, might we not discover the presence of some assumption or intention or qualification which will remove these supposed defects from his paragraphs?

This undertaking finds one justification in the character of Anselm himself. It hardly seems likely that a man of his obvious intellectual capacity and dialectical skill could search for an argument with intense effort over a long period of time and then produce only a pure paralogism, which he would mistakenly find so compelling for his purposes that he would see it as a gift from God himself.[14]

More important, there are details in the argument which this standard, conceptualistic interpretation simply cannot explain. Why, for instance, does Anselm begin with such a peculiar "idea"—the notion of "that than which nothing greater can be conceived"? Why does he not consider God directly, in terms of God's own infinite or perfect reality, instead of merely comparing him with the resources of human thought? Again, if this is a typical ontological argument, why does he give so much emphasis to the role of Christian faith?[15] And what of his repeated insistence that God is inconceivable, and that we men can no more have an idea of God in this life

[13] John Duns Scotus, *Opus oxoniense* I, Dist. 2, Q. 2: "Anselm's reason about the *summo cogitabili* can be *colarari*." Leibnitz, *New Essays Concerning Human Understanding* (New York, 1896), p. 502: "What Descartes has borrowed from Anselm is very beautiful and really very ingenious, but it still has a gap that needs to be filled." Hegel, *Lectures on the History of Philosophy* (London, 1896), vol. III, p. 64: "It is to be remarked about Anselm's argument that . . . the content indeed is right, but the form faulty."

[14] *Prosl.* Preface (I. 93.10-19): "I directed my thought to the search for this argument *saepe studiosque*." *Prosl.* IV (I. 104.5f.): "My thanksgiving to you, good Lord, my thanksgiving to you. For what I first believed through your giving I now understand through your illumination."

[15] *Prosl.* I (I. 100.18f.): "For I do not seek to understand so that I may believe, but I believe so that I may understand. For I also believe this, that 'unless I believe, I will not understand' (Isa. 7:9)."

than we can have the beatific vision?[16] Such points cannot be readily accommodated into the conventional view.

Finally, it has recently become clear that Anselm's own work, the *Proslogion*, was not known either by Immanuel Kant or Thomas Aquinas, the two classic critics of the argument. Kant was occupied exclusively with the version of the argument formulated by Leibnitz. The latter did everything possible to make it a purely analytic proof, and therefore he substituted the idea of a "necessary being" for that of "something than which nothing greater can be conceived." Kant's whole discussion is molded accordingly.[17] As for Thomas, although he is closer to Anselm in time, his criticisms are even further removed from the *Proslogion*. For as far as we can tell today, Anselm's argument was totally ignored throughout the twelfth century. When it did appear in the first half of the thirteenth century, it was extracted from its context in the *Proslogion* and was mixed in with a number of other isolated citations to prove the thesis that God's existence is self-evident and therefore need not—and cannot—be demonstrated. This was the only way in which Thomas knew the argument, and this was what he criticized.[18] The question therefore remains whether these criticisms will stand up when measured, not against Leibnitz or certain textbooks of the thirteenth century, but against a meticulous reading of the *Proslogion* itself.

Such are the concerns and the justifications of the recent historical study of Anselm's argument. Work in the last few decades has concentrated particularly on three distinct problems, and these will now be surveyed in turn.

[16] *Prosl.* XVI; *Monol.* LXV.

[17] See especially A. Koyré, *L'idée de Dieu dans la philosophie de S. Anselme* (Paris, 1923), pp. 231-234: "Kant did not know the *Proslogion*; he makes no mention of Anselm, and does not seem to be aware that he was the real author of the ontological argument. He presents it as 'the celebrated demonstration by Descartes.' But it is not this demonstration either which he analyzes and criticizes. It is the very different one by Leibnitz—in the form which Christian Wolff had given it."

[18] The classic work on this topic is A. Daniels, "*Quellenbeitrage und Untersuchungen zur Geschichte der Gottesbeweise in Dreizehnten Jahrhundert*" (in *Beiträge zur Geschichte der Philosophie des Mittelalters* [Munster, 1909], vol. 8, parts 1 and 2). He shows (1) the complete absence of the argument in the literature of the twelfth century (pp. 111-115); (2) the proof-text manner of using sources in the thirteenth century (p. 121); and (3) the precise ways in which the thirteenth-century versions of the argument differed from Anselm's statement (pp. 131ff.). See also on this problem J. Chatillon, "L'argument de S. Anselme chez les premiers scholastiques du XIIIe siècle," in *Spicilegium Beccense* (Paris, 1959), pp. 209-231.

II. *The Complexity of Anselm's Argument*

One of the most important recent developments has been a recognition that *Proslogion* II and III were seen as a unity by Anselm himself, and that his argument therefore has a complexity which has often been ignored.

The reasoning of these two chapters obviously falls into three units. There is first a syllogism (*Prosl.* II) to prove to the fool that "something than which nothing greater can be conceived" must exist not only in the understanding but in reality as well. The steps of this syllogism may be paraphrased as follows:

1. The fool who denies that "God" exists is at least able to understand the meaning of this longer phrase when he hears it. That is, he is able to think about something than which nothing greater can be conceived, and is able to recognize some of the features which it must have as the bearer of this characteristic, even though he does not as yet realize that it exists.

2. The fool must also acknowledge that something which is in the mind and also in reality is greater than something which is only in the mind.

3. Therefore, something than which *nothing* greater can be conceived must possess this greater condition; it must be both in thought and in reality. Otherwise, we would be faced by an impossible contradiction: That than which we cannot possibly conceive of a greater would be that than which we could easily conceive of a greater.

This is the first unit of Anselm's reasoning, and the one to which the most attention has been given.

In the next unit (*Prosl.* III, first part) he continues to consider something "than which nothing greater can be conceived." but this time in order to prove, not that this something exists, but that it exists in such a way that it cannot even be conceived by the human mind as not existing. The argument may be paraphrased:

1. Consider something which cannot possibly not exist, and which we therefore cannot even conceive of as not existing. This is obviously something greater than that which is capable of not existing and which we can conceive of as not existing.

2. Therefore whatever is "that than which nothing greater can be conceived" cannot be conceived not to exist, even hypothetically. For if that were possible, then it would not be that than which *nothing* greater can be conceived.

The question which immediately issues from this point—namely, if the human mind cannot even conceive of this as not existing, how does it happen that the fool can deny God's existence?—is considered by Anselm in *Proslogion* IV. His answer is that the fool can certainly deny the existence of "God," because that term by itself does not tell him what kind of a reality it designates. When he denies the existence of "God," he is identifying the word either with nothing at all or with a nondivine reality.

In the third and last unit of reasoning (*Prosl.* III, second part), Anselm takes a different direction and tries to prove that the subject under discussion—namely, that which has been shown not only to exist, but also to exist in such a way that it cannot even be conceived not to exist—is actually the Lord God, Creator of heaven and earth. He offers two reasons, which may be paraphrased as follows:

1. The Creator is the one reality which man as a creature cannot surpass with his mind, and which he cannot judge by trying to create the idea of something greater. A creature who could do this—who could devise in his mind something greater than his Creator—would in that regard be superior to his Creator, which is absurd.

2. The human mind can conceive of any created reality as not existing because (as Anselm explains more fully in his *Reply* to Gaunilo) such a thing does not have a full unlimited existence. It receives its reality from beyond itself, and therefore has a nature that is objectively capable of not existing. When we consider something which we cannot even conceive of as not existing, that is, something which in its very nature is incapable of not existing, then we are conceiving of something which does not derive its existence from elsewhere—either from our minds or from God. This underived something must be God himself.[19]

Thus, the final point is established: The subject reasoned about in the first and second units of the discussion is indeed the Lord God.

Such is the complex pattern of Anselm's argument, and obviously a satisfactory account can ignore no part. The fact remains, however, that until recently no attention was paid to this whole sequence. The usual method was simply to ignore *Proslogion* III entirely. Anselm's

[19] Cf. *Reply* IV (I. 134.2-6): "In fact, all those things—and only those things—can be conceived not to be which have a beginning, or an end, or a combination of parts, and . . . which do not exist everywhere and always in their totality. But that alone cannot be conceived not to be which has neither a beginning nor end nor combination of parts, and which thought finds existing always and everywhere in its totality." *Reply* I (I. 131.30-32): "What is composed of parts is capable of being dissolved by thought and of not existing. Therefore, whatever does not exist fully . . . even if it does exist, can be conceived not to exist."

first unit of reasoning was isolated as a self-contained proof for the existence of God complete in itself, and the only problem was to discover how his syllogism was supposed to work. Gaunilo took this view of the matter nine hundred years ago, and today we still find it dominant in philosophical circles. Thus, Étienne Gilson can write a piece on "The Proof of the *Proslogion*" without once mentioning *Proslogion* III.[20]

There is one superficial justification for this approach. When Anselm entitles his chapters, he calls Chapter II "That God Truly Is (*vere sit*)," and Chapter III "That He Cannot Be Conceived Not To Be." This would seem to indicate that the former is concerned with God's existence, but the latter with the human mind and with what it can or cannot conceive. Of course, these titles cannot be ignored, because all the textual evidence indicates that they go back to Anselm himself.[21] At the same time we cannot attribute to them the same value which chapter titles have in our day. In the eleventh century, theological works were not carefully organized into chapters, but had the character of an unbroken continuity. Anselm himself sees his *Proslogion* as a "single argument" which by itself "proves . . . *whatever* we believe regarding the divine substance."[22] Even the way in which chapterization is handled in the oldest manuscripts reinforces this sense of continuity. For they offer a list of chapter titles and corresponding numbers at the very beginning of the work, but within the text itself a chapter is only indicated by its number appearing at an appropriate place in the margin.[23] It was not Anselm but his later editors, therefore, who inserted the chapter titles into the text and so broke up its continuity into what look like self-contained and definitively entitled units. In conformity with the practice of his times, Anselm's titles briefly mention some important idea from each portion of his work, so as to provide his readers with a rough and ready means for referring to particular points in the total argument. They were a device for reference, not a resumé of content or a cata-

[20] In his work *History of Christian Philosophy in the Middle Ages* (New York, 1955), pp. 132ff.

[21] Also see Anselm's remark in the Preface to *Cur Deus homo?* (II. 43.46-47).

[22] *Prosl.* Preface (I. 93.5-10). Cf. Eadmer, *Life of Anselm* XIX: "It came into his mind to investigate whether that which is believed and preached about God . . . could be proved by *uno solo et brevi argumento*." There are still scholars today who cannot conceive of how everything which a Christian believes about God can be made part of a single argument, and who therefore construe Anselm's "one argument" as only concerned with God's existence.

[23] See *Opera omnia St. Anselmi* I. 4.

logue of the decisive theses argued in the work.[24] For that reason, there are no grounds for *presuming* that Chapter II is a self-contained unit; that Anselm meant it to establish the existence of God with conclusive finality, so that he could then turn to other matters in Chapter III; or even that in his reasoning here he had God's existence in mind, and was not simply preparing a link for a thesis that would only come to full expression in a later chapter.

Recognizing that *Proslogion* II cannot be isolated, another traditional approach has seen Chapters II and III as parallel arguments for the same point. According to Thomas Aquinas and the textbooks of citations which he used, both of these chapters demonstrate that God's existence is self-evident, Chapter II from the meaning of the term "God," and Chapter III from the fact that God's nonexistence is inconceivable.[25] In our day both Charles Hartshorne and Norman Malcolm find an independent proof for God's existence in both chapters, but they maintain that the argument in the first part of Chapter III is the logically superior one.[26] It is certainly the case that *we* can take the reasoning which Anselm offers in Chapter III and use it to prove the same conclusion demonstrated in Chapter II. What is very dubious is that Anselm himself had this in mind. For there is some kind of shift from the theme of Chapter II, that "God exists both in relation to the mind and in reality," to Chapter III's concern that God "exists so truly that he cannot even be conceived not to exist." The latter seems to be a refinement or development of the former, rather than a strict repetition, as Thomas and Hartshorne propose.

The decisive break from these two traditional approaches was made in 1931 by Karl Barth.[27] He proposes a way to see Chapters II and III

[24] D. M. Cappuyns, *op. cit.*, p. 325 n. 40; Anselm Stolz, pp. 204ff. The latter points to the striking discrepancy between the title and contents of *Prosl.* XVII.

[25] Thomas Aquinas, *op. cit.*, I. 10, thc paragraph *Illa enim* for the argument of *Prosl.* II, and the paragraph *Item, cogitari* for that of *Prosl.* III. See also Bonaventura, *Questionum disputarum: De mysterio Trinitatatis* Q. I, a. 1, 22 (the argument of *Prosl.* III) and 23 (that of *Prosl.* II).

[26] Hartshorne's essay "What Did Anselm Discover?" and Malcolm's essay "Anselm's Ontological Argument" are reprinted below, pp. 321ff. and pp. 301ff., respectively.

[27] Karl Barth, *Fides quaerens intellectum,* first German ed. 1931, Chr. Kaiser Verlag, Munich; second German ed. (unchanged) 1958, Evangelische Verlag, Zollikon. English translation by Ian Robertson, *Anselm: Fides quaerens intellectum,* 1960 SCM Press, London, and John Knox Press, Richmond, Va. Barth's discussion of *Prosl.* III is reprinted below, pp. 135ff.

as two indispensable *phases* of Anselm's proof. The purpose of Chapter II, he argues, is simply to demonstrate that God has extramental reality, that he exists *in re*, as well as *in intellectu*. It establishes that God has at least the existence which characterizes every other actual object, that he is real in the same fashion as sticks and stones. In Barth's vocabulary, Chapter II proves God's "general" existence.

Barth's thesis, however, is that such a proof is not adequate. Anselm would never have been content simply to leave God as one of that class of things which are extramental, for, in fact, God does not exist in the same way as sticks and stones. He is the origin and creator of all extramental reality, and therefore his existence is *not* properly established by a proof that he exists outside the human mind. There must also be a demonstration of what Barth calls God's "special" existence, the existence which distinguishes God from all other existence.[28] This is the demonstration which Barth finds in *Proslogion* III.

According to Barth, Anselm's procedure here is to show that God cannot even be conceived in theory not to exist, that by no inventiveness can the human mind think of God as not existing. His existence is such that even in thought the possibility of his nonexistence is excluded. No such exclusion confronts thought in the case of other things. As Anselm makes clear again and again in his *Reply* to Gaunilo, the mind is able to think of them as possibly not existing, no matter what kind of factual existence they may have. "Everything can be conceived not to be," Anselm writes, "except that which is the highest."[29]

[28] *Ibid.*, German pp. 147f., English p. 130.

[29] *Reply* IV (I. 134.1f.). It must be noted that, although Anselm clearly affirms the *fact* of this limitation upon human knowledge, and shows in *Prosl.* III that it is entailed in God's unsurpassability, he is not clear about the ultimate *grounds* for it. (1) One possibility is that God's nature is ontologically inseparable from existence. His essence is to exist, and his existence is in this sense necessary. This is what limits the human mind: it can find nothing in God which would allow it to think of God in abstraction from his act of existing. The evidence is not clear that Anselm himself had this in mind. (2) A second interpretation focuses on man's creatureliness. Because for Anselm God is the Creator, whose existence is the premise of every actual or possible existence, there is nothing, therefore, which would enable the mind to think of existence apart from God, and therefore no vantage point from which it could think of God apart from existence. The point here is not that God necessarily exists, but that every creaturely experience and thought takes place within horizons of God's existence. Anselm's remarks in *Reply* I (I. 131.18-132.2) indicate that he may have been thinking in these terms. (3) Barth (*op. cit.*, German p. 176 n. 1, English p. 153 n. 1) suggests a third possibility. The inability of human thought in relation to God is not an absolute inability, grounded either on God's nature or on man's creatureliness, but is a relative inability. It depends on men seeing themselves in the presence of

Barth claims that Anselm really has two different things in mind when, in the title of Chapter II, he explains his purpose as proving "That God Truly Is." In *Proslogion* II he is concerned with God's "true" existence from the human standpoint, i.e., God's objective. extramental existence. But in *Proslogion* III he is concerned with God's "true" and unique existence as God, the existence which God has as the origin and basis of all that exists apart from him.[30]

Barth's essential thesis is simply that Anselm means *Proslogion* III to lift the concept of God's existence right out of the plane of the general concept of existence. While there are beings who exist extramentally in their own right, and while God is a being who has such existence, Chapter III is meant to prove that God alone is a being who exists in a manner beyond the power of thought to deny.[31] Here Anselm brings his argument to its decisive point, demonstrating not simply that God exists, but that to the human mind he exists as *God*. In this light Barth can maintain that for Anselm *Proslogion* II has no significance whatsoever, except as it leads to and is completed by *Proslogion* III. When philosophers like Gaunilo take Chapter II as a proof in and by itself, they are quite happy to find in God the same kind of existence as is found in sticks and stones, and to measure God's being by the same criterion of extramental reality that creatures possess. Such an aim, according to Barth, is impossible for Anselm; he is too acutely aware of the difference between the creature and the Creator.[32] As he says in the *Monologion*, to have merely the extramental reality of the creature is "to be almost nonexistent and to exist scarcely at all."[33] Barth can even maintain that "according to Anselm's own account," if God only exists in the way demonstrated in *Proslogion* II, if he only has general existence *in re*, then *he does not exist at all*.[34] According to Barth, then, never for a

---

their Creator, and being willing to conduct their thinking in a way that is proper for such a situation. They know that they are "prohibited" by the command of their Creator from surpassing him. Insofar as they are obedient to him, therefore, they "cannot" conceive of him as lacking, even in theory, the existence which they constantly receive from him.

30 Barth, *op. cit.*, German p. 102 n. 2, p. 109 n. 2, pp. 112 and 179f.; English p. 94 n. 2, p. 100 n. 1, pp. 101 and 155f.

31 *Ibid.*, German pp. 153 and 179f., English pp. 134 and 156. See pp. 137, 157.

32 *Ibid.*, German pp. 103-105 and 177f., English pp. 95f. and 154f. See p. 156.

33 *Monol.* XXVIII (I. 46.3): *fere non esse et vix esse.*

34 Barth, *op. cit.*, German p. 178, English p. 154: "If God only had general existence, in the manner of all other beings, then not only would he not exist as God, but according to Anselm's own account in *Reply* III (I. 133.11f.) he would

moment does Anselm intend to prove the existence of anything but that which is the origin and truth of all creaturely existence. Never does he see *Proslogion* II except as completed by the first part of *Proslogion* III.

One of the chief values of Barth's interpretation is that it helps explain Anselm's response to Gaunilo. For although the latter focuses his criticism almost entirely on the syllogism in *Proslogion* II —because, he says, it is the one glaringly weak point in an otherwise *verax*, *praeclarus*, *magnificus*, *utilis*, *pius* and *sanctus* little book[35]— yet Anselm in his *Reply* works mainly to restate and develop in new ways the thesis of *Proslogion* III. The fact that he should answer Gaunilo's attack with an expansion of precisely that phase of the argument which Gaunilo largely ignores is an indication that the real focus of his interest is where Barth locates it.[36]

On two points, however, Barth's position has been attacked for not going far enough. On the one hand, he fails to take the second, praying part of *Proslogion* III seriously. In spite of the fact that Anselm himself apparently finds this section essential to his argument and does not challenge the fool's denial until after he has completed it, Barth tells us just the opposite. This, he says, is not part of Anselm's proof. It simply expresses the devout obedience with which all Christian thinking about God must be conducted.[37] On the other

---

not exist at all for he did not create himself and therefore he does not possess the general existence which is granted to creatures."

35 Gaunilo, *op. cit.*, 8 (I. 129.20f.). In paragraphs 2-4 Gaunilo argues that "that than which a greater cannot be conceived" does not exist in the mind, or if it does, it is no different from an idea of any doubtful or nonexistent thing. In paragraphs 5-6 he argues that its existence in thought provides no ground for inferring its existence in reality. Only in paragraph 7 does he consider *Prosl.* III.

36 In *Reply* I Anselm explains the characteristics of that which *cannot be conceived not to exist*. In *Reply* III he argues that actually conceiving of "that than which nothing greater can be conceived" prevents the mind from *conceiving of its nonexistence*. In *Reply* IV he contrasts the act of conceiving and the act of understanding God's nonexistence. In *Reply* V he rejects Gaunilo's formula—"that which is greater than all things"—on the ground that, unlike the being described by his formula, something greater than all things might still be able to be conceived not to exist. In other words, the whole point of his formula is that it leads beyond *Prosl.* II to *Prosl.* III. In *Reply* VII he explains the advantage of his formula over the name "God," in that there is nothing in the latter term to prevent the fool from conceiving of its nonexistence. In *Reply* IX he shows how it is possible for the mind to conceive of something whose nonexistence is impossible and therefore inconceivable. It might almost be said that in the *Reply* Anselm spontaneously thinks of God as *quod non potest non esse cogitari*, rather than as *quo maius cogitari non potest*.

37 Barth, *op. cit.*, German p. 173, English p. 150: "The chapter could have

hand, when Barth assigns two quite different meanings to the phrase *vere esse*—signifying ordinary extramental existence in *Proslogion* II but unique divine existence in *Proslogion* III—he may be letting a verbal formula conceal a radical disjunction. Can general existence and special existence be two grades along a single continuum, as Barth claims, so that the God whom we first discover to exist in the same way as everything else turns out finally not to exist in the same way as everything else?[38] Can that which is the origin and truth of all beings also be *a being*, a something that exists objectively outside the mind? The two meanings which Barth tries to put in sequence may be not only different, but contradictory.[39]

Two years after Barth's volume appeared, Father Anselm Stolz, a Benedictine theologian, found a way to avoid these weaknesses by moving far beyond anything Barth had envisioned.[40] For Stolz does not simply find a place for *Proslogion* III after *Proslogion* II. He sees *Proslogion* III as the heart of the argument, with *Proslogion* II serving only a preliminary function. Anselm, he contends, has *no thought whatsoever* of proving the fact of God's existence, of showing that God has at least as much reality as sticks and stones. Anselm wants *only* to prove God's unique manner of existing as God, his *Seinsweise*, and not his *Dasein*. According to Stolz, it is only by an "optical illusion" that readers see a proof of God's existence in the *Proslogion*.

Initially, Stolz does not appeal to anything in the argument itself, but to Anselm's review in Chapter XIV of what his thinking has "discovered" up to that point.[41] There Anselm lists three items.

---

closed with the preceding sentence, for with that sentence the proof as such is completed."

[38] According to Barth, *Prosl.* II proves that "God has at least as much objective reality as all other beings" (*ibid.*, German p. 179, English p. 155). "Why should not this sign of true existence belong as much to Him as to every object created by him?" (*ibid.*, German p. 147, English p. 130).

[39] This problem is emphasized by Paul Tillich, "Two Types of Philosophy of Religion" in *Theology of Culture* (New York: Oxford, 1959), pp. 13-15. For what Tillich calls the ontological type, God is the principle of knowledge, the first truth in the light of which everything else is known. He is the identity of subject and object, and precedes any cleavage into subject and object. Tillich argues that there can be no logical transition from such pure Being to *a* highest being, from a principle which is beyond subject and object to something that exists objectively over against our minds like other things.

[40] Anselm Stolz, "Zur Theologie Anselms im *Proslogion*," in *Catholica* (Paederborn), I (1933), pp. 1-24. This essay is translated below, pp. 183ff.

[41] See p. 194.

The second is that God is life itself and light itself and wisdom itself (which covers the material in Chapters V-XII), and the third is that God is everywhere and always (which corresponds to the discussion in Chapter XIII). Therefore, Stolz argues, the first item that Anselm mentions in his review must represent his understanding of Chapters II-IV. And what he says is that "My soul . . . has discovered that God is that *summum* of all things than which nothing better can be conceived."[42] Stolz calls attention to two features of this statement. First, it makes no mention of God's existence, but only of establishing God's *way* of existing as the *summum* of all things. Secondly, it speaks as if Chapters II-IV do this by proving that "that than which nothing greater can be conceived" is God. Anselm makes the same point in *Proslogion* V. He speaks there as if what he has just proved in the preceding chapters is that God is "that than which a greater cannot be conceived," and as if this by itself establishes the fact that God is the supreme reality.[43]

On this basis, Stolz contends that the conventional view of the argument is doubly wrong. It is wrong in supposing that Anselm wants to settle the question of whether God exists, when in fact he betrays no awareness of such a question. It is also wrong in supposing that God's identity as "that than which nothing greater can be conceived" is something which Anselm takes purely on faith, something settled wholly outside the argument. In fact, according to Stolz' reading of the summary in Chapter XIV, it is precisely *this* which Anselm wants to prove. For it is this which establishes God's unique way of being as the *summum* of all things. "Therefore," Stolz concludes, "on the basis of Chapter XIV, *Proslogion* II-IV would seem to be only a matter of proving that God (whose existence is fully assumed throughout) is really that than which nothing gteater can be conceived."[44]

Stolz then analyzes the argument as having two stages. In the first stage, consisting of *Proslogion* II and the first part of *Proslogion* III, it investigates the *kind of existence* possessed by something than which nothing greater can be conceived. Here Anselm proves

[42] *Prosl.* XIV (I. 111.8-11).

[43] *Prosl.* V (I. 104.11f.): "What are you, then, O Lord God, than whom nothing greater can be conceived? What are you, except that *summum* of all things which exists through itself alone." That is, since you are that than which nothing greater can be conceived (as has just been proved), that means that you are also the *summum* of all things.

[44] Stolz, see p. 196f.

that this something must have *esse in re*, and not just *in intellectu* (*Proslogion* II); and further that it must have such a *maxime esse*, an *esse* so completely devoid of nonbeing that it cannot even be conceived not to exist (*Proslogion* III, first part). For Solz, however, the decisive fact is that during this first stage the argument is *not about God*.[45] Anselm's careful formulations make it quite clear that "God" is not the subject which, according to Chapter II, exists *in re*, and that "God" is not the subject which, according to the first part of Chapter III, we cannot conceive of as not existing. As far as the argumentation in both of these syllogisms is concerned, the stated subject is simply an "*aliquid*," a *something* which is that than which nothing greater can be conceived.

The second stage of the argument, Stolz continues, consists of the second part of Chapter III, and there Anselm offers his two reasons to prove that this "something" must indeed be the God worshiped by Christians as the Creator of heaven and earth. Far from being a mere addendum to the argument, then, as Barth holds, this second part of Chapter III is viewed by Stolz as the very heart and climax of Anselm's reasoning. Here the "something" than which nothing greater can be conceived is rationally identified with God. Here *God* is shown to be the one with such *maxime esse* that he cannot even be conceived not to exist. He is shown to be the unique reality which has absolutely no possibility of not being and whose nonexistence therefore is inconceivable. In other words, because of the second part of *Proslogion* III, the argument does just what Anselm reports in his review in Chapter XIV: It proves that God is the *summum* of all things.

There is one obvious textual difficulty with Stolz' view. Several times Anselm speaks of *Proslogion* II-III as proving "that God truly is" (*Deus vere est*), and at the end of Chapter IV he thanks God for enabling him to understand "that you are."[46] Does not this preoccupation with the question of God's *esse* mean that Anselm is concerned with the fact—and not with the supreme manner—of God's existence?

Not at all, says Stolz. Because modern readers are preoccupied with the problem of subjective illusion, they naturally take Anselm's phrase "true existence" to mean objective, extramental existence.

45 *Ibid.*, p. 202.

46 *Prosl.* Preface (I. 93.7); *Prosl.* II (I. 101.2); *Prosl.* III (I. 102.6; 103.1; 103.3). At the end of *Prosl.* III (I. 103.7f.) the phrase becomes *verissime et maxime esse*.

They assume that for him, as for them, God's existence is *verum* so far as it stands over against the human mind with an actuality of its own. Stolz argues, however, that this assumption is completely wrong.[47] "True existence" (*vere esse*) was a technical term used by Augustine and early medieval theology to designate that which has such full and absolute being that it cannot change in any way, either by enhancement or reduction (in that sense, it "truly exists"), and to contrast this being with other things that are only partially and derivatively real and that are therefore capable of an alteration in their being.[48] The phrase *vere esse* identifies "true" being, not as objective in contrast to the unreality of subjective illusions, but as unchangeable in contrast to the unreality of mutable creatures.[49]

Stolz contends that this is Anselm's framework also. In the *Monologion* he clearly identifies "untrue being" and "nonbeing," not with mental fictions, but with mutable creatures.

Since [created things] are in a transient, most brief and scarcely existent present, they scarcely exist at all. Therefore, since they are as mutable as this, they are rightly denied a simple, perfect and absolute being, and are asserted *not to exist* and *to exist scarcely at all.*[50]

Could Anselm, Stolz asks, have treated creatures in their objective reality as "almost nonexistent" in 1076, and then a year later, in the *Proslogion*, have considered this mutable, momentary, objective kind of existence as "true being," and have seriously tried to prove that God possesses it?

47 See Stolz' article "*Vere esse* im *Proslogion* des hl. Anselm," in *Scholastik* IX (1934), pp. 400-409.

48 Stolz refers to Augustine, *De Trinitate* VII.5 (10): "He alone truly is (*vere est*) because he is immutable." *Sermon* VII.7 (*P.L.* 38.66): "The name *esse* means unchangeability. For everything which is changed stops being what it was and begins to be what it was not. True being, genuine being, pure being is not possessed, except by the one who is not changed." In *The Morals of the Manicheans* I (1), Augustine speaks of "that which remains always the same, which cannot be corrupted or changed in any part and which cannot now be anything but what it was before. To be in this way is what is called *esse verissime*, for this term signifies a nature that subsists in itself and is unchangeable. We can say that this nature is nothing else than God."

49 See Augustine, *Confessions* VII.11 (17): "I considered all the other things which are beneath you, and I saw that they are neither altogether real nor altogether unreal. They are real insofar as they are from you; but they are unreal in that they are not what you are. For only that truly is (*vere est*) which endures unchangeably." *Ennaration on Psalm* 134.4: "God is such that by comparison with him the things which are made are not. When not compared with him they are, because they are from him. When compared with him, however, they are not, because true being (*verum esse*) is unchangeable being and this is God alone."

50 *Monol.* XXVIII (I. 46.13-16). Italics added.

In Stolz' view, then, Anselm's *vere esse* designates God's unique *way* of existing, in contrast to the *non esse* or *vix esse* of mutable creatures. In identifying *Proslogion* II-III as a demonstration that God "truly is," he is simply using this technical Augustinian phrase to state what he expresses in another way in his summary in Chapter XIV: "I have discovered that God is the *summum* of all things." *Proslogion* II-III is wholly concerned with the manner—and not the fact—of God's existence, with his *vere esse*, with the way in which he exists just as we believe, namely *proprie*, *absolute*, *maxime* and *verissime*. Stolz contends that Anselm even hears the fool's denial in this Augustinian perspective. He thinks of the assertion "God is not" as denying, not God's objective existence, but his "true existence," and as attributing to God the transient *non esse* of a creature.[51] Stolz therefore claims that the answer to the fool does not occur in *Proslogion* II but in *Proslogion* III.

The works of Barth and Stolz point to the significance of *Proslogion* III as part of Anselm's argument, Barth emphasizing the first part of this chapter and Stolz the second. They have clearly shown that a decision about the extent and complexity of the argument is tied up with the question of its meaning and purpose. It also must be observed, however, that since the 1930s, when these studies appeared, discussion of this whole problem has been largely dormant.

III. *The Purpose of the Argument*

A second problem that has figured in recent studies is the question of Anselm's *motive* in undertaking his argument. According to some, he means to prove God's existence to the autonomous reason, so that any normal man, who lets himself be guided by his natural intelligence, cannot help being convinced by it. In that case, Anselm is a rationalist and, in the vocabulary now popular, is doing "philosophy." According to others, he wants his argument to proceed from *within* the Christian faith, only for the purpose of illuminating what the Christian believes, and therefore only relevant for members of the Christian Church. In that case, he is said to be doing "theology." There are still others who find Anselm intent upon securing a religious vision of God, so that his reasoning has an essentially "mystical" purpose.

[51] Stolz, *Scholastik* IX (1934), pp. 408f.

Each of these views is able to appeal to certain statements within Anselm's corpus, and therefore to offer a certain justification for its position.[52] This means that the real problem lies in deciding how to weigh these various statements and in finding a coherent interpretation that will do justice to them all. We should take note of them in all their diversity, in order to appreciate the depth and delicacy of this problem.

1. THE RATIONALISTIC ANSELM

In one group of texts, Anselm insists on the importance of proceeding *sola ratione* "(by reason alone"). The opening sentence of the *Monologion* is typical.

If someone—either because he has not heard or does not believe—is ignorant of the one supreme nature . . . and of the many other matters which we necessarily believe about God and his creatures, I think that such a person, even if he has only a mediocre mind, can still in a large measure convince himself of these things *by reason alone*.[53]

Such a person, Anselm seems to be saying, does not have to believe the Bible or the Church or the preacher in order to be grasped by the meaning of Christian truths. He can understand them simply by the use of his reason, and by the use of a reason that has no special endowments. It is Anselm's plan, apparently, to address this person. When he reasons silently with himself in the *Monologion*, therefore, he explains that he will urge "absolutely nothing in Scripture on the authority of Scripture," but will use ordinary *argumenta* and simple *disputatio*. He wants his assertions about God to be supported simply by "the necessity of reason" and "the clarity of truth"—qualities which will impress a person completely ignorant of Christianity.[54]

Anselm follows this same procedure in other writings. In the

[52] Anselm offers the most important accounts of his purpose in the *Monol.* Preface, I, LXIV (written 1076); *Prosl.* Preface, I, XIV-XVII (writen 1077-1078); *Epistola de Incarnatione verbi* I and *Letter* 136 to Bishop Fulcon (both written 1092 after the Synod of Sens, to explain clearly the difference between his own view and the heretical doctrine of Roscelin on the Trinity); *Cur Deus homo*? Preface, I.1-4 and 25, II.22 (written 1094-1098); and the *Letter* in which Anselm commends this last work to Pope Urban II (written 1098).

[53] *Monol.* I (I. 13.5-11). Italics added.

[54] *Monol.* Preface (I. 7.7-11). Cf. Eadmer, *Life of St. Anselm* I.xix, trans. by R. W. Southern, p. 29: In the *Monologion*, "putting aside all authority of Holy Scripture, he seeks and discovers by reason alone what God is, and with invincible reason he proves and demonstrates what the faith holds true regarding God."

Proslogion, even though he says that here his *faith* seeks understanding, his thesis is that what Christians believe about the divine nature and persons "can be proved *by necessary reasons* without the authority of Scripture."[55] When he argues against a Trinitarian heretic like Roscelin, he makes no appeal to the authority of the Scriptures, because, as he explains, Roscelin either does not believe in these books or misinterprets them. "His error must be demonstrated by the very reason on which he relies."[56] Even in his investigation of such a fundamental Christian mystery as the Incarnation, Anselm "leaves Christ out of view" so as to prove the matter "*by necessary reasons*"; he "leaves out what was taken from the Bible" in order to satisfy unbelievers "*by reason alone*"; he "sets aside Christ and the Christian faith as if they had never been" in order to understand the matter "*by reason alone*."[57]

Anselm has full confidence in the reliability of logical reason. Whatever is concluded by good argumentation from sound premises, he says, "should not be doubted at all,"[58] and if it concerns God, it should be "believed" and accorded the certainty of faith itself.[59] Anselm even insists on this point with reference to the highest Christian mysteries. He acknowledges, for instance, that God's triune being completely transcends the scope of the human intellect. Nevertheless, although we cannot understand *how* God is in this way (*ratio quomodo ita sit*), he assures us that we can have complete certainty *that* God is in this way (*ratio quia ita sit*), because this can be conclusively demonstrated by "necessary proofs."[60] Or again, he says that we may not be able to use our intellect to grasp how a man can be saved by Christ; that is, we may not be able to know the steps of this process or the precise ways in which God brings them about. Nevertheless, "even if we do not understand the reason how this is (*quomodo sit*), we ought not to doubt that it is (*quod sit*) when this is inferred by necessary reason." In fact, Anselm even goes so far as to say that anyone is a "fool" who denies what must "necessarily" be the case, simply because he does not understand how (*quomodo*) it can be the case.[61]

According to the rationalistic view, however, Anselm is not simply

[55] This is the account of his purpose which he gives in the *Epistola de Incarnatione verbi* VI (II. 20.17-19).

[56] *Ibid.*, II (II. 11.5-8).

[57] *Cur Deus* Preface (II. 42.11-13); II.22 (II. 133.6-8); I.20 (II. 88.4-6).

[58] *Ibid.*, I.25 (II. 96.2).

[59] *Ibid.* (II. 96.1f.); *Monol.* LXIV (I. 75.4f.).

[60] *Monol.* LXIV (I. 75.8f.).

[61] *Cur Deus* I. 25 (II. 95.15-20; 96.2f.).

interested in satisfying his own intellectual appetite for knowledge. He values reason, not only because it discloses what must be objectively true, but also because it has a unique power *subjectively*. According to those who stress his rationalism, he thinks that it is able to persuade the human mind, and, with regard to the religious questions that concern him, this means to convince the unbeliever and correct the heretic. As he says in the passage from the *Monologion* quoted above, he directs his reasoning to anyone who does not know or does not believe the Christian faith, in the conviction "that such a person, even if he has only a mediocre mind, can still in a large measure convince himself of these things *simply by reason* ALONE."[62] Anselm is convinced that a strictly rational proof does force the mind to give its assent to whatever is demonstrated. "The intellect," he says—and by this he means *any* intellect—"is compelled by reason (*constringitur per rationem*) to acknowledge what is shown to be valid (*ratum*)."[63] Therefore, any argument that is executed in a sound and precise way should make an irresistible claim upon the men who hear it, even if they have mediocre minds and completely irreligious hearts.[64] In fact, since believers do not need to have the Christian faith proved to them by reason, Anselm obviously feels that his dialectical powers give him a special mission to help the unbelievers.[65]

Therefore, in the *Monologion*, for the unbeliever who does not know the faith, Anselm relies on reason alone in order to "lead him rationally to those matters of which he is ignorant irrationally" and to "convince" (*persuadere*) him of the truth of Christian beliefs.[66]

62 *Monol.* I (I. 13.5-11). 63 *Ibid.*, XVI (I. 30.32f.).

64 Anselm clearly believes that his reasoning will make sense to men of *mediocris ingenii* (*Monol.* I, I. 13.10) and *tardi intellectus* (*Monol.* VI, I. 19.20), and to the many *illiterati* (*Cur Deus* I. 1, II. 48.6). And he also expects it to impress the *pagani* (*Cur Deus* II. 22, II. 133.8), the *impii* (*Letter* 136, III. 280.37) and the *insipiens* (*Reply* VII, I. 137.4).

65 *Letter* 136 (III. 280.34ff.): "Our faith is to be defended by reason against unbelievers, but not against those who confess that they delight in the honor of a Christian name. For it is rightly demanded of these latter that they firmly keep to the pledge which they made at their baptism. Unbelievers (*impii*), however, must be shown rationally those things for which they despise us irrationally."

66 *Monol.* I (I. 13.16). *Monol.* VI (I. 19.16-20): "I do not want to neglect any simple or even silly objection that occurs to me in this discussion. For in that way, first of all, I can proceed with more certainty to what follows, because I have left nothing ambiguous in what precedes; and secondly, if there is some other person, even one who is slow-minded, whom I may want to convince of what I have glimpsed, *he* can easily accept what he hears from me, because every kind of obstacle, even the slightest, has been removed."

Again, in the *Cur Deus homo?*, it is because Anselm wants to "satisfy" unbelievers about the reason for the Christian hope that he sets Christ aside completely, makes no appeal to the New Testament fulfillment of Old Testament signs, and seeks only to "prove" everything with "necessary reasons."[67] As Boso remarks,

> You so prove that God became man of necessity that, even if the few things which you have derived from our sacred books are set aside, such as God's three Persons and Adam, you satisfy both Jews and pagans by means of reason alone.[68]

Anselm develops the same technique with heretics and schismatics. He tries to turn Roscelin from his heresy of tritheism by avoiding Scripture and using only "that same reason on which Roscelin relies to defend himself."[69] And when he addresses the Greeks on the question of the Holy Spirit, he begins with what they accept without question, and then leads them "rationally" to what they do not believe by means of *certissimis argumentis*.[70] In the interests of communication, then, Anselm believes that it is incumbent upon him to explain the articles of his Christian creed by reason alone. For *ratio*, he says, is sought by all men, and, although unbelievers want to see the rationality of Christian dogmas for quite different reasons than do believers, "what we both seek is *unum idemque*, one and the same.[71]

Out of all these texts there comes a clear picture of Anselm as a *rationalist*, in the sense of someone who is concerned above all else to meet the demands of autonomous reason. It is maintained that he seeks the kind of technically rigorous argumentation which demonstrates what is necessary and which is therefore able to "convince" any person of ordinary intelligence. He is dominated by the desire to transpose various articles of the Christian faith into terms of pure reason. In Eadmer's concise words, "he seeks

[67] *Cur Deus* Preface (II, 42.12f.), I.1 (II. 47.10-48.1), I.4 (II. 52.3-6).

[68] *Ibid.*, II.22 (II. 133.5-8).

[69] *Epist. de Incarn. verbi*, rev. ed., II (II. 11.5-8).

[70] *De process. Spirit. Sanct.* I (II. 177.7-10, 15-17): "If the Greeks would rather acquiesce to solid truth than to contend for a worthless victory, I hope that by the help of this same Holy Spirit they can be led rationally through what they confess without ambiguity to what they do not yet accept. . . . I will make use of the faith of the Greeks and of the things which they believe and confess without question, in order to fashion absolutely certain arguments that will prove what they do not believe."

[71] *Cur Deus* I.3 (II. 50.16-20).

and he finds what God is by reason alone."[72] Therefore, if he offers us a proof for God's existence in the *Proslogion*, the proponents of this view contend that he does so with the belief that his starting point, his middle term and his conclusion are all readily available to the intelligence of any man.

The greatest problem facing this interpretation of Anselm is his clear insistence on the primacy of faith over reason. If he is the kind of rationalist we find portrayed here, why would he say of himself, "I do not seek to understand in order that I may believe, but I believe in order that I may understand"?[73] And why would he deliver what almost sounds like a curse upon the rationalists of his day: "May it happen that . . . those who first try to ascend the ladder of faith by means of their understanding be forced to descend into all sorts of error because of the defectiveness of their understanding"?[74]

Advocates of the rationalistic Anselm have proposed two very different answers. According to some, the "faith" which he stresses in these texts has nothing to do with the intellectual act of believing some truth. It is an exclusively volitional act, a matter of what he calls in one passage "right willing" (*rectitudo voluntatis*), namely, of *wanting* what the faith teaches and of *seeking* it with humility and purity of heart.[75] Anselm, say these interpreters, believes that this right willing comes only as a gift from God,[76] and for that reason he asserts that it must precede any activity that is to be called "Christian," including the activity of rational inquiry. He requires that faith have primacy, not for there to be a rational understanding of Christian truths, but for that understanding to be part of a man's redeemed life in Christ. He makes it quite clear, in fact, according to these interpreters, that prior to faith and apart from faith, men of the most ordinary intelligence, who hear Christian preaching, *can* conceive of what these words mean and can therefore reflect conceptually upon Christian truths.[77] Anselm, they say, is writing to these men.

Other commentators believe that, while Anselm does intend to

[72] *The Life of St. Anselm* I.19, R. W. Southern's ed., p. 29.

[73] *Prosl.* I (I. 100.18).

[74] *Epist. de Incarn. verbi*, rev. ed. I (II. 7.10-8.1).

[75] *Ibid.*, (II. 7.10-9.19), and *De concordia praesc.* III. 2 (II. 264.26-265.7). Adolf Kolping, *Anselms Proslogion-Beweis der Existenz Gottes*, pp. 15-20, gives a full statement of this view.

[76] *De concordia praesc.* III.3 (II. 266.8-267.4), quoted on p. 160 n. 35.

[77] *Ibid.*, III.6 (II. 271.7-9): "The mind's conceiving [of the meaning of the preacher's words] by itself does not produce faith . . . but faith is produced through grace, when rectitude of will is added to conceiving."

demonstrate the articles of faith to natural reason, he sometimes contradicts himself and speaks as if Christian faith were a necessary precondition. In him, they say, we see the new Aristotelian notion of theology as a science of rigorous argument coexisting side by side with the older patristic concept of theology as the elaborated wisdom of faith. In practice he is a "rationalist," writing in terms of strict reason for unbelievers, but he sometimes describes his work as believing theology.[78]

This rationalistic view of Anselm has been severely challenged in recent decades, although it still finds broad support.[79] It results in very different judgments of Anselm, however. Some commentators are enthusiastic. They see him as the person who freed reason from the kind of blind repetition of authoritative statements which marked the Dark Ages, and who recalled the minds of men to the pursuit of genuine inquiry. His rationalism, they say, initiated the intellectual renaissance of the high Middle Ages.[80] They also find a significant evangelistic value in this quality of his work, and praise him for "using all his intellectual gifts in the service of evangelism, to bring unbelievers to the point at which they must hear unmistakably the Word of the living God."[81]

Other commentators criticize Anselm for his reliance on reason. Thomists especially speak of his "recklessness" and "indefensible pretentions" in trying to prove the Trinitarian processions and the Incarnation with necessary reasons.[82]

2. THE BELIEVING ANSELM

Another set of passages in Anselm's writings points in an entirely different direction. Here we find not an admonition to proceed *sola ratione*, but an insistence on the primacy of faith and on the exclusively *Christian* context of all fruitful reasoning about God. In these passages Anselm seems to be speaking as a medieval

[78] See M. J. Charlesworth, *St. Anselm's Proslogion*, pp. 34-40, and Dom Vagaggini's remarks in *Spicilegium Beccense*, p. 106.

[79] See p. 62 n. 103.

[80] So A. Dufourcq: "S. Anselme: Son temps, son rôle," in *Revue de philosophie* XV (1909), pp. 598f., 601f. See also A. Kolping, *Anselms Proslogion-Beweis der Existenz Gottes*, pp. 19f.

[81] J. McIntyre, "The System of St. Anselm's Theology," in *Spicilegium Beccense*, p. 101.

[82] E. Gilson, *Reason and Revelation in the Middle Ages* (New York, 1950), p. 26; J. V. Bainvel, *Revue de philosophie* XV (1909), p. 737.

monk, every moment of whose waking life is shaped by a craving and hunger for God. The commentators who focus on these passages deny that there is any trace of rationalism in Anselm. In his dialectical works, they say, he is controlled by exactly the same purpose as in his *Prayers* and *Meditations*—not to vindicate Christian faith to the demands of pure reason, but to arouse his readers' minds to the love and enjoyment of God. The passages which support this view of Anselm may be arranged in the following two groups to form a coherent picture.

In the first group of passages, these interpreters see Anselm as insisting on the primacy of faith, that is, on the fact that men must first believe what is said in the sacred writings of the Christian Church before they try to reason. By their sin, he says, they have cut themselves off from God, so that now even their intellects—the very "senses of their souls"—are debilitated and "covered with darkness."[83] Therefore, when God in his mercy offers them the truth of himself and himself as the truth through these holy writings, men are initially incapable of receiving this gift with their darkened reasons. They can gain fruitful contact with it only by *believing* what these writings say, only by *holding unshakably* to the sometimes unintelligible content which they present.

According to the advocates of the believing Anselm, this is the meaning of his insistence that "the right order demands that we first believe the deep matters of the Christian faith before we presume to examine them by means of reason."[84] Since reason is what needs strengthening and correction, men obviously cannot rely on their rational judgments to lead them into all truth. They have another road: *faith*, which means faith in the redeeming *content* of the sacred writings and therefore faith in *sacred writings themselves* as reliable expressions of this content. For Anselm, men only come into contact with the divine truth when they cease insisting upon their *own* autonomous judgment and willingly let their minds be guided by these writings. And since there can be no comparison between the truthfulness of these God-given documents and the truthfulness of human reason, Anselm holds that *faith should be completely independent of all rational judgments*. It should not need the approval of reason, it should not be shaken by the perplexities of reason and it should not seek the support of reason.

[83] *Prosl.* I (I. 99.2-6); *Prosl.* XIV (I. 112.1-5); *Prosl.* XVII (I. 113.14f.).
[84] *Cur Deus* I.1 (II. 48.16f.).

Certainly if I, a contemptible little man, attempt to write something to reinforce the strength of the Christian faith, as if it needed my defense with so many wise and holy men present everywhere, we may presume that I will definitely appear, and be judged to be, ridiculous.[85]

Such conduct, Anselm continues, would be as if someone were to try to stabilize Mount Olympus by tying it down with ropes and pegs. Reason simply has no strength of its own to confirm or enhance the reliability of God himself in his revelation.

A second group of texts quoted by advocates of the believing Anselm concerns the *motive* of his intellectual work. Here he makes the point that the Christian cannot be merely docile and passive, cannot *merely believe*. The Christian, he insists, is alive with a desire and striving for God. In fact, that is his defining mark: to love God as his only good with all his heart and soul and mind.[86] This striving must characterize his faith as well. Therefore, Anselm defines faith as an active striving, not just *toward* God (*tendere ad Deum*), but *into* God (*tendere in Deum*). "By believing the supreme being," he says, "the human soul strives into it."[87] On the one hand, Anselm says that, if a man's faith has no striving, it has no love, which means that it is no different from the "dead faith" which the Epistle of James describes as belonging to the devils.[88] On the other hand, Anselm warns that a faith which involves no striving is valueless for men. It does not gather them into the divine life. To strive into God is to participate (although always in a creaturely manner) in God's *own* mode of being, in *his* aseity and glory. "Whoever will come to him by striving, will not remain outside of him but will remain within him."[89] Against the traditionalists of his day, Anselm maintains that the essential element of Christian faith

[85] *Epist. de Incarn. verbi*, rev. ed., I (II. 5.7-19).

[86] *Prosl.* XXV (I. 118.15-19): "Why, O slight man, do you wander about through many things, seeking goods for your soul and body? Love the one good in which are all goods, and that will suffice. Desire the simple good which is the whole good, and that will be enough. What do you love, my flesh? What do you desire, my soul? Here it is, here is whatever you love, whatever you desire."

[87] *Monol.* LXXVI (I. 83.18).

[88] *Monol.* LXXVIII (I. 84.16f.) on James 2:16, 26. Anselm derives this analysis of faith from Augustine. See the latter's warning against mere faith in *Tractates on the Gospel of St. John*, VI.21: "Faith is mighty, but without charity, it profits nothing. What does James say? 'The devils believed and trembled.' They confessed Christ. . . . They had faith but not charity; hence they were devils. Boast not of faith; to that extent you are only on a level with the devils."

[89] *Monol.* LXXVI (I. 83.27f.). On this point, see Karl Barth, *op. cit.*, German p. 6, English p. 17.

is the striving (and not the *docility*), the believing *into* (and not the believing).

In the presentation of the believing Anselm, we now reach a decisive point, a point connecting faith with reason. For if the Christian wants God and hungers for God, if his faith is a genuine striving for and into God, then, says Anselm, his faith will naturally *seek to understand God.* For what else does a lover ever want but a richer and better understanding of his beloved? What else does a man want who seeks God as his total joy but to *know* him, even slightly, in his enjoyableness and ravishing desirability? Because faith is a striving, *it* is what prompts men to investigate the faith rationally and to secure whatever understanding of God they can. And *it* is what enables men to experience their rational insights as joy, as the joy of satisfied love.

According to the advocates of the believing Anselm, these are the two groups of texts which show his orientation and explain the decisive features of his writings. They claim that the primacy of faith means that in every act of reasoning he takes *something from revelation as his premise.* In this technical sense he always reasons from the faith. He treats an article of the faith as an unknown *x*—not disbelieved, but not yet understood. Then he seeks for another article of the faith, another and undoubted statement in the divine writings, from which he can infer this by irrefutable logic.[90] In the argument of *Proslogion* II, for example, he uses his reason to derive one revealed dogma (that God exists) from another revealed dogma (that God is that than which nothing greater can be conceived).[91] This view therefore takes the position that the method which Anselm describes in the *Cur Deus homo?* controls his entire work.

> Let us suppose (*ponamus*) that there never was an Incarnation of God or any of the things which we say concerning that man; but let us take as true (*constet inter nos*) the fact that man is made for a beatitude which cannot be attained in this life, that no one can reach this God unless freed from sin . . . and the other things which must be believed for eternal salvation.[92]

In short, this view maintains that Anselm always proceeds as a

[90] Karl Barth gives this account of Anselm's method in *Anselm*, German pp. 54-60, English pp. 55-59.

[91] *Ibid.*, German p. 82, English p. 78; and P. Vignaux, *Philosophy in the Middle Ages*, pp. 42f.

[92] *Cur Deus* I.10 (II. 67.12-16).

theologian, inferring one article of the faith from others.[93] This means, of course, that he can have absolutely no "apologetic" aims, in the modern sense of that word. According to these interpreters, he engages the fool and the unbeliever only to *oppose* them. He wants his reasoning to confound them or silence them, but not to convert them.[94]

The second group of passages, those in which Anselm describes the quest for rational understanding as a work of love, is seen to account for his insistence on proceeding *sola ratione*. He refuses to quote authoritative texts, not out of any desire to meet unbelievers on their grounds, but solely because of the desire of his *Christian love for God* to understand the one he loves. That is why de devotes himself so "often and strenuously" to finding the best rational arguments for his Christian beliefs. That is why he considers that every Christian is obligated to undertake this same enterprise. And that is why he shares his investigations even with men of "dull mind" and "little knowledge," so that they, too, may fulfill the intention of their striving faith with a little understanding, and to that extent may enjoy a foretaste of heavenly bliss.[95]

Such, then, is the textual basis for the picture of Anselm as a Christian theologian, who argues within an attitude of believing faith, from the data of revealed faith, and for the satisfaction of loving faith. Eadmer, Anselm's biographer, was the first to propose this view, but it has always had its advocates.[96] Recently, however,

93 G. Sohngen, *Die Einheit der Theologie in Anselms Proslogion* (Braunsberg Program, W.S., 1938-1939), calls this procedure *Konklusionstheologie*.

94 Letter commending *Cur Deus* (II. 39.3f.). See Alexandre Koyré, *L'Idée de Dieu dans la philosophie de S. Anselme*, p. 205: "Certainly this argument [in *Prosl.* II] has never persuaded an unbeliever, effected a conversion, or led anyone to believe in God. But this was not its purpose. We do an injustice to a great theologian if we examine his argument from this point of view." *Ibid.*, pp. 204f.: "Let us be clear: Anselm's proof was not made to convince the fool; it cannot do this. But it can show him the insufficiency of his criticism; it can make him see that his denial of God does not reach or touch and cannot break the faith of the believer." Karl Barth, *Anselm*, German p. 117, English p. 106: "He has absolutely no thought of coming to an understanding with his dialogue-partner . . . on the basis of a shared minimal knowledge of God, let alone of starting to move toward his partner's own basis of argument. . . . He *speaks* and the other has to *listen*."

95 *Monol.* I (I. 13.10) and VI (I. 19.20).

96 *Life of St. Anselm* I. vii: "He had so much faith in the divine writings that he believed with unbreakable firmness that there was nothing in them which deviated in any way from the path of solid truth. Hence, with supreme effort he directed his mind to this end, that according to his faith he might be found worthy to perceive with his reason those things which he felt were hidden by deep obscurity in the sacred writings." See also M. Scheeben, *Mysterien des Christentums*

it received its most forceful and thoroughgoing presentation in Karl Barth's 1931 essay, *Fides quaerens intellectum: Anselms Beweis der Existenz Gottes.* He first presents an elaborate analysis of Anselm's general theological program, according to which Anselm seeks to discover the rational interconnections which lie between the different articles of the Christian Creed and thus to expose the rationality inherent within the revealed truth itself.[97] Then Barth gives a line-by-line commentary on the text of *Proslogion* II-IV, to show that the argument is a strictly theological investigation and should be dissociated completely from the "ontological proof" which we find in Descartes and Leibnitz.[98]

It is important to remember that Barth devotes himself to Anselm's argument because of his own theological principles. He is convinced, as he explains in his *Church Dogmatics* II/1, that what differentiates God from everything else and even from his own nonexistence is not any separation which he maintains between himself and other things, but is simply *his own inner act of being.* He does not need a basis by which to define and delimit himself in differentiation from what he is not or from his own nonexistence. To be himself he does not have to stand over against the world, as its cause and Lord. He himself is his own basis, and *as such* he differentiates his being from what he is not, and from his own nonexistence, and finally from every creaturely thought of his nonexistence. This is the true meaning of God's aseity, and the mark which distinguishes his existing from all other existence.[99]

On this basis, Barth contends that any proof for God's existence must reflect his aseity. That is, it must be a proof, not of a God who

---

(Freiburg, 1865), # 107.2; J. B. Franzelin, *De Deo Trino* (Rome, 1874), p. 321; F. Overbeck, *Vorgeschichte und Jugend der mittelalterlichen Scholastik*, Lectures given in 1891 and 1893 (Basel, 1917), pp. 213f.; Martin Grabmann, *Geschichte der Scholastischen Methode* (Freiburg, 1909-1911), I, p. 278 n. 2; A. Koyré, *L'Idée de Dieu dans la philosophie de S. Anselme* (Paris, 1923), pp. 36f.

97 Barth, *op. cit.*, German pp. 54-60, English pp. 54-59.

98 *Ibid.*, German pp. 198f., English p. 171: "God *gave* himself to be the object of Anselm's knowledge and God *illuminated* Anselm's mind so as to become knowable to him as an object. Apart from this event there is no proof of God's existence, that is, of God's objectivity. But in the power of this event there is a proof worthy of gratitude. . . . That Anselm's proof for God's existence should have been repeatedly called the 'ontological' argument, that people should not have seen that it stands in a different book from the well-known teaching of Descartes and Leibnitz . . . —all this was a thoughtlessness on which no more words should now be wasted."

99 *Church Dogmatics* II/1, p. 309.

causes the world and for that reason is different from the world and has an identity only by standing in contrast to the world, but of a God who exists so fully out of himself and whose existence even as God lies so fully within himself that just his own existing—and not anything he does to or for the world—differentiates him from all his creatures, from his own nonexistence and from the thought of his nonexistence. If one follows out this principle, obviously no datum can be used to prove God's existence, since his existence would then be defined by its relationship to and difference from that datum. Only his own actual existing can prove his existence in terms of its genuine aseity, and every human rational proof can do no more than simply repeat this proof.

For Barth, it is the peculiar excellence of Anselm's argument in the *Proslogion* that it fulfills this condition. As Barth sees it, it established God's existence from the fact that God did and does and will *demonstrate himself*, that he gives himself to be the object of human awareness and reveals himself to be men's creator and re-creator whom they cannot surpass. According to Barth, Anselm rests his proof for God's existence entirely on God's self-revelation of his unsurpassability.[100]

Nevertheless, although Barth finds in Anselm a close affinity to his own theological concerns and has often been charged with making Anselm into a mirror-image of himself,[101] his interpretation has had an absolutely decisive influence in every quarter. In fact, it can be said that he has been responsible for shifting the general climate of opinion. Many of the major historians of medieval thought—including P. Vignaux, A. Hayen, H. Rondet, J. de Finance, H. de Lubac—now accept his basic contention that Anselm works as a theologian.[102] Primarily because of his essay, the rationalist picture of Anselm, which was largely taken for granted at the beginning of the century, has now become a merely debatable hypothesis.[103]

[100] *Ibid.*, pp. 304f.

[101] See E. Gilson, *Arch. d'hist. et lit. du Moyen Age* IX (1934), p. 23 n. 1; and M. J. Charlesworth, *St. Anselm's Proslogion* (Oxford, 1965), pp. 41 and 44. Barth anticipates this objection in *Anselm*, German p. viii, English p. 9.

[102] This means that these historians must also distinguish between Anselm's faith-oriented formulation of the argument and the purely rational version of it which became popular in the thirteenth century. See J. Chattillon, "L'Argument de S. Anselme chez les premiers scolastiques du XIIIe siècle," *Spicilegium Beccense*, pp. 227f., 231.

[103] We have an indication of the changed situation if we compare the collection

There has been one important modification of the theological interpretation of Anselm since Barth's essay. Several French-speaking Roman Catholic scholars insist on the importance of faith, but they question Barth's further thesis about Anselm and the fool.[104] How, they ask, can Barth say that Anselm constantly sets himself "against" the fool, that he refuses to have anything to do with him in his unbelief and only "lets him go on repeating his counterthesis until the last day"?[105] Surely Anselm deliberately seeks to engage unbelievers in discussion, not meeting them on the grounds of their unbelief, to be sure, but expecting that his display of the rationality of revelation will make some impact on them.[106]

André Hayen has broken fresh ground on this point by examining the role of the fool in *Proslogion* II-IV in terms of Anselm's *monastic vocation*.[107] As a member and then an abbot of the Benedictine order, Anselm is controlled in all his work not only by faith in God, as Barth stresses, but also by an apostolic love for his neighbor. Because of this love, Hayen holds, he wants to include all men in his meditations on the rationality of Christian truth. He wants to think with a truly universal reasoning that will not only delight the monks at Bec and other Christians, but will also engage the thinking of all actual men. Because he has dedicated himself to being a servant of Christ, and because his charity therefore extends to *all* those for whom Christ died, "his own search for the *intellectus fidei* will not be true or complete as long as it excludes the fool."[108]

Hayen makes it quite clear that there is no question here of

---

of articles on Anselm published by the *Revue de Philosophie* in December 1909, with the collection *Spicilegium Beccense* published in 1959. In the former, two authors present Anselm as a believer (pp. 607, 641), while four see him as a rationalist (pp. 601f., 700f., 735). In the latter, however, he is viewed eleven times as a believer (pp. 13, 25, 79f., 156, 173, 196, 227f., 234, 265f., 302, 315f.) and only four times as a rationalist (pp. 98f. 105, 187f., 350f.).

104 See, for instance, Henri Bouillard, "La Preuve de Dieu dans le *Proslogion* et son interpretation par Karl Barth," in *Spicilegium Beccense*, pp. 198-200, 205f.

105 Barth, *op. cit.*, German p. 115, English p. 105. As long as the fool remains in his unbelief, Barth explains (German p. 67, English p. 65), he and the believer "march along side by side with nothing in common, and once this is recognized, they can both save themselves all the trouble and excitement involved."

106 Barth himself clearly recognizes the weakness of his interpretation at this point. He spends seven pages (German pp. 67-75, English pp. 65-72) trying to explain Anselm's "extraordinary mildness" toward the fool and his "astonishing recognition" of solidarity with the unbeliever.

107 Hayen's article "The Role of the Fool in St. Anselm and the Necessarily Apostolic Character of True Christian Reflection" is translated on pp. 162ff.

108 *Ibid.*, p. 166. See also p. 167.

apologetics in the modern sense, no plan to justify the truths of revelation by means of the self-evident principles of reason.[109] Anselm sees the fool as someone who is not yet wise, because his reason has not yet recovered the normal play of its natural exercise in faith. "Yet *already* when listening to believers, *already* when thinking the ideas which they teach him, the fool is *already* caught up in the movement of faith, moving along the road *toward* wisdom, along the road *toward* the liberation of the light of his reason under the illuminative control of faith."[110] According to Hayen, then, Anselm does not expect his reasoning on matters of faith to convert unbelievers—only God's direct agency can do that—but he does think that it will advance and attract them toward their conversion by showing them something of the light contained in revelation.[111]

Hayen acknowledges that Anselm's perspective sets faith in radical opposition to evil. It is the opposition determined by Christ's redemptive work, however. It is not against fools and unbelievers, as Barth claims, but against *the devil* for the sake of fools and unbelievers. It is against the Prince of this world, against that power of darkness and foolishness which continues to deny God in monks, as well as in fools.[112] Because he carries an apostolic—or evangelical—responsibility, and means his work to be an instrument of Christ's redemption of lost men from the power of the devil, Hayen holds that Anselm cannot seek even for an argument of God's existence without engaging the mind of one of those lost men. "Without the fool's intervention, Anselm's meditation would be devoid of charity. And if devoid of charity, then it would cease to be contemplative and to know God in an effort of love."[113]

3. THE MYSTICAL ANSELM

Advocates of both the rationalistic and the believing Anselm agree that he is primarily concerned with *technical reason*. In their view he wants to see how far the various Christian truths can be transcribed into logically incontrovertible arguments. He wants to satisfy the most rigorous demands of dialectical reasoning.

Certain features of the *Proslogion*, however, throw some doubt

[109] *Ibid.*, pp. 170ff. [110] *Ibid.*, p. 178. [111] *Ibid.*, p. 171. [112] *Ibid.*, p. 169.
[113] *Ibid.*, p. 170.

upon this assumption. They suggest that Anselm is not concerned with logical arguments for their own sake, but with an *experience of God* which he expects these arguments to produce. Anselm Stolz has presented this view most elaborately and persuasively.[114] The *Proslogion*, he says, represents an effort of the soul to raise itself to a kind of vision of God, by means of a dialectical investigation of the rationality of Christian dogmas. In short, he contends that it is a work of *mystical theology*.[115]

In support of his thesis, Stolz emphasizes two things: the language of prayer in which much of the *Proslogion* is written, and Anselm's repeated references to "approaching" God, or "finding" God, or "beholding" God or "seeing" God's face.

As to the first point, Stolz observes that if we examine Anselm's writings by their style, they fall into two distinct groups.[116] On the one hand, there are the doctrinal tracts (*Lehrhaften*) which strive for logical precision and consist entirely of a sequence of dialectical arguments. These include the *Monologion*, dialogues like the *De veritate* and the *Cur Deus homo*?, and the works of controversy against Roscelin and the Greeks. On the other hand, other writings like the *Orations or Meditations* have the form of prayer and are addressed directly to God.

Stolz believes that the *Proslogion* belongs to this second group. He rejects the view that its prayer passages represent sentimental interruptions of what is meant to be pure theological reasoning, and that they may be safely dismissed by serious students of the work as pious decorations.[117] He tries to show that, far from being accidental, prayer constitutes the essential style of the entire *Proslogion*. In some cases, he observes, like Chapter VIII, the whole speculative deduction is carried through in the language of prayer. In other cases like Chapter VI, there is a bit of dialectical reasoning in an impersonal style, but this *always* issues in a prayer passage. That is to say, in the *Proslogion* every single proof, without exception, is either conducted in the form of prayer or concludes in prayer.[118] On this basis, Stolz argues that the prayer form cannot be dismissed

[114] Stolz's most important essay, "Anselm's Theology in the *Proslogion*," is translated on pp. 183ff.

[115] *Ibid.*, pp. 185f.

[116] A. Stolz, "Das *Proslogion* des hl. Anselm," in *Revue bénédictine* XLVII (1935), p. 336.

[117] Stolz, "Anselm's Theology in the *Proslogion*," p. 199.

[118] *Ibid.*, pp. 199ff.

as unimportant. Just the opposite seems to be the case. The logical reasoning exists to bring about and enrich the prayers, so that each dialectical passage only comes to its conclusion at the moment when the prayer begins, or rather, in that prayer itself. In the case of *Proslogion* II for instance, this means that the reasoning there is not intended simply to prove that a "something" than which nothing greater can be conceived does exist in reality. It is meant to lead the mind to the point where it can address *God himself* directly. This happens only in the second half of *Proslogion* III.[119] Stolz emphasizes, in fact, that as long as the discussion is conducted in the style of dialectical reasoning, Anselm refuses to make any reference to God. For his real concern is to address God, not to argue about him.[120] In general Stolz warns us that if we forget Anselm's own reminder that *Proslogion* means *alloquium* ("an address"),[121] and if, by ignoring the prayers, we treat the dialectical passages as independent sequences of reasoning, then "we will cut ourselves off from the meaning of the *Proslogion*."[122]

The other feature of the *Proslogion* to which Stolz appeals is Anselm's explicit account of its purpose: to excite and elevate the mind to the contemplation of God. This is how he describes his aim in the *Orations or Meditations*, and this, Stolz says, is what he means to do in the *Proslogion* also.[123] In Chapter I of the latter—entitled *Excitatio mentis ad contemplandum Deum*—he calls upon his soul to withdraw into itself from the tumults of the world and to "seek your face, O Lord." But, recognizing the power of sin to obstruct this effort, he petitions God to show his face, to reveal himself, to give him the joy of beholding him somewhat. According to Stolz, this chapter clearly proves that the *Proslogion* is Anselm's effort not to satisfy the demands of technical reason, but to attain a vision of God; not to "investigate (*investigare*) those matters which he does not know by silent reasoning with himself" (this is his purpose in the *Monologion*), but to "approach" God, to "see"

[119] *Ibid.*, p. 201. [120] *Ibid.*, p. 202.

[121] *Prosl.* Preface (I. 94.13). *Alloquium* was actually Anselm's original title for this work, cf. *Epistle* 109 (III. 242.11).

[122] Stolz, "Anselm's Theology in the *Proslogion*," p. 200.

[123] *Orations or Meditations*, Preface (III. 3.2-4): "The orations or meditations which follow are written to excite (*excitare*) the mind of the reader to the love or fear of God, or to a meditation (*discussio*) upon him." *Prosl.* Preface (I. 93.21-94.2): "I have written the following little work in the person of one who strives to elevate (*erigere*) his mind to the contemplation of God and who seeks to understand what he believes."

God, to "eat the bread of angels."[124] Of course, in this way he cannot secure a full, eternal vision of God, which is impossible in this life, but only a vision "from afar, from the depths," or, as Stolz prefers to say, an *experience* of God.[125]

Stolz finds the decisive evidence regarding Anselm's basic intention in the over-all structure of the *Proslogion*.[126] Viewing the work as a technical investigation of intellectual problems, most commentators divide it into two sections, Chapters II-IV, on God's existence, and Chapters V-XXVI, on God's nature.[127] Stolz rejects this as arbitrary and completely unrelated to Anselm's text. What is obvious in any reading is the structural significance of Chapter XIV. For at this point, Anselm interrupts the rational inquiry which has been proceeding since Chapter II in order to review what he has done and to see if he has attained his original aim of experiencing God. He confesses that he has failed: "Still you are hidden from my soul, O Lord, in your light and blessedness."[128] He has not attained what he wants, a *sensus* of God. As he explains more precisely in Chapter XVI, he has found the unapproachable light in which God dwells, but not God himself. Echoing many of the phrases of Chapter I, he again acknowledges the obstructive power of sin and again petitions God to "cleanse, heal, sharpen and enlighten the eye of my mind so that it may gaze (*intueatur*) upon you." He then begins a second sequence of rational inquiries, and this time, according to Stolz, he succeeds in his effort. He does find the joy of an experience of God,[129] and interprets this joy as a foretaste of eternal beatitude.[130]

Thus, for Stolz the *Proslogion* consists of a two-phase movement to attain a mystical contact with God through a rational investigation of Christian dogmas. Each phase consists of thirteen chapters, and each begins with the same kind of prayer: a call to the soul to seek a vision of God, a recognition of the obstruction of sin and a petition for God's help. Stolz contends that this structure clearly establishes the fundamentally mystical intention of the work.

124 Stolz, "Anselm's Theology in the *Proslogion*," p. 185.

125 *Ibid.*, p. 189. It was F. Cayré who first developed the notion that in Augustine and the Augustinian tradition, dialectical reasoning may function as the instrument for mystical contemplation. See his *La contemplation augustinienne* (Paris, 1927) pp. 16f., 239, 244.

126 Stolz, *op. cit.*, pp. 191-194.

127 Barth, *op. cit.*, German p. 1, English p. 13.

128 *Prosl.* XVII (I. 113.8).

129 *Prosl.* XXVI (I. 120.25f.): "I have found a joy that is full, and more than full."

130 Stolz, *op. cit.*, pp. 190f.

Stolz' proposal is undoubtedly the most radical of all the interpretations yet made of Anselm's purpose. For it repudiates three widely accepted principles. (1) It maintains that Anselm does *not* have a single theological program, and does *not* pursue a uniform and unvarying purpose in all his writings. The *Proslogion* has its own peculiar intent, which corresponds to its distinctive literary form of prayer.[131] (2) Stolz' proposal challenges the custom of reading the *Proslogion* from the viewpoint of the *Monologion*, which immediately precedes it, or the *Reply* to Gaunilo, which supplements it. The fact that these two works move at the level of technical reason, Stolz warns, should not cause us to ignore the very different style and purpose which we find in the *Proslogion*. The *Reply* proves conclusively that Anselm attached great importance to the logical value of his reasoning, but it does not prove that this reasoning has no mystical function.[132] (3) Finally, and most important, Stolz' view collides with the modern assumption that logic and prayer are completely distinct and mutually exclusive areas of discourse. People today so objectivize logic and so sentimentalize prayer that each can only be seen as the negation of the other.[133] By indicating a deep interconnection between these two elements within the *Proslogion*, Stolz seriously challenges this modern prejudice. In fact, he raises the question of whether large portions of earlier Christian literature have not been profoundly misunderstood in recent times because of this prejudice.[134]

[131] Stolz, *op. cit.*, p. 184. Stolz, of course, is chiefly attacking Barth's notion of "*The* Theological Program" in Anselm (*Anselm*, German p. 4, English p. 15). But this idea is a commonplace in Anselmic studies. See, for instance, John McIntyre, "Premises and Conclusions in the System of St. Anselm's Theology," in *Spicilegium Beccense*, p. 95: "St. Anselm employs a uniform method throughout his works. . . . This systematic procedure, which I shall call 'the Anselmic method in theology,' remains the same, no matter the subject with which he happens to be dealing at any one given moment."

[132] Stolz believes that the controversy with Gaunilo has produced a two-fold distortion in the reading of the *Proslogion*. It has focused undue attention upon Chapters II and III, so that the work has not been examined as a whole, but solely from the viewpoint of these opening chapters. It has also encouraged the neglect of the prayer passages, in favor of a one-sided preoccupation with the dialectical arguments. See Anselm Stolz, *Anselm von Canterbury* (Munich, 1937), p. 20; and "*Vere esse* im *Proslogion* des hl. Anselm," in *Scholastik* IX (1934), p. 400.

[133] Joseph Bochenski's remark is typical, in *The Logic of Religion* (New York, 1965), p. 25: "A logical analysis introduced into an act of prayer would most probably damage if not destroy this act as such." Every chapter of the *Proslogion* disproves this assertion and, in that regard, must be incomprehensible to people who share Bochenski's view.

[134] See A. Stolz, *Theologie der Mystik* (Regensburg, 1936).

Chiefly because of this prejudice, perhaps, very little further work has been done along the lines indicated by Stolz' view.[135]

IV. *The Logic of the Argument*

Historical studies have largely concentrated on the syllogism in *Proslogion* II. The aim has been to discover an interpretation of this chapter that remains faithful to the words of the text, and yet at the same time presents an argument that a monk of the eleventh century like Anselm would have found lucid and compelling. This project is complicated, however, by the fact that there are not just one, but three distinct points of uncertainty, corresponding to the three steps of the syllogism.

There is first the question of Anselm's starting point. For he asserts that the idea of something than which nothing greater can be conceived is readily understood and is in the understanding. But is it? By Anselm's own account in *Proslogion* XV, something "than which a greater cannot be conceived" not only cannot be surpassed by thought; it cannot even be attained by thought. For that which is itself too great to be conceived is greater than that beside which the mind cannot conceive of something *else* that is greater. However, if this something is inconceivable, then Anselm is wrong in claiming that this is understood and truly stands in relation to the understanding. Furthermore, the objection is made that Anselm's initial statement does not give us enough information to identify the subject under discussion. The statement refers to *our* mental inability to conceive of anything greater than it, but we are told nothing about its actual nature. For that reason, we can form no notion of this object, and are therefore incapable of judging whether it exists. The initial statement informs us only about ourselves and our limits, and leaves us still within the circle of our own subjectivity.
the first. But, it is objected, can such a comparison be made? Is

Secondly, there is the question of the argument's middle step. Anselm asks us to think of this as existing in thought alone; then to think of it as existing also in reality; and finally, by comparing these two conditions, to recognize that the second is "greater" than there any difference between our idea of a hundred real dollars and

[135] Two exceptions are Paul Vignaux, *Philosophy in the Middle Ages* (New York, 1959), pp. 39f., 51; and Henri de Lubac, "Sur le Chapitre XIV du *Proslogion*," in *Spicilegium Beccense*, pp. 299-302.

our idea of a hundred purely imaginary dollars? If I am thinking of the table that stood in my dining room this morning, and if I suddenly learn that my wife is redecorating the room and has had this table removed and destroyed, does this mean that now when I think of the table, I must change my idea of it in some respect, because it no longer exists? Does the existential status of a thing have any bearing at all on its ideational content? Moreover, is this comparison possible in terms of the object? For the principle of identity requires that the attributes be of the same nature as the subject, real if the subject is real, purely conceptual if the subject is purely conceptual. Therefore, when Anselm tries to compare the *same thing* as existing and as not existing, he abuses the nature of identity. That which exists is a completely different subject from that which is nonexistent. His way of making the comparison is impossible, because it requires two different subjects, not two conditions of the same subject. The comparison which constitutes the middle phase of the argument is therefore challenged both noetically and noematically.

Finally, even if we can accept the first two steps in Anselm's reasoning, there is some question whether we can draw from them the conclusion which he desires, namely, that "that than which nothing greater can be conceived" truly exists in reality. For this seems to be an illegitimate passage from the order of thought to the order of reality. The first two steps do allow us to draw a conditional conclusion, to the effect that *if we think* of "that than which nothing greater can be conceived," *then* we are logically bound to *think* of it as existing. But the fact that the initial idea entails this *logical* consequence does not of itself prove that the idea represents an actual reality and is therefore a true idea.

All these criticisms turn on exactly the same point: They affirm that human thought cannot make any judgment about what is real simply by analyzing or comparing or drawing implications from its own subjective ideas. In order to speak of "existence," the mind must in some way be grasped by what lies beyond its ideas.

The historical studies of Anselm's reasoning in *Proslogion* II have been shaped by this formulation of the difficulty. Where, they ask, does Anselm see God's existence impressing itself upon the human mind, so that the mind is not forced to draw that existence out of its own ideas? What is Anselm's unspoken assumption which allows him to see his argument not just as moving within the closed circle of subjective reasoning, but as providing a compelling *demonstration* of God's real existence?[136] And historians have usually answered these questions by reconsidering the *starting point* of the argument. As long as the starting point is a doubtful, man-made idea, there is simply no way at all to reach a conclusion about God's existence without a fallacy. Historical knowledge of Anselm and the eleventh century is therefore marshaled to show that Anselm begins with something more than a mere "idea."

Historical studies may therefore be classified into groups, according to their particular proposal for re-interpreting this idea. In what follows an effort is made to provide a fairly comprehensive typology of such theories.

I. A REALISTIC IDEA

One widely held interpretation accepts the fact that the argument begins with an idea. It maintains, however, that even Anselm would be offended by an inference about objective reality from subjective thought. According to this interpretation, therefore, the "idea" with which Anselm begins cannot be an idea in the subjective modern sense, a fabricated hypothesis, a concept which the mind fashions out of its own inventive power in order to throw light on the turgid world of experience. For Anselm this idea, even as an idea, must *already* stand in the sphere of the real. That is to say, Anselm's argument is grounded on an "idea" in the realistic sense, on an idea that for one reason or another is taken as an apprehension of the real. This means specifically that the idea of "something than which nothing greater can be conceived" is the mind's real knowledge of God as the unsurpassable, of God as a greatness (or perfection) which utterly exceeds the whole power of human thought. At the beginning of the argument, then, Anselm is not looking at or thinking about some mental notion and wondering whether this is a true notion which represents a real object. *Through* this idea he is looking at and thinking about reality, specifically about the unique perfection of God's nature. There is an *aliquid*, a real something which stands over against his mind and which he initially knows in one of its aspects, namely, as that which is too "great" for his

[136] Anselm speaks of his argument as *probans solum ipsum* (Preface, I. 93.6), *procul dubio* (*Prosl.* II, I. 102.2), *planum* and *consequens* (*Reply* II, I. 132.21, 27) and *satis necessarium* (*Reply* X, I. 138.28).

conceiving to surpass. From the start, his mind is in touch with God's reality, and no fallacious movement from the realm of mere thought to the realm of objective existence is involved. As Adolf Kopling says, "for Anselm, mere thought is more than an abstraction of our mind. . . . With regard to its content, it already pertains to the reality that transcends the mind."[137]

From this initial knowledge of God's unsurpassable greatness, Anselm reasons that any reality which has such greatness must exist, for otherwise it would not have this greatness. This is no purely logical unraveling of a hypothetical definition. Nor does it require some impossible comparison between a mere idea of something as not existing and another mere idea of it as existing. Throughout the syllogism the mind is probing a real something, at first aware only of its unsurpassability, but then, through this syllogism, becoming cognizant also of its real existence. Thus, the realistic interpretation obviates some of the chief weaknesses in the argument by making it genuinely "onto-logical," in the pre-Kantian sense of that word. Anselm never worries about breaking out of the realm of mere thought, because from the beginning he has attributed to the mind a direct understanding (*logos*) of God's essence (*ontos*).[138]

According to the realists, then, since Anselm begins with a direct cognition of God's reality, it is better not to call this an "idea" at all, but an awareness.[139] Some say that he views it in this way

[137] Adolf Kolping, *Anselms Proslogion-Beweis der Existenz Gottes*, pp. 68f., 137f.

[138] Kant, who held that the mind has no contact with external reality, except in sensory experience, used the word "ontological" to designate that thinking which deals only with pure concepts, that is, with the *a priori* forms of the intellect which are devoid of all objective (that is, sensory) content. (*Critique of Pure Reason*, pp. 494, 500.) This use was directly contrary to the older meaning of the term, according to which "ontological" designated an understanding or science (*logos*) of the real, essential being (*ontos*) of things. Today the word normally carries the Kantian meaning, but this is not always the case. See, for instance, Alexandre Koyré: "A truly ontological demonstration, a direct proof that would reason from the very essence of God to his necessary existence, must presuppose a perception—a clear and distinct notion—of the divine essence." (*L'Idée de Dieu dans la philosophie de S. Anselme*, p. 201 n. 1.) The realistic interpretation finds in the *Prosl.* an "ontological" argument in precisely this older, non-Kantian sense of the word.

[139] This view actually goes back to Gaunilo, who insisted that Anselm's proof could only be valid if it began with an indubitable knowledge of God. *On Behalf of the Fool* 2 (I. 125.17-126.1): The argument is valid "if that being's reality is so firmly established that it cannot be conceived in the same way as every false or dubious thing. But in that case I am not said to 'conceive' of it or to have it in my 'conception,' but to 'understand' it and to have it in my 'understanding.'

because of his Platonic doctrine of ideas.[140] He can presume that his opening idea of God constitutes an awareness of God's reality because *every* human idea represents a cognition of what is real. He is an epistemological realist.[141] Other historians explain this realism as the product of a decisive religious experience. Anselm, they say, bases his argument on an experience of God's being, which shows itself to be so imcomparably real that every question about its objective uncertainty is settled immediately.[142] For both of these interpretations, the opening phrase—"that than which nothing greater can be conceived"—has the character of an experience-pre-supposing term, like perception words ("red," "yellow") or sensation words ("ache," "tickle") or emotion words ("anger," "joy"). Such terms as these cannot be abstractly defined. We can learn their meaning only experientially, by referring to the actual objects or experiences which they designate. So also with the starting point of Anselm's argument: Unless we have this awareness of God constantly before us, the argument will seem to hang in suspension, unrelated to anything real. According to the realists, therefore, those who deny the conclusion cannot be accused of a logical blunder. They simply fail to recognize the awareness which is being analyzed.[143]

The realists often admit that Anselm's way of formulating this awareness is peculiar. The mind, he says, is first aware of the object as "a greatness unsurpassable by human thought." He then argues that, since existing is greater than nonexisting, anything with this unsurpassable greatness must exist. Otherwise, if it did not exist,

---

Only then would I not be able to conceive of it except by understanding it, that is, except by comprehending rationally that it exists in reality." This peculiar kind of "comprehension" which Gaunilo describes here—and which he dismisses as impossible—is exactly the starting point proposed by the realistic interpretation.

[140] For a study of this feature of Anselm's thought, see Domet de Vorges, *S. Anselme* (Paris, 1901), pp. 141-167; and Martin Grabmann, *Die Geschichte der Scholastischen Methode* (Freiburg-in-B., 1909), I, pp. 293-311.

[141] See, for instance, Michael Schmaus, *Katholische Dogmatik*, vol I (5th ed., Munich, 1953), p. 184: "The validity of Anselm's argument stands and falls with the validity of the conviction which the Platonic spirit has always cherished, namely, that knowing is contact and, indeed, a union with real actuality. Once this is accepted, then the idea of God as the highest reality cannot be a mere content inside the consciousness. It refers to a spiritual reality which is encountered."

[142] See, for instance, Maurice de Wulf, *History of Mediaeval Philosophy*, vol. I (London, 1952), p. 163.

[143] On this point see N. Rescher, "The Ontological Proof Revisited," in *Australasian Journal of Philosophy* 37 (1959), p. 140.

it could not possibly have the greatness which the mind has actually encountered in it, namely, a greatness unsurpassable by human thought. But why express its greatness in this way? Later thinkers proposed simpler and more emphatically ontological formulations: Let us begin with the awareness of God as "the best" or "the absolutely perfect."[144] The realistic interpreters, however, are not primarily concerned with these fine technical points. In their view the power of the argument does not depend on the validity of its *logic*, but on the initial awareness which it elaborates. They want to see in the *Proslogion* a celebration of God's greatness as immediately apprehended, not an exercise in technical reason. That is why they warn us against taking the logic too seriously and thus being misled into thinking that Anselm wants his readers to rest their knowledge of God's objective being upon the validity of his syllogism. Beckaert even suggests that his dialectical style is "an error of presentation," used by him in conformity to the tastes of his times but actually obscuring the decisive intuition of God which he wants to explore.[145]

The great value of the realistic interpretation has been its insistence on seeing the argument as an *analysis* of something certain, rather than as a *verification* of something uncertain, as a recognition of God in his presence, rather than a questioning inquiry about him in his absence.[146] This means that the function which "proving" has

[144] One variant proposes that we designate the content of the initial awareness as "the best," rather than as "a greatness unsurpassable by thought." This was first proposed by William of Auxerre (see A. Daniels, *Geschichte der Gottesbeweise*, p. 26), but it was formulated most concisely by Richard Fishacre, *In Lib. I Sent.* Dist. III, a. 8 (see Daniels, *ibid.*, p. 23): "Existence is included in what is good. But existence is such a great good that everything seeks it. Therefore existence is included in our understanding of what is best. Therefore, just as snub-nosed cannot be understood without nose, so what is best cannot be understood without existence. Therefore, if [what we are thinking about] is the best, then it exists. But the best [which we are thinking about] is the best. Therefore, [that which we are thinking about] does exist." Descartes repeats this in *Meditation* V, although using mountain and valley instead of snub-nosed and nosed: since existence is a perfection and since God is the absolute of all perfection, "existence can no more be separated from the essence of God than the idea of a mountain from that of a valley. . . . It is no less impossible to conceive of a God who lacks his existence, i.e., of a supremely perfect being who lacks a perfection, than to conceive of a mountain without a valley." If we know God as the supremely perfect, then we know that he must exist.

[145] See the essay by Beckaert which is reprinted below, pp. 111ff.

[146] See P. Evdokimov, "Aspect apophatique de l'argument de S. Anselme," in *Spicilegium Beccense*, p. 254: That from which the argument proceeds "is always a disclosure. . . . It presents itself and imposes itself with absolute certitude, which is a dimension wholly different from intellectual certitude. Every question about the possibility of an illusion or about the reality of the content of this disclosure

had in the modern world cannot be projected back upon Anselm. Modern science and philosophy have been controlled by a fundamental suspicion of spontaneous, unexamined thought. The mind, it is believed, easily deceives itself by fabricating notions, so that no idea can be given credence unless it has first been *verified*; that is, unless reason has found some assurance that it is true, beyond the fact of its mere presence in the mind. Descartes formulated this axiom of modern knowledge as well as anyone: "It will be useful to reject as false everything about which we can imagine the *least doubt*, so that we may discover with greater clarity those things which are absolutely true."[147] This means that ideas are *presumed false* until proved otherwise. If they are not shown to be "absolutely true," if they are not tested and confirmed by some kind of convincing rational evidence, then they must be treated as if they were false, mere hypotheses or prejudices that an undisciplined mind has generated.

It has been easy for modern readers to identify the proof with this distrust of unsubstantiated ideas. Does not Anselm himself begin by asking whether the idea of God which is "in the understanding" is in the understanding "only" (and is therefore false) or is in reality "also" (and is therefore true)?[148] And does this not mean that he intends his proof to function in the modern way, that is, to remove all uncertainty from this idea by demonstrating that it is the idea of a genuinely existent reality?

The realistic interpretation points out, however, that once Anselm's argument is read in these terms, it turns out to be outrageously fallacious. If the problem is to remove uncertainty about some idea of God, obviously nothing is gained by elaborating the logical implications of this idea. Such a procedure only exhibits what is contained *within* the circle of uncertainty; it does not break out of that circle. As Gaunilo, who anticipated the modern spirit in a remarkable way, said, "since I can have all sorts of uncertain and even false things in my understanding, the fact that I can think of something unsurpassably great is no proof that it really exists."[149] "It first must be made certain to me that this great thing is really

---

is beside the point. Religious experience as such admits of no preliminary, reflective state, but, on the contrary, postulates a receptive nudity, a space free from ourselves and totally open to grace. Religious experience is the immediate presence of God, who precedes and in this way totally suppresses every question."

147 Descartes, *Principles of Philosophy*, Part I, Principle 2. Italics added.

148 *Reply* VI (I. 136.5-8).

149 *On Behalf of the Fool* 2 (I. 129.8-13). Also 5 (I. 127.29f.): "It cannot possess real existence simply by standing in relation to the understanding."

somewhere"—i.e., there must be other evidence than just the idea of it—"before I can accept your analysis of the idea as an account of some real thing."[150] Assuming that Anselm wants his proof to verify a questionable subjective idea, we must join Gaunilo and condemn his effort as wholly misguided.

The realistic interpretation rejects this assumption on the ground that there is no warrant for imputing a modern (and Gaunilian) distrust of thought to Anselm. For one thing, the whole *Proslogion* is pervaded by such a strong awe and reverence for the divine reality that it would be incongruous for it to present God initially as a questionable hypothesis that needs proof. Furthermore, could Anselm say in *Proslogion* III that God's nonexistence is completely unthinkable for man, if in *Proslogion* II he himself had asked us to think of God merely as a dubious idea?

Further still, there is a theological consideration. Anselm's doctrine of God excludes the kind of hypothesis-confirmation procedure which is identified with "proving" in the modern world. Anselm affirms that absolutely no parity can exist between God and the immanent activities of his creatures. Anselm would never take seriously some idea of God that men devise in their own heads and would never wonder whether some objective reality might correspond to it. God is no planet Neptune, dreamed up first as a hypothesis in the mind of some religious Leverrier and then later "proved" to correspond with something in reality. No creature has the intellectual power to invent an idea adequate for the reality of his Creator. If Anselm ever were to come upon such a "God-hypothesis," he would dismiss it as referring to some fictitious God that is proportioned to man's measure. In his perspective, the only idea of God worth taking seriously is the one which comes from God's own reality and not from the human mind.[151]

Finally, according to advocates of the realistic interpretation, Anselm does not share the modern belief that subjectivity is the main threat to human knowledge. He knows nothing of the sharp distinction made everywhere today between the logical (or subjective) order and the ontological (or objective) order, for this distinc-

[150] *Ibid.*, 5 (I. 128.11-13).

[151] P. Evdokimov, *Spicilegium Beccense*, p. 255: "This coincidence [in Anselm] of intuitive contemplation with transcendent reality, this grasp of ultimate truth takes place only in God and by God. . . . For we can speak truly of God only with God, we can never move toward God except by proceeding from God and being in God."

tion was not sharply made until the thirteenth century.[152] Therefore, when he refers to something as *esse in intellectu* ("being in the understanding"), this phrase does not carry for him a skeptical nuance. He is not using these words to suggest that this something may be a mere illusion. For him, as for his age, the important source of untruth is not the uncritical thinking of the human mind, but the *diabolus*, who still exercises power in the world. If sin cuts men off from the truth, it is not because it has released some irresistible principle of illusion *within* their souls, but because it has subjected them to the *rule of the devil*. This perspective would find it rather naive for men to seek security for their unreliable ideas in objective evidence. That would be to turn, not from darkness to light, but from the darkness of sin that lies within man to the darkness of the world and the devil that surrounds him. Anselm makes it quite clear that in his view the real truth—even the truth of things in the world—lies only in God Himself.[153] Men therefore remain bound in uncertainty until they are freed from the power of darkness by God's illumination. Then they share in *his* view of the truth and see everything by *his* divine light.[154] According to the realistic interpretation, then, Anselm would not find confirmation for his idea of God in any logical syllogism or objective evidence, but only by an encounter with the reality of God himself. Only God's own presence can vindicate, as only it can provide, the true idea of God. Once again we cannot attribute to Anselm the modern conviction that "proof" is designed solely to confirm uncertain ideas.

Without question, the realistic interpretation has been the most broadly favored by historians. It was adopted by nearly all the major studies in the nineteenth century, and it is the usual statement

[152] Kolping, *op. cit.*, pp. 138, 149f.

[153] In Anselm's view, "it is obvious that in the [divine] Word through which all things were created there is not the likeness of these things but their true and simple essence" (*Monol.* XXXI, I. 50.7-9). Anselm can therefore say that "every created substance exists that much more truly in the Word, i.e., in the understanding of the Creator, than in itself, as the Creator exists more truly than the creature" (*Monol.* XXXVI, I. 55.4-6). As with reality, so with truth. As nothing is real by itself but only by participating in the supreme being, so nothing is true by itself but "only by participating in the supreme truth" (*De verit.* II, I. 177.16), which supreme truth "causes" the truth in everything else (*De verit.* XIII, I. 199.27-29). And so also with knowledge: Something is known only through the model of it which God has in his understanding (*Monol.* X, I. 24.24f.; 25.27).

[154] It is no accident that, when Anselm considers the power and certainty of his proof, he attributes it to God and offers a prayer of thanksgiving, "that what I first believed through your gift I now understand through your illumination" (*Prosl.* IV, I. 104.5f.).

in textbooks today. By not resting the probative force of the argument on its merely technical validity, and by viewing Anselm's thought as working within a transcendent awareness, instead of groping for contact with the objective world, it offers a picture much closer to the intellectual climate of Anselm's day and to Anselm's own religious motives in the *Proslogion.*

One very serious difficulty facing this interpretation, however, has persuaded many commentators to seek another solution. For how can the argument be based on a direct awareness of God, when Anselm makes so many strictures *against* any such direct awareness? Because created things are "not comparable" to the divine, he warns that our words and concepts, since they properly signify created things, are also not comparable to the divine.

The supreme essence is so above and beyond every other nature that, if ever anything is said of it by means of words which it shares with other natures, there is no common meaning at all. . . . Therefore, if the customary meaning of my words is alien to the supreme essence, whatever reasoning I do does not pertain to it.[155]

God, in other words, is truly *incomprehensibilis* and *ineffabilis*, "because he cannot be described with words just as he is."[156] Therefore, when men try to understand God from the vantage point of their present experience, they have available only the most "shadowy significations," and quickly learn that "he transcends all human understanding."[157]

It thus appears that the opening phrase in *Proslogion* II—"something than which nothing greater can be conceived"—cannot be identified with any direct human experience or awareness of God. The words clearly direct our attention not to God himself, but only to the *inability* of our minds in relation to God. And should any doubt on this matter still remain, Anselm removes it in his *Reply*: "When the expression 'that than which nothing greater can be conceived' is spoken, what is heard can undoubtedly be conceived and understood, even if *the reality itself cannot be conceived or understood.*"[158]

[155] *Monol.* LXV (I. 76.2-9). On the basis of this principle, Anselm affirms the inadequacy of such key words as "wisdom" and "essence" (I. 76.29-77.1): "The word 'wisdom' is not sufficient to show me that through which all things are made and preserved from nothing; and the word 'essence' cannot express to me that which is far above all things through its unique sublimity, and is completely beyond all things through the attributes of its own nature."

[156] *Monol.* LXIV (I. 75.6f.); LXV (I. 77.1f.). [157] *Monol.* LXV (I. 76.22-29).

[158] *Reply* IX (I. 138.9-11). Italics added.

If this evidence is valid and if God for Anselm is beyond human thought, then the realistic interpretation must be discarded. Erich Frank, in fact, finds that the question of God's existence has a special urgency for Anselm because of this feature which the realists overlook. How can anyone be certain of the existence of a being which transcends everything men know, even their capacity for thought?[159] Frank believes that Anselm turns this problem into a solution: Because God is beyond thought, the fool who considers God to be an illusion which thought has fabricated cannot be thinking about God at all.[160]

2. A NOETIC DATUM

As Anselm formulates his argument, he obviously attaches great importance to the fact that "that than which nothing greater can be conceived" is understood and is in the understanding. It is therefore suggested that, instead of immediately identifying this idea with the presence of some actual entity, after the fashion of the realists, we should recognize Anselm's clear emphasis on its conceptual character. He states that it is "in the understanding," and from this he infers that it must "be *conceived* to be" in reality also.[161] Far from starting with the mind in touch with reality, he actually seems to move in just the opposite direction. Until the last step in the argument, he has the mind aware only of its own immanent contents.

On this basis, the proposal is made that what Anselm really does is to propose God as the *cause* of these psychological data, of the idea itself or of the logical necessity which the mind discovers in this idea. In other words, for all its appearance of being "ontological" in the Kantian sense and of inferring God's existence directly from our idea of him, the argument is actually cosmological. It begins with a contingent datum—namely, an idea or an inference in our

159 Erich Frank, *Philosophical Understanding and Religious Truth* (New York, 1952), pp. 34f., p. 51 n. 26: "The Anselmian argument signifies the beginning of a new epoch of philosophical thought. . . . Greek philosophers like Plato, Aristotle and Plotinus still believed that they could directly grasp being through *nous*. A Christian philosopher like Anselm knows that it is no longer possible through thought alone to conceive of God."

160 *Ibid.*, p. 51 n. 30.

161 *Prosl.* II (I. 101.16f.): "If it is at least in the understanding, it can be *conceived* to be also in reality, which is greater."

minds—and it points to God's real existence as the only possible cause for this datum.

Dom Beda Adlhoch gives one version of this interpretation.[162] He contends that Anselm argues from two *empirical* psychological facts. First, men do have an idea of God "in their understanding," an idea which is a mental *res* located in the mind and which, like everything else in the mind, must be "caused." The second psychological fact is that this idea is the highest notion—the "psychological maximum"—which the human mind can form (". . . a greater cannot be conceived"). Now such a mental *res* cannot be produced by the mind itself or by anything in the created world. Therefore, Adlhoch claims, "by inferring from effect to cause according to the law of causality and sufficient reason," Anselm concludes that a supreme being must exist as the cause of this idea.[163] In short, Adlhoch reads *Proslogion* II in terms of the argument in Descartes' *Third Meditation*.[164]

[162] D. B. Adlhoch, "Der Gottesbeweis des hl. Anselm," in *Philosophische Jahrbuch der Görres-Gesellschaft* VIII (1895), pp. 52-69, 372-389; IX (1896), pp. 280-287; X (1897), pp. 261-274, 394-416. The doctrine that the human intellect has God as the immediate and proper object of its knowledge—a view called "ontologism"—was officially condemned by Pius IX in 1861. See Denzinger—Rahner, *Enchiridion Symbolorum* # 1659-65. Certain Italian Roman Catholic theologians suspected Anselm of this error, especially in the 1880s, when the realistic interpretation of the argument began to gain currency. In these articles, Adlhoch seeks to clear Anselm of this charge by showing that his proof is cosmological and not ontological, and that it begins with data from the human mind and not with a direct awareness of God. Adlhoch's view was given some refinements by Adolf Dryoff, "Der ontologische Gottesbeweis des hl. Anselmus in der Scholastik," in *Probleme der Gotteserkenntnis*, by Dryoff *et al.* (Munster, 1928), pp. 90ff.

[163] Adlhoch, *op. cit.*, VIII (1895), pp. 375, 378; X (1897), p. 413.

[164] Descartes' reasoning in the *Third Meditation* is very careful and precise, and it may be compared with Anselm's argument. It has six steps.

(1) We do have the idea of an infinite, eternal, all-knowing and all-powerful substance, from which everything else derives its reality. This is not just the empty negation of all finite qualities, but is the positive representation of such a substance.

(2) This idea represents a more supremely perfect level of reality than any of the ideas of finite substances which the mind has.

(3) The efficient and total cause of anything, whether an object or an idea, must have at least as much reality as that which it causes. Since to "cause" means to "communicate reality" to another, a cause can only produce in the effect such reality as it itself already possesses.

(4) Formally speaking, an idea is only a mode of the human consciousness, and in that respect it has no more reality than what it receives from that consciousness. But an idea also has a *representative* reality. That is, it "represents" something to the mind for consideration. In this respect, it cannot exist in the mind

Étienne Gilson has proposed a more subtle form of this interpretation. Anselm, he contends, appeals to God's reality as the cause, not of the initial idea as such, but rather of the *logical necessity* which the mind discovers in analyzing this idea. Gilson recognizes that Anselm himself does not present his proof in this way in the *Proslogion.* He only demonstrates that thinking of the nonexistence of that than which nothing greater can be conceived is "certainly impossible" for the rational mind. God must be thought of as existing. Then, from this logical necessity, he moves immediately to the conclusion that God must exist in objective reality.

Gilson's point is that, for the argument not to be empty of meaning, we must insert into it a doctrine of truth, according to which the *logical* necessity of affirming the existence of something can only be caused by, and is therefore an infallible sign of, the *ontic* reality of that thing. Or, in its more general form, this doctrine is that every logically necessary proposition is true because it is *caused* by the reality to which it refers. Gilson believes that this is just the principle which Anselm actually develops in his *De veritate* II (I. 177.18).[165]

According to Gilson, then, the argument as stated by Anselm is inadequate. It only presents the datum for a proof. Anselm himself find its satisfactory, however, because he sets it in the context of a causal theory of truth which he takes for granted.

> In St. Anselm's doctrine the necessity of God's existence is the cause of the necessity of affirming that existence. But he never says—and apparently does not even think—that proving God's existence consists in showing how his necessity causes the necessity of our affirming his existence. . . . That is why his argument gives to every philosopher the impression of floating in a vacuum. . . . He simply poses God's existence as necessary in itself, because it is necessary for thought.[166]

---

unless it is put there by a cause which contains *at least as much reality* as whatever is "represented" to the mind by the idea.

(5) The reality represented by the idea of God is so great, however, that the mind is immediately convinced that it itself does not contain such reality formally or eminently, and therefore cannot be the cause of this idea. "I who am a finite being could not have the idea of an infinite substance, unless it were given to me by some actual substance, infinite in reality."

(6) "It is a necessary consequence, then, that I am not alone in the world, but that besides myself there is some other being who exists as the cause of this idea."

This is the argument which Adlhoch finds crudely formulated in *Prosl.* II.

165 É. Gilson, "Sens et nature de l'argument de S. Anselme," in *Archives de l'histoire doct. et lit. du moyen age* IX (1934), pp. 9f., 13f.

166 *Ibid.*, pp. 17f. Cf. also É. Gilson, *The Spirit of Mediaeval Philosophy* (New

The chief objection to this interpretation asks whether Anselm construes the intellectual life in the Cartesian manner, as data inside the head which are somehow "caused" by realities that are outside. For him the intellect is the *intentional* phase of human being. It is man's active openness toward reality, toward real entities through "understanding" and toward possible entities through "conceiving." It is never a self-enclosed place, within which certain phenomena occur, such as ideas and inferences, because of causes operating upon it from without. In other words, the intellect for Anselm is a realm of *relationship*. Therefore, while he does thank God for "giving understanding" to his faith (*Proslogion* IV), while he does speak of objective things as being the "cause" of the truth in statements (*De veritate* II) and of God as being the "cause" of all truth in thought and speech (*De veritate* X), and while he does wonder about the existence of something that is "at least *in intellectu*" (*Proslogion* II), he never thinks of this "understanding" which is given or this "truth" which is caused or this something *in intellectu* which is doubted as being *an entity inside the human mind*. In every case, Anselm explicitly tells us, he is thinking of a "rectitude" *between* the human mind and the object. This correct *relatedness* is what God gives; this correct *relatedness* is what God causes; and this correct *relatedness* is what anything *in intellectu* seems to—but may not—have.[167] Anselm never under-

York, 1940), p. 60: "Where St. Anselm went wrong . . . was in failing to notice that the necessity of affirming God, instead of constituting in itself a deductive proof of his existence, is really no more than the basis for an induction. In other words, the analytical process by which St. Anselm draws the necessity of God's existence from the idea of God is not actually a proof that God exists, but might very well become the initial datum for such a proof. We might try to show that the very necessity of affirming God postulates God's existence as its sole sufficient reason."

[167] M. J. Charlesworth, *St. Anselm's Proslogion* (Oxford, 1965), p. 63: "It is obvious enough that when St. Anselm speaks of 'that than which nothing greater can be conceived' as existing 'in the mind' (*in intellectu*), he does not mean this to be taken in any psychological sense, as though there were existents of two distinct kinds, real existents and mental existents. For something to exist 'in the mind' simply means, for St. Anselm, that it is thinkable, or conceivable, or intelligible, or logically possible; in other words, we know what it would be like for that thing to exist, but we do not know whether it actually exists or not." A. Koyré, *op. cit.*, pp. 208f.: "To have something 'in the understanding' is only the most general manner of saying that this thing is the object of an intellectual act. . . . The being which we have 'in the understanding' is not a copy, image, representation or symbol of the real being. It is that very being itself. *In intellectu esse* only means: to be the object of an intellectual intention, to have an intentional existence."

stands the processes and contents of thought as subjective data externally caused. He would therefore never use causal induction to explore his thoughts about God, although he would use it (and does so in the *Monologion*) to find the cause of objective things.[168]

3. A LIMIT TO "CONCEIVING"

There is another subjective interpretation which, like the preceding view, finds Anselm assuming that the human mind is somehow constrained by God's reality. In this case, however, the divine is not said to "cause" a datum in the mind, but to "limit" a certain mental operation.[169]

Attention is focused on the "conceiving" (*cogitare*), which is referred to in the key phrase. In his *Reply*, Anselm clearly distinguishes this activity from what he calls "understanding" (*intelligere*), in that the latter only occurs in relation to what stands directly before the mind with its own actuality. He agrees with Gaunilo that, "according to the proper meaning of this word, false matters cannot be 'understood,' although they can certainly be 'conceived.' "[170] *Cogitare*, then, is an activity by which the human consciousness breaks away from what actually confronts it and contemplates what is not the case. It designates the mind's freedom from factual necessity, or, as Anselm prefers to call it, "subsequent necessity."[171] "Even though you know (*scire*) with complete certainty that you exist," he says to Gaunilo,

[168] *De verit.* II (I. 178.25), X (I. 190.6f.).

[169] Although no individual has developed this interpretation with consistent thoroughness, commentators often make fragmentary use of it. See, for instance, P. Michaud-Quantin, "Notes sur le vocabulaire psychologique de S. Anselme," in *Spicilegium Beccense*, p. 25.

[170] *On Behalf of the Fool* 7 (I. 129.12-14); *Reply* IV (I. 133.24f.).

[171] *Cur Deus* II. 17 (II. 125.5-22): In the past anything which was going to be the case took on the character of necessity, simply because it was going to happen. "This is nothing more than saying, it was necessarily the case that this would be, because this was actually going to be. Necessity of this kind, however, does not compel something to be, but the fact that it is establishes the [factual] necessity of its actuality (*esse rei facit necessitatem esse*). For there is an antecedent necessity which is the reason (*causa*) that anything is, but there is also a subsequent necessity, which the thing establishes. . . . This subsequent necessity runs through all time: Whatever was, it is necessarily the case that it was; whatever is, it is necesssarily the case that it is and it will necessarily be the case that it was; whatever is going to be, it is necessarily the case that it is going to be." According to Anselm, the human consciousness is bound by this factual necessity with regard to everything that has been or will be in any way actual. Yet it is not completely bound, because by its power of "conceiving," it can consider what is false, that is, what has not been and never will be the case.

"you can *cogitare* yourself as not existing." And you can do this, not by making a real judgment, but by *imagining* (*fingendo*) that things are as you conceive of them.[172] In Latin the term *cogitare* has always suggested this element of inventiveness, of mentally fashioning something that is not actually the case.[173]

The distinction between "understanding" and "conceiving" figures in Anselm's development of his argument. He maintains that the fool "understands" his key phrase and has its content "in his understanding," because the phrase is obviously a real datum confronting the fool's mind. It is therefore grasped by that mental activity which is reality-oriented. Next, when Anselm asks the fool to consider this content as also existing in reality, he shifts to the word "conceive."[174] And he does so, it may be argued, because he knows that God does not stand immediately before the fool's mind, like a datum with factual necessity. He knows that the fool will only be willing to consider God's existence with that mental activity which breaks free from the real and reaches beyond what is directly given. In other words, against the realistic interpretation, this would indicate that Anselm does not assume in the fool a direct knowledge of God's reality.

Given this inventive power of "conceiving," Anselm is able to say that we can conceive of the nonexistence of anything that is, with one important qualification—provided that it does not exist in its totality everywhere and always, that is, provided that there is some objective possibility of its not existing. If something is composed of parts, so that, wherever and whenever it exists, it does not exist in its totality, then, Anselm writes, "it is capable of being dissolved by *cogitatione*." Conceiving is able to fragment it and to imagine reality without any —and all—of these parts.[175] Similarly, if there is any place or any

[172] *Reply* IV (I. 134.7-10).

[173] Cicero: "I do not just 'conceive' of you, I see you;" "I 'conceive' of the walls of Babylon and the face of Homer." Augustine: " . . . these things of heaven which we do not see, but believe and 'conceive' of according to our feeble human capacities." See *Thesaurus linguae Latinae* (1905-1958), on "cogito," vol. III, col. 1467.

[174] *Prosl.* II (I. 101.19). This shift in vocabulary comes through with great force in Anselm's restatement of the argument in *Reply* II (I. 132.22-30).

[175] *Reply* IV (I. 131.23-32): "If the individual parts of something are not where or when its other parts are, all its parts—and therefore the whole of it—can be conceived to be never and nowhere. . . . Just as the individual parts of time do not exist when the other parts do, they can be conceived (*cogitari*) to exist never. And just as the individual parts of the world do not exist where the other parts do, so they can be conceived (*subintelligi*) to exist nowhere."

time where something does not exist, we can expand that condition of nonexistence in our conceiving, and can conceive of that thing as existing never and nowhere.[176] Even if there is only the theoretic possibility of its nonexistence at some time, if we can conceive of it to have a beginning or an end and can therefore conceive of its being absent from reality at some moment, then we can also *conceive* of it as being absent from reality altogether and totally nonexistent.[177] And, of course, these conditions which make it possible for us to conceive of the nonexistence of real things also enable us to conceive of the existence of unreal things.[178] As Anselm tries to show in *Proslogion* III and *Reply* IV, however, there is one reality which lacks these conditions:

> Everything can be conceived not to be, except that which is supremely. . . . That alone cannot be conceived not to be in which conceiving discovers neither beginning nor end nor combination of parts, and which it finds existing always and everywhere in its totality.[179]

What does all this mean? It means that although conceiving is inventive and is able to break free from what is actual, yet it is not completely free. It cannot make up anything at all. For Anselm seems to be saying that by the power of conceiving, the human mind can only devise that which is in some sense *objectively possible*, that which *could* be the case *in reality*. Objective possibilities determine what the mind can initially posit to itself. They establish the absolute limit for conceiving which no ingenuity or effort can surpass. What is nonsensical and ontologically impossible—such as a square circle or a rational beast or a created God—cannot stand before the mind, even though empty verbal statements may be made about such things. In Anselm's phrase, no one can "really conceive" (*vero cogitare*) of them.[180]

The purpose of Anselm's rational analysis, according to this inter-

[176] *Ibid.* (I. 131.18-22): "Whatever does not exist in some place or at some time, even if it does exist in some other place or at some other time, can nevertheless be conceived to exist at no time and in no place, just as it does not exist at some time or in some place. For that which did not exist yesterday and does exist today can be conceived (*subintelligi*) never to exist, just as it is understood (*intelligitur*) not to have existed yesterday."

[177] *Reply* IV (I. 134.2f.): "Everything can be conceived not to be which has a beginning or an end." *Reply* III (I. 133.15f.): "If something could be conceived not to be, it could also be conceived to have a beginning and an end."

[178] *Reply* I (I. 131.3f.): "Whatever can be conceived to be and actually is not can be conceived to be through a beginning."

[179] *Reply* IV (I. 134.1-6).

[180] *Reply* III (I. 133.14f., 18).

pretation, is to show *why* something is impossible and excluded from our conceiving. He employs it, for instance, in *Proslogion* II to demonstrate that a something-than-which-a-greater-cannot-be-conceived which does not exist would be a something-than-which-a-greater-can-be-conceived. The logic shows us, then, that such a nonexistent something-than-which-nothing-greater-can-be-conceived would be an absolute impossibility. It is therefore not really something within the province of our conceiving, not something our minds can devise. Prior to this analysis, we may be under the impression that we can reasonably deny God's existence. The analysis proves, however, that regardless of what we may say with words, nonexistence can have no place, even in our initial conception of God. It shows us those false and empty assertions which we may have been making but which have absolutely no mental content. It discloses to us where we are speaking like fools.

What Anselm designates by *cogitare*, then, has a peculiar character. For all its freedom to move beyond the real, it still has a realistic aspect. It might be called the cognition of objective possibility, just as *intelligere* is the cognition of objective actuality. That is why he can state so confidently in his *Reply* what human conceiving "can" and "cannot" do. It *can* conceive not to be *only* that which is genuinely able not to be. It *cannot* conceive not to be *only* that which has neither a beginning nor an end nor a combination of parts.[181] And because its limits are wholly determined by what is objectively possible and not by what is subjectively preferred, Anselm can examine it to determine what actual possibilities there are. In fact, since conceiving reaches beyond the actual to the possible, it is able to probe into the ontic roots of things far more deeply than "understanding." It offers us a way to "discover" their fundamental metaphysical status, the possibility (or impossibility) of their not existing.[182]

If we now turn to *Proslogion* II and keep in mind that the "conceiving" mentioned in the key phrase is not a free-floating, purely subjective imagining but a peculiar relation of the mind to the real, then we may see that this has a decisive bearing on the argument. For it means that Anselm locates his discussion, not in the realm of the actual (the province of *intelligere*) nor in the realm of the merely

[181] *Reply* V (I. 134.31f.); *Reply* IV (I.134.2-6).

[182] *Reply* IV (I. 134.6), where Anselm calls upon *cogitatio* to "discover" whether there is a beginning or an end or a combination of parts in anything.

fanciful, but in the realm of the objectively possible. In that realm, according to the key phrase, there is nothing greater than God. God is not only unsurpassable by anything in fact; he is also unsurpassable by anything in theory. There is simply not the remotest possibility of there being anything to surpass God. Therefore, because conceiving is rigorously limited to the possible, the fact that nothing *can be* greater than God means that nothing *can be conceived* greater than God. Anselm does not ask the fool to begin with some factitious idea, dreamed up in his head and arbitrarily labelled "God." He refers him to what can be "conceived" (*cogitari*), not "contrived" (*excogitari*).[183] But neither does Anselm join with Gaunilo and simply adopt the entire viewpoint of the fool, conceding to God "no other reality (if this can be called 'reality') than of something which is absolutely unknown to the mind, but of which the mind tries to conceive on the basis of a word merely heard."[184] Whether the fool knows it or not, he, too, stands in a universe where all real and possible things are grounded in God, and his conceiving is affected accordingly. He is able to conceive of every sort of weird and preposterous thing—except that which is objectively utterly impossible. Conceptually he can soar beyond and deny everything that is—except that which *cannot possibly* not be. This is the one actuality which even the fool's conceiving cannot surpass. And if he imagines that God is some easily dismissed illusion, this is only because he is not thinking of the real God.

According to this interpretation, then, the connection between conceiving and the possible provides the key to the argument. This is the hidden assumption which puts Anselm's reasoning in touch with the real, and prevents it from being a mere exercise in empty thought. The proof begins, not with an idea, but with a noetic limit, imposed by, and therefore indicative of, reality itself. The logic simply demonstrates that this initial limit whereby the mind is not able to conceive of anything greater than God, involves other limits, such as its not being able to affirm (*Proslogion* II) or even to conceive of (*Proslogion* III) God's nonexistence.

This interpretation thus puts the argument in the context of the Christian doctrine of creation, according to which all real *and possible* existence depends on God. Since effects never exceed their cause, this

[183] William of Auxerre was the one who presented Anselm's key phrase as *aliquid quo maius excogitari non potest* in his "Summa aureae" I, Q. 2 arg. 4, in A. Daniels, *Geschichte der Gottesbeweis*, p. 27.

[184] *On Behalf of the Fool* 5 (I. 128.5-7).

means that nothing can surpass God, even in the realm of objective possibility. The novelty of Anselm's discovery is located precisely at this point: It postulates God as the Lord and limit of all *possibilities*, and recognizes, therefore, that the inventive mental activity by which we consider what is possible is as much bound to God as objective reason. In fact, it might be argued on theological grounds that anyone, like Gaunilo, who denies the validity of this argument and who maintains that God can only function for us as the cause of the actual—but not as the limit of the possible—does not recognize God's full transcendence.

It is certainly true that the major critics of Anselm's proof do not capitalize on the fact that God is the ground of all real possibilities, and do not interpret "conceiving" as a responsible relation to the real and as an activity which may be used to probe the metaphysical status of things. On the contrary, they are convinced that, once we leave *intelligere* and step beyond the actual, we are in the realm of the doubtful and the false. We have lost touch with the one reference point that can save us from illusion. Gaunilo speaks for all these critics when he challenges Anselm with this problem.[185] He tells him that, before speaking of God's greatness, he should first prove God's existence by an "indubitable" and "most certain" argument—that is, by an argument which shows that the divine "is actually somewhere" and "exists as a genuine and undeniably real thing."[186] In short, Gaunilo takes for granted the pagan belief that the divine can be taken seriously only if it belongs *within* the sphere of the actual, but not of the possible.[187]

The same picture of the mind is found in modern philosophy. Existence, it is said, is not a predicate, an accidental perfection which the intellect can readily dissociate from things. Existence in space and time is a brute thereness, too immediate to be thought and too real to need explanation. It functions like a pagan absolute, which the

[185] *Ibid.*, 2 (I. 126.10-12): "This [argument]—that this object stands in relation to my understanding, since I understand what is heard—will not do, because I believe that all sorts of uncertain or even false things can stand in relation to my understanding in this way, since I understand the words for them."

[186] *Ibid.*, 2 (I. 126.9); 5 (I. 128.2); 7 (I. 129.7).

[187] *Ibid.*, 5 (I. 128.11-13); 6 (I. 128.30-32). According to Thomas Aquinas, also, man is only connected with the real through what is empirically actual. He can say, therefore, that "no difficulty arises in holding that God does not exist" (*Summa contra Gentiles* I.11), because in his view when the mind turns from the actual, it is not constrained by any limit, by any "cannot," at least with respect to God. It is quite able to conceive of God's nonexistence.

mind cannot handle but only honor with reverence.[188] According to the interpretation of the argument reviewed here, Anselm would have nothing to do with this kind of homage. It gives to ordinary existence a mastery over thought which he reserves to God alone. In his view, it is claimed, far from being bound in helpless dependence on factual existence, the mind can easily surpass and dismiss it. God alone is the only reality that cannot be surpassed or denied in this way.[189]

The chief difficulty with this interpretation is that it must discredit Anselm for thinking that his argument is valid "by itself alone." In fact, it portrays *Proslogion* II as not an argument in the proper sense at all. It says that that which makes the reasoning probative is nothing explicitly stated in the text, but is a noetic limit which every mind is supposed to experience because of a radical doctrine of creation. The proof works, not chiefly because of its logical rigor, but because anyone who seriously tries to surpass God will actually encounter this limitation, and will *then* have the knowledge necessary for appreciating the argument. The question remains, however: How can Anselm, in an argument which he thinks is autonomous, take such an elaborate and unusual psychology as something that can be assumed?

4. A REFLEXIVE DISCOVERY

Recent developments in continental philosophy have led to a further portrayal of the argument in subjective terms.[190] This view is based on a fundamental distinction between what may be called "projective" and "reflexive" thought. In every moment of consciousness the mind reaches outward away from itself toward some object; it thus acts intentionally and projectively. At the same time, however, while grasping for things, the mind is also aware of its own operations, of its own intellectual, moral and emotional processes. In other words, alongside the knowledge which each man has of the world, he also possesses a *reflexive knowledge* of himself as an

[188] The question of whether existence can be a predicate is examined in two articles printed below, pp. 219-245.

[189] To show that contingent existence is a thinkable and accidental perfection, Anselm appeals to the fact that "everything which has a beginning or an end can be conceived not to be" (*Reply* IV, I. 134.2f.).

[190] For the contribution of some French philosophers to this interpretation, see the essay by Aimé Forest, "St. Anselm's Argument in Reflexive Philosophy," which is reprinted below, pp. 275ff.

inner spiritual activity, as an *élan*, or dynamism, of consciousness and will.

According to this interpretation, what reflexive knowledge discovers is that, as an activity, the human intellect is always stretching beyond its immediate objects. It is seeking for the universal and the essential and the unconditioned, even though it is confronted by things which are particular, accidental and contingent. In short, it is gripped and haunted by the *idea of God*, which makes it dissatisfied with the meager content of immediate experience, and which keeps it always discovering generalities, building systems and reaching for ultimates. Since, however, this idea of God corresponds to no datum that the mind has encountered, no determinate and specifiable object that can be set alongside and over against other objects, it cannot be an "idea" in the usual sense, that is, a mental representation of something out there. God never stands before the human consciousness as a "something out there." What kind of an "idea" is this, then, and, if it is not generated in the mind by some objective datum, how does it arise?

According to those who emphasize reflexive knowledge, the idea of God is simply the mind's recognition of what lies at the root of its *own* intellectual activity. Human thinking has the idea of God and is constantly seeking for God in all its outgoing action, because it is sustained and activated *from within by God.* This is an idea in the *active* sense. It is that *by which* and *toward which* the mind is moved and provoked in all its thinking. And here, these thinkers claim, we have the key to a responsible knowledge of God. For God is to be known, not as the cause or ground of the outer world, but as the mystery which sustains man's spiritual activity from within. That is to say, he is not discovered inductively from evidence or deductively from concepts, but reflexively, by the mind's consideration of the inner roots of its own activity. Therefore, the idea which men have of him actually arises from their self-knowledge and not from their world-knowledge. It is a *reflexive*—and not a *representative*—idea. According to Ravaisson, when the soul examines itself reflexively, "it does not discern itself only, but also at its foundation, the absolute from which it arises."[191] These writers therefore maintain that we are mistaken in our habit of equating ourselves with ourselves. The presence in our thought of this active idea of God shows that there is more in us than ourselves. When we look at our-

[191] Ravaisson, *Rapport sur la philosophie contemporaine en France*, p. 271.

selves reflexively and become conscious of what we are, we recognize what Aimé Forest calls "an interior beyond" within ourselves, a transcendent mystery that is constitutive of the vital dynamism of all our thinking.[192]

The claim is made that this reflexive discovery of God is what Anselm recognizes and makes explicit in his proof. Anselm begins by showing the fool that he does conceive of God, not of God as some object out in the world, but of God as the absolute maximum of the mind's conceiving, as something than which nothing greater can be conceived. By his opening formula, then, Anselm initiates the fool into a *reflexive inquiry*. The fool is made to realize that his intellect is thinking of something not objectively identifiable, and therefore possesses—or rather, is possessed by—an activity that exceeds the data of his consciousness.

According to the proponents of this interpretation, once the idea of God is seen to be in the mind, there immediately follows the recognition that God himself is present there, activating it to think this idea. But they are quite emphatic that God's existence here is not the conclusion of a logical syllogism or a cause merely postulated to account for a psychological fact. It is something genuinely *perceived* from within the thought that tries to think of him. In other words, it is claimed that, in his argument, Anselm does not want to reason *to* a truth, but simply to give a clear understanding of the divine presence which has always been manifesting itself in the mind's own activity. His argument does not discover what is given to consciousness, but what is at the *foundation* of consciousness. It moves in a regressive manner, from an activity to its inner ground. It produces an awareness and appreciation of what the mind does not embrace in any of its objective representations, but of what embraces it and stands at the origin of its dynamism. Donald Nicholl describes Anselm's project in the following way:

He uses the same philosophical method as Marcel, Heidegger or Sartre, the phenomenological method, which is neither inductive nor deductive, but reflexive (would St. Anselm have said "meditative") . . . . If we interpret the argument in this way, it says that when a person has an idea of a "being than which nothing greater can be conceived," then that person, by reflection, is aware of the existence of such a being. . . . One awareness passes smoothly into another awareness—or rather, one awareness is discovered *in* another awareness. . . . A person realizes that a "being

[192] See p. 281.

than which nothing greater can be conceived" does exist because the very act of his conceiving, on its reverse side, is an operation of God. The human person . . . is conscious of himself as the subject of this divine operation. He discovers himself *in* God.[193]

Jacques Paliard makes the same point: Anselm's argument "does not at all consist in passing from the logical to the real, but in grasping at the very heart of an intellectual experience the reality which conditions it and which it means to reflect. You would not affirm me, it could be said, if you did not already possess me."[194]

It must be made clear that the reflexive activity emphasized here is not to be confused with "introspection." In the latter the mind turns away from the world and looks at its own mental processes as if they were objects. Introspection requires thought to substitute for the objective world an objectivized version of itself. Reflexive knowledge, on the other hand, is what the mind learns about itself *while in the process of thinking about objects*. It accompanies, and does not replace, projective thought. Now this, it is claimed, is exactly what we find in *Proslogion* II. Anselm presumes, even in the unbelieving fool, a genuine projective effort to conceive of God. He expects the fool to try to think about something than which nothing greater can be conceived, to try to understand this and to have it in his understanding. According to the reflexive interpretation, however, Anselm does not mean his proof to help the fool to carry through and complete this projective effort. He demonstrates that this effort, quite apart from whether it succeeds, discloses the existence of God where the fool least expects it, not somewhere out there, where he has been habitually looking, but within and behind this very mental effort in himself.

The chief difficulty facing this reflexive interpretation has to do not with the inward direction which it proposes, but with the identity which it postulates between the idea of God and God's own active reality. To say that human thinking of God is an operation of God certainly echoes the lofty value given to human rationality in modern times, but it does not at all accord with Anselm's perspective. He will have nothing to do with some theandric principle within man, or with the notion that when we have touched the highest in man, we have touched what belongs properly to God. God may be and

193 D. Nicholl, "An Anselmian Soliloquy," in *Downside Review*, 1950, pp 172-181.

194 J. Paliard, "Prière et dialectique," in *Dieu vivant* 6 (1946), p. 57.

may operate in every creature (*Monologion* XX), and by grace he may restore his own image in man's rational activities (*Proslogion* I, *Monologion* LXVII), but Anselm never allows these points to obscure the immense difference between creative and created reality, and never lets an activity immanent within the rational creature to be confused with the divine as such. Moreover, his way of using his key phrase puts the emphasis less on *our conceiving* than on *the something* for which our conceiving reaches. That is, a projective focus on the object is put into the foreground. Also, in his *Reply*, when he argues that the fool can form the idea of something unsurpassably great, he makes no reference to reflexive knowledge, but only to the fool's experience of great things in the world.[195]

5. A REVEALED RULE FOR THOUGHT

A very different view of the argument is proposed by those, like Karl Barth, who see Anselm working exclusively as a theologian. They are particularly concerned to free him from the taint of apologetics. He has no interest, they say, in trying to satisfy the rational demands of unbelievers and in convincing them of God's existence on grounds which they would accept. He is seeking simply to understand the rationality of THE faith (*ratio fidei*), the rationality of that which has been divinely revealed through Christ and is now embodied in the Church's Creed. Since a man's only contact with that revelation comes through an inner attitude of faith, these critics hold that Anselm can no more argue God's existence from the viewpoint of an unbeliever than he could paint a landscape from the viewpoint of a blind man. He may take up an unbeliever's statement as a problem for his own reflections—as here in the *Proslogion* he takes up the fool's denial of God—but he does so in faith and with faith, for a better understanding of the faith. "For Anselm," Barth writes, "the possibility of a discussion with the unbeliever on the latter's ground was . . . the excluded, the forbidden, the impossible possibility."[196]

Now this view requires Barth to reassess *Proslogion* II. For this means that Anselm's discussion about how well the fool can understand the phrase "that than which a greater cannot be conceived" forms *no part of the argument itself*. Anselm does not mean his reasoning to depend on what is in the fool's mind. Barth contends that all Anselm is doing here is to show that the question of God's existence

[195] *Reply* VIII. [196] Barth, *op. cit.*, German p. 72, English p. 69.

is a question which even the fool, for all his disbelief, can view as an intelligible question. That is, because the fool understands the key phrase when he hears it, he does have the idea of something unsurpassable to human thought. He does confront it, a least as an object of his thought, with an objective existence that still has to be investigated.[197] In this way, according to Barth, Anselm shows that the question under discussion is not unintelligible nonsense, even for an unbeliever. He has introduced the fool to the problem of God's existence—as a problem—but nothing more than that.[198] Anselm, Barth insists, is not so foolish as to use the fool's idea *also to solve* this problem. He does not offer, as proof for God's reality, a mental notion in the mind of someone who denies God's reality altogether. Anselm, says Barth, only means to speak "in opposition to" the fool.[199] Therefore, his efforts to show the fool that he understands the words denoting God are only intended to engage the fool in opposition. They are not part of the argument proper.

Barth's position here is not clearly supported by the text, as we shall note later. But it has been of service in showing how the question of apologetics can profoundly affect one's understanding of the structure of the argument. If one takes the position that Anselm means to convince the fool on his own grounds, and therefore seeks a proof that entails nothing which the fool does not already know and accept, then one naturally sees Anselm arguing from the idea of God, which even the fool will admit having in his mind, and trying to infer God's existence solely from that idea. In other words, one is led to interpret the argument as a patent fallacy. By dissociating Anselm completely from any apologetic concern, Barth does not have to locate the argument wholly *within* the circle of the fool's understanding, or to find its starting point in some idea of God which the unbeliever is supposed to have in common with the believer. He thinks he has found a way to exonerate Anselm from simple-mindedly confusing the order of thought with the order of reality.

According to Barth, then, Anselm's argument finds its starting point and leverage, not in some universally accessible human idea about God, but in the self-revelation of God which is reliably articulated by the Credo and in which Christians firmly believe. Specifically, it begins with the revelation that "you are something than

197 *Ibid.*, German pp. 119f., 133, English pp. 108f., 118f.

198 *Ibid.*, German pp. 138f., English pp. 122f.

199 *Ibid.*, German p. 64, English p. 62.

which nothing greater can be conceived." From this given revelation the argument proceeds. But how? By what mechanism does it infer God's existence? Not, Barth maintains, by unraveling the *content* of this description of God.

In support of this Barth appeals to the literal meaning of the key phrase, which says nothing directly about God's nature but only about human thinking. Its content is noetic, rather than ontic. Instead of giving a positive description of God himself, it specifies what the human mind *cannot do* in relation to God: It cannot conceive of anything greater.[200] Barth is quite insistent that nothing here gives us grounds for establishing the argument on an ontological basis, as Gaunilo and the theologians of the thirteenth century did. They all made the proof proceed from some ontic assumptions about God's reality, such as that God is "greater than all things" (Gaunilo), or that God is "the simplest" (Richard Fishacre), or that God is "the truth" (Alexander of Hales).[201] Barth holds that, in associating Anselm's proof with such ontic assumptions, these writers ignore the fact that what Anselm starts with is not any direct description of God's nature, but *a God-given rule for human thinking* (*Denkregel*).[202]

Furthermore, Barth points out that, in Anselm's view, truth belongs primarily to objective reality, and that thought becomes true only secondarily, insofar as it conforms to what is objective.[203] To understand God's objective existence, Anselm must raise his knowledge of God to the level of truthfulness, and for this no analysis of the mere idea of God, no merely intellectual acquaintance with him

[200] *Ibid.*, German p. 78, English p. 75: The key phrase "does not say *that* or *what* God is. . . . Nothing is contained in it in the way of statements about the existence or about the nature of the designated object." Also, German p. 113, English p. 102f.: "It conceals no declaration about the nature of God, and still less (concealed in this) a declaration about the existence of God. The formula simply repeats the prohibition, imposed on a believer's thinking by revelation . . . that he is not to think of anything greater than God, on the pain of the consequence that the thought of a 'God' who can be set beside something greater would immediately cease to be the thought of the real—that is, of the revealed and believed—God."

[201] *Ibid.*, German p. 93 n. 1, English p. 87 n. 1. See A. Daniels, *Geschichte der Gottesbeweise*, on Fishacre, pp. 22f., #s 1, 6 and 8; on Alexander, p. 28 # 1 and p. 30 #s 7-9; on Bonaventure p. 40 # 23.

[202] Barth, *op. cit.*, German pp. 84, 93, English pp. 80, 87. Also, German p. 96, English p. 89: "*Quo maius cogitari nequit* is designed to exclude just this conceivability of God's nonexistence or imperfection which lies in the background of every ontic idea of God—to exclude it with the thoroughness and force of the Creator's prohibition to the creature: *non eritis sicut Deus*."

[203] *Ibid.*, German pp. 99-101, 139f., English pp. 92f., 123f.

is sufficient, even if that acquaintance is derived from revelation itself.

It is Barth's proposal, then, that instead of trying to unravel the idea of God which is communicated to us by the key phrase, Anselm's strategy is to use the key phrase as it is meant to be used: as a *criterion for judging the various assertions about God* which men make. Barth sees the argument as having four steps, which we may paraphrase as follows.[204]

1. Anselm asks us to conceive of "that than which a greater cannot be conceived" in two ways: first as something that is purely intramental (*esse in solo intellectu*), and then as something that is both intramental and extramental (*esse et in re*).

2. Anselm then observes that the second is "greater" than the first—not quantitatively but qualitatively greater. In fact, it is so much greater that what is conceived in these two different ways cannot be the same thing at all. We cannot add extramental existence to our idea of an intramental God without thereby conceiving of an essentially different and "essentially greater" being.

3. Up to this point Anselm has been moving wholly within the inner circle of what is thought. Now he takes the decisive step. Using as his criterion the revelation that God is "that than which a greater cannot be conceived," he determines that the God conceived in the first way above, the purely intramental and essentially lesser God, cannot be God at all. Because we can easily conceive of something greater than him, he does not possess that characteristic which the real God has truthfully *revealed* to be his. What Anselm does is to show that when men think of God "properly," that is, when they think of him in accord with the key phrase that has been revealed, they cannot think of him as existing only in thought.

4. Anselm then draws his conclusion: Since the first way of conceiving of God—as something which exists in thought alone—is false, the other way of conceiving of God must be true, for it stands in conformity with God's own self-revelation. Therefore, since the notion that God "exists both in the understanding and in reality" is true, God must really exist in reality.

Let us note a number of features of this interpretation.

1. Barth believes that the proof breaks out of the circle of human thought by means of the key phrase, considered as something divinely revealed, or, as he prefers to say, considered as God's "revealed name." This is what enables the argument to attain objectivity. Anselm's critics, Barth believes, fail to appreciate this crucial point. Like Gaunilo, they do not understand how Anselm can pre-

[204] *Ibid.*, German pp. 140-146, English pp. 124-129.

sume the givenness and reliability of this formula. They see it only as the expression of some idea in the fallible human mind, and as being merely the statement of a false or dubious thing. Therefore, they plead with Anselm first to prove God's existence by a rigorous argument, before appealing to this questionable idea.[205] According to Barth, however, "it is in no sense Anselm's intention to produce this formula out of his own head."[206] He sees it as part of what "we believe," part of the divinely authorized Credo. It therefore provides a genuinely objective reference point, by which to test various human statements about God.[207] For Barth, then, Anselm attains objectivity in the formula itself, considered as divine revelation, and to disregard this fact is to leave the argument in a vacuum.[208]

2. In this interpretation the key phrase plays its role not by giving us any direct knowledge of God, but by serving as a *norm* by which we can judge whatever ideas we may have concerning God. It confronts us with a prohibition that must be obeyed, rather than with a concept that must be thought. According to Barth, Anselm considers the human mind quite capable of transgressing this prohibition. In fact, the fool who denies God's existence actually attributes *less* reality to the divine than to any stone or mosquito which actually exists. He "can" conceive of many things greater than God. The mental inability designated by the formula pertains to men only insofar as they see themselves standing in the presence of their Creator and offer to him their total obedience, which is to say, only insofar as they have become his faithful servants and have abandoned all efforts to make themselves superior to him.[209] For them this revealed prohibition has absolute force and requires them never to conceive of God as nonexistent. In this way, Barth makes good his contention that Anselm presumes no ontic knowledge of God in his argument. For according to this analysis, what the proof gives us is not a knowledge of God, but only a knowledge of the truth or falsity of *our thoughts* about God.

3. Since the key phrase provides us with a norm for our thoughts, rather than with any direct knowledge of God, it cannot function

205 E.g., Gaunilo *op. cit.*, 2 (I. 125.15f.), 5 (I. 128.5-7,9-11), 6 (I. 128.26-30). Barth, *op. cit.*, German p. 127, English p. 114: "For Gaunilo *quo maius cogitari nequit* is just one *percepta vox* among many others, and is not a dynamic word of revelation; it is not the name of God that is revealed and believed."

206 Barth, *op. cit.*, German p. 81, English p. 77.

207 *Ibid.*, German p. 175, English p. 152.

208 *Ibid.*, German pp. 149f., English pp. 130f.

209 *Ibid.*, German p. 176 n. 1, English p. 153 n. 1.

alone. It requires another element, namely, *acts of thinking which it can judge*. Barth remarks that the traditional view that Gaunilo inaugurated—to the effect that Anselm means to prove God's existence by using the key phrase and nothing else—could only succeed if the key phrase offered us an immediate vision of God. But it does not. It simply states a rule for human thinking about God, and this by itself can never settle the question of God's existence. To do so would be, as Barth says, to "produce knowledge of God's existence out of a vacuum—a real *creatio ex nihilo*."[210] In Barth's view, therefore, alongside the revealed rule for thought, the proof also contains a "second element of knowledge," a "second assumption": namely, fallible human thoughts about God which are to be proved, and thus raised to the status of genuine knowledge, by means of this rule.[211] In this sense, Barth maintains that the argument is synthetic and not analytic.[212]

4. By having the proof depend on an extrinsic norm which men receive from the divine revelation, Barth says that Anselm is able to let human thinking be just what it is—subjective, unreliable, partly receptive but also partly inventive—without thereby undercutting the proof. In other words, he does not have to impute to the mind a reliable awareness of God, which the argument simply unravels. He does not have to relate human thinking directly to God, thus compromising his own insistence on the *indirectness* of all knowledge which men have of God in this life.[213] He only requires that his readers conceive of God, first as an object of thought alone and then as a real existent, and that they do so with the same confused, problematic and often misguided thinking which is normally theirs. To be sure, the second possibility—namely, that God truly exists—is contained in the articles of faith, but, Barth maintains, Anselm carefully avoids appealing to this to settle the question.[214] God's existence is at this stage simply something to be conceived of by the mind in the ordinary way, like any other dubious thing. One of Barth's major points is that Anselm transposes this conceiving to the status of truth, not by arbitrarily conferring upon it some special infallibility, but by assessing it *against the rule of thought* which the Christian derives from revelation.

5. One elusive feature of Barth's interpretations is that it requires

[210] *Ibid.*, German p. 85, English p. 81.
[211] *Ibid.*, German pp. 78f., 85, English pp. 75, 81.
[212] *Ibid.*, German p. 95, English pp. 88f.
[213] *Ibid.*, German pp. 83-85, 127-129, English pp. 79f., 113-115.
[214] *Ibid.*, German pp. 39f., English pp. 42f.

the formula to *function in two different ways*. In steps 1 and 2 the phrase expresses something conceived by the human mind, conceived first as a purely mental object and then as an object in reality. In this form the phrase described is a very uncertain thing which stands within the problematic circle of human thinking. It constitutes the *material* element in the argument, that which must be raised by proof to the level of rational certainty. In step 3, however, the formula begins to function as a divine revelation, which Christians believe and which imposes a stringent prohibition upon their thinking. In this form it consistutes the normative and *formal* element of the argument, that which gives a demonstrative force to the reasoning. In Barth's view, everything depends on catching this difference between the material and the formal components, between the formula as humanly conceived and the formula as divinely revealed and believed.

6. Barth recognizes the very limited conclusion to which this reasoning leads. He emphasizes that it does *not* prove God's existence directly. It only shows that God's nonexistence "cannot be" (*hoc esse non potest*), that we are not allowed to conceive of a nonexistent God when we proceed in accord with divine revelation. According to Barth, Anselm's further assertion—that God must therefore actually exist both in the understanding and in reality—"does not spring from the proof and is in no way derived from it. It is demonstrated by the proof only insofar as the opposite statement about God's merely intramental existence is shown to be absurd."[215] For Barth, however, far from weakening the argument, this indirectness is precisely what Anselm desires. For he does not seek a direct proof, that is, a proof which we would only have to think through in order to have God's existence securely before our minds. That would mean that we would not have to wait upon God's free self-revelation for our knowledge of his existence. The proof would take the place of revelation, and God's existence would be an item at the easy disposal of human reasoning.[216] In Barth's view, however, Anselm has no desire to carry his proof in this direction. He wants it to function within—and not in place of—God's revelation. Therefore, since the positive statement that God exists is given and must be continually given by revelation, and since it is therefore not something which the human mind can envelop and take full possession of by its own rational efforts, all that reason can do is what Anselm sketches in

[215] *Ibid.*, German p. 146, English p. 128
[216] *Ibid.*, German pp. 34f., English pp. 38f.

Proslogion II: It can take the opposite statement, that God only exists in the mind, and can reduce it to an absurdity by means of a rule of thought taken from revelation. Barth thus sees the limited conclusion of the proof as part and parcel of Anselm's conception of Christian gratitude and obedience. Men, even in their reasoning, can only acknowledge and recognize that their fruitful dealings with God depend completely on his prior communication of himself to them.[217]

With these distinctive features of Barth's view in mind, it is easy to see how much they depend on his thesis that Anselm is a theologian, working only within the Christian revelation for the benefit of his fellow Christians. Criticisms of Barth's view therefore concentrate chiefly on this question, rather than on this detailed study of the argument. There are several fundamental points in his analysis, however, which do not find support from the text of *Proslogion* II.

Barth maintains, for example, that, as a theologian, Anselm does not argue from the viewpoint of the fool. He wants to help faith seek understanding, not to convert unbelief by means of a rationality that is supposed to be stronger than pride and sin. According to Barth, then, his discussion of the fool's understanding of the key phrase has no place in the argument. It is simply a preliminary remark. By completely identifying Anselm with revelational theology, Barth finds that he must posit a discontinuity in the text, between the statements which describe and engage the unbeliever in terms of what the believer knows, and the argument itself, which, by the application of a revealed rule of thought, gives understanding to the Christian believer. The text itself, however, indicates no such discontinuity, either in its style or train of thought. In fact, it creates just the opposite impression. After showing that "something than which nothing greater can be conceived" is in the *fool's* understanding, Anselm opens what Barth calls "the proof proper" by saying that this something "cannot be in the understanding alone."[218] Does Anselm here give any hint that now he has ceased to be concerned with what the fool understands and has suddenly become interested only in the believer? Does he not build upon his description of the fool, arguing that what he has just shown to be in the *fool's* understanding cannot be in *that* understanding alone? The whole proof seems to be based on what is in the fool's mind. Furthermore, this initial statement of

[217] *Ibid.*, p. 173, English pp. 150f.
[218] *Ibid.*, German p. 139, English p. 123.

the "argument proper" begins with the words "*et certe. . .*," which heighten the sense of continuity with the preceding sentence.

The same difficulty faces Barth's appeal to a datum of revelation. According to his analysis, in the early stages of the argument the key phrase characterizes for us a hypothetical something, which we are to conceive of first as not existing, and then as existing. But in the later stages, Barth tells us, when these two ways of conceiving are assessed by their conformity to the key phrase, this phrase then represents a datum of revelation, carrying the authority and reliability of God himself. Barth's whole effort to save the argument from fallacy depends on thus shifting the formula from a material to a formal status, The text, however, indicates no such shift. When it says that a nonexistent God cannot be something "than which nothing greater can be conceived," it seems to be appealing to the key formula just as it was presented four lines earlier—not as a divine revelation, but as something in the fool's understanding. The text seems to be exhibiting *to the fool* a purely intellectual contradiction in his own mind, and not warning Christians against the transgression of a God-given command. Here, again, Barth posits a discontinuity which does not find support in Anselm's statements.

Finally, Barth's view makes the proof an argument from authority, for he says that the norm by which Anselm decides between the two ways of conceiving of God is established not by reason, but simply by the fact that it is revealed. "How," Barth asks, "do we know that God is really named 'that than which a greater cannot be conceived'? We know it because that is how God has revealed himself, and because we believe him just as he has revealed himself."[219] As Barth explains at another point, the formula can have meaning in the argument only if we hear it as coming from our Creator, only if it expresses the lordship which God possesses over us when we stand in his presence. If we do not receive it in this way, we do not understand it at all.[220] This means that the power and the leverage of the argument depend wholly upon *authority*, not upon the authority of the key phrase as such, of course, but upon the authority of God in his revealed presence. Here we find Barth colliding not only with Anselm's explicit disavowal of all appeal to authority,[221] but also

[219] *Ibid.*, German p. 175, English p. 152.

[220] *Ibid.*, German p. 176 n. 1, English p. 153 n. 1.

[221] See *Epist. de Incarn. verbi*, rev. ed., 6 (II. 20.17-19): " . . . my two little works, the *Monologion* and *Proslogion*, which are especially (*maxime*) written to this end, that what we hold by faith about the divine nature and persons (except

with his clear desire to resolve the issue at the level of "evident" dialectics and "well-known" words, rather than at the level of religious encounter.[222]

6. AN IDEA PROVED IN THE MONOLOGION

All the interpretations which we have examined so far are based on the assumption that Anselm takes his initial idea for granted and for that reason does not give a clear account of its origin and status. He simply presents us with the fool thinking about the key phrase and proceeds from there. But why does he believe that this first act needs no explanation? Does it represent a direct and primordial intuition of God (according to his realism in the *Epistola de Incarnatione verbi*)? Is it a universal reflexive discovery (in conformity with his strong self-awareness in *Proslogion* I)? Or is it a revealed truth which can be assumed in his medieval society (for he explicitly says that this is something "we believe")?

There are a number of interpreters, however, who find that all this speculation is beside the point. Of course, an explanation of the status of this idea is necessary, they say. Anselm himself admits that not only his argument for God's existence, but his entire reasoning throughout the *Proslogion*, depend on the "strength" (*vis*) of the key phrase.[223] It is therefore out of the question that he would fail to explain it. By his own reckoning such a failure would cripple his work. According to these interpreters, if we find no explanation in the *Proslogion*, the reason is as obvious as it is simple: he has already given it in the *Monologion*.

In this earliest of his writings, Anselm seeks to prove the existence of a *summum magnum* from the existence of things in this world. He starts with the partial goodness (*Monologion* I) or greatness (*Monologion* II) or existence (*Monologion* III) or relative superiority (*Monologion* IV) of the objects which we find around us. In each case he argues that the cause by which all these objects are good (or great or existent or superior) in their particular ways must itself be some *one thing* which is greater in its goodness (or greatness or existence or

---

for the Incarnation), can be proved by necessary reasons without the authority of Scripture."

[222] *Consequentius* (*Reply* II, I. 132.27); *palam* (*Reply* III, I. 133.10); *nota lingua* (*Reply* II, I. 132.12).

[223] *Reply* X (I. 138.30-139.3).

supremacy) than all these, which in fact is good (or great or existent or supreme) through and by itself alone, and which therefore cannot simply possess these attributes, but must itself be the very essence of goodness (or greatness or being or supremacy).[224] Some writers therefore propose that when Anselm wrote the *Proslogion*, he not only had these proofs from the *Monologion* clearly in mind, but he actually *presupposed them* in his reasoning. That was why he could expect his readers to take for granted that the idea of a *summum magnum* unsurpassable by thought had a secure basis in reality. Instead of worrying about this point again, he simply assumed its validity as proved in the *Monologion*, and spent his efforts subjecting it to a detailed logical analysis. According to this view, then, the *Proslogion* was intended to be read as the extension of, or appendix to, the *Monologion*. For that reason, every effort by modern readers to find a starting point for the argument within the *Proslogion* itself is doomed to failure. No such starting point exists there.[225]

The main evidence for this interpretation comes from the *Reply*. When Gaunilo objects that Anselm's key phrase is as much beyond human understanding as God himself, in other words, when he questions the status of this initial idea, Anselm simply repeats the reasoning which he developed in *Monologion*. He shows how our minds can ascend from lesser goods to greater goods, and how, from the things through which we do conceive of something greater, we can learn "a great deal" about "that than which we can conceive of nothing greater."[226] Further evidence for this view has been found in the key phrase itself. For God is characterized there by the words "nothing greater," which means that Anselm thinks of him not as he is in himself, but as the supreme term in a scale of "great things."[227] This idea of God is therefore derived from the structure of and the items in this scale, and this is just what Anselm demonstrates in the *Monologion*.

[224] *Monol.* V, VI and XVI.

[225] Before the realistic interpretation became popular, it was standard practice for nineteenth-century historians to base the argument in *Prosl.* II on the proofs in the *Monol.* See, for instance, H. Bouchitte, *Le rationalisme chrétien* (Paris, 1842); C. de Rémusat, *S. Anselme de Cantorbéry* (Paris, 1854), p. 454; A. Stockl, *Geschichte der Philosophie des Mittelalters* (Mainz, 1864), vol. I, pp. 264f.; Van Weddingen, "Essai critique sur la philosophie de S. Anselme," in *Mémoires couronnes* (Brussels, 1875), pp. 320ff. For a contemporary statement of this view, see the essay by A. Beckaert reprinted on pp. 111ff.

[226] Gaunilo, *op. cit.*, 4 (I. 126.31-127.2). Anselm, *Reply* VIII (I.137.14-28).

[227] See Austin Farrer, *Finite and Infinite* (London, 1943), p. 12 n. 1.

It would be a relief to be able to dispense with all the historical speculations which we have surveyed and to fill in elements missing from the argument with reasoning directly presented in the earlier work. Unfortunately, such a procedure flatly contradicts Anselm's own unambiguous statements. In the Preface he explains that the whole point of his *Proslogion* is to escape a complex tangle of reasoning (*concatenatio multorum argumentorum*) and to find a completely autonomous argument which would require for its proof "nothing else but itself alone" (*nullo alio quam se solo*).[228] In the proof itself, and again in the *Reply*, he goes out of his way to emphasize that men have only to hear and understand the words of the key phrase for the argument to convince them. On their part "no other work is needed."[229] He could hardly be more explicit. He may have been mistaken, of course, about this ideal of autonomy, and his argument may actually require the sort of reasoning that he offers in the *Monologion*. But it is difficult to claim that this linkage was part of his deliberate intention.

7. CONCLUSION: THE NEXT PROPOSAL

From this survey it is certainly clear that the investigation of *Proslogion* II has not yet been completed. The traditional view, that the argument simply analyzes a subjective concept, has fallen out of favor, but no broadly accepted alternative has been found. In fact, considering the labor that has been expended and yet the continuing failure of every interpretation to escape points of awkwardness, we might conclude that the project is impossible, that sufficient data do not exist—either in Anselm's own corpus or in the extant remnants from his age—to settle our questions about his argument. Apparently any commentator can look at the text from his own perspective and can find just enough evidence there to warrant his own particular theory.[230] Yet the actual situation is even more chaotic than has yet been indicated. For very few interpreters adopt one or another of the "pure" positions sketched above. Recognizing the hopeless complexity of the evidence, they hedge their bets, so to

[228] *Prosl.* Preface (I. 93.4-7).

[229] *Reply* V (I. 135.19f.); *Reply* X (I. 138.31).

[230] Cf. Paul Evdokimov, in *Spicilegium Beccense*, p. 234: "The argument is like one of those inns in Spain to which each person brings his own food and drink."

speak, and combine fragments from different theories in all kinds of ways. One popular strategy is to connect the argument with the proofs in the *Monologion*, but at the same time to ground it *both* on the data of Christian revelation and on a realistic awareness of God.[231] According to another proposal, Anselm assumes that God is vitally related to every soul, yet with his logic he argues for God's existence as the cause of our idea of him.[232] Within a single paragraph Étienne Gilson is able to coordinate Anselm's theological effort to understand revelation with his Platonic realism.[233]

It is possible, however, to make a different judgment of this situation. Perhaps all of these proposals, in spite of their variety, are actually shaped by a common but unrecognized principle, and perhaps that principle is so alien to Anselm that no fully satisfactory interpretation can be achieved. There are clear indications not only that such a principle has been present everywhere, but also that it has had the effect of falsifying the most vital point in the argument.

In both *Proslogion* II and the *Reply*, Anselm gives a perfectly clear account of where his reasoning begins. The proof, he says, only requires someone to *hear and understand ordinary words*, specifically, the words of the key phrase. "Yet when this very same fool hears what I say, when he hears of 'something than which nothing greater can be conceived,' he certainly understands what he hears."[234] Yet Anselm goes further and relies on these ordinary words, not only to begin his proof, but also to draw out its conclusion. He argues that "something than which nothing greater can be conceived" must exist in reality, because otherwise it would contradict *the meaning of these words*. [235] Since he makes no efforts to authorize and verify his phrase, Gaunilo directs some of his most vigorous attacks against this point. How can anything true ever be known simply on the basis of a word heard?[236] In the face of this criticism, however, Anselm simply reaffirms his position. "In my argument nothing else

[231] So Adolf Dyroff, "Der ontologische Gottesbeweis in der Scholastik," in Dyroff, Elfes *et. al. Probleme der Gotteserkenntnis* (Munster, 1928), pp. 91, 84, 90f; and A. Faust, *Der Möglichkeitegedanke* (1932), vol. II, pp. 132, 164-167, 149.

[232] See Dom Illtyd Trethowan, *An Essay in Christian Philosophy* (London, 1954), p. 105.

[233] Étienne Gilson, *History of Christian Philosophy in the Middle Ages* (New York, 1955), p. 135.

[234] *Prosl.* II (I. 101.7f.).

[235] *Prosl.* II (I. 101.18f.); *Reply* I (I. 131.13-15); *Reply* II (I. 132.23-133.2): "In that case 'that than which a greater cannot be conceived' would be that than which a greater can be conceived, which is utterly absurd."

[236] Gaunilo; *op. cit.*, 4 (I. 127.13f.).

is needed except uttering (*sonat*) the words, 'that than which a greater cannot be conceived.' "[237] He is convinced, apparently, that hearing words is an event of genuine knowledge; that words themselves have the power to initiate some kind of relation of "understanding" between the listening mind and reality. They present to the mind not just the subjective thoughts of the man who speaks them, but the actual entities to which they refer. Anselm is so certain of their noetic power, in fact, that if anyone claims to be unaffected by them, he says that he will dismiss such a person as either impudent or feeble-minded.[238]

With regard to words about God, however, Anselm recognizes that their power is severely limited. They cannot present the divine reality as they do the reality of ordinary objects, because in the present life God completely surpasses human cognition. Nevertheless, Anselm is convinced that they do convey something to the listening mind.

When [the expression] "that than which a greater cannot be conceived" is spoken, what is heard (*quod auditur*) can undoubtedly be conceived and understood, even if that very reality (*illa res*) cannot be conceived or understood.[239]

Anselm never gives a clear account of this peculiar knowledge and never explains how we are able to understand the "what" of a statement about God without understanding God's "*res*." He seems to be groping toward the distinction between perceiving the literal meaning of the verbal statement, along with its dialectical consequences, and gazing upon the full reality which bears this meaning.[240] In any

[237] *Reply* V (I. 135.19f.).

[238] *Reply* II (I. 132.12f.): "Whoever does not understand when familiar words are spoken to him either has no understanding at all or a very obtuse one." *Reply* IX (I. 138.11-15): "Even if anyone were so foolish as to say that 'something than which a greater cannot be conceived' does not exist, he still would not be so impudent as to say that he could not understand or conceive what was said. Or, if such a person were found, his words should be discredited (*respuendus*) and he himself denounced (*conspuendus*)."

[239] *Reply* IX (I. 138.9-11).

[240] *Reply* I (I. 132.7-9): "Certainly 'that than which a greater cannot be conceived' is understood and does stand in relation to the understanding *at least to this extent*, that these matters concerning it [i.e., these matters grasped by dialectical analysis of its meaning] are understood." In *Monol.* X (I. 24.27-29) Anselm identifies only two kinds of knowledge that involve words: We may think of the *voces* as such, or we may have an intellectual vision of the *res ipsae* which the words signify. These are exactly the same categories used by Gaunilo. He points out that the fool who is supposed to "understand" the key phrase must do so

case, he is quite emphatic that this *intelligere quod auditur* represents a genuine knowledge, and that it is produced in the mind by intelligently hearing the words of the key phrase. He never intimates that his formula functions merely to express an idea or awareness that stands inside someone's head. By virtue of its intelligibility, it is able to relate the minds of those who hear it to the real God (although not directly to God's reality)—provided, of course, they hear it intelligently in terms of its meaning and not stupidly as a string of verbal noises.[241]

There is nothing new or unique in this confidence which Anselm shows in the power of language. In the Christian tradition it had its source in the Pauline passage: "How are men to believe in the Lord of whom they have never heard? And how are they to hear without a preacher? . . . Therefore, faith comes from what is heard, and what is heard comes by the word of Christ," i.e., by preaching (Rom. 10:14-17). On this basis, Augustine argues that an understanding of human words must always precede Christian faith. "No man can believe in God unless he understands somewhat. . . . Since 'faith comes from what is heard and what is heard by the word of Christ,' how can anyone believe him who preaches the faith if he . . . does not understand the language that is spoken?"[242] The same point is made by Anselm.

When Paul says that faith is from what is heard, it is to be understood

---

either *secundum vocem* or *secundum rem* (*On Behalf of the Fool* 4, I. 127.13; 126.31). The first would mean that the fool only thinks about the words themselves, without having any notion of what they signify, and "it would be astonishing if he ever hit upon the truth of God's reality in this way" (I. 127.13-21). *Secundum rem* would mean that the fool now possesses a direct vision of God and thus has a truer knowledge than any living Christian (I. 126.31-127.3). In either case the argument seems to collapse. It is in the face of this criticism that Anselm in his *Reply* moves beyond his position in *Monol.* X and proposes a third kind of knowledge, not of the mere words of his formula (*secundum vocem*), nor of God's reality (*secundum rem*), but of "what is heard," of what the words mean—*secundum significationem*, so to speak. In this way, Anselm tries to escape the stark choice of either total vision or total ignorance posed by Gaunilo.

[241] As Anselm points out in *Reply* VII (I. 136.30-137.5), the word "God" can only be an empty verbal noise, because it is a technical term which conveys nothing in the realm of normal discourse. His formula, however, consists of ordinary words and therefore presents not only its verbal exterior, but also its meaning to anyone with ordinary intelligence. That is why, he explains, it can be used to introduce the fool to the knowledge of God.

[242] Augustine, *In Ps.* 118, *Sermon* XVIII. 3. Also *Sermon* XLIII.vii.9: "Understand in order that you may believe my words; believe, in order that you may understand the Word of God."

that faith is from *what the mind conceives through what is heard*—not that the mind's conceiving alone produces faith, but that faith cannot be without conceiving.[243]

Anselm makes it clear that this verbal knowledge produces faith in people only if divine grace moves their will to *want* what the words say. Without this gift of right willing, they receive no blessing or newness of life from their knowledge.[244] Anselm also explains that conceiving of something through its verbal description does not convey knowledge of whether the thing described is actual. By hearing what the words mean, a person is only able to conceive of the thing as a thinkable possibility and nothing more. If he wants to encounter its actuality, he must go to experience.[245] In this way, Anselm keeps knowledge-through-words (which he identifies with "conceiving") carefully distinct from knowledge-through-experience (which he calls "understanding").

The description of "conceiving what is heard" from the preacher is exactly parallel to the account of the atheist which Anselm gives in *Reply* VII.[246] In the one case, the believer would never have faith if the preacher's *words* had not first communicated *their meaning* to him. In the other case, the unbeliever denies what is called "God" because he does not know the *meaning of this word*. Both passages make the same point: Ordinary words in themselves have such communicative power that anyone who hears them can naturally "conceive" their meaning, even if he cannot tell whether their meaning is true.

When, therefore, an unbeliever is addressed by statements of Christian belief—such as the key phrase in *Proslogion* II—even though he does not believe what they say, he is able to grasp their meaning intellectually, provided they are expressed in the ordinary words which he understands.

It might be argued, then, that, in *Proslogion* II, Anselm rests his argument on the power of verbal statements to convey their objective meaning. This would explain why he thinks it enough for the fool simply to hear and understand the words of his key phrase. This

243 *De concordia praesc.* III.6 (II. 271.5-8). Italics added.

244 *Ibid.* (II. 271.14-17).

245 *Epist. de Incarn. verbi* original ed., 4 (I. 284.26-29), rev. ed., I (II. 9.5-8): " 'He who has not believed will not understand' (Isa. 7:9). For he who has not believed will not experience, and he who has not experienced will not conceive. For as much as experience surpasses something heard, so much does the understanding (*scientia*) of what is experienced surpass the conceiving of what is heard."

246 *Reply* VII (I. 136.31f.).

would also explain why he is confident that this statement of Christian faith will mean something to an unbeliever—enough at least for him to follow a purely conceptual argument. In the generations after Anselm, thinkers continued to have confidence in the noetic power of language and to keep a sharp contrast between knowledge-through-words and knowledge-through-experience.[247]

Without exception, all modern interpreters of the argument reject the principle that words can produce knowledge. However vigorously they may champion Anselm's argument, on this point they agree with Gaunilo that "something true can rarely, if ever, be known in this way." They consider language to be a mental epiphenomenon, a tool for subjectivity. Men use it to *express* or *externalize* whatever lies within their minds. Words, they believe, do not produce thought —thought produces words and gives them whatever significance they may have. This means that if we want to find the meaning of any statement, we must discover what those who use it *have in mind.* We must penetrate their subjectivity.

Every interpretation of the argument written during the last two centuries has been controlled by this hermeneutic principle. Although Anselm says that he begins with the fool hearing and understanding the words of the key phrase, it is assumed that this is just his way of expressing and appealing to something *already present* either *in* the fool's mind or *in* his own. The historian's task is to get behind these words and to determine, on the basis of historical evidence, what subjective item Anselm most likely has in mind. Perhaps it is a purely mental creation, an "idea" which the fool concocts in his head in response to the formula. On the other hand, perhaps it is a subjective awareness of something real—an immediate intuition or a reflexive discovery or an encounter with revelation or a cosmological inference. In any case, it is agreed that the historian must get behind and subjectivize Anselm's appeal to the words of his formula. Here we have a principle which has shaped all modern interpretations of

[247] See, for example, Hugh of St. Victor, *De sacramentis christianae fidei* II.x.3: "By *cognitio* we understand a knowledge of things—not that knowledge which is comprehended from the presence of the things themselves, but that which is received only from what is heard and is made manifest by the meaning of words. When he who hears understands what is said, even if he does not know whether or not it really is as it is said, knowledge still exists insofar as he understands and knows what that is which is said. This knowledge is *cognitio*." One could hardly ask for a clearer statement of the kind of knowledge which Anselm requires for his argument and which he produces in the mind of anyone willing to hear his key phrase intelligently.

the argument, and which, if it is false to Anselm, seriously reduces their value.

That language is merely derivative and expressive is an axiom inherited from the seventeenth century. Modern science arose out of the conviction that, in order to understand the truth about nature, men must disregard everything that has been said and rely only on direct experience. That is, they must conduct experiments. For the rationalistic philosophers, clear and distinct ideas were somehow produced in the mind directly by reality, without any mediation of language. And the theologians crowned everything by replacing the words of Scripture either with a personal message of salvation (the subjectivity of hope and fear) or with a Hebrew record of history (the subjectivity of memory).

Today, for the first time in centuries, a serious challenge is being raised against this subjectivistic theory of language. Words, according to Martin Heidegger, are not primarily the tools by which men express what is already in their heads. Rather they are the *instruments of reality itself*, the medium through which being discloses itself, using man's voice as its spokesman. Language is not about reality, it is reality in the state of unveiledness, and in every statement it is the subject matter—not the subjectivity of the author—which addresses man's thought.[248]

This view has begun to liberate readers from the axiom that language expresses merely *human* ideas. We may expect, therefore, that eventually it will lead to a new approach to *Prologion* II. When that occurs, interpreters will give full weight to Anselm's *intelligere quod auditur*, and will be able to understand why he thinks that nothing else is needed except uttering the words "that than which a greater cannot be conceived."[249]

[248] See especially Heidegger's collection of lectures and essays entitled *Unterwegs zur Sprache* (2d ed., 1960). For the revolution which this view of language has already effected in Biblical studies, through the work of Gerhard Ebeling and Ernst Fuchs, see *The New Hermeneutic*, ed. by J. M. Robinson and J. B. Cobb, Jr. (New York, 1964).

[249] The kind of reassessment that awaits Anselm has already been achieved in the case of Parmenides by Eugen Fink, in his *Zur ontologischen Frühgeschichte von Raum-Zeit-Bewegung* (The Hague, 1957), pp. 65-74.

IV

A. BECKAERT

A Platonic Justification for the Argument *a Priori*[1]

When we hear Anselm speaking of God, we cannot fail to be struck by a double contrast. There is first the association of contemplative and wholly Platonic realism with an abstract, determined and subtle dialectic. This association leads us to think that this realism is that of an idealism, for which the intellectual order is the most real and provides the condition for concrete reality; that abstract thought is an intellectual experience rooted in sensible experience; and that abstract thought is the expression of the real (being and truth are convertible, in the Augustinian understanding of truth), because thought maintains a nourishing contact with the real through a fundamental intuition.

Secondly, and no less striking, Anselm shows a conviction about the validity of his thought that continues even in the face of a full awareness of the meaning and seriousness of the objection raised against it. This conviction is likewise realistic in its intent and dialectic in its manner. Anselm's conviction and authority suggest that a certain perspective of thought is involved here, a peculiar illumination, and that if we wish to avoid the dissatisfaction which this objection causes, we must recover this perspective. This dissatisfaction and this objection arise from the dialectical apparatus whose appearance of logical rigor obliterates the impression of realism.

Let us try to get away from the abstract covering, which may have been an error of presentation that conformed to the tastes of the

[1] *Spicilegium Beccense* (Paris: J. Vrin, 1959), pp. 185-190. Trans. by Arthur C. McGill.

times, if this helps us to restore Anselm's method as the appeal to an intuition which is grounded on the concrete. In that case, his method will not be a passage from the logical order (from which its form gives it the appearance of moving) to the ontological order (where it is directly established throughout by an intuition).

I

There are two conditions explicitly required for Anselm's argument: that it be concerned with a perfect Being, and that the mind be led to think of this Being, or, to be more precise, that the idea of this Being be imposed as if from outside. The conclusion then is that the idea of God (which is in fact imposed) is in itself absurd without an internal necessity for existence; that the intuition of God (which is in fact given) would be impossible (as an act of thought) if it were not objective; and that God is "unthinkable" in abstraction from (and *a fortiori*, with the negation of) his existence: "He cannot be conceived not to be."[2]

Therefore, if the idea of God is imposed, it will carry its objectivity with it. This is an idea which contains the guarantee of its objectivity in the very fact that it is imposed on us, and which collapses as a "thinkable" idea the instant objectivity is detached from it.[3]

[2] *Prosl.* III. This is not to say that the distinction essence-existence is rejected by Anselm. "For it is one thing for a thing to stand in relation to our understanding; it is another thing for us to understand that it really exists" (*Prosl.* II); there is "knowing an idea in its terms" (without affirming it or believing in its objectivity), and there is "understanding the thing as a thinkable object" (*Prosl.* IV and *Reply* IV; we will come upon this distinction again). Essence and existence are certainly distinct and separable in the abstract notion of the contingent—inseparable although distinct in the concrete intuition of the contingent (distinct, because by itself the contingent could not be real). Cf. *Reply* I. These are inseparable in God, however, because they are not even distinct in him: God is Being. This suggests Anselm's starting point, which the beginning of the *Monol.* will confirm.

[3] This is not to say that existence is to be considered an element of essence, necessary for the fulfillment of the essence. The essence is viewed in such a way, however, that its perfection implies the power to realize itself, a power dynamically realized. If God is thought of as being able not to exist, then he is an essence subject to beginning and end (*Reply* I), an absurd implication for the idea of God. That which is only in the understanding is less than that which also exists outside of it, less than contingent reality. Such is obviously the meaning of *Prosl.* II and *Reply* II (and the meaning to be found in Descartes), so that he who denies God is not truly thinking of God, who can only be thought of in an objective perspective (*Reply* I).

The question, then, is this: Does such an idea actually impose itself upon us? Let us understand this clearly: Is it imposed on us in spite of ourselves, as if from the outside, from a source and with a power that excludes subjectivity?

The answer is: yes, provided such an idea is *truly* thought. Not simply "if it is perceived and its terms understood," without any belief about it being involved, but rather if this idea in fact presents itself and establishes itself as thinkable (*Proslogion* IV).

An analogy can clarify this precise point. A theoretical calculation allowed Leverrier, the astronomer, to affirm the existence of a planet (Neptune) and to plot its orbit; another allowed Newton to demonstrate the reality of solar gravitational attraction; etc. We know how many times a mathematical and purely dialectical analysis has been shown to be a fruitful instrument for discovery. We appreciate the condition for this: The analysis proceeds in the one case from the observed irregularities in the orbit of Uranus, in the other case from the observation of the planetary ellipses, and in every case from some observation which imposes on the calculation those data that ultimately will establish the objectivity of its conclusion. It is necessary—and sufficient for this conclusion to be imposed, undoubtedly in the name of the initial observations, but with such *freshness* as the dialectical mechanism of thought demands.

Is this the Anselmic condition? The *Proslogion* is content to pose the hypothesis that the idea of God is thought. It then shows that thinking of this idea will not be simply a matter of representing the terms of it to oneself, but of appreciating that it is a proper and even well-founded idea.[4] Nevertheless, the *Proslogion* means to present a new argument, distinct from the reasoning in the *Monologion*. He begins in the same terms: For Anselm it is always a matter of contemplation. (*Proslogion* I and II: On its side faith gives to thought the object, "that than which a greater cannot be thought.") Yet the *Monologion* has described at length this Platonic-Augustinian contemplation (see St. Augustine, *Confessions* VII. 11ff.): Everything that participates is a tributary of a *summum* (see *Monologion*, the first chapters and Chapter LVI). In his *Reply* (in favor of our argument), Anselm will expressly return to this starting point:

[4] *Prosl.* II, to which *Reply* IX returns with insistence. Again: The one who denies God is not truly thinking of God; only the contingent can be thought of as not existing (*Reply* I); in the case of everything that can be thought to be false, the fact of our thinking of it does not establish it as an existent (*Reply* VI).

The idea of God is imposed by sensible contemplation, as the Source which justifies the perfections observed in the contingent (*Reply* VIII). This Source is thought of as the absolute of everything "that it is better to be than not to be" (*Reply* X). We recognize here the Platonic procedure which, moving in the "intelligible" order, means to remain in touch with the objective when it is raised to the absolute —which is the mind's proper orientation. The In-Itself, which is induced or rather (according to Plotinus) perceived in its radiance, is also the By-Itself, since it exists neither through an efficient cause, nor through a material cause, nor through an instrumental cause, nor again, since it is not derived *ex nihilo* through an efficient cause or through itself. "Otherwise, it would not be the highest" (*Monologion* VI). Rather than constituting a demonstration, this exhaustive exclusion of the "through another" is a comprehensive analysis of the By-Itself, and indeed this is what Anselm means by "the highest" in the *Monologion*, and by the "that than which nothing greater can be conceived" in the *Proslogion.* The ontological Truth which Augustine perceived in measured realities (*Confessions* VII. 15 and 17), the Plotinian One, the radiantly absolute Being in the being of beings, the Platonic good which is the synthesis and the power informing all intelligible realities—this is what there is in Anselm's perfect Being: the Being which exists necessarily and by itself. The contemplation of being in its contingency (when one follows the radiance from the reflection to the source) is elevated into the contemplation of Being in itself and by itself, in its necessity, where reality is Existence because it is the justification of existence. And when we pass from the contingent to the Source of being, the possibility of being or of not being (and similarly the possibility of thinking of the nonbeing of the object of experience) is replaced by the necessity of being (and similarly by the necessity of thinking of the being of the object).

II

We have come to the heart of the question. In Anselm's thought, will not this ascent be the psychological genesis of the argument? As early as the *Monologion*, and whether in terms of the investigation "of the world" or in terms of the revelation by faith, the procedure is double. It is a procedure which seems to be dependent on the realism of the Platonic dialectic, and which depends first on the observation of contingent being and *then on the intuition of being itself*. Or if one wishes, we can say that the procedure of thought with contingent being has itself become revelatory for Anselm. There is reflection upon this procedure, and this is the *Proslogion* (whose title suggests an appendix to the *Monologion*).[5] The *Monologion* is contented with the purely objective point of view of the ascent into being; the *Proslogion* marks off the critical point of view as valid through itself—but not as valid by itself alone, as if it were a matter of an arbitrarily improvised thought (what Descartes will call "a factitious idea"). The dialectical perspective ought not distract us from the fact that Anselm constantly moves in a realistic perspective of observation (or in a perspective of faith, understanding this as a living contact, not as some neutral perception of the object). In his discussion of the argument, Anselm gives us reminders that the idea of God is suggested by sensible contemplation; he gives us a constant parallel with contingent being, which keeps the argument in contact with its objective starting point; he specifies that to think truly is to think an object and not to stop at a theoretical expression, even to the point that the denier of God is not truly thinking of God, since his idea is inadequate. In fact, we here reach the conclusion of the Augustinian method of "degrees," or of the Plotinian perception of Being, where there is imposed on the one hand the necessity of the absolute Source, and on the other hand the disclosure that the intuition of this absolute would be impossible if it were not objective. At this point the impression of manifestness (either intuitive or mystical) is so strong that the idea thus obtained "is valid by itself." But this is the first aspect (namely, the intuitive grasp of Being), which serves as the condition for the second aspect (namely, that the idea of God, when truly thought, is imposed as objective). If this idea of absolute Source is imposed as an intellectual necessity, it imposes its object as real: "If it stands in relation to any understanding, it does not stand only in relation to the understanding."[6]

5 For a full discussion of the ontological argument as a reflexive analysis, see pp. 275ff.

6 *Reply* II. We should observe that Anselm's argument is not concerned to justify the appearance of the idea as a simple psychological fact (as Maine de Biran would interpret Descartes), as if the appearance of the idea postulates as a fact the object which causes it, independently of the content of the idea. Descartes considers the idea of God in man as the mark of the Creator, and focuses less on the presence of the idea than on its meaning. For Anselm, it is first a matter of the practical impossibility of "thinking Being as nonexistent," insofar as one has in view necessary Being (*Reply* III and *Prosl.* II). On the other hand, he judges that

Throughout the whole Platonic-Augustinian ascent which opens the *Monologion*, we observe being where it need not be. At the summit, however, at the infinite, we must acknowledge that being is necessary. Consequently, the expression "when this being is thought" is not a theoretical hypothesis (for which it would be enough to think the words for the idea of God). It refers to an experience. It signifies: If the ascent toward Being (or the adherence to faith) succeeds in posing the Being which is the Source, that is, the perfect Being, then it poses a necessary, and therefore existent, essence.

The need for objectivity thus seems to be connected with the principle of causality in its Platonic form, according to which the measured reality postulates the absolute of which it is a participation. In safeguarding the realism that allows real existence to be inferred, however, are we not justifying the argument only at the price of its originality? No, for in fact the nerve of this demonstration is that *once the idea of infinite being is posed to and imposed upon the understanding*, and without anything further, this idea cannot be treated theoretically, and cannot be thought of as a factitious idea (like the idea of the Blessed Isles), without an internal contradiction. The reason is that, as the idea of a perfect essence, this idea implies that in that essence there is a virtuality to exist, a virtuality which, for the same reason, cannot but be realized (cf. *Monologion* VI). Therefore, the nerve of the new argument is the principle of identity, under the form of noncontradiction.

Consequently, our hypothesis is that at the conclusion of the somewhat inductive investigation in the *Monologion*, it occurred to Anselm that his vision of Being-by-itself is itself a proof in its own right, because this vision is imposed as soon as it is posed by, or even detached from, the data which have occasioned it but without which it could not have occurred.[7] Here we are in the presence not of

---

the knowledge of God "from the world" finds a special and directly expressive datum in the human mind as such: "The mind is mirror and image" (*Monol.* LVI-LVII), in the Pascalian sense that we seek because to some extent we have already found. Faith provokes the reflexive analysis of the intuition itself, as the operation of a mind that is endowed with the being and image of God.

7 The argument in the *Prosl.* is "second" in two ways: It is distinct from the induction in the *Monol.* but it presupposes that induction in order that the idea of God not be arbitrary. This "second" argument is more than a confirmation, however. It is given as sufficient in itself, even when the first argument is not brought fully into the foreground. The condition for it is simply that the mind be brought by the first inductive argument—or by faith—to think of God as an object really furnished from outside.

a debate over the extension of a conceptual inference, but of an intuition which, when it attains the One and the Infinite, goes beyond its experiential and contingent basis and its purely dialectical conditions. Philo of Alexandria said that in the case of such an intuition the Object is its own light, or the light which enables us to see is the very Object which is seen. This is a unique vision, the very fact of which, independently of its preparation (through experience, or faith, or dialectic), confirms the reality of the Object. According to Plotinus, in the case of this intuition, the contingent realities which are possible and virtual, including the measured objects which serve as the basis for it, are effaced, because in the One every possibility is fully actualized. The vision of the One is outside of time and its conditions; there the True is objectively confounded with Being. In contingent reality, what is thinkable is realizable to the extent that it is thinkable. We are certainly aware that the existence of the Blessed Isles, or of any other of Descartes' factitious ideas, is not "necessary," and that it depends on us. If we had the power to objectify such ideas, Descartes observed, we could even elevate the idea which we have of ourselves to the infinite. Being is thinkable as necessary only if it is necessary. We feel constrained to think of the necessary as existent, and if we feel constrained to think of this necessary Being at all, we are constrained to think of it as existing. And that is why St. Anselm points out that the case of perfect Being, duly thought of as necessary and by itself, is valuable and unique (*Reply* III and V).

In conclusion, we cannot criticize from a purely logical point of view, as an abstract idea, something which Anselm always defines as a concrete thought. We do not recognize the image that a painter has seized from an unusual angle; we are astonished by a doctrine that does not immediately agree with our familiar categories, so long as we are not placed in that order of thought where the doctrine has been able to impose itself upon an exacting intelligence.

One can say as much of the Cartesian version of the argument. Without historic references, it shows such surprising similarities to Anselm's version that we must conjecture some analogous foundations and the same kind of relationship joining thought to reality. In the case of Descartes, however, there is an original recourse to a psychological intuition; there is the consciousness of the mind's constructive activity in the matter of factitious ideas, and of the objectivity of the ideas which it does not construct; there is finally the understanding of a physico-mathematical objectivity which furnishes the basis for the argument. In Anselm this basis is assured by the Platonic-Augustinian contemplation of being, and by the presentation of the divine Object in a faith which is the light emanated by the Object. In both Anselm and Descartes there is the perception of the absolute in the very fact of relativity, and the perception of objectivity as the condition for thought.

We might extend the application of this principle to the argument "by universal consciousness." Human thought as such, taken in its entirety and with such a historic range as practically excludes exceptions (according to the norms of probability), cannot be deceived about the objectivity of an idea which is in fact universally imposed upon it.

In short, is not the rational intuition that "the True is identified with Being" the ontological complement (and the inseparable complement, in spite of the fallacious impression which Anselm's abstract logic gives) of this concrete intuition, that the measured being which we experience reveals the absolute Being that justifies its existence?

V

Karl Barth

A Presupposition of the Proof: The Name of God[1]

In *Proslogion* II-IV Anselm wants to prove the existence of God. He proves it by assuming a Name of God, the meaning of which implies that the statement "God exists" is necessary (that means, that the statement "God does not exist" is impossible). In *Proslogion* V-XXVI Anselm wants to prove the *Nature* of God (that means his Perfection and Unique Originality). He proves it on the presupposition of the same Name of God, the meaning of which implies that the statements, "God is perfect and originally wise, mighty, righteous, etc.," are necessary (that is, all statements to the opposite effect are impossible). The lever in both cases, the *argumentum* in his analysis of both parts of the *Proslogion*, is therefore the Name of God that is presupposed[2] concerning which the author tells us in the Prologue how he sought it and how, after he had abandoned the search, he suddenly found it.

At the beginning of *Proslogion* II, where it appears for the first time, this Name is rendered by the words "something than which

[1] From Karl Barth, *Anselm: Fides quaerens intellectum*, transl. by Ian Robertson (London: SCM Press and Richmond, Va.: John Knox Press, 1960). This work appeared in German in 1931, under the title *Fides quaerens intellectum* (Munich: Chr. Kaiser), and was reissued with no change in the text in 1958 (Zollikon: Evangelische Verlag). Slight changes in the translation have been made and the Latin has been trans. by Arthur C. McGill.

[2] *Reply* (I. 138.30ff.): "The signification of this key expression [which simply me ns the Na me of God that is presupposed] is in itself so forceful that, by the ve ry fact that it is understood or conceived, the reality which it expresses is proved by necessity actually to exist, and to be whatever we are bound to believe about the divine substance."

nothing greater can be conceived." The actual formulation is not fixed either in the *Proslogion* itself or in the essay against Gaunilo: instead of "something" Anselm can also say "that." It can even be further abbreviated by omitting the pronoun. As for "nothing . . . can," *possit* can be replaced by *potest* and occasionally by *valet*; *nihil* also by *non*; *nihil* (or *non*) . . . *possit* (or *potest*) also by *nequit*; and also, quite frequently, *maius* by *melius*. Only this last variant is important for an understanding of the formula.

In the first place the literal meaning of the formula is clear. It can be quite easily translated into French: "*Un être tel qu'on n'en peut concevoir de plus grand*"[3] or even better, "*Quelque chose dont on ne peut rien concevoir de plus grand.*"[4] In German it can be paraphrased: "*Etwas über dem ein Grösseres nicht gedacht werden kann.*" (Something beyond which a greater cannot be conceived.) Here "great" suggests, as is shown by the variant *melius* and by the whole application of the formula, quite generally the large mass of all the qualities of the object described and therefore as much its "greatness" in relation to time and space as the "greatness" of its spiritual attributes or of its power, or of its inner and outward value or ultimately the type of its particular existence. The "greater" which cannot be conceived beyond the thing described is therefore quite generally: anything *superior* to it. And from the application which the conception is given, particularly in *Proslogion* II-IV, the definitive sense can be taken to be: the being that stands over against it as a fundamentally higher mode of being.

For a thorough understanding of the literal meaning of this Name the first thing that has to be noticed is what it does *not* say: It does not say—God is the highest that man has *in fact conceived*, beyond which he can conceive nothing higher. Nor does it say—God is the highest that man *could conceive*. Thus, it denies neither the former reality nor the latter possibility, but leaves open the question of the givenness of them both. Clearly it is deliberately chosen in such a way that the object which it describes emerges as something completely independent of whether men in actual fact conceive it or can conceive it. It is so chosen that its actual conception, as well as the possibility of its conception, emerges as being

3 So Bainvel in the *Dictionnaire de théol. cath.*, vol. 1, column 1351.

4 So A. Koyré, *S. Anselme de Cantorbéry, Fides quaerens intellectum* (Paris, 1930), p. 13.

dependent upon an essentially unexpressed condition.[5] All that the formula says about this object is simply this one thing, this one negative: Nothing greater than it can be thought; nothing can be thought that in any respect whatsoever could or would outdo it; as soon as anyone conceives anything which in any respect whatsoever is greater than it, insofar as it can be conceived at all—then he has not yet begun to conceive it or has already ceased.

It remains to be said: We are dealing with a concept of strict *noetic* content which Anselm describes here as a concept of God. It does not say *that* God is, or *what* he is, but rather, *in the form of a prohibition* that man can understand, *who he is*. It is *une définition purement conceptuelle*.[6] It contains nothing in the way of statements about the existence or about the nature of the object described.[7] Thus, nothing of that sort is to be derived from it on subsequent analysis. If it is to be of any use in proving the existence and nature of God, then a second assumption, to be clearly distinguished from this first one, is necessary—the prior "givenness" (credible on other grounds) of the thought of the Existence and of the Nature of God which with his help is to be raised to knowledge and proof. "Something than which nothing greater can be conceived" is therefore on no account the condensed formula of a doctrine of God that is capable of later expansion but it is a genuine *description* (*significatio*), *a Name* of God, selected from among the various revealed Names of God for this occasion and for this particular purpose, in such a way that to reach a *knowledge* of God, the revelation of this same God *from some other source* is clearly assumed. All that can possibly be expected from this Name is that, in conformity with the program of Anselm's theology, it should demonstrate that between the Name of God and the revelation of his Existence and Nature from the other source there exists a strong and discernible connection. *Only in that way* and to that extent will statements about the existence and Nature of God inevitably follow from an understanding of this Name.

5 It goes without saying that there was a serious misunderstanding when William of Auxerre (died 1232), in his report on Anselm's proof, thought that he could interchange—that is, interpret—Anselm's *cogitari* ("conceive") by *excogitari* ("invent"). See A. Daniels, *Geschichte der Gottesbeweise*, p. 27.

6 A. Koyré, *L'Idée de Dieu dans la philosophie de S. Anselme* (Paris, 1923), p. 203.

7 It was also a crucial misunderstanding when John Peckham (died 1292) quoted Anselm's proof as "the argument undertaken from a definition." See A. Daniels, *op. cit.*, p. 44.

From what has been said we have first of all to establish that the presupposition of this Name has without any doubt a strictly *theological* character. Notice how the formula is introduced—"and we *believe* that you are something (*aliquid*) than which a greater. . . ."[8] What is said here is confirmed by the conclusive statement in which Anselm later guarded against the possible rejection of this Name for God, that is, against the fact that it is unknown to the Christian: "I use your *faith* and *conscience* as a most certain argument that this is false."[9] In this statement the *fides* of Gaunilo, who is being addressed, is itself to confirm his acquaintance with this Name of God and his "conscience" is to confirm his acquaintance with the one designated by this name: As a believing Christian Gaunilo knows very well who the "that than which a greater cannot be conceived" is. With this we ought also to compare the remarkable accounts given by Anselm in the Prologue to the *Proslogion* of the discovery of this concept. He sought it "often and diligently," sometimes thinking he was to find it the next moment, sometimes thinking he would never find it. Eventually he gave up the attempt as being an impossible undertaking and decided, so as not to waste further time on it, not to think about it any more. As soon as he did that, however, the idea began to force itself upon him for the first time in the right way. "One day, therefore, when I was wearied from violently resisting its urgency, that for which I had despaired offered itself to me in the very conflict of my thoughts, so that I eagerly seized the conception which I was anxiously repelling."[10] Is this a scientific report on an investigation or is it not rather a—perhaps quite typical—account of an experience of prophetic insight? However that may be, Anselm did not regard this designation for God as a nonbinding theologoumenon and certainly not as a constituent part of a universal human awareness of God,[11] but as an *article of faith*. If we assume for a moment that there were for Anselm, alongside the explicit statements of the text of the revelation, consequences arising directly from these to which he attached

[8] *Prosl.* II (I. 101.4f.). [9] *Reply* I (I. 130.15f.).

[10] *Prosl.* Preface (I. 93.10ff.). See also Eadmer, *The Life of St. Anselm*, ed. and trans. by R. W. Southern (London, 1962), I. 19, pp. 29f.

[11] This was how he was understood to a large extent later on. Bonaventure speaks of "Anselm who says that according to the universal conception of the human mind, God is that than which nothing greater can be conceived" (in A. Daniels, *op. cit.*, p. 38). According to John Peckham, "Anselm argues: According to all men, God is that than which nothing greater can be conceived" (*ibid.*, p. 43).

equal weight,[12] then we will have no difficulty over the fact that naturally the "that than which a greater cannot be conceived" does not admit of proof by appeal to any text that was authoritative for him.[13] Thus, in no sense is he of the opinion that he produced this formula out of his own head, but he declares quite explicitly the source from which he considers it to have come to him: When he gives God a Name, it is not like one *person* forming a concept of another *person*; rather it is as a *creature* standing before his *Creator*. In this relationship which is actualized by virtue of God's revelation, as he thinks of God he knows that he is under this prohibition: He can conceive of nothing greater, to be precise, "better", beyond God without lapsing into the absurdity, excluded for faith, of placing himself above God in attempting to conceive of this greater.[14] "That than which a greater cannot be conceived" only appears to be a concept that he formed for himself; it is in fact as far as he is concerned a revealed Name of God.[15]

Thus, we see at once (how could it be otherwise after the immediately preceding closing words of *Proslogion* I?) that at the very outset of his Proof of the Existence of God and indeed precisely there, Anselm is fully and legitimately engaged in the exposition of his theological program. It goes without saying that for him the Existence of God[16] is given as an article of faith. This Existence of

[12] *De processione Spiritus Sancti* 11 (II. 209.14ff.): "Therefore, we ought to acknowledge with certainty not only the things which are read in Holy Scripture, but also what follows from these things by rational necessity, provided that it is contradicted by no other reason."

[13] In comparision, we may recall in this connection Luther's *sola fide*.

[14] *Prosl.* III (I. 103.4ff.): "For if some mind could conceive of something better than you, the creature would become superior to its Creator and would judge its Creator. This is obviously absurd." Perhaps it is not an accident that just at this point, as an exception, Anselm uses the word "better" (*melius*), instead of "greater" (*maius*).

[15] Among the later scholastics who dealt with Anselm's proof, Bonaventure (see A. Daniels, *op. cit.*, p. 39) and Thomas Aquinas (*ibid.*, pp. 65f.) saw correctly that what was involved in the concept that Anselm presupposed was the "Name of God." In Agidus of Rome (died 1316, *ibid.*, p. 76) there is a sentence which could be the most exact interpretation of Anselm's intention—"to demonstrate that God exists is to declare what is introduced by this name God"—if Agidus did not unfortunately continue, "which is evident from all the demonstrations that prove this." For from this it follows that the "Name" in the sense of "all" these proofs did not mean for him a "personal Name" but an "essential Name" of God, that is, the nature of God. That is how it stands with Bonaventure and Thomas as well. But in Anselm himself the "that than which a greater cannot be conceived" has the meaning and plays the role of a "personal Name."

[16] *Prosl.* II (I. 101.3f.): "Give to me, so that . . . I may understand that you are, just as we believe."

God which is accepted in faith is now to be recognized and proved on the presupposition of the Name of God[17] likewise accepted in faith and is to be understood as necessary for thought. Thus, here the Name of God is the *a*[18] taken from the Credo by means of which the Existence of God now represented as *X* is to be transformed into a known quantity from one that is unknown (not disbelieved but as yet not realized): "No one who understands what God is can conceive that God is not."[19] Starting from this point of the Credo, *the other thing, the Existence of God, must make itself—not credible* (it is that already)—*but intelligible.*

The choice of this particular point, the discovery of this particular Name of God, was the first step along the path that was to commit Anselm to the development of the Proof. That it had a vital significance for him follows just as much from the manner in which he reports his discovery in the Prologue as from the manner in which he defended it later against Gaunilo. We can be certain: At all events this first step does not lead away from the constraint of specifically theological thinking but rather leads right into it; it concerns the choice of the concrete limit which so far as this question is concerned appears to make knowledge possible.

We are combining further comment on the Name of God which was normative for Anselm's Proof with a discussion of Gaunilo's two misunderstandings which followed immediately on this first step.

1. Gaunilo develops the thought, especially in Para. 4-5 of his reply, that when men hear the Name of God, they are unable, for lack of any kind of intuitive response and therefore of any suitable universal concept, to grasp more than a mere word (*vox*), to grasp at the same time the "truth of the reality" (*rei veritas*), truth in relation to God. Whether it be the word *Deus* or Anselm's formula, the word itself could not provide him with a knowledge of God unless some extension of what the word is meant to denote

[17] Anselm's references to the revelatory-theological character of the vital assumption of his proof are overlooked when this is understood, as is frequently done especially by Thomas Aquinas, as an answer to the question: "whether the existence of God is self-evident." For Anselm there is no such "self-evidence" in theology, no insights which do not stand under the seal of faith.

[18] The Nature of God accepted by faith and already indispensable for the definition of the conception of the existence of God certainly comes under consideration as *b*; further points in the Credo may stand more or less visibly in the background, as *c*, *d*, *e*. . . .

[19] *Prosl.* IV (I. 103.20f.).

were also given to him from another source. There are no less than four points here that are at cross-purposes with Anselm.

(*a*) In his skepticism of the possibility (maintained by Anselm) of a knowledge of God, Gaunilo appears as a great champion of the concept of the *incomprehensibility of God.* Ought there really to be a word capable of giving knowledge of God; should any human word about God be more than a reasonably meaningful symbol of a human, an all too human, desire, that is never fulfilled, to comprehend the incomprehensible? These are the questions he feels compelled to address to Anselm. And it is quite remarkable that in so doing he felt compelled to appeal directly to Anselm.[20] Surely just a glance at *Monologion* XXVI-XXVII and LXIV-LXV would have been enough to show to anyone directing such questions to Anselm that in so doing he was merely beating the air. Also in the *Proslogion* itself he might equally well have read in the first chapter: "In no way do I compare my understanding with [your sublimity];"[21] or in *Cap.* XV: "Therefore, O Lord, you are not only that than which a greater cannot be conceived, but you are something greater than can be conceived";[22] and in *Cap.* XVI-XVII a whole succession of most impressive declarations of the total hiddenness of God even for those who know him in faith. The only explanation for Gaunilo's obvious failure to take such passages into account is that he did not realize that for Anselm even the statement of the incomprehensibility of God was an article of faith not in any sense denied by the presupposition of the Name of God, that the whole point of the presupposition was to raise this article of faith (as well as others) to knowledge by means of the Name of God and that he indeed proved it logically in the *Proslogion* using this same Name of God.[23] How then do we know that God is incomprehensible? How do we come to assert the inadequacy of all concepts of God formed by men? Certainly for Anselm, like everything we know of the Nature of God, we know this in and by faith: In faith we are given and by faith we recognize a designation for God which is not totally inadequate, not just a symbol, etc., for

[20] Gaunilo, *On Behalf of the Fool* 4 (I. 127.2f.): "As you yourself assert, His reality is such that it cannot be similar to anything."

[21] *Prosl.* I (I. 100.16).

[22] *Prosl.* XV (I. 112.14f.).

[23] In *Prosl.* XV (I. 112.15ff.) it is proved in this way: "Since something of this kind [namely, something greater than can be conceived] can be conceived to exist, if you, O Lord, are not this one, something greater than you can be conceived. Yet this cannot be done."

the simple reason that it expresses nothing about the nature of God but rather lays down a rule of thought which, if we follow it, enables us to endorse the statements about the Nature of God accepted in faith (for example, the statement of his incomprehensibility) as our own necessary thoughts. This necessary thought which is endorsed, the Proof itself, stands of course under the shadow of the incomprehensibility of God; it stands with the proviso that thinking is merely speculative, simply through similitudes (*per similitudinem*) not through what belongs to God (*per proprietatem*), with the proviso that in itself it is an empty shell ever requiring to be filled from above, by the Truth itself. But this proviso is also its protection: Within the limits in which all theology is contained it is true, and an inviolable validity attaches to it. Against which we must seriously ask whether the incomprehensibility of God that Gaunilo so favors is anything but a statement of purely secular gnosis, not based on faith and incapable of providing any basis for a knowledge of God, and therefore whether it can really possess the critical force which it ought to have.

(*b*) But now Gaunilo desires and seems to regard as possible a *second element of knowledge* which operates in conjunction with the supposedly empty Name of God. If he had understood Anselm, then he must have been aware that not even Anselm is trying with his Name of God to produce knowledge of the Nature and Existence of God out of a vacuum—a *creatio ex nihilo* indeed—but that for Anselm it is axiomatic, as the contents of the *Proslogion* indisputably show, that the element of knowledge deriving from the other source is presupposed in the articles of faith concerning the Existence and Nature of God, only that now these are treated—in respect of their knowledge content (*not* in respect of their truth content!)—as unknown, that is, as articles that are true but still not understood. Gaunilo could not have overlooked these facts had it not been that by the second element of knowledge which he postulated he was thinking of something quite different from what Anselm was thinking. It is quite clear that when he demands an "incontestable argument,"[24] when he wants to be sure "that this greater is actually somewhere," in order thereby to know God's Existence by means of the concept of God,[25] when he calls for the demonstration of a "genuinely and undeniably real thing,"[26] the

[24] Gaunilo, *op. cit.*, 2 (I. 126.9f.).
[25] *Ibid.* 5 (I. 128.12f.).
[26] *Ibid.* 6 (I. 128.31).

demonstration of the *esse* of that "nature which is greater and better than everything,"[27] he does not mean the givenness of an article of faith from another source which fills out the concept of God and which is to be proved by means of this concept, but quite simply he is thinking of the givenness of a corresponding idea. That this is in fact what he meant follows from the two illustrations which he himself gave of his objections. First, when someone speaks to him about knowing "God," he would like to know as much about "God" from other sources as he knows at least in general from his acquaintance with other men about a particular man who may be unknown to him personally.[28] Secondly, he compares the unknown Existence of God to that of an unknown island in a far-off sea, whose existence he will not allow to be proved by a description of its perfection but only by the same method as that in which men have habitually proved the existence of hitherto unknown islands.[29] That shows how lightly he took *his* statement about the incomprehensibility of God! The element of knowledge other than the Name of God of which Anselm was thinking in these circumstances must have seemed to him of little note and little comfort.

(*c*) For Gaunilo "that than which a greater cannot be conceived" is *any concept* as it can be formed by man with or without regard to the object concerned. Therefore, he can bring into the discussion the incomprehensibility of God as an argument against the validity of knowledge in Anselm's formula. Therefore, he can postulate that this formula, in order to become valid for knowledge, must be completed by an idea. For him a word in itself is in all circumstances "only" a word, an empty word, which can, however, be delivered from its emptiness where a corresponding idea is given. Where the intended content is God, the word must remain in its emptiness. It is clear that from here he would only have rejected Anselm's element of knowledge from the other source, and that he could also have described the article of faith about the Existence of God in respect of its epistemological validity as nothing more than an empty *vox*. That there ever could be words which even in themselves do not remain "mere" words but are a divine revelation in the guise of something "conceived" by a human brain in accordance with human logic and expressed in human Latin—that, in complete contrast to Anselm, was for him a totally foreign concept.

(*d*) In one breath Gaunilo described the "that than which a

[27] *Ibid.* 7 (I. 129.8f.). [28] *Ibid.* 4 (I. 127.4ff.). [29] *Ibid.*, 6 (I. 128.14ff.).

greater cannot be conceived" and the word *Deus* as epistemologically invalid.[30] Without giving the special content of the formula more careful consideration, he saw in "that than which a greater cannot be conceived," as well as in *Deus*, a definition of the Perfect Nature of God which as mere *vox* was invalid. This will come out still more clearly later on. He overlooked the fact that this *vox* is to be distinguished from the "word 'God' which is somewhat intelligible," just because its content is only of a noetic and not of an ontic nature. Anselm had of course expressly declared: "I do not seek, O Lord, to penetrate your sublimity, but I desire to understand your truth in some measure."[31] Just because of the concept of God in the *Proslogion* this "in some measure" cannot signify a quantitative limitation of the range of human insight into the nature of God simply because this Name of God is lacking in ontic content. In that case it can only describe the noetic mediation of this Name of God. This Name of God conceives God only in that sphere in which he can be conceived,[32] not "in his sublimity," but with great hesitation and reserve—by conceiving the manner in which he is not to be conceived. He is not to be conceived in such a way—this possibility is ruled out by the revelation-faith relationship to him—that anything greater than him could be imagined or even imagined as conceivable. Obstructing any thinker who has a hankering in this direction, the revealed Name of the Lord—his Name is "that than which a greater cannot be conceived"—stands as effective

[30] *Ibid.*, 2 (I. 126.4ff.): "It can hardly be credible that when this something is spoken of and heard, it can be conceived not to exist in some other way than the way in which 'God' can be conceived not to exist."

[31] *Prosl.* I (I. 100.15ff.). See *Reply* I (I. 132.3f.): "Do you think that that about which these matters are understood can be partially (*aliquatenus*) conceived or understood, or can be partially in conception and in the understanding?" *Reply* VII (I. 136.27ff.): "Furthermore, if that which is partially understood is sometimes denied, and if that which is not understood at all is altogether denied, is it not easier to prove the reality of something doubtful from that which is partially understood than from that which is not understood at all? Therefore, is it not credible that someome should deny the reality of that than which a greater cannot be conceived, of which he has heard and which he partially understands, simply because he denies the reality of 'God,' the meaning of which he does not know at all. Furthermore, if the former is denied because it is not perfectly understood, nevertheless, is it not easier to prove the reality of that which is somewhat understood than the reality of that which is not understood at all?"

[32] *Reply* VII (I. 137.3ff.): "In order to prove against the fool that God exists, I have not been irrational in using 'that than which a greater cannot be conceived.' For while he does not understand 'God' at all, he has some understanding of this."

deterrent.[33] Since theology adheres to this command; since the noetic *ratio* of faith follows the *ratio* of the object of faith and consequently the ontic *ratio*; and since, therefore, theology assents to that Name of God as an article of faith and presupposes it for all that follows—it is able to illumine the noetic necessity of faith (that means the impossibility of denying the existence and the perfect nature of the God designated by that Name) by the roundabout route of ontic necessity which is inseparable from ontic rationality. Thus, theology can know what is believed, that is, prove it. In this sense, as already illustrated, the conception of God in the *Proslogion*, just because of its limitation, possesses epistemological validity. According to Anselm, to want to take "partially" as a "not at all" or deny validity of knowledge to this Name of God, because it does not happen to be identical with God's own conception of himself, is the same as maintaining that we cannot see the daylight because our eye in fact is not able to see the light of the sun from which the daylight proceeds.[34] Anselm is not to be blamed for such wanton misinterpretation of this Something into Nothing.

2. Gaunilo persistently so understood Anselm's formula and in numerous passages so quoted it as if Anselm had actually written in the *Proslogion* which he was criticizing: "something which is greater than all things." We may well wonder at the gentleness with which Anselm protested[35] at this substitution and at the fact that even despite this negligence on the part of his opponent, so confusing for all concerned, he did not hesitate to acknowledge at the end of his reply Gaunilo's goodwill.[36] By this negligence Gaunilo failed most seriously to appeciate that the formula which Anselm used in the *Proslogion* did not simply have a more particular content but a different content altogether from the definitions which he utilized

33 Compare *Monol.* XV (I. 29.17ff.): "It is impious to think that the substance of the supreme nature is such that something not it is in any way better than it."

34 *Reply* I (I. 132.5ff.): "If you say that this is not understood at all or is not in the understanding because it is not understood completely, you should also say that the man who cannot look directly at the pure light of the sun does not see the daylight which comes from the sun."

35 *Reply* V (I. 134.26f; 135.22f.): "Nowhere in all my writings is such a proof to be found. . . . You inaccurately accuse me of saying what I did not say." By "all my writings" the *Prosl.* is primarily intended, to which alone Gaunilo was referring. However, the *Monol.* can also be intended, insofar as there too the "greater than all things" is not applied to the proof of God's existence.

36 *Reply* X (I. 139.11): *benevolentia.*

in the *Monologion* in connection with Augustine.[37] The restlessness with which Anselm searched for a new *argumentum* in the Prologue to the *Proslogion* and the joy with which he reports having found it could not be explained had he been able to accept one of these older definitions as equivalent to his new *argumentum*. In the same passage he declared what the new *argumentum* that he was seeking ought to achieve: Namely, it ought to be sufficient as *unum argumentum* to prove the Existence and Nature of God.[38] And certainly it ought to have such force of proof that in its structure it may correspond to what faith holds to be the Nature of God and therefore be able to be used to prove God in a manner befitting God. Thus, God's Nature is soon transcribed as follows: God alone is the "supreme good which needs nothing else and which all things need in order to exist well." That, however, means that the Name of God, on the presupposition of which the Existence and Nature of this God are to be proved, must be so formed that in view of the Existence of God believed but not proved, or Nature of God be-

[37] The conception of God to which Gaunilo was obviously listening in the *Monol.* meant: the greatest or highest or best. *Monol.* II (I. 15.22f.): "something which is greatest (*maximum*) and best (*optimum*), that is, the highest (*summum*) of everything that is." *Monol.* XV (I. 29.19): "It is necessarily the case that [the substance of the supreme nature] is whatever it is absolutely better to be than not to be." *Monol.* LXXX (I. 86.20f.): God is "the substance which [man] considers to be above every nature that is not God." This is in fact, although not literally, Gaunilo's "that which is greater than all things." In this respect compare Augustine, *On Christian Doctrine* I. 7: God "is thought of in such a way that the thought seeks to attain something than which there is nothing better or more sublime." Thus, God is the greatest that can be imagined. Perhaps this was the passage that formed the starting point from which Anselm aspired to his later formula, although his is characteristically different from this Augustinian one: "No one can be found who believes that God is that than which something is better." In this second sentence we may notice how Augustine again moved away from the direction in which Anselm proceeded further. The same is true in the following sentence from *On Free Will* II. 6 (14): "I will certainly admit that God is that than which nothing is considered superior." We can see Anselm's whole relation to Augustine on this matter condensed in this passage from *Reply* X (I. 139.3ff.): "Concerning the divine substance we believe anything which to our thought it is absolutely better to be than not to be [Anselm goes this far with Augustine]. . . . Nothing of this sort, however, can fail to belong to that than which a greater cannot be conceived. Therefore, it is necessary that 'that than which a greater cannot be conceived' is whatever should be believed about the divine essence." Here we are dealing with those thoughts of Anselm that are independent of Augustine.

[38] *Prosl.* Preface (I. 93.6ff.). By way of criticism he calls the *Monol.* "a chain of many connected arguments," and is thus obviously objecting that there the Name of God has none of the systematic significance which he now wants to give it.

lieved but not proved,[39] it is enough to conceive this Name or express it, in order thereby to complete the required proof.[40]

The formula corresponding to Anselm's previous position, which was carelessly drawn into the discussion by Gaunilo, "that which is greater than all things"—would not conform to these conditions. This can be seen at once to be simply a transliteration back into ontic terminology of the noetic terminology which Anselm is now deliberately choosing and to which he is careful to give point. Neither is it in the narrow, strict sense a designation or Name of God like "that than which a greater cannot be conceived," but in itself it is a brief paraphrase of the Nature of God. As such, therefore, as far as proof is concerned both of the Existence and Nature of God as these are held by faith, it is insufficient. It is no accident that although in various passages[41] in the *Monologion* Anselm *asserts* the Existence of God as held by faith, he did *not* try to prove it. The insight that such proof is impossible on the basis of the conception of God assumed in the *Monologion*, is perhaps a later achievement. It comes to formal expression in the answer to Gaunilo[42] and is based on the fact that "that which is greater than all things" might also be conceived of as *not existing*. As long, however, as the conception that is presupposed does not in itself rule out that possibility and as long, therefore, as the nonexistence of God, is conceivable without the presupposed conception of God being destroyed, this conception is not amenable to proof; because a proof of the Existence of God is only being discussed when this Existence is demonstrated as necessary to thought (that is, as impossible not to be thought). But in the same context Anselm also declares—and that by way of public self-correction apropos the *Monologion*—that that conception would not be sufficient to prove what faith holds to be the Nature of God and for the reason that once again "that which is greater than all things" does not preclude the possibility that a "greater than it (even if not actually existing)"

39 Of course, the prior givenness of a subject of the proof cannot be excluded by the "aseity" of the Name which is presupposed.

40 *Prosl.* Preface (I. 93.6f.): " . . . an argument which requires for its proof nothing else but itself alone." *Reply* V (I. 135.19ff.): "In my argument nothing else is needed except the utterance of this: 'that than which a greater cannot be conceived'. . . . 'That than which a greater cannot be conceived' provides proof by and through itself." Cf. *Reply* X (I. 138.30ff.).

41 Explicitly in *Monol.* VI; implicitly in *Monol.* XXXI and XXXIV.

42 *Reply* V (I. 134.27ff.).

could at least be conceived.[43] However, even the exclusion of such a possibility would have to be accomplished by a real proof of the originally perfect Nature of God.

Obviously Gaunilo could not have attempted anything more devastating than his ill-considered retransliteration into ontic terms of the new formula that Anselm introduced in the *Proslogion.* The very thing that Anselm intended should make it valid as a proof, its austere character as a rule for thinking about God, was thereby taken away from it, and it is hardly surprising that, on the basis of *this* presupposition, Gaunilo was not able to appreciate Anselm's actual Proof. Again, he is just beating the air when he thinks it necessary to inform Anselm that by means of this conception the Proof is not possible.[44]

The invalidity for proof which Anselm himself asserted of the "that which is greater than all things" stood in very close connection with a second consideration, namely that as a Name of God this formula did not possess that *self-sufficiency* that belongs to and befits the nature of its subject. For the "that which is greater than all things" to become admissible as proof, it required certain presuppositions not contained within itself. That is, in order to be the highest, it must first presuppose the existence and nature of "all things," that is of objects which in their existence and nature point beyond themselves to the "highest" which forms their peak. Without the rest of the pyramid the peak could not be a peak. "By ascending from lesser goods to greater goods" (as Anselm described it, still in his *Reply* to Gaunilo) do we arrive at the conception of the "best, greatest, highest." It is only from other heights that the highest comes into view. From the existence and nature of the lower we may "infer" (*conicere*), form tentative conclusions about, such a

[43] *Reply* V (I. 135.14ff.): "Suppose that someone says that there does exist something greater than all the things that are, but that nevertheless this can be conceived not to be and that a greater than it, even if not existing, can be conceived. In that case, can it be so obviously inferred that therefore this something is not really greater than all the things that are?" Not only in the *Prosl.* but also in the later work *De veritate* I (I. 176.12), where once again Anselm gives a proof of God's nature, we see him therefore working with the "it is impossible to conceive. . . . "

[44] The fact that Anselm's proof became known in wider theological circles during the thirteenth century was in the end unfortunate. The first ones to take it up—Richard Fishacre, William of Auxerre, Alexander of Hales (A. Daniels, *op. cit.*, pp. 24, 27, 20f.)—immediately compromised it by introducing it within a series of proofs of God's existence clearly based on ontic assumptions, every one of which Anslem had declared to be ambiguous.

highest. The unbeliever is to be reminded that we can do this and the believer is to be reminded from Romans 1 : 20 that our ability to do this is a truth of revelation.[45] But—in so doing—neither the nature nor even the existence of the "highest" as such is known or proved. For why should it not be conceived of as not existing, or, if existing, capable of being surpassed?[46]

In order to be valid for proof the conception of the "highest" requires in the second place to be supplemented by such another concept as excludes the very possibility of this mode of thinking. This vital concept is just the "that than which a greater cannot be conceived." Insofar as the "greater than all things" is thought of as identical to the "that than which a greater cannot be conceived," the existence and perfection of what it describes can be proved—but *not* otherwise.[47] Therefore, it has none of that self-sufficiency with which it would correspond to its object. This self-sufficiency does, however, belong to the Name of God discovered in the *Proslogion*. The designation of God as the "that than which a greater cannot be conceived," does not assume the existence or nature of any creature, certainly not of God himself, neither as actually conceived nor as being conceivable. It simply says that *if* God

45 *Reply* VIII (I. 137.18,27ff.).

46 It is just in *Reply* VIII, where the inherent continuity between Anselm's new formula and the conception of God in the *Monol.* comes out most clearly, that he lays great emphasis on the fact that the question "whether or not there is in reality something of this kind" cannot be answered along the road taken in the *Monol.* (namely, by a *via eminentiae*).

47 From this standpoint also, Gaunilo's "Lost Island" analogy is shown up as a useless notion. Gaunilo takes the "that than which a greater cannot be conceived" as a definition of the nature of God, and takes Anselm's proof as deriving God's existence from God's nature as that is thus established. In actual fact, for Anselm the proof of God's nature follows just as much as the proof of his existence from the "that than which a greater cannot be conceived," and indeed it does so in such a way that the latter is prior to the former. Anselm, too, does not think first of the perfection of that "Lost Island" in order to know its existence; he, too, wants to know first of all of its existence but most certainly from a less unreliable source than the general experience of which Gaunilo is clearly thinking. And to that extent he also wants to know of its perfection, which is not to be confused with any other. *Reply* V (I. 135.26ff.): "That than which a greater cannot be conceived can never be understood except as that which alone is greater than all things. Therefore, just as that than which a greater cannot be conceived is understood and is in the understanding, and on that basis is asserted to be in reality, so also that which is called 'greater than all things' is understood and is in the understanding, and on that basis its existence in reality is inferred by necessity. You now see how correct you were to compare me with that fool who asserts that a 'Lost Island' really exists solely because he understands the description of it!"

should or could be conceived—that both these are in fact so is obviously the other assumption, the substance of the Proof—then nothing else may be conceived of as greater than God. For all its formal, or noetic, insufficiency it stands on its own feet. The Proof that is to be worked out on the assumption of this designation of God will not be an analytic but a synthetic proposition.[48] In that it corresponds to its object.[49] And likewise it can now be valid as a proof: It is able to perform the same function as the presupposed Name of God is to perform in a Proof of God. With "that than which a greater cannot be conceived" the enemy (denial or doubt) is sought out on his own ground, in thought itself, on which ground this enemy is repeatedly calling in question the knowledge of God on the assumption of an ontic conception of God. Here this enemy is placed under the sign of the Name of God and is thereby challenged to necessary knowledge of God. "That than which a greater cannot be conceived" is designed to exclude just this *conceivability* of the nonexistence or imperfection of God which lurks in the background of every ontic conception of God—to exclude it with the radicalism and force of the Creator's own injunction to the creature "you shall not be like God"—and likewise to establish knowledge of the truth of the existence and perfection of God.

We may say that the motive that led Anselm to choose this particular Name was completely misunderstood by Gaunilo. Otherwise the "greater than all things" would not have appeared at all. Our understanding of Anselm's intention will depend on our avoiding right from the start this erroneous substitution by Gaunilo.[50]

[48] Above all, the argument proves itself, as Anselm stated in the passages quoted above, p. 131 n. 40. Therefore, the argument may also be used as a means of proof.

[49] Cf. Anselm's earlier statement on the aseity of God in *Monol.* XV (I. 28.13ff.): "If none of those [created] things ever existed, in relation to which this nature is called 'the supreme' and 'the greater,' then this would be understood neither as 'the supreme' nor as 'the greater.' Nevertheless, it would not therefore be any less good or suffer any detriment whatsoever to its essential greatness."

[50] How remarkable it is that even so clever and independent a historian as Franz Overbeck, in his *Vorgeschichte und Jugend der Mittelalterlichen Scholastik* (Basel, 1917), p. 220, could not rise even a little above the level of the common but false explanation of the basic concept of Anselm's proof.

VI

Karl Barth

Proslogion III: The Special Existence of God

Quod non possit cogitari non esse. (I. 102.5)	That he could not be conceived as not existing.

This heading denotes the second, more specific meaning of "he truly exists" (*vere sit*): God exists in such a way (true only of him) that it is impossible for him to be conceived as not existing.

Quod utique sic vere est, ut nec cogitari possit non esse. (I. 102.6)	Which so truly exists that it cannot even be conceived as not existing.

We have now to take a look at a second, narrower definition of of the general existence of God ("so truly exists"). Of course in this closely defined way existence is being asserted of the God described by "that than which a greater cannot be conceived." And not only in this way, as *Proslogion* II showed. But in this definite manner *only* of God. This second definition reads—he does not only exist; there is no possibility of his being conceived as not existing.

We might object (and the reason why *Proslogion* III is frequently overlooked or taken lightly may be implicitly based on this objection), that this second statement that is now to be proved is *identical* with the first statement that was proved in *Proslogion* II, insofar as this is accepted as proved. If the existence of God is proved there, then it must mean that it is impossible for him to be conceived as not existing. The antithesis between a God who exists only in thought and One who exists objectively (and therefore genuinely) as well as in thought showed—God would not be God if this "God" who exists only in thought were God. We are not thinking of the true God when we think of this God. Thus, it is impossible for us to conceive of the true God as not existing. To what extent is the thesis of *Proslogion* III *more* than a mere repetition or underlining of this result from *Proslogion* II?

Reply to this objection: in *Proslogion* II the concept of existence was expressly the general concept of existence in thought and in reality. On that basis it was proved that it is impossible to conceive of God if his existence in thought and in reality are denied. But the very impossibility of thus denying the existence of a being *can* be understood as a merely *factual* denial that accompanies a recognition of this being's existence in fact, although insisting that *in theory* it might be possible for it not to exist. What we know as existing "in the understanding and in reality" we cannot in fact at the same time conceive as not existing. But we cannot deny that we *could* think of it in itself as not existing (assuming that the factual impossibility would not hinder us). In *Proslogion* II it was then shown that in actual fact God cannot be conceived as not existing. Not of course on the ground of positive knowledge of his existence. With the existence of God there is absolutely no question at all of a knowledge of his existence such as we can have of the existence of other things, and the knowledge of it that we certainly have from revelation was definitely eliminated here as a basis of proof. But on the basis of the revealed Name of God, which cannot possibly apply to a being that does not exist "in the understanding and in reality," the question arises of the God who exists "in the understanding and in reality" and who, as bearer of this Name, is known only by revelation. Whoever hears and understands this Name can in fact apply this Name to no mere object of thought but only to the God who makes known his existence in the same revelation. To that extent it is actually already proved in *Proslogion* II that it is impossible for us to conceive the true God as not existing. However, it has not so far been proved, and the *question* now arises, whether it is true that the reason that prevents the actual denial of the Existence of God can also debar even the hypothetical conception of the non-existence of God. Could this reason not be of the same type as our positive acquaintance of the existence of other things on the ground of the knowledge that we have of them? This acquaintance certainly has the power to render impossible for us the thought that these things do not exist, but it does not have the power to withhold from us the thought that their nonexistence *might* be conceived. The concept of existence assumed in *Proslogion* II is the general concept, applicable to all things that exist. A thing that we know as existing cannot at one and the same time be conceived as both existing and as not existing. But we can quite well conceive, simultaneously with the thought of its existence, that it possibly might not exist were it not known to us as existing. The question is now: whether, despite the proof just demonstrated, we are in such a position in respect of God that, knowing his existence, we have to reckon at the same time at least hypothetically with his nonexistence; or whether God is an *exception* in the case of the knowledge of his existence, so that the knowledge that we have of him renders impossible in practice not only the thought of his nonexistence, but also—likewise in practice—the thought of the very *possibility* of his nonexistence. Must this impossibility in practice mean also the absolute exclusion of our *conceiving* God's nonexistence?

Our chapter answers this question. It lifts the concept of the existence of *God* right *out* of the plane of the general concept of existence.[1] The limitation on the concept of existence—"existence in the understanding and in reality"—with which it was applied to God in *Proslogion* II, now disappears. Our chapter affirms the *exception* that is made here: The revealed Name of God has more power than the positive knowledge that we can have of the existence of other things "in the understanding and in reality." It compels in him who hears and understands it a recognition not only of the factual impossibility of the thought that God does not exist but also of the impossibility of that thought ever being *conceived*. Beyond the recognition that God exists, the Name of God as it is heard and understood compels the more precise definition that God does not exist as all other things exist whose nonexistence we cannot reject in theory even when the vindication of this theory is impossible for us to conceive in practice. But God exists—and he alone—in such a way that it is impossible even to conceive the *possibility* of his nonexistence. That is the thesis of *Proslogion* III. And that is not a repetition but a vital narrowing of the result of *Proslogion* II.

[1] C. in this respect: B. Adlhoch, "Der Gottesbeweis des heiligen Anselm," *Philos Jahrb. der Görresgesellschaft*, vol. VIII, Part 1 1895, pp. 380; K. Heim, *Das Gewissheitsproblem*, 1911, p. 78; R. Seeberg, *Dogmengeschichte* vol. 3, 1913, p. 150f.; A. Koyré: *L'Idée de Dieu, etc.*, 1923, pp. 193f.

At this point we insert an account of the essence of Gaunilo's comments on *Proslogion* III that were put into *On Behalf of the Fool*[2] Para. 7 and also of Anselm's reply given in *Reply* IV. Gaunilo's objection is important because it is in it that his own position becomes relatively clearer than anywhere else. And Anselm's reply ought to be the best proof that the interpretation that we have just attempted of *Proslogion* III is correct.

Leaving everything else aside, Gaunilo's main objection is to the whole manner in which the chapter *puts the question.* Instead of "God cannot be conceived as not existing" (*cogitari*), on his view Anselm would have been better to have said, "we cannot *know* God as not existing or as possibly not existing" (*intelligi*). Thereby denial of or doubt as to God's existence would be characterized as "something false," as Gaunilo thinks it ought to be. For "false things cannot be understood" (*intelligi*): Knowledge is ever knowledge of truth. However, that "false things" and therefore also this particular "false things" *can* be *conceived*, as is obviously the case with the fool, Anselm had no intention of disputing. From this point onward—just from the point where in its own way it becomes interesting—Gaunilo's exposition becomes sketchy:

"I know (*scio*) myself as existing and also at the same time as possibly not existing. On the other hand, I know God as existing but it is impossible for me to know him as possibly not existing. In knowing myself as existing, can I at the same time conceive of myself as not existing? I do not know. If I *can* then I can also do it for everything else whose existence I know with the same certainty. If I *cannot*, then the fact that I cannot conceive an existence as not existing is not true only in respect of God."[3]

We see here (apart from the general statement in the last chapter this is the *only* occasion in his essay, but here it is very definite) that even Gaunilo *asserts* the existence of God, indeed the "under-

[2] What is not of the essence in this paragraph by Gaunilo is the repetition of the objection (I. 129.1-10) that the "genuinely real being" of God must first of all be made known, or have been made known otherwise than by means of the mere expression, before any sort of conclusions about his existence can be drawn from his perfection which that expression declares. Gaunilo's confusion between "that which is greater than all things" and "that than which a greater cannot be conceived" (see above pp. 129ff.) has a particularly disastrous effect here—in fact he paraphrases here Anselm's alleged "that which is greater than all things" with "the nature that is greater and better than everything else that is" and with "the supreme reality."

[3] Gaunilo, *On Behalf of the Fool* 7 (I. 129.10ff.).

standing" (*intelligere*) of the existence of God, although of course we also see at once that what he understands by it is something quite different from what Anselm understands. His "understanding" is synonymous with a "knowing" (*scire*) which for some reason or another is a "most certain knowing."[4] It may be that what he wants this to describe, if it is a case of "understanding that God exists," is the same as Anselm describes[5] as the certainty of faith that is already well established prior to all theology. But perhaps he is familiar rather with the "completely certain argument" which he is always missing in Anselm and what he has in mind is some empirical knowledge of God, perhaps somewhat in the manner in which Thomas Aquinas later made it credible to many. Certainly he wants to be sure that his "understanding" is understood differently from all pure thinking and vice versa, pure thinking also—of course to its shame—as independent from what he styles "understanding." Gaunilo "recognizes" or "knows" not a little: he knows, for example, even "with complete certainty," that he himself exists. He certainly also knows the limited nature of this his existence and therefore of the possibility of his nonexistence. On the other hand, he does *not* know—and he does not want to make up his mind merely "by thinking"—whether despite this his knowledge of his existence he could or could not *conceive* of himself as not existing. His position in respect of God is exactly the same. He knows God as existing and indeed even that it is impossible for him not to exist. But one sentence expressing this (perhaps on the ground of tradition, perhaps of experience or perhaps of both) would satisfy his claim to characterize the opposition of the fool as "something false." Against which he expects nothing from a special effort of thought in this realm (perhaps in any realm). Normally "conceiving" (*cogitare*) is just the simple reproduction of "understanding" (*intelligere*), and "understanding" means "knowing" (*scire*). On the other hand, abnormally, thinking that is not identical with the reproduction of the thing known seems to him in all circumstances to be hopeless: just as much when it asserts (with Anselm) the existence of God as when (with the fool) it denies it. Do I exist? Does anything exist? Does God exist? What thinking could decide

4 With this passage cf. also *ibid.* 2 (I. 125.20ff.): "Only then would I not be able to conceive of this except by understanding it, that is, except by comprehending rationally that it exists in reality."

5 See above [in K. Barth, *Anselm*], German pp. 19ff., English pp. 26ff.

these conclusively? Be my knowledge in all these points ever so sure, pure thinking as such is here as free as it is insufficient to make this decision. We *can* conceive of God as not existing.[6] Let us then abide by the thinking that is identical with the reproduction of knowledge.[7] The end of the passage is particularly remarkable. What does the "either—or" mean with which Gaunilo ends? The question as to the necessity of the thought of his own existence was obviously dragged into the discussion because he assumed that behind Anselm's doctrine of the impossibility of the thought of God's nonexistence there stood a general doctrine of necessary thoughts ultimately based on that of the necessity of his own existence. In my opinion he regarded him as standing where Descartes later stood. And so he thinks Anselm has only this alternative: either his statement "the thought of one's own existence is necessary" is false—in which case all corresponding statements collapse with it, including the statement, "the thought of God's existence is necessary." Or this statement is correct—in which case the statement about the existence of God has at least a parallel and that finishes the uniqueness of the existence of God which Anselm asserted. It can be maintained that these last words of Gaunilo's polemic are the most spiritually valuable in his whole work, and yet they are the least relevant to Anselm.

Anselm replied to this as follows. Just because the point at issue is the proof of the existence which is *peculiar* to God, our thesis must be: "God cannot be *conceived* as not existing." It is certainly true that God cannot be *known* as not existing, since "something false" can never be an object of knowledge. But supposing he, Anselm, had put forward *this* thesis, would Gaunilo not have replied to him (and correctly) in the sense of his closing sentence: This statement is applicable to all that exists and not only to God.[8]

[6] Later, in his *Summa contra Gentiles* I. 11, Thomas Aquinas will not be afraid to say, "No difficulty arises in holding that God does not exist."

[7] Bouchitté (*Le rationalisme chrétien*, p. 306) is no doubt right to give this compliment to Gaunilo, although in connection with a different passage: "Men accustomed to philosophic studies certainly recognize that in this passage and in the one that follows there is something not discredited by the experimental and sensualist philosophy of our day."

[8] *Reply* IV (I. 133.24ff.): "You yourself say that according to the proper meaning of this word nothing false can be 'understood.' Therefore . . . you would probably have objected that nothing which is can be 'understood' not to be. . . . Therefore, the impossibility of being understood not to be is not a property peculiar to God."

Whereas the statement, "God cannot be *conceived* as not existing," can only have *one* subject, "God." For all that exists apart from God can be conceived as not existing.[9] The proof of this follows from the Nature of God.[10] *All* things finite and divisible (but *only* these) can be conceived as not existing: In view of what is beyond their spatial and temporal limits, in view of their partial nonidentity with themselves, obviously the thought of their possible non-existence must occur, however assured we may be that their existence is known.[11] The Infinite and Indivisible, which is *God* (and it *alone*), *cannot* be conceived as not existing (insofar as on other grounds it must be conceived as existing). Insofar as it has no bounds and in its totality is identical with itself, its existence (assuming it to possess such) cannot be denied.[12] Thus: If the existence of God is to be proved, then it must be proved that he cannot be *conceived* as not existing. But Anselm has no intention of relating this to any analogous statement about his own existence, let alone of setting it in a relation of dependence on such a statement, as Gaunilo seems to take for granted. There is *no* analogous statement (Anselm is not Descartes) concerning man's own existence. Of course, Gaunilo can say that he does not know whether he *could conceive* himself as not existing while *knowing* his existence. Naturally he is able to do that as certainly as he is capable of creating a *fiction* by ignoring what he knows of his existence. The nature of man as distinct from the Nature of God will not put any obstacle in the way of such a fiction.[13] Anything at all (except God) we can conceive as not

[9] *Ibid.*; (I. 133.29ff.): "If one examines the matter closely, this objection cannot be made against 'conceiving.' For even if there is nothing existing which can be 'understood' not to be, nevertheless everything can be 'conceived' not to be, except that which is supremely."

[10] Once again it is to be noted that the point here in *Reply* IV is not the question of the existence of God, a question which is assumed to be still open, but the question as to what "existence" can and does mean when it refers to God. This question is to be answered from the nature of God. See above [in K. Barth, *Anselm*] German p. 105 n. 2, English p. 97 n. 1.

[11] *Reply* IV (I. 134.2f.): "In fact, all those things—and only those things—can be 'conceived' not to be which have a beginning or an end or a combination of parts."

[12] *Ibid.*, (I. 134.4ff.): "That alone cannot be conceived not to be which has neither beginning nor end nor combination of parts, and which thought finds fully existing always and everywhere."

[13] *Ibid.*; (I. 134.7ff.): "You must realize therefore that even though you know with complete certainty that you exist, you can 'conceive' of yourself as not existing. It surprises me that you say that you do not know this. For we do 'conceive' of the nonexistence of many things which we 'know' to exist, and we

existing: That is to say, although we know its existence and although in fact we are not able to vindicate the thought of its nonexistence, we can create the hypothesis or fiction that would correspond.[14] Thus, in reply to Gaunilo's skeptical statement that he does not know whether he could conceive himself as not existing, it has to be said that *in actual fact* he cannot do this (prevented by knowledge of his existence), but can do it very well *hypothetically*, as a fiction. And the same is true of our thinking in respect of all things apart from God.[15] Thus, there is no general doctrine of necessary thoughts standing behind the thesis of *Proslogion* III. That there are also things other than God that cannot in fact be conceived as not existing is a different matter. What is represented by Anselm in *Proslogion* III is this sentence, of which God alone can be the subject: Even in this second sense, even *hypothetically*, God cannot be conceived as not existing.[16] Anselm comes to terms in *Proslogion* IV with the fact, dealt with so disastrously by Gaunilo, that nonetheless the fool asserts that he can conceive the nonexistence of God.[17] What had to be shown here was that in *Proslogion* III Anselm is concerned with a problem which for all his vaunted positivism Gaunilo has not yet even seen. Just here, where Gaunilo is at his cleverest, all that he can show is that he is completely at cross-purposes with Anselm for the reason that where his work ends, Anselm's begins.

---

do 'conceive' of the existence of many things which we 'know' not to exist. We do this, not by making a real judgment, but by *imagining* that these things are as we conceive of them."

[14] *Ibid.*; (I. 134.10ff.): "In this sense [meaning I], we can 'conceive' that something is not when we 'know' that it is, because at one and the same time we can 'conceive' of the former and yet 'know' the latter. In another sense [meaning II], we cannot 'conceive' that something is not when we 'know' that it is, because we cannot conceive of something as both existing and not existing at the same time."

[15] *Ibid.*; (I. 134.13ff.): "Therefore, if anyone distinguishes in this way between these two meanings of the word 'conceive,' he will understand that whenever something is 'known' to be, it cannot be 'conceived' not to be [in the sense of meaning II]; and yet that whatever is, except that than which a greater cannot be conceived, even if it is 'known' to be, can still be 'conceived' not to be [in the sense of meaning I]."

[16] *Ibid.*, (I. 134.16ff.): "Therefore, it is the peculiar property of God that he cannot be 'conceived' not to be [in the sense of meaning I], while many things, so far as they exist, cannot be 'conceived' not to be [in the sense of meaning II]."

[17] *Ibid.*, (I. 134.18f.): "As to how it is *said* that God is conceived not to be, I think that I have said enough about this in my little book."

Nam potest cogitari esse aliquid, quod non possit cogitari non esse; quod maius est, quam quod non esse cogitari potest. (I. 102. 6ff.)	It is possible to conceive as existing something which cannot be conceived as not existing; and which is greater than what can be conceived as not existing.

What follows now is the narrowing of the proof in *Proslogion* II achieved in the sense of the opening sentence that sets the theme of the chapter. It is taken as proved and admitted that existence *in general*, "existing in the understanding and in reality," applies to God; on the other hand, the *special* brand of true existence, applicable only to him (his "existing so truly that") and which according to the opening sentence consists in the fact, not yet established in the proof, that he so exists that he cannot be conceived as not existing—that is taken as still open to question. Just because it is not a case of a second proof (nor indeed of a repetition of the first), but rather a case of narrowing the *one and only* proof, admittedly in a way that is decisive, without further preparation this narrowing is combined with the first general statement; it can and must be essentially the same proof as before, except that now right along the line a second reflection on the impossibility of the nonexistence of God is to be carried to the length of the impossibility of even *conceiving* his nonexistence.

Anselm starts from the possibility of conceiving side by side a being who exists and who cannot be thought of as not existing, and then another being who likewise exists but who can be thought of as not existing. The "existing in the understanding and in reality" in the sense of *Proslogion* II applies to both; but they are distinguished from each other in that theoretical denial of this "existing" is impossible in the case of the first being but possible in the case of the second. The opening statement is thus: These two beings and their comparison side by side are conceivable.

Let us suppose that we did conceive of these two beings alongside each other. We must admit that once more we have conceived first of a "greater" and of a "smaller" being, a being of a higher and of a lower order. The principle of progressive orders which Anselm here assumes could be the same as that in *Proslogion* II, only that this time we have a higher degree within the same series. It is now no longer a contrast between something that exists on the one hand merely in thought and on the other hand in thought and objectively, but a contrast between something that certainly exists objectively as well as in thought but yet which is conceivable as not existing and on the other hand something existing objectively and in thought but which is not conceivable as not existing. Out of the general *vere esse* there now rises significantly before us a "true existing" whose reality has its basis neither merely subjectively nor merely subjectively and objectively, but is based beyond this contrast *a se*, in itself. A being to which "true existing" in this latter sense applies, whose existence is therefore independent of the antithesis between knowledge and object, such a being is obviously a "greater." It belongs to a higher level of existence than a being to which "true existing" still applies merely in the general sense, which, however genuinely it may exist, is still subject to this antithesis and whose existence can therefore be denied in theory by the same thinking as has to assert its existence in fact. This first being exists not only in the truth but exists as the truth of existence itself, as the criterion of all existence and nonexistence which is always presupposed in all thinking of the existence and nonexistence of other beings; consequently, it cannot be conceived as not existing. Whoever thinks of these two beings side by side has conceived this "greater" over against a "smaller."

Quare si id quo maius nequit cogitari, potest cogitari non esse: id ipsum quo maius cogitari nequit non est id quo maius cogitari nequit; quod convenire non potest.

(I. 102.8ff.)

When, therefore, "that than which a greater cannot be conceived" can be conceived as not existing, then "that than which a greater cannot be conceived" is not "that than which a greater cannot be conceived." Which is a contradiction.

For the sake of argument God is identified with this second being, who although existing, is however conceivable as not existing. Why should God not exist within this limitation, as is the case with all other beings known to us? As the most exalted Being in the universe at the head of many others? The gods of the heathen seem to manage it. But that very fact raises the question whether these "gods" justify their name. It is by the revelation of the Name of God that this question is decided. The God who is revealed is called "that than which a greater cannot be conceived." And from that we again have this intolerable contradiction: This God who although existing can be conceived as not existing, is *called* "that than which greater cannot be conceived" and yet *is not* that. That a "greater" is conceivable has just been shown. "Which is a contradiction." Once again it is obvious that a pseudo-God has to be unmasked and the Name of God denied to a being who cannot be seriously taken as God. Whether this "God" exists "in the understanding and in reality," he does *not* exist *as God.* God cannot possibly exist *merely thus.* In order to be identical with God, over and above his identity with a being who exists in this manner, he would have to be identical with this conceivable "greater." Whether distinct from or similar to this latter, he shows himself up for what he always is—not God.

Sic ergo vere est aliquid quo maius cogitari non potest, ut nec cogitari possit non esse (I. 103.1f.)	Therefore, "something beyond which nothing greater can be conceived" exists in reality in such a manner that it cannot be conceived as not existing.

Again the conclusion is drawn: What is described as "something than which a greater cannot be conceived" exists in such a way that it cannot be *conceived* as not existing. To what extent is this conclusion binding? Clearly first of all, we repeat, only insofar as a "God" conceivable as not existing is not disqualified from being God by the contradiction between the Name of the God *who is revealed* and the manner of existence of *this* so-called "God." God as he is *revealed cannot* in any circumstances exist in that way. But once more the actual conclusion stretches out beyond this negative that can be proved; from the impossibility of the revealed God having *such* an existence a conclusion is drawn as to the existence that is *peculiar* to him and which no thinking can question. And again it has to be said: This last, vital *positive* statement appears (after the opposite statement—that God's existence may be questioned by thinking—has been proved absurd), *without* its *following* as a consequence from the preceding line of thought. It is brought in as a possibility of thought alongside another ("it can be conceived that something is . . ."). If it is to remain, if it is now supposed to be *proved,* "therefore it so exists in reality," then this can make sense only if an *article of faith,* fixed in itself as such, has been proved in such a way that the opposite statement would be reduced *ad absurdum* by means of the statement of the Name of God which is likewise assumed to be revealed and believed. This article of faith (regarding that existence of God which is not only genuine but also incapable of being denied even theoretically) was introduced first of all disguised as a possibility of thought alongside another, and it remains before us as the positive result after this opposite statement has been dropped. Responsibility for the *givenness* of this statement (for the last "reason as to how it is") is not for the theologian to bear.[18] To "understand" (*intelligere*) means to see into the noetic rationality and therefore into the noetic necessity of the statements that are revealed, on the basis that they possess ontic rationality and necessity as revealed statements, prior to all "understanding," to all "proof" and therefore not based on proof. This can only happen in theology as such. But it *can* happen, and it is what in fact has happened here.

Before following *Proslogion* III to its climax, for the sake of completeness we must turn once again to Anselm's Apology against Gaunilo. As already mentioned, in one passage there he plainly repeated the simple proof of *Proslogion* II.[19] On the other hand, in a whole succession of passages—a further indication of where and in what his interests lay—he continually offered his opponent new *variations* of the narrowed-down proof of *Prosologion* III. We summarize them shortly so as to show: (1) that the decisive thought of *Proslogion* III is not bound to the form which it is given there but is capable of variations; (2) that what these passages in fact deal with are variations of the narrowed-down proof of *Proslogion* III.

1. *Reply* IX.[20] We start with this last passage because it is here that we find ourselves nearest to the form which the argument takes in

[18] See above [in K. Barth, *Anselm*], German pp. 19f., English pp. 27f.: "On the basis of the completely unquestioned assumption *that it is* just as he, a Christian, believes [*dass es so ist*], the man who asks for Christian knowledge asks *in what way is it so* [*inwiefern es so ist*]. . . . A science of faith which denied or questioned the faith (that is, the *Credo* of the Church), would *ipso facto* cease to be either faithful or scientific."

[19] Reply II (I. 132.2ff.).

[20] *Reply* IX (I. 138.19ff.): "That which cannot possibly not be is obviously something that can be conceived and understood. He who conceives of this conceives of something greater than he who conceives of that which has the possibility of not being. Therefore, when he is conceiving of that than which a greater cannot be conceived, if he conceives that it has the possibility of not being, he is obviously not conceiving of that than which a greater cannot be conceived. However, the same thing cannot be conceived and be not conceived at the same time. Therefore, he who conceives of that than which a greater cannot be conceived is not conceiving of what can, but of what cannot possibly, not be. For that reason, what he is conceiving must necessarily exist, because whatever is able not to exist is not that of which he is conceiving."

Proslogion III. Again, something that is conceived as "greater" is compared with something conceived as "smaller." Again, the Name of God shows that God cannot be identical with this "smaller." And finally it is again taken to follow (on the basis of the already given article of faith)—as he cannot be the "smaller," God is the "greater." The difference between this and the basic form of *Proslogion* III consists in the fact that here the "greater" is defined as the "that which *cannot* not be" and the "lesser" as "that which *can* not be," and that in consequence this result follows: When someone conceives of that than which a greater cannot be conceived, "what he conceives must necessarily be." This distinction obviously involves an *abbreviation*; for rationality necessity is at once substituted, surely intimating that the proof consists in demonstrating that it is impossible to *conceive* of God as not existing.

2. *Reply* III.[21] Here Anselm replies to Gaunilo's island analogy: What is described as "that than which a greater cannot be conceived" could not be conceived as not existing because it exists (if at all) in virtue of the rationality (and therefore on the basis) of Truth itself. If it did not exist thus, it would not exist at all. The island analogy is nonsense because it overlooks the fact that it is only the existence of God (and therefore not the existence of this island) that can be proved as Anselm has proved it. And then the argument proceeds: Anyone who denies the existence of God must face the question whether he is really thinking of him who is called "that than which a greater cannot be conceived." If he is not thinking of him, then obviously he does not deny *his* existence. If he is thinking of him, then he is thinking of one whose existence cannot be denied. For

[21] *Reply* III (I. 133.10ff.): "It is now obvious, however, that that than which a greater cannot be conceived cannot be conceived not to be, because it exists with the undoubted ground (*ratio*) of truth itself. Otherwise it would not exist at all. Let us suppose that someone says that he does conceive that this does not exist. In my view, when he is conceiving in this way, he is either conceiving of 'that than which a greater cannot be conceived,' or he is not conceiving of it. If he is not conceiving of it, then it is not this which he thinks does not exist. On the other hand, if he is really conceiving of it, he at least conceives of something which cannot be conceived not to be. For if it could be conceived not to be, it could also be conceived to have a beginning and an end. But this is impossible [in the case of 'that than which a greater cannot be conceived']. Therefore, whoever really conceives of this conceives of something which cannot be conceived not to be. Whoever really conceives of it, then, does not in fact conceive that it is not. Otherwise he would be conceiving of something which cannot be conceived. Therefore, 'that than which a greater cannot be conceived' cannot be conceived not to be."

could his existence be denied, then he would have to be conceivable as finite. But he is not conceivable as finite. (Whoever thinks of him who is called "that than which a greater cannot be conceived" is never to think of a finite being, but rather of "the ground (*ratio*) of truth," and so of a being that does not exist in the manner of finite beings.) Therefore, whoever thinks of *him* thinks of one whose existence cannot be denied. Thus, the existence of him who is called "that than which a greater cannot be conceived" cannot be denied.

Here too we immediately recognize the nerve of the proof of *Proslogion* III: By what his Name forbids, God is fundamentally distinguished from all beings that can be conceived as not existing. The proof of course cannot establish *that*, even if we deny his existence, we still conceive of him and therefore *must* conceive of him in this his uniqueness as the *infinite* Being and therefore as existing. All it tries to prove and all it can prove is that *if* we really conceive *him*, we conceive him as existing of necessity, as so existing that he cannot be conceived as not existing. This reminder of God's infinity alludes to one of the statements of revelation about the *Nature* of God. But the fact that God is infinite does not prove that he exists. Rather, the fact that God is infinite proves that (if he exists) he exists differently from beings who are not infinite—that is, he does not exist in such a way that his existence can be denied. The positive conclusion that he exists does not follow from the statement quoted here concerning his Nature. That remains at the point where he who is called "that than which a greater cannot be conceived" is conceived and where therefore his existence too is an article of faith.

3. *Reply* I (where Anselm gives the proof successively in three different forms). We are confronted first of all[22] with an inversion of the form just given under 2. He who is called "that than which a greater cannot be conceived" can be conceived as existing. But who is it who is then conceived? A being whose existence is infinite. A being whose existence could be denied would have to be conceived as a finite being. If then he who is called "that than which a greater cannot be conceived" is not conceivable as a finite being, then his

[22] *Reply* I (I. 131.1ff.): "If this can ever be conceived to be, it necessarily follows that it exists. For 'that than which a greater cannot be conceived' cannot be conceived to be, except without a beginning. However, whatever can be conceived to be and actually is not can be conceived to be through a beginning. Therefore, it is not the case that 'that than which a greater cannot be conceived' can be conceived to exist, and yet does not exist. Therefore, if it can be conceived to be, it necessarily is."

existence cannot be denied. If he can be conceived as existing, then of necessity he must exist, and that means he must be conceived as existing of necessity. Of the "abbreviation" that is applied, the same is to be said as under 1; of the appeal to the infinity of God, the same as under 2. For the rest we again recognize the basic form— separation of God's existence from that of all other beings. Consequently, this existence, unlike that of all other beings, cannot be disputed. Conclusion (the positive article of faith remains): God exists of necessity.

4. *Reply* I in a second passage:[23] Anselm takes as his starting point the assumption that at least the concept as such expressed in the Name "that than which a greater cannot be conceived" (no matter whether the existence of its bearer is accepted or denied) is capable of realization. Supposing then someone were to deny or doubt his existence. That man could nevertheless neither deny nor doubt that *if* he, who bears this name, did exist in accordance with his Name, then he would *have* to exist, and with ontic objectivity (*actu*) as much as for our knowledge (*intellectu*). His Name forbids that he should be reckoned as one of those beings who merely exist in fact, that is, who are recognized as existing. A purely conceptual being that does not really exist could never be obliged to exist: even if it did exist, it could obviously either exist or not exist, be known as existing or as not existing; at best it would be a being existing in fact and known as existing. The "if then" statement is therefore not applicable to a purely conceptual being that does not really exist but only to a being who can be conceived and who really does exist, of whom at the same time it can be said what is in fact to be said of God: It is impossible for it not to exist or to be conceived as not existing.

A highly complicated feature, but one that is very significant for Anselm's thought and intention in this matter, is that at first the question as to the general existence of God (in the sense of *Proslogion* II) is expressly left open. It is only the Name of God that is

[23] *Ibid.*, I (I. 131.6ff.): "Further, if it can be conceived in any way at all, it must necessarily be the case that it exists. For while someone may deny or doubt the existence of something than which a greater cannot be conceived, he will not deny or doubt that, if it does exist, then in fact and for the understanding it is impossible for it not to be. Otherwise it would not be that than which a greater cannot be conceived. As for things which can be conceived and yet do not exist, in fact and for the understanding it is possible for them not to be. Therefore, if 'that than which a greater cannot be conceived' can be conceived at all, it cannot not be."

introduced by the hypothesis: "It can be conceived." Then the Name of God extorts the admission that he who has this Name, *if* he existed (in the sense of *Proslogion* II), would exist *of necessity* (in the sense of *Proslogion* III). Then this "if" is whittled down by the assertion that a purely conceptual being, even if it did exist (in the sense of *Proslogion* II), would not exist of necessity. And then it is concluded (we would have appreciated a transitional step)—God (no mere conceptual being but one existing in the *Proslogion* II sense) is a necessarily existing Nature. The procedure is then—first the question of *Proslogion* III is answered hypothetically and then by means of this hypothetical answer (!) the question of *Proslogion* II, and, following from it, the question of *Proslogion* III, are answered categorically.

5. And now in a third passage[24] of *Reply* I, Anselm goes yet a step further. The question of *Proslogion* II is to be taken not just as being open, but as being denied, and there is only the possibility of conceiving the thought content of God's Name. Again two "if then" statements of similar content now appear but in reverse order from that in the form given previously: *if* a purely conceptual being not really existing were to exist, then as such (for obviously even if it were a being that existed it would not be one that existed of necessity) it would not be identical to God. Therefore, *if* God were to exist as such a merely conceptual being not really existing, then he would not be identical with himself. Therefore, this hypothesis is absurd. Therefore, in conceiving the thought content of this Name, all we can assume is the existence of its bearer. The Name of God thus demands that his existence, even if it is denied, cannot (and incidentally this renders its denial impossible) be conceived merely as an existence in fact, but only as one that is necessary.

6. *Reply* V[25] is worked out with the same material. Again the hypothesis is on the one hand the nonexistence of God and on the other,

[24] *Ibid.*, (I. 131.12ff.): "Let us nevertheless suppose that, even if it can be conceived, it does not exist. Now whatever can be conceived and is not, if it were, it would still not be 'that than which a greater cannot be conceived.' Therefore, if it were 'that than which a greater cannot be conceived,' it would not be that than which a greater cannot be conceived—which is utterly absurd. Therefore, if something than which a greater cannot be conceived can be conceived at all, then if is false to say that it does not exist."

[25] *Reply* V (I. 134.ff): "For what does not exist is capable of not existing. And what is capable of not existing is capable of being conceived not to exist. As for whatever can be conceived not to exist, if it does exist, it is not that than which a greater cannot be conceived; and if it does not exist but might exist, it would not be that than which a greater cannot be conceived. However, with

the conceivability of his Name. From the first would follow the possibility of his nonexistence and from the second its conceivability. However, something conceivable as not existing, even if it does exist, is not the legitimate bearer of the Name "that than which a greater cannot be conceived." And if it does not exist, it would not be the legitimate bearer of this name, even if it were to exist, for alongside him there would be a greater conceivable, who could not be conceived as not existing. This impossibility of regarding it as the legitimate bearer of the Name of God is the characteristic distinction between God and every being that is conceivable as not existing. Thus, God would have to be a being distinct from himself in order to be a being conceivable as not existing. And so he cannot be a being conceivable as not existing. With the inconceivability of his nonexistence, its very possibility also collapses and incidentally with it the reality of his nonexistence that was the hypothesis.

In all six of these variants the *object* of the Proof (in agreement with *Proslogion* III) is not the existence that God has in common with beings who are different from him, but rather that peculiar, indeed unique and in the end only true existence which, over and above this general existence, applies only to him—the absolutely necessary, because the original existence, "of the *ratio* of truth." Incidentally forms 4-6 reach conclusions that refer back to general existence and so to a strengthening of the Proof of *Proslogion* II. But only incidentally. There can be no question but that in these last three forms too Anselm's primary and decisive interest was in the "it cannot *be conceived* not to be." In all its six forms the Proof consists (again agreeing with *Proslogion* III) in demonstrating: It is impossible to conceive him who is called "that than which a greater cannot be conceived" as existing in the way that other beings are conceivable as existing, that is, in such a way that his nonexistence could be conceived. His Name and his Nature exclude this.

In demonstrating this, the way is prepared for the positive statement: God so exists that his nonexistence is inconceivable. This statement as such is not proved. On the contrary, it stands, like the

---

regard to 'that than which a greater cannot be conceived,' we cannot say that even if it does not exist, it is still not that than which a greater cannot be conceived or that if it were to exist, it would not be that than which a greater cannot be conceived. It is evident therefore that neither does this not exist, nor is it capable of not existing, nor is it capable of being conceived not to exist. For otherwise, if it does exist, it is not what it is called, and if it were to exist, it would not be what it is called."

general statement of *Proslogion* II, "God exists," as an article of faith by itself. What happens in the Proof and its variants is that sometimes this statement is directly attained through the Proof, at other times its opposite is directly excluded through the Proof, that is through the interpretation of the revealed Name and Nature of God. That is the "understanding "of God's Existence corresponding to Anselm's program.

Et hoc es tu, Domine Deus noster. Sic ergo vere es, Dominine Deus meus, ut nec cogitari possis non esse: et merito. Si enim aliqua mens posset cogitare aliquid melius te, ascenderet creatura super Creatorum et indicaret de Creatore, quod valde est absurdum. (I. 103.3ff.)	And this thou art, O Lord our God. Thou dost exist in truth in such a way that thou canst not be conceived as not existing. And that with reason. For if any and every mind were able to conceive of something better than thee, then the creature would be rising above the Creator and judging the Creator. This would be most absurd.

Whether we understand this part of the text perhaps determines for every reader of Anselm whether the whole is understood or not. The chapter could have closed with the preceding sentence, for with that sentence the Proof as such is completed. But the chapter does not close, and anyone who does not heed this, anyone who does not take what Anselm now inserts at least as seriously as the actual Proof will most certainly misunderstand the Proof itself.

In the first place Anselm resumes the form of *address* to God, that is, he passes from the language of theological inquiry to the language of prayer. Or rather—once again[26] he shows that the whole theological inquiry is intended to be understood as undertaken and carried through in prayer. In prayer, and surely that means: by presupposing in the most positive manner the object of the inquiry, its Presence and its Authority for the course and the success of the inquiry concerning him. This "object" who is worshiped and thus investigated is, however, *Dominus Deus noster = Dominus Deus meus*, the God who is Lord of the *Church* and as such is the God of the inquiring *theologian*, who is Lord in this double relationship and to whom only devout obedience is possible. Theology is devout obedience. Could Anselm interpret his "I believe so that I may understand" more clearly than by revealing this attitude in which he pursues his study and more obviously than by insisting that it is on

[26] Cf. the opening sentences of *Prosl.* II.

this that the course and outcome of his inquiry depend? Even formally his inquiry is distinguished by a provocative lack of all doubt, including all "philosophic doubt," of all anxiety, including all apologetic anxiety and in this connection by a no less provocative intellectual coolness. Can it be otherwise when theology is what it is for him: assent to a decision coming from its object, from the "Lord," acknowledgment and recognition of the "Lord's" own communication of himself? It is certain that we cannot take Anselm's attitude that is so manifest here as proof that his thinking is based on received revelation. But it does assuredly prove that he *means* his thinking to be thus based and it is in that way that he wants to be undersood as a thinker. If anyone interprets his argument as an a priori philosophical system then he will certainly have Anselm himself against him at every point. Anselm's own words have to be quietly altered and abbreviated if he is to be so interpreted. Just as, for example, Anselm's critics, beginning with Gaunilo of Marmoutiers, have discreetly taken no notice of this passage and all that follows from it. We can interpret his Proof only when, *along with* Anselm, *in Anselm's own* sense, we share the presupposition of his inquiry—that the object of the inquiry stands over against him who inquires not as "it," not even as "he," but as "thou," as the unmediated "thou" of the Lord.

"And *this* thou art. . . ." "This" refers to "something than which a greater cannot be conceived." It was in fact the assumption made at the beginning of *Proslogion* II—"We believe that you are something than which nothing greater can be conceived." Now at the end of the inquiry it is again brought to remembrance. It is not just of anything, but of God the Lord, whom we believe because he has revealed himself, because he stands unmediated over against us as God the Lord, it is of him that it is proved that he exists—since *he* exists thus: "in truth," and that now means in such a way, "that thou canst not be conceived as not existing." He who is present in unmediated form to the thinking churchman and who is worshiped by him, he is not only the One whose existence can be thought of as sure in itself, but in relation to him even thinking is not free; he renders impossible the very thought of his nonexistence, so certainly is he the One "beyond whom a greater cannot be conceived."

But this equation which is vital for the Proof in its general and special form, is it valid? Does God really bear this Name? Must everyone who conceives of God really conceive of the prohibition expressed in this Name? Anselm does subsequently establish this basis of the whole—theologically as is appropriate. There is a "we understand" that also corresponds to the "we believe" at the beginning of *Proslogion* II. How do we know that God is really named "that than which a greater cannot be conceived"? We know it because that is how God has revealed himself and because we believe him as he has revealed himself. But this knowing can be explained: We know it because on the basis of revelation and faith, we know that when we stand before God, we do not stand as any one being before any other being, but as a *creature* before his *Creator*. As such, and from him who stands over against us, we unfailingly hear this Name of God and we unhesitatingly accept the prohibition it expresses. To what extent? To the extent that the creature stands absolutely *under* his Creator and remains there and therefore in his thinking cannot set anything above the Creator. Along with his existence, he also has his thinking about existence, its values and its degrees, all entirely from the Creator. His thinking can be true only insofar as it is true in the Creator himself. The conception of a "better" beyond the Creator would mean for the creature an ascent (*ascendere*) to a point where by nature he cannot stand, a judgment (*indicare*) by a standard of truth or value which by nature he cannot possess. Conceiving a greater than the Creator would therefore mean absurdity—not a physical but *the* great logical-moral and therefore forbidden absurdity. For the creature as such, the Creator as such is absolutely "that than which a greater cannot be conceived." Should the creature fail to hear this Name of God and the prohibition it contains, then that can only mean that he has not yet understood the Creator as such nor himself as creature. It is in faith that he understands him and himself within this relation and so hears his Name and the prohibition against conceiving anything greater than him.[27] And so

[27] We note here two further objections which Thomas Aquinas raised against the proof of *Prosl.* III. The first appears in his *Commentary on the Sentences* (Bk. I, Dist. III, Q. 1, a. 1 and 4; printed in A. Daniels, *op. cit.*, p. 65), and is given as Anselm's interpretation. "Anselm's reasoning is to be understood in this way: After we understand God, we cannot understand both that God is and that he can be conceived not to be. Nevertheless, from this it does not follow that a person cannot deny God or conceive of God as not existing. For he may think that there exists nothing of the sort than which a greater cannot be conceived. His reasoning therefore may proceed from this supposition, which takes the place of the view that something than which a greater cannot be conceived does exist." This exposition is as unlike Anselm as it possibly could be, and can only be taken as criticism. Of the exposition itself we can say: For Anselm the view that God cannot be conceived as not existing does not under any circum-

Anselm, who has proved that it is impossible for him who is called "that than which a greater cannot be conceived" not to exist, can say with a clear conscience that he has proved it impossible for *God* not to exist.

Et quidem quidquid est aliud praeter te solum, potest cogitari non esse. Solus igitur verissime omnium et ideo maxime omnium habes esse: quia quidquid aliud est, non sic vere, et idcirco minus habet esse. (I. 103.6ff.)	And so it stands: Whatever exists apart from thee, the Only One, can be conceived as not existing. Thou alone of all beings hast really true existence—and therefore thou alone of all beings hast perfect existence. For anything other than thee[28] does not possess this manner of existence and therefore possesses but imperfect existence.

Anselm has proved that it is impossible for *God* not to exist. That means, however, that he has proved what can be proved only of God. For that reason, then, the main point that Anselm wanted to make did

---

stances follow "after we understand God," that is, from some *a priori* understanding of God. It follows from the article of faith that "God is called 'that than which a greater cannot be conceived," just as insight into this article of faith follows in its turn from the article of faith that "God is the Creator." In Anselm, that "something than which a greater cannot be conceived does exist" is not a "supposition" but the revelation apart from which there is no theology at all. Here it is the revelation of the Name of God and of the prohibition which that Name expresses. To be sure this prohibition "can" be transgressed. We "can" therefore "conceive that there is nothing of the sort than which a greater cannot be conceived." When Anselm says that we "cannot" conceive of this, he says it in the presence of God and therefore as one who cannot transgress this *prohibition*. In his criticism Thomas unfortunately disregards *this* sense of "cannot."

The second objection, now explicitly formulated as an objection, appears in *Summa contra Gentiles* I. 11, and reads: "If God can be conceived not to be, it does not necessarily follow . . . that something greater than God can be conceived. For the fact that he can be conceived not to be is not due to any imperfection or uncertainty in his being, since his being is in itself supremely manifest, but to the weakness of our understanding, which can contemplate (*intueri*) God, not in himself, but only through his effects." We can compare this with the final words of *Prosl.* III to catch a glimpse of the contradiction between two worlds that is disclosed here. When Anselm speaks of revelation and faith, Thomas disputes the possibility of a "contempation of God in himself." When Anselm sees "stupidity" and "foolishness" at work against the background of divine reprobation, when he sees God offended by the creature's exalting himself above his Creator, as in *Cur Deus homo?* I. 15 (II. 72.29ff.), Thomas sees the problem of creaturely imperfection, to which Thomas can reconcile himself by remembering God's unassailable "manifestness" in himself, and by demonstrating the "contemplation of God from his effects."

[28] A. Koyré: "Everything that is not you . . . "

not come until the narrowed-down Proof of *Proslogion* III and it was not the general Proof of *Proslogion* II. Of course, in *Proslogion* II he had also proved that God certainly did exist, that is possessed not just reality in thought but objective reality. But what a complete misunderstanding it is to think that *this* Proof formed the substance of his purpose! If God were to exist merely generally, in the manner of all other beings, then not only would he not exist as God, but according to Anselm's own account[29]—he did not create himself and therefore does not possess existence as such, as is granted to the creature—he would not exist at all. All that his existence has in common with that of other beings is objective reality as such. But the objective reality of all beings apart from him is such that they can be conceived as not existing and indeed in a special sense have to be conceived as not existing. This to the extent that the existence of all beings apart from him is conditioned by his existence and is an existence that is bestowed from out of his existence. The reason why there is such a thing as existence is that God exists. With his existence stands or falls the existence of all beings that are distinct from him. Only fools and their theological and philosophical supporters, the Gaunilos, could think that the criterion of general existence is the criterion of God's existence and could therefore either not get beyond *Proslogion* II or take *Proslogion* III as conditioned by *Proslogion* II. Whereas it is all the other way around: It is the existence of God that is the criterion of general existence, and if either of these two chapters of Anselm is ultimately or decisively conditioned by the other, then it is *Proslogion* II by *Proslogion* III, and not *vice versa*. It is the existence of *God* that is proved *when* it is proved that God cannot be conceived as not existing. Thus, with the prohibition against conceiving anything greater than him and with this prohibition ruling out the thought of his nonexistence—thus does God alone confront man. Thus, he and he alone is objective reality. Because God exists in the inexplicable manner which thought cannot dismiss, as he does exist as bearer of his revealed Name, for that reason there is objective reality and the possibility of its being conceived and so there is also the possibility of conceiving of God as existing at all (in the sense of *Proslogion* II). In which case absolutely everything that exists apart from him exists, as it were, coupled to his existence and is therefore conceivable

[29] *Reply* III (I. 133.11f.): That than which a greater cannot be conceived "exists with the undoubted ground of truth itself. Otherwise it would not exist at all."

as existing only in relation to the conception of his existence (that cannot be denied) and so, apart from this connection, is ever conceivable also as nonexisting. God *alone* is incapable of not existing and therefore he alone can be the subject of the Proof of *Proslogion* III. Therefore, the One and Only God—we cannot emphasize too strongly or take too seriously the fact that Anselm says all this in the second person singular—has existence that is utterly true (*verissime*) and therefore perfect (*maxime*).

"He truly exists" was how it was put in *Proslogion* II, and what was meant was quite generally that God has at least as much objective reality as all other beings. Then *Proslogion* III qualified this thesis—"that he exists *so truly* that he cannot be conceived not to be." But the same "so" that does the qualifying also designates the truth of God's existence as being different from that of the existence of all other beings: "Thou hast utterly true (*verissime*) existence." The superlative (and we may equally well add even the superlative *maxime*) is a faltering phrase for that fusion of truth and appropriateness in which all existence different from God himself must be found in order to be true and proper; the fusion in which *Proslogion* II and the existence of God himself are found; the fusion which according to *Proslogion* III is identical with the insoluble but intellectually inevitable existence of God as Creator. There are beings who exist. Even God is a Being who exists. But God alone, the Creator, is a being who exists in a manner insoluble and beyond the power of thought to deny, in relation to whom true and appropriate existence is also given to other beings. *Verissime* and *maxime*, in the truth and appropriateness which is the criterion of all existence, God alone has existence. While the "existence" and even the "true existence" are not to be denied to these beings that are distinct from him who is inconceivable as not existing, nevertheless the "so existing" or "so truly existing," the truth and appropriateness of their existence come from God and remain God. What God has in perfection (qualitative and not quantitative) they have only in imperfection (qualitative and not just quantitative)—existence, objective reality. No one, nothing else at all confronts me as thou dost—in such a way that this "ascending" above and "passing judgment" on the object is made impossible for me and the only question is of obedience or disobedience. And so in fact (the result of the previous consideration of the Name of God is confirmed)—the existence of *God* is proved when it is proved that God cannot be conceived as not existing.

Cur itaque "dixit insipiens in corde suo: non est Deus," cum tam in promptu sit rationali menti te maxime omnium esse? Cur, nisi quia stultus et insipiens? (I. 103.9ff.)	On what ground, then, did the fool say "there is no God" when to the rational mind it is quite plain that thou of all beings dost exist in perfection? On what other ground than that he is stupid and foolish?

Anselm comes back to the starting point of his inquiry. Alongside the believer, who in relation to the existence of God now stands within appropriate limits as one who knows, there still stands, unmoved like a block of wood, the fool with his "There is no God." The formal, inner necessity of the statement "there is such a nature"[30] is demonstrated, but that does not create any necessity in fact to take it as a positive statement instead of as a question. Although, in fact just because, this demonstration was a self-contained circle, it is confronted (Anselm does not need any Gaunilo to say it) with the assertion, "God is not a real object," with the same kind of consistency about it as presumably belongs to a self-enclosed circle. The analysis of this actual (physical) possibility of the thesis of unbelief (Anselm is certainly as passionately concerned with it as any Gaunilo) is treated as a special problem at the end of *Proslogion* IV. Here it concerns him—in complete contrast to the knowledge of faith that has been achieved—only as fact. He has not forgotten and has no intention of overlooking this other person who keeps on saying and is obviously able to say and perhaps is bound to say, "There is no God." He does not forget or overlook him just because he himself stands so very close to him and because by this opposition he himself is faced with the question which is now answered. "We both seek one and the same thing!"[31] Did he not have to know his opponent's case very intimately and expound it very forcibly in order to defeat him and so raise faith to knowledge? Is not he, who obviously was so well able to conceive and expound this opposite point of view, himself in some way and at some point a fool too? Or at least is the solidarity between him and his opponent not so entirely broken that he could always understand him as well as he understands himself? It is enough that side by side with the man who says, "only God really exists," there is the man who says on the other hand, "there is no God." And with him the question arises, "Why does he talk thus? Where is he from? Who is he?"

[30] *Prosl.* II (I. 101.6).

[31] *Cur Deus homo?* I. 3 (II. 50.19f.).

The question: "*How* did the fool say . . .?" of *Proslogion* IV[32] is *not the same* question. It is, as it were, a question as to the *nature* of the negative statement. At the moment all that Anselm is concerned with is its reality as such (*cur*?). One possible reason that might lead a man to say, "There is no God" is now rejected in accordance with the Proof just presented: he is no longer able to say that he cannot understand the article of faith on the existence of God as such or that he cannot understand the necessity of its content in relation to the other articles of faith. For the present all that could be done for such understanding has been done—according to Anselm better results are admittedly in reserve. As a matter of fact "sound human understanding" can tell us not only that God exists, but that of all other beings he alone exists in perfection, *verissime*, *maxime*. It is certainly astonishing that Anselm so obviously ventures to describe denial of the existence of God as an impossible possibility which is simply excluded for the "rational mind" in view of the possibility of theological instruction and especially in view of his theologoumenon just concluded which quite openly and admittedly was brought about with the help of very different material from "sound human understanding." And it is even more astonishing that after this reason for the denial has collapsed, all that he appears to be able to consider is one other reason—divine reprobation of whoever can deny the existence of God. But if from false theological pride or with an unkind severity, anyone could argue against an earnestly seeking fellow mortal, once again the vital condition involved in Anselm's thinking would be ignored. We saw that this thinking is achieved—and this is the most important thing that can be said about it—as it continues in worship.[33] The subduing of the "rational mind," which he describes here as happening once for all, is for him the being subdued by the object, the "by our Lord God," before whose face he has been theologizing; the being subdued which he himself has experienced and which he can and must also assume to be the case with anyone who has been truly theologizing with him. According to Anselm there are no theological problems that are finally settled, so surely must we, when we have prayed, pray again and continue to pray. But it would be prayer devoid of faith in the hearing of prayer (and therefore not prayer) if theological thinking in the act of its ful-

[32] *Prosl.* IV (I. 103.13).

[33] In order to be quite concrete, perhaps we ought to add: in worship that is within the framework of the Benedictine *opus Dei*.

fillment were not entirely sure of its case and so unwilling to venture forth at its own level with its unconditional demand. And it is exactly the same with the basis which Anselm describes as the only possible basis for the statement "There is no God." From what has been already said and in this whole context, the commonplace explanation "because he is stupid and foolish" is quite impossible—that the man who says, "There is no God" is a clown who is incapable of following the proof because he cannot think logically. That would be a completely unjustifiable affront to one's fellow mortal. Anselm comes nowhere near it: We will hear in *Proslogion* IV that he explained the meaning of the statement "There is no God" entirely on the assumption that from the intellectual point of view he who holds it is to be taken seriously. Neither is any moral defect directly expressed by the "stupid and foolish." That it signifies *both* intellectual *and* moral perversity is of course undoubtedly true. Obviously the "stupid" inserted into the quotation reinforces the statement in this direction. But the point is not a perversity that is, as it were, physical but technical, and here again not a perversity of individual functions but of the whole position. The fool may be quite normal intellectually and morally. Only that, whether normal or not, he is just a fool; one who accomplishes what is not physically impossible but what it is forbidden to attempt; one who puts himself (the inner impossibility is not an outward impossibility for him) in a position where as a human being, normal or otherwise, he can only fall.[34] Anselm did not ascribe it to any quality of his own, but to the grace of God, that he himself was not a fool doing the same thing and that for him the inner impossibility was at the same time an outward one.[35] For that

[34] *De casu diaboli* IV (I. 241.4f.): "By wanting something which he ought not to have wanted, he abandoned righteousness (*iustitia*) and thus sinned." *Ibid.*, XXVII (I. 275.21ff.): "He abandoned righteousness because he wanted what he ought not to have wanted; in this way, that is, by wanting what he ought not, he abandoned righteousness. Why did he want what he ought not? No cause precedes this wanting, unless it is the fact that he was able to want. Or did he want what he ought not simply because he was able to want? No, because a good angel was similarly able to want and yet did not want something he ought not. . . . Why therefore did the devil want what he ought not? For no other reason but that he wanted. This wanting has no further cause. . . . It itself, so to speak, was the efficient cause of itself and the effect." See F. R. Hasse, *Anselm von Canterbury* (1852) vol. II, p. 427: "For Anselm the actual origin of evil is an 'unfathomable' fact, which means that it is a fact devoid of say inner or outer necessity."

[35] *De concordia*, Q. III. 3 (II. 266.8-267.4): "Can someone who does not have this rectitude [of will] gain possession of it by himself in any way? Obviously he can only gain possession of it by himself either through wanting or not wanting.

reason, the otherwise fearful reproach, "You are stupid and foolish," is not a direct reproach. It is only by the grace of God that Anselm's solidarity with him has been ended. The fool thinks and speaks as one who is not saved by the grace of God. That is the reason for his perversity, and why he can say, "There is no God." *This* reproach does not imply any uncharitableness. It is with just this reproach on his lips that Anselm takes his place as near as it is possible to be and therefore with as much promise as there could possibly be, alongside this fellow mortal whose action is so unintelligible. It is precisely with this reproach that, at the end of his attempt "to prove" the article of faith about the existence of God, he has to declare the possibility of a statement that contradicts it. This contradictory statement is the statement of unbelief, of the corrupt will, of man unreconciled.

By wanting, however, no one can obtain a rectitude of will by himself, because unless his will already has possession of such a rectitude, he cannot want it. On the other hand, it is unthinkable that someone lacking this rectitude of will can attain it by himself by not wanting. Therefore, a creature cannot in any way gain possession of it by himself. But neither can a creature gain possession of it from another creature. For just as no creature can save another, so also no creature can give to another that by which he is saved. It follows therefore that no creature gains possession of rectitude of will . . . except by the grace of God. . . . Grace alone can save a man, since no act of his free choice . . . will give him that rectitude of will to which he submits himself by an act of free choice. And although God does not give this rectitude to all men, since 'He has mercy on whomever he wills and he hardens whomever he wills' (Rom. 9:18), nevertheless he gives it to no one in consideration of some preceding merit, since 'who has ever first given a gift to God that he might be repaid?' (Rom. 11:35). However, if the will . . . merits either an increase of bestowed righteousness or a power to produce good desires or some other reward, these are all the fruits of primary grace and of 'grace on behalf of grace' (John 1:16). Consequently, all this is to be imputed to grace, for 'it does not depend on the wanting' which a man wills 'nor on the exertion' which he exercises, 'but on the mercy of God' (Rom. 9:16). For it is said of everything but God alone: 'What have you that you did not receive?' (I Cor. 4:7)." See also *Meditation* VII.4 (*Patrologia Latina* 158.744): "I know that just as I cannot fraudulently snatch or steal any of your goodness, so also I cannot obtain by any merits of my own all that goodness for which I turn to you and delight in you. For what can be owed to my merits, unless it is the penalty of eternal death? I know that it lies in your holy good pleasure to annihilate me according to the multitude of my crimes . . . or to reform me and make me acceptable to yourself according to the wealth of your inestimable mercies—you who alone are the re-maker of the creatures whom you alone have made." *Ibid.*, (*P.L.* 158.744f.): "I take refuge with you, knowing that for me there is no flight from you except toward you. Who but you alone can deliver me from your hands? . . . Look, I pray, upon yourself, to whom supplications are never made without the hope of favor. For only in yourself will you find the source and cause for compassion, according to the abundance of your sweetness and vastness of your mercy. Do not, I pray, look upon me, for in me you will find nothing but what merits your wrath and is worthy chiefly of eternal death." [Recent critical studies cast doubt that Anselm was the author of the meditation cited here.]

VII

ANDRE HAYEN

The Role of the Fool in St. Anselm and the Necessarily Apostolic Character of True Christian Reflection[1]

THIS study divides naturally into two parts. First we will establish the fact of the intervention of the fool in the meditation practiced by St. Anselm and the monks of his abbey. Next we will discover that this intervention is necessary for the exercise of their meditation. Such will be the two sections of Part I.

Part II will draw out the implications of this intervention, both those antecedent and those consequent, which is to say, both the reason why this intervention is necessary and its full significance. The reason for it is the "revealability" of the creation. The significance of it is the apostolic purpose of true Christian reflection. The latter can only be developed under the impetus of the ardent preoccupation of radiant apostolic charity. Its genuine development is completely in the service of this effective radiance.[2] Hence the division of Part II into two sections.

I. *The Intervention of the Fool in St. Anselm's Meditation*

I. THE FACT OF THIS INTERVENTION

We are not the first to investigate this. Paul Vignaux has written that *Fides quaerens intellectum* is "a study of matters of faith which

[1] From *Spicilegium Beccense* (Paris: J. Vrin, 1959), pp. 69-85. Transl. by Arthur C. McGill. This represents the second part of an article which Father Hayen entitles, "S. Anselme et S. Thomas: la vraie nature de la théologie et sa portée apostolique." In the first part Anselm and Thomas are compared in terms of both their differences and their common intellectual intention.

[2] As John S. Dunne rightly remarks about St. Thomas (in *Theological Studies*, 1958, p. 443), if a participation in God (*le théologal*) is at the source of his metaphysical effort, metaphysics in its turn is "a source of his theological achievements."

seeks to discover in them a reason, a necessity."[3] Undoubtedly the "necessary reasons" for which Anselm seeks[4] "are not, however, simple probabilities adapted for use with this or that questioner: They claim the *universality* of truth."

The word "universality" which we have just emphasized should be compared with a remark by Vignaux that gives us the key to the Anselmian "dialectic": The necessary reasons "are offered to the mind in the course of a dialectical investigation which has the form of *at least a virtual dialogue*."[5]

The phrase just italicized should be compared in its turn with still another observation by Vignaux: Anselm's faith seeking understanding is "a dialectic born of love,"[6] and the love from which it arises is that expressed by the prayer in the very opening lines of the *Proslogion*. Anselm's at least virtual dialogue arises from a love that in advance unites the Christian to the unbeliever, and this love is nothing else but the pure love of the contemplative, who is held in hope by the unique desire for the divine possession.[7]

The assertion just made demands justification. It goes beyond Vignaux' explicit statements, but it is not opposed to them. As a matter of fact, this author continues:[8]

To put it briefly, the unbeliever is a person whom St. Anselm does not address directly, but whom he cannot do without. . . .[9] The prior speaks to his Benedictines. But if they ask him for reasons to overcome all their objections,[10] his investigation will take the form of a discussion and the

[3] Paul Vignaux, *La philosophie au moyen age* (2d ed., Paris, 1957), p. 32. English translation by E. C. Hall, *Philosophy in the Middle Ages* (New York: Meridian, 1959), p. 36

[4] See *Epistulo de Incarnatione verbi*, rev. ed., VI (II. 20.16-19): " . . . my two little works, the *Monologion* and *Proslogion*, which were especially written so that what we hold by faith concerning the divine nature and persons, although excluding the Incarnation, could be proved by necessary reasons (*probari necessariis rationibus*) without the authority of Scripture."

[5] Vignaux, *op. cit.*, French p. 32, English p. 36. Italics added.

[6] *Ibid.*, French p. 37, English p. 40. Italics added.

[7] *Prosl.* I (I. 100.10f., 15-18): "Let me seek by desiring you, let me desire by seeking. Let me discover by loving, and let me love by discovering. . . . I do not seek, O Lord, to penetrate your sublimity . . .; but I desire to understand to some extent your truth, which my heart believes and loves."

[8] Vignaux, *op. cit.*, French pp. 40f., English p. 44. Italics added.

[9] E. Gilson emphasizes this "not directly" in "Sens et nature de l'argument de S. Anselme," in *Archives d'histoire doctrinale et littéraire du moyen age*, ix (1934), p. 21 n. 2.

[10] Two pages earlier Vignaux gives a more precise account of this inquiry by monks: They ask without anxiety, without any desire to strengthen their certi-

person objecting will enter upon the scene. . . .[11] The matter for debate is the object of faith itself. The adversaries[12] are both the believer, who accepts it, and the unbeliever, who rejects it. The first is bound to the second:[13] In accomplishing the "unless you believe you will not understand," the believer also satisfies another law inscribed in sacred Scripture, for I Peter 3:15 expresses the wish that you "always be ready to satisfy everyone who asks you for the reason for the hope that is in you. . . ."[14] Some twenty years after writing the *Proslogion*, St. Anselm cites this passage at the opening of his *Cur Deus homo?* In that treatise St. Anselm shows how the study of the faith should make a place for the objections of infidels. It provides a beautiful formula for *the unity of men, otherwise divided, in the face of revelation*:[15] "While the unbelievers seek for a reason because they do not believe, and we because we do believe, nevertheless what we both seek is one and the same. . . ."[16] Indeed, St. Anselm has resolved not to have recourse to authority, but rather to move in the realm of the necessary, which is to say, in the realm of the universal.[17] As Karl Barth has said,[18] without having "abandoned the shelter of the

---

tude or any concern to free themselves from doubt. Vignaux, *op. cit.*, French p. 38, English p. 42. See p. 167.

[11] As we shall see below, properly speaking there is no discussion. We shall also see that the "person objecting" does not *enter* onto the scene, since he is there *from the beginning*. It would even appear that this person who objects—that is, the fool who is already enveloped in that theological charity from which St. Anselm's contemplation proceeds—was present from the very beginning of his meditation, from the first sentence of the first chapter of the *Proslogion*.

[12] We must stress the importance of the point made in the preceding note, for Vignaux himself will make this point a little later in St. Anselm's own terms. The care not to treat any thinker as an adversary—however profoundly he may disagree with us in the face of the truth—is for the scholastics not simply an apostolic requirement of charity. Charity requires this solicitude, and this solicitude will be apostolically fruitful only because it is *first of all* a fundamental requirement of *scientific method*: Without this solicitude, implicit but effective, theology and philosophy will never be anything more than pseudo-sciences, not knowing, when they speak of God, what they want to say or to whom they speak. Compare the formal statement in I John 4:7b-8: "He who loves is born of God and knows God. He who does not love does not know God, for God is love."

[13] We emphasize this statement of cardinal importance. It is now a matter of discerning the profound nature, the "divine root" of that "original bond" which unites them in Christ the Savior and in view of him. See Colossians 1.

[14] This passage continues: ". . . yet do this with gentleness and reverence."

[15] Italics added.

[16] *Cur Deus homo?* I.3 (II. 50.18-20). This important text, which speaks of "the dynamism" of the fool, drawn by the Father toward the Son, is cited twice on pp. 179f.

[17] This universal is the genuine universal. It is the absolute truth, for as soon as it *begins* to reveal itself to every mind, it does so with that "irresistible force" which can lead by necessity those who do not evade it to the absolute certainty that they ought to adhere to *the* faith by *their* faith.

[18] Karl Barth, *Anselm*, German pp. 62f., English p. 61.

Church for one instant" in his search for a common ground with the unbeliever,[19] the author of the *Proslogion* in addressing the monks speaks *against* the unbeliever.[20]

The unbeliever inserts himself into the faith seeking understanding. Just as the Virgin's *Magnificat* replies to St. Elizabeth by turning towards God, so also Anselm's *Proslogion* responds to the invitation of the monks with a meditation that is essentially a prayer. But this prayer does not praise God or adore him or contemplate him except by being addressed to the fool. This is not a prayer of which the fool could become conscious by himself, should he so wish. It (virtually) summons him, it requires him to hear Anselm and to understand what he says. Whether we like it or not, the prayer relates itself to the fool to the extent that he pays some attention to Anselm and to the latter's interpretation. Anselm's meditation would not be a true prayer if it were not genuinely open to the fool.

This is an openness that solicits the necessary cooperation from the unbeliever before opening to him a share in the riches which Anselm already possesses. The latter does not invite the fool simply to pick up some crumbs that fall to the ground, while he himself, safely installed at the table of the Lord, savors the banquet of divine contemplation. Unquestionably as soon as he hears Anselm, the unbeliever draws near to the lavish repast which the Lord has reserved for those who fear him. But this unbeliever is not confined just to receiving. *He gives*, first and foremost to the monk whose meditation cannot do without him. His *act* of hearing, his attentiveness as a questioner play an integral part in St. Anselm's argumentation.[21]

[19] He has not abandoned the Church for the simple reason—which is constantly being lost from view by our lack of reflection and by lapses in our "apostolic contemplation"—that he is already on a common ground with the unbeliever, or, in Vignaux' phrase, that there is a "unity of men, otherwise divided, in the face of revelation." See p. 164 n. 11.

[20] This last sentence by Vignaux is perfectly correct except for the word "against," which we have italicized and which expresses the very opposite of the intention of St. Anselm himself and of the Anselmian dialectic. Nothing is easier than to begin following this distraction, this mistake, since we are completely habituated to conceiving of the relations of reason and faith in terms of symbiosis, or harmony, or conciliation. See, for example, the remark which Georges Duby makes in the course of two otherwise admirable pages on Anselm: St. Anselm "works along the way to rational theology, in close association with philosophy which has the task of *conciliating* revelation and reason." *Le Moyen Age* (Paris 1955), p. 283. Italics added. (This book is volume III in *L'Histoire generale des civilizations*, under the direction of Crouzet.)

[21] A questioner, not an adversary. The fool's objections play a collaborating role in St. Anselm's effort, in his contemplation.

Indeed, in order to develop, in order to have a religious meaning and not be a speculative evasion that ceases to contemplate the *actual reality* of God and his love, this argumentation requires the *real existence* of the fool, and not merely the abstract possibility that there is a fool who can conceive of God just as Anselm conceives of him. In fact the *act* of hearing St. Anselm (*audire*) and of "understanding in faith" (*intelligere*) lays the foundation in the *Proslogion* of its argument, i.e., of its contemplation, which is wholly preoccupied with the loving search for the knowledge and possession of God.[22]

This is why no violence is being done to the fool by St. Anselm. The fool is not a "protégé" of the prior, someone benevolently invited to the doorstep of the cloister to profit from the monks' contemplation. This is a secret invitation, an invisible guest whose collaboration is awaited because it is necessary for the very life of the monastery, for its contemplation of God.

But from where does this necessity arise?

2. THE NECESSITY OF THIS INTERVENTION

The fool plays a necessary role in St. Anselm's meditation on account of the latter's inspiration, that is, on account of his contemplative vocation. No meditation can be an integral part of Christian contemplation unless it is sustained by charity. Yet charity is universal, extending to all those for whom Christ died. That is why Anselm's search for the *intellectus fidei* will not be true or complete so long as it excludes the fool and is not pursued in liaison with him. Such is the meaning of the *unity* of rational inquiry which embraces the believer and unbeliever: "Nevertheless, what we both seek is one and the same."[23]

But Anselm's inspiration—or *intention*—is not at odds with the very structure of his reflection. That is why the intervention of the unbeliever is required not only with respect to *the intention and exercise of the act of meditating*, but also with respect to *the very essence of the Anselmian meditation.*

[22] Here is the text from *Prosl.* II (I. 101.7-9) where the *act* of the fool intervenes in the argument: "When the fool *hears* me saying 'something than which nothing greater can be conceived,' he *understands* what he hears; and what he understands is in his understanding, even if he does not understand that it exists." We will see below the necessity for this intervention of the fool in St. Anselm's meditation.

[23] *Cur Deus homo?* I.3 (II. 50.20). See pp. 178ff. on the unity of understanding between believer and unbeliever, which their common investigation renders more and more nearly perfect.

The two divisions of this section correspond to the two aspects which we have just distinguished.

A. The Fool and St. Anselm's "Christian Intention"

St. Anselm's meditation, Vignaux observes, "begins by faith: One should never dispute about the object in which one believes as if it might not be; rather, without ever ceasing to affirm it and love it, one will seek for a reason why it is the way it is. . . . Here we have another aspect of the medieval mind: a very firm faith in search of very strict reasoning."[24]

How should this search be understood? Vignaux continues: "Here we should not think of an unbeliever who demands reasons to make him believe, or of troubled believers who want to strengthen their certainty and thus free themselves from doubt."[25] No, Anselm is neither an unbeliever nor a troubled believer. He is, along with the entire *community* of his monastery, a contemplative. Vignaux demonstrates it in this way:

A prayer precedes the argument and forms the first chapter of the *Proslogion.* But this should *not at all be neglected* as a vague piece of pious rhetoric, a banal call to self-composure. One rather will find portrayed there *the human situation out of which the proof is born.* It is a dialogue of the creature with his Creator: *quaero vultum tuum,* "I seek your face." This desire to see the face of God lies in a creature—in ourselves—who have been created precisely for this vision. Nevertheless, we have never done that for which we were made. The possibility of this vision has been lost for the whole race by the first man: Original sin explains the absence of God. In his own need for the vision of God the monk recognizes the universal grief of all the sons of Adam, a sort of world-weariness. For Anselm [and for his followers] it is a matter of recovering something of human knowledge as it was before the fall, of reestablishing man—at least partially—in that state from which he has fallen. But to remake what has been destroyed, to accomplish a kind of re-creation, is a superhuman task, is strictly the work of grace. Hence the prayer of the man who speculates. It must never be forgotten that for Anselm man cannot seek

[24] Vignaux, *op. cit.*, French p. 38, English pp. 41f.

[25] *Ibid.*, French p. 38, English p. 42. We should focus on the singularly penetrating and illuminating pages where Karl Barth studies the role of the fool in St. Anselm, *op. cit.*, German p. 63, English pp. 61f. In particular, it is not altogether exact to say that Anselm discusses the question of "in what way [*in wiefern*] that which he believes is true," or to say that this question "troubles" him and that this uneasiness "is sufficient . . . is appropriate and significant."

unless God teaches him, and cannot find unless God reveals himself. *Doce me quaerere te et ostende te quaerenti*, "Teach me to seek you, and show yourself to the one who seeks." Such is Anselm's petition.[26]

The phrases italicized in this passage of "genuine history" allow us to determine St. Anselm's "situation" vis-à-vis the fool, what Barth calls his "peculiar situation as the opponent of the heathens, Jews or heretics."[27]

As we have already remarked,[28] although with his pen he many times writes *contra insipientem*, it is never St. Anselm's intention to set himself *against* the fool. The fool is instead, as Barth calls him, "the one addressed by the proof."[29]

It is certain that Anselm wants to "address the fool," but it seems evident to us that he does not want simply "to reduce him to silence."[30] On the other hand, it is evident that he does not address the fool *directly*. The *Proslogion*, for example, is not a book of apologetics.[31] Like the *Monologion*,[32] the *Proslogion* strives to progress in "intellectual certainty"; that is, it strives to conceive the object of its meditation "more and more distinctly," in order to facilitate access to this same understanding for any future hearer.

An actual visible encounter with such a fool is not at all necessary. What is indispensable for the Anselmian meditation is the interior preoccupation with this kind of an encounter.

Quilibet intellectus, any hearer whatsoever. Yet why does Anselm always address not the "reasonable man," but the fool? For the reason which Paul Vignaux has just stated: "It is a matter . . . of re-establishing man—at least partially—in that state from which he has fallen . . . of accomplishing a kind of re-creation." More precisely, it is a matter of participating in the redemptive work of the first born

[26] Vignaux, *op. cit.*, French pp. 35f., English pp. 39f.

[27] Barth, *op. cit.*, German p. 64, English p. 62.

[28] See p. 164 nn. 11, 12.

[29] Barth, *op. cit.*, German p. 64, English p. 62.

[30] Both statements are Barth's, *op. cit.*, German pp. 70 and 64, English pp. 67 and 62.

[31] *Ibid.*, German p. 64, English pp. 62f. This has also been emphasized by É. Gilson, *op. cit.*, p. 21 n. 2.

[32] Cf. *Monol.* VI (I. 19.16-20): "I do not want to neglect carelessly any simple or almost silly objection that occurs to me in the discussion. The reason is not only so that I may be able to proceed with more certainty to what follows because I have left nothing ambiguous in what precedes; but also so that, if by chance I should want to convince someone with a dull mind of what I have discovered, he can easily accept what he hears from me because every kind of obstacle, even the slightest, has been removed." Cited by Barth, *op. cit.*, German p. 63 n. 1, English p. 62 n. 1.

from the dead, of entering into the struggle of Christ against the devil, into the victory achieved by Jesus, who must continue to reign "until he has placed all his enemies under his feet, so that God may be everything to everyone" (I Cor. 15:25, 28), which is to say, so that God may be everything in the reason of the fool, just as he is everything in the mind of Anselm and the monks, and in that of the blessed who already contemplate the Father face to face.

In this way the expectation of the creation, which "waits with eager longing for the revealing of the sons of God" (Rom. 8:19), will be fulfilled. In this way the fool cooperates in realizing his hope that he too will be liberated from his enslavement to corruption, in order to enter into that liberty of glory which belongs to the children of God. The fool, just as much as the monks, ought to participate in that liberation. Conversely, without him the monks at Bec cannot accomplish their own salvation, their participation in the unique salvation of all men, for already they possess the first fruits of the Spirit, and groan inwardly as they await the redemption of their bodies (Rom. 8:20, 23).

It is a matter of vanquishing the Prince of this world, the *insipientia*, the principle of foolishness which struggles against God in all the fools, and also in all the monks who by their austere life keep offering penance for their own sins. The quest for understanding which the monks undertake with the fool, with whom they stand in solidarity, is a common effort of redemption. By this quest they enter into a more profound communion with him;[33] they and the fool together enter into the perfect fullness of communion which all the children of God have with the Father and his Son, Jesus Christ.[34]

Such is the elementary practice of "contemplative charity" at the Abbey of Bec, as attested by St. Anselm's meditations.[35] The fool plays a necessary role because of the universal mercy of the One who had to die in order to bring into unity the scattered children of God.[36]

33 I John 1:7: "If we walk in the light, as he is in the light, we have fellowship with one another."

34 *Ibid.*; 1:3f.: "That which we have seen and heard we proclaim also to you, so that you may have fellowship with us; and our fellowship is with the Father and his Son Jesus Christ. We are writing this in order that our joy may be complete."

35 According to the definition of the contemplative life which St. Thomas (*Summa theologiae* II-II, Q. 180, a. 1 *contra*) learns from St. Gregory (*In Ezech.* II.2, in Migne, *P.L.* 76.953): "to hold firmly to the love of God and our neighbor with our whole mind, and to cling only to a longing for the Creator."

36 John 11:51f.: "Being high priest that year, Caiaphas prophesied that Jesus

Without the intervention of the fool, Anselm's meditation would be devoid of charity. And if devoid of charity, then it would cease to be contemplative and to know God in an effort of love. "Whoever loves is born of God and knows God." Consequently, "whoever does not love has not known God, for God is love" (I John 4:7f.).

Because Anselm is a monk, and because his meditation is inscribed into his life, which is contemplative in the largest and most profound, as well as in the strictest, sense of that word—therefore, before taking assistance from anyone else, he will seek out the help of the fool, whose heart is furthest separated from that truth which Anselm's heart "believes and loves,"[37] but to whom Christ is closer for that very reason. For Christ is the One who came not to call the righteous but sinners (Mark 2:17); the One who inspires the "meditation" of the monks at Bec, and prompts the concern for the fool which Gaunilo carries in his heart; the One who has already inspired the "monastic contemplation" of the monks of St. Andrew who listened to St. Gregory; and the One who will later inspire the "scholastic contemplation" of St. Thomas, as the latter dictates his *Summa theologiae* to explain Aristotle to the young Dominicans of St. James.

It is no more a matter for St. Anselm than for Karl Barth of surpassing revelation and faith and grace, of walking hand in hand with the unbeliever and giving himself to the free work of reconstructing Christian knowledge with pure reason.[38] There is no such thing as "pure reason" for Anselm, and he does not work to reconstruct a noetic edifice which he first would have made a show of dismantling. Rather, within his faith in Jesus, Anselm strives to continue the work which was begun by Jesus, by his "afflictions"[39] and his victory,[40] and which is nevertheless still uncompleted, the work of building up the Body of Christ, at the end of which we *all* attain to realizing that *unity of the faith and knowledge of the Son of God*, and to establishing that perfect and mature Man who realizes the fullness of Christ (Eph. 4:12-13).

---

should die for the nation, and not for the nation only, but to gather into one the children of God now scattered abroad."

37 *Prosl.* I (I. 100.17f.).

38 Barth, *op. cit.*, German p. 65, English p. 63: It is impossible that Anselm admitted a conception of reason which permitted him to "walk arm in arm with the unbeliever for the sake of making an arbitrary reconstruction of Christian knowledge 'from pure reason.' "

39 Col. 1:24: ". . . and in my flesh I complete what remains of Christ's afflictions for the sake of his body, that is, the Church."

40 John 16:33: "I have said this to you, that in me you have peace. In the world you have tribulation, but be of good cheer, I have overcome the world."

It is no more possible for St. Anselm than for Karl Barth to free himself from foolishness by himself, or to attain to the true *ratio* without being illuminated by the *ratio* of faith. For this liberation is the work of the *ratio veritatis* which comes from on high,[41] because it is God himself. However, this illumination is at once interior and exterior. It is produced in that arduous and dogged communion of investigation[42] which occurs between the still-unbelieving fool and the community that meditates with Anselm in the God-given light of faith.

This common meditation, this unique dialogue is at the same time both a flowering of the monks' contemplation in the light of faith, purifying them of all sin,[43] and an advance of the unbeliever's conversion toward that light and under its attraction. Undoubtedly this common meditation constitutes the authentic reality of what we today call "apologetics."[44]

Here also Barth's position is justified. For St. Anselm there is no place for an apologetics "alongside" a theology properly speaking.[45]

Does this mean that between scholastic theology and metaphysics there is no place for distinguishing a "middle term" that both opposes and connects these two extremes, a dialectic, or rather, a *dialogue*, a *community of intellectual inquiry*, whose theological face (invisible to the fool, but known with certainty by the believing community) is a *theology of conversion* (that which the Anselmian meditation elaborates)—and whose philosophical face (directly accessible to the fool)[46] is a *philosophy of action* (such as presented by Blondel in his first *L'Action*, and irreducibly distinct from the metaphysics of the act of being)?

[41] Barth, *op. cit.*, German p. 66, English p. 64.

[42] *Cur Deus homo*? I.3 (II. 50.20): ". . . nevertheless that which they both seek is one and the same." See p. 180.

[43] I John 1:7: "If we walk in the light, as he is in the light, we have fellowship with one another, and the blood of Jesus his Son cleanses us from all sin." This purification extends to the intelligence and faith, as to the will and charity.

[44] St. Anselm's meditation could indeed be peculiarly close to the dialectic of Maurice Blondel. Will it not, so to speak, be like the theological face (still insufficiently distinguished by St. Anselm from scholastic theology in the strict sense) of an intellectual effort of which Blondel's philosophy of action will be the philosophic face (still insufficiently distinguished by Blondel from the metaphysics of the act of being in the strict sense)? The explanation which we have given elsewhere for "the continuity of the Blondelian dialectic" in his book *L'Action* invites an affirmative reply. Cf. *Convivium* (1959), pp. 157-180.

[45] Barth, *op. cit.*, German p. 70, English p. 67.

[46] The fool plays the role which we attribute to the "reader-philosopher" in our article on "the continuity of the Blondelian dialectic."

Like the middle terms in one of the "syllogisms" which the metaphysicians employ, this dialogue is first.[47] It is at the *origin both* of the nonphilosophic reflection of the theologian in the strict sense, *and* of the nontheological reflection of the metaphysician.

That is why Barth, Gilson and Vignaux have good reason for emphasizing that St. Anselm never once departs from the shelter and soil of the Church (that is, speaking quite concretely, from the cloister of his monastery). There is no need for him to seek some common terrain where he might encounter his adversary, still less to penetrate into the realm of his adversary in order to battle with him there on his own terrain. The fool is already present among the monks, invisibly yet so genuinely. St. Anselm does not exhort or teach him from the elevation of his serene faith, as one might stand on the shore and light a beacon or throw out a lifebuoy for a castaway in a storm. In the still impure serenity of their faith, in the still imperfect ardor of their love, in the humble and eager straining of their hope, Anselm and all the monks at Bec still share in the sin, the obscurity and the unbelief where the fool flounders. The latter is already in communication (although not yet in communion) with the serenity of their faith, with the ardor of their love, with the straining of their hope, by the very fact that he questions them or raises an objection against them. There is no encounter to be made or contact to be established. There is simply this communication to be recognized and accepted, to be accepted fully until it is consummated in communion.

Anselm's communication with the unbeliever is the insertion of the entire Church into the world. For Anselm and his monks, in their life together in the abbey, form only one cell of the Church. Although written at the request of his brothers and continued by them, his mediation is still that of the entire Church, which will not attain to the perfect knowledge of Christ, to the full flowering of the intelligence that enables us to penetrate the mystery of God, to the knowledge of the love of Christ that surpasses all knowledge, unless we all together become one in the faith (Eph. 4:13), unless we are tightly

[47] Should we not say that this dialogue *is* the situation, which is concretely ordered to the supernatural, and which the metaphysician ought to "reflect"? In this sense, does not the dialogue constitute the true "point of departure for metaphysics" (J. Maréchal), its "first concrete principle" (P. Scheuer, "Notes de Métaphysique," in *Nouvelle revue théologique*, 1926, pp. 329-334, 447-451, 518-525; and G. Isaye, "La justification critique par rétorsion," in *Revue philosophique de Louvain*, 1954, pp. 205-235).

knit together in love (Col. 2:2). For one only receives the grace to understand the mystery of Christ together with all Christians.[48]

Yet, as St. John reminds us, the unity of the Church extends to all the children of God who are still scattered abroad, to all the sheep which Christ will shepherd.[49] That is why, like St. John's first letter and Paul's letter to the Colossians, which are open to all men, in the hope of glory among the pagans,[50] St. Anselm's meditation also should extend to the fool, under the penalty of otherwise being unfaithful to its original inspiration and of deserting the contemplation of God.

B. *The Fool and the "Technical Structure" of St. Anselm's Meditation*

The fact which we have been discussing is a necessary fact: The fool's intervention into St. Anselm's argument lays the foundation for this argument.

The method which the monks stipulate for their prior compels recognition. Anselm ought to follow it. His meditation certainly proceeds from the faith, is made fruitful by the faith, and is developed entirely within the faith. Not for an instant does St. Anselm dream of putting his faith in question: His sole concern is to be faithful to the obligation of his baptism. He seeks understanding by fidelity to this obligation, not by anxiety for greater certainty, and this understanding is the personal fruit of his effort of fidelity: In attaining to this, the contemplative will taste a true joy. This is what St. Anselm vigorously affirms in his letter to Fulcon, the Bishop of Beauvais.[51]

[48] Eph. 3:17-19: ". . . so that you, being rooted and grounded in love, may have power to *comprehend with all the saints* what is the breadth and length and height and depth, and to know the love of Christ which surpasses knowledge."

[49] John 11:51f.: ". . . he prophesied that Jesus should die for the nation, and not for the nation only, but to gather into one the children of God who are scattered abroad." John 10:16: "I have other sheep that are not of this fold; I must bring them also, and they will heed my voice. So there shall be one flock, one shepherd."

[50] I John 1:3-4: "That which we have seen and heard *we* proclaim to you, so that you may have fellowship with us. . . . And *we* are writing this to you so that *our* joy may be complete." Col. 1:27f.: "To his saints God chose to make known how great among the Gentiles are the riches of the glory of this mystery, which is Christ in you, the hope of glory. Him we proclaim, warning every man and teaching every man in all wisdom, so that we may present every man mature in Christ."

[51] *Letter* 136 (III. 280.32ff.): "It is most foolish and senseless to summon up doubt in an uncertain question, simply because something which is firmly established on solid grounds is not understood. For our faith is to be defended by reason against unbelievers, but not against those who confess that they delight in the

The *Monologion* confirms this assertion and makes it more precise. The joy of understanding is that of a greater certitude, which, it seems, is nothing but a more explicit unfolding within faith, a conceptually more distinct flowering of the initial certitude of faith itself.[52]

The "speculative"[53] or "contemplative"[54] understanding which Anselm attains in this way is difficult to define. In 1934 Gilson asked whether this is a *gnosis*. Of the eight characteristics of *gnosis* which he then proposed, let us mention the following: The Anselmian meditation is sought by faith itself; faith remains transcendent over it; it proceeds by necessary reasons towards a vision by the intelligence; within faith, it aims at that which can be known by the reason and seen by the intelligence; and, finally, this vision by the intelligence does not eliminate faith, but only contemplates the intelligibility of it.[55]

But for St. Anselm, understanding is not the contribution which reason makes to complete or enrich faith. It is the completion of the intelligence illuminated, opened and transfigured under the control of faith.[56]

In St. Anselm's view it is clear that reason does not devote itself to the objective investigation of an exterior given, namely, the articles of faith. It "reflects," that is to say, it offers itself to the illuminative control of God-given faith. It abandons itself to the supernatural light which reveals the revealable (cf. p. 180 below). It is the consecration

---

honor of a Christian name. For of these latter it is rightly demanded that they firmly keep to the pledge (*cautionem*) which they made at their baptism. Unbelievers, however, must be rationally shown those things for which they irrationally despise us. For the Christian ought to make progress toward understanding through faith, but not to acquire faith through understanding or to abandon faith if he cannot understand. When he can attain understanding, however, he should enjoy this; but when he really cannot, he should venerate what he cannot grasp."

[52] *Monol.* VI (I. 19.17f.): Anselm tries to meet every possible objection "so that I may be able to proceed *with more certainty* to what follows because I have left nothing ambiguous in what precedes." Cf. *Cur Deus homo?* I.25 (II. 96.6f.), where Boso says, "I did not come for you to remove doubt from my faith, but to show me the *ratio* for my certainty."

[53] *Monol.* VI (I. 19.19): ". . . if by chance I should want to convince someone of what I discern [*speculor*]."

[54] *Prosl.* Preface (I. 93.21f.): ". . . in the person of one who strives to elevate his mind to the contemplation of God."

[55] Gilson, *op. cit.*, p. 50, # 1, 3, 6, 4 and 7. The last two points are in Gilson's own words, and require a clarification. The principle for this may be found in the important chapter which he devotes to the *revealable* in the later editions of his *Le Thomisme* (transl. into English as *The Christian Philosophy of St. Thomas Aquinas*).

[56] St. Anselm affirms this many times. See, for instance, *Letter* 136 as quoted on p. 173 n. 51; or *Prosl.* I (I. 100.17-19); or *Monol.* I (I. 14.1-4).

of the intelligence which is assumed by the divine light, by the light creative of the intellectual act that submits itself to it. For this is "the life of every being, which was the light of men" (John 1:4).

St. Anselm and his brothers devote themselves to this effort, which is essential for monastic contemplation and for every Christian contemplation. And that is the reason why the monks ask Anselm to set aside the authority of Scripture (they do not speak of *faith*), in order to follow a strictly (and purely?) rational method.[57] On his part St. Anselm believes that this method is legitimate and fruitful,[58] provided that it is executed in a solid and exacting way.[59] It will delve into reason, and will draw out the implications of which the latter is pregnant. To the unbeliever who objects against the faith, one may demonstrate his error by means of the very reason from which he takes his objections. One may do the same with the heretic: One may expose Roscelin's error, not by the authority of Scripture, but by the reason which he uses to justify his Trinitarian heresy.[60]

The Anselmian method uproots ignorance,[61] and it often ridicules difficulties[62] by an effort of wisdom, by an advance of reason.[63]

57 *Monol.* Preface (I. 7.5-11): "More in accord with their will than with the easiness of the thing or with my ability, they have prescribed for me the following form for the writing of this meditation: that absolutely nothing in Scripture should be urged on the authority of Scripture, but that in a plain style, with nontechnical proofs and with simple argumentation, rational necessity should concisely prove and the clarity of truth should openly show that whatever is claimed as the conclusion of each investigation is actually the case."

58 *Monol.* I (I. 13.5-11). "If someone is ignorant—either because he has not heard or *does not believe*—of the one supreme nature [of God] . . . and of the many other things which we *necessarily* believe about God and his creatures, I think that such a person, should he have only a mediocre mind, can still in large measure *convince himself* of these things *even by reason* ALONE." Italics added.

59 *Cur Deus homo?* I.4 (II. 52.3-6): "Therefore, we first must exhibit the *rational solidity* of the truth, that is, the *necessity which proves* that . . .; then, in order that this so-to-speak body of truth may shine more fully, we must display the harmonies [Eve and Mary, etc.] in the so-to-speak picture of this body."

60 *Epist. de Incarn. verbi*, rev. ed., II (II. 11.5-8): "We must not reply to this man with the authority of the Holy Scriptures, because either he does not believe in them, or he interprets them in a perverse way. For what do the Scriptures say more openly than that God is one and unique. *Therefore, we must demonstrate his error by the very reason on which he relies to defend himself.*" Italics added.

61 See n. 58.

62 *De casu diaboli* XXVII (I. 275.3): ". . . a fatuous question." *Monol.* VI (I. 19.16): "I do not want to neglect any simple or almost silly objection." Cited on p. 168 n. 32.

63 *Letter* 136 (III. 280.37f. cited above p. 173 n. 51): Unbelievers "must be shown rationally that for which they despise us irrationally." *De casu diaboli* XXVII (I. 275.4f.): "It is certainly not always easy to reply wisely to foolish inquiries."

That is, under the guidance of reason,[64] St. Anselm's method seems to liberate the light of reason[65] from the confusions which have obscured it and have prevented it from enlightening us, from unveiling the truth to us, from giving us understanding.

But why should a contemplative who does not wish to meditate except by proceeding from his faith, be concerned to place Scripture in a parenthesis and to proceed only by reason alone? In order, we believe, to protect himself against the temptation of complacency and sloth: in order to avoid simply repeating the formulas of Scripture; in order to be compelled *really to think his faith*, that is, in order to offer to the supernatural control of his God-given faith a reason that is genuinely alive, genuinely in the act of living and of working as reason.

Yet for St. Anselm this reason in its actual exercise is not a mere "faculty", and still less, a mere abstraction called "Reason." It is the concrete existing reason, which is in exercise in every reasonable man—by whom is meant those who, because deprived of faith, are incapable of releasing the wise (*sapienter*) and reasonable (*rationabiliter*) effort of this reason. Thus, St. Anselm's meditation *should be open* for *eventual* participation by every fool.[66] And this is why the monks ask their teacher never (*penitus nihil*) to use the authority of Scripture.[67] Their care to "exclude" Scripture is commanded by their concern to "include" within the divine control of faith the whole of reason, the "concrete reason"—that is, the truly universal reason, the reason of all actual men and not just that of monks or of believers.[68]

Anselm accedes to this request by letting the fool's *concrete* act of thinking *necessarily* intervene in his argument.

This necessary intervention appears especially in the explanation of the argument in the *Proslogion* and in the *Reply* to Gaunilo. In his reasoning Anselm proceeds from an idea of God, and he thinks this idea *while listening to* a Christian who thinks this idea under the

[64] *Monol.* I (I. 13.13f.) and VI (I. 19.12f.): "It is evident that at some time . . . with reason leading and that [unbeliever] following, the latter [who, either because he has not heard or does not believe, is ignorant of God] will advance rationally to those matters of which he is irrationally ignorant." ". . . those things concerning the supreme substance which I have considered by the light of reason."

[65] It is extremely important not to introduce here a precision which will only plunge us into ambiguity. In spite of Descartes' esteem for the argument of St. Anselm, the latter has in mind the light of reason in a wholly different sense from the *natural* light of the mind conceived by Descartes.

[66] *Monol.* VI (I. 19.20): ". . . and if by chance I should want to persuade anyone of that which I discern . . ."

[67] See p. 175 n. 57.

[68] See p. 169.

prompting of the loving desire of the "faith that seeks understanding." The idea of God, which is the hinge of the argumentation in the *Reply*, is not isolated by Anselm from the actual exercise of the act of thinking this idea in a dialogue that proceeds from faith and from love.

The *Reply* to Gaunilo, in fact, is not addressed to "a" fool, to some vague, indeterminate personage, but to a very specific speaker who defends the viewpoint of the fool,[69] and whose act of thinking is going to provide the foundation for Anselm's response. In fact, the latter relies in an absolutely emphatic way on Gaunilo's *faith* and *conscience*,[70] in order to convince him that God—the "that than which a greater cannot be conceived"—is really and truly in the act of being thought. St. Anselm does not argue from the certitude which his faith gives to Gaunilo. He invites Gaunilo to reflect *on the exercise of the intellectual act* of believing in God: Even if he only reflected a little on the actual exercise of *his* faith and *his* conscience, Gaunilo would not be able to doubt that the "that than which a greater cannot be conceived" is an "intelligible"[71] that has reality in the mind which actually thinks it.

Here, in fact, is Anselm's thesis: "To deny that the idea 'that than which a greater cannot be conceived' is thought, that is to say, to deny that the idea *really* is in the mind which thinks it—this is to deny that God is that than which a greater cannot be conceived, or at least to deny that God is thought, that is to say, that God is really in the mind."[72] But this last denial is absolutely false, which Anselm proves in this way, by inviting Gaunilo to reflect and to recognize with an absolute certainty that he thinks God and that God is really in his intelligence, in his thought: "That this is false I use *your* faith and conscience as a most compelling argument."[73]

69 *Reply* I (I. 130.3-5): "Since . . . the one who refutes me is not the fool but *a Catholic on behalf of the fool*, it is sufficient for me to reply *to the Catholic*." Italics added.

70 *Reply* I (I. 130.15f.): "I use your faith and conscience as a most compelling argument."

71 The scholastics will prefer to call this: a *ratio*. To commit such an anachronism, especially in order to avoid speaking of the content of the consciousness, would be the worst misunderstanding.

72 *Reply* I (I. 130.12-15): "I say: if 'that than which a greater cannot be conceived' is not understood or (*vel*) conceived, and (*et*) is not in the understanding or (*vel*) in conception . . ." Note the careful choice here of terms that are conjunctive (*et*), disjunctive (*aut*) or that mark a simple synonymy (*vel*). In our translation we have added "that is to say" to the text two times in order to highlight what is already emphasized by the use of these three terms in Latin.

73 *Reply* I (I. 130.15f.).

As St. Anselm explains to Gaunilo, the whole argument of the *Proslogion* is thus grounded on the *real existence*, in the mind in act, of the idea of the "that than which . . ." But this real existence in the mind in act is the immanence of the idea to the *concrete act* of thinking, which is to say, to the concrete act of the fool who *understands*, *by listening to*, the Catholic who speaks to him.[74]

The fool's "communion of inquiry" with the monk[75] necessarily forms an integral part of the Anselmian meditation. Or to put this more exactly, *sit venia verbis*, this communion is the substantial form of St. Anselm's technical argumentation.

II. *Implications*

I. PRESSUPPOSITIONS

The fool's collaboration would be superfluous and illusory if he did not genuinely participate with his own effort of "wisdom" and "rationality" in Anselm's effort.[76] The fool is, and can only be, a speaker who is *not yet* wise, whose reason has *not yet* recovered the normal play of its natural exercise by and in faith. Yet *already* when listening to the believers, *already* when thinking the ideas which they teach him to conceive, the fool is *already* caught up in the movement of faith, moving along the road *toward* wisdom, along the road *toward* the liberation of the light of his reason[77] under the illuminative control of faith.

This "dynamic" role should not surprise us. It is the indispens-

[74] *Reply* II (I. 132.10-20): "I said that *when the fool hears* 'that than which a greater cannot be conceived' stated, *he understands what he hears*. To be sure, whoever does not understand when familiar words are spoken to him either has no understanding at all or a very obtuse one.

"I then said that *if this* [*expression*] *is understood, it is in the understanding*. But how can that be in no understanding which is demonstrated to exist necessarily in reality? You say, however, that even if it is in the understanding, it still does not follow that it is really understood. Consider how its being in the understanding follows from the fact that it is understood. For just as that which is conceived by conception, just as it is conceived, so it is in conception—in the same way that which is understood is understood by the understanding, and what is understood by the understanding, just as it is understood, so it is in the understanding." Italics added.

[75] Cf. above p. 169, and also Vignaux' remark cited above pp. 163-165 about the passage from *Cur Deus homo*? I.3: "This treatise . . . gives a beautiful *formula* for the unity of divided men before revelation." Actually we are in the presence not only of a formula, but of the exercise of this unity.

[76] See p. 175 n. 63.

[77] See p. 176, and the sentence from *Monol.* I cited in n. 64 on that page.

able function and attitude of every speaker in any kind of dialogue. *Already* bound to the one to whom he listens with the attention that he gives him, he does *not yet* know what the other should propose to him, what he has to receive from the other to *come* into communion with him, that is, to receive from the other and to give to him, which is to say, *to express ourselves between ourselves*.[78]

The unique understanding which faith seeks by means of this dialogue with the fool becomes clear in the light of this dynamism. On the one hand, this understanding is the delightful[79] flowering of the faith of Anselm and his brothers. It is a very certain knowledge of the mystery of this faith, of its "necessity" and yet at the same time of the impossibility of our understanding it.[80] On the other hand, the same intellectual investigation seems to lead the unbeliever "wisely" and "rationally" *to the threshold* of faith, to the certainty that he ought to give his adherence of faith to the truths discovered by such reasons. The text of *Monologian* LXIV which has just been cited in the preceding note continues as follows:

Nor should the certainty of faith be given any less to those things which are validated by necessary proofs, provided that no other reason opposes them, even if they do not admit of being explained because of the incomprehensibility of their own natural sublimity.[81]

Yet there is only one single *intellectus fidei* for both the unbeliever and the believer. As Boso says in *Cur Deus homo?*:

Allow me therefore to use the words of the unbeliever. For it is proper that when *we strive to inquire into the reason for our faith* I put forward the objections of those who *do not at all want to submit to this same faith*

78 The dynamism proper to the fool alone: Unlike us, he does not yet "have fellowship with the Father and with His Son Jesus Christ" (I John 1:3). The dynamism common to the fool and St. Anselm: Our joy is not yet complete (I John 1:4).

79 See above p. 173, and *Letter* 136 (III. 281. 40f.): "When [the Christian] can attain understanding, he should enjoy this; but when he really cannot, he should venerate what he cannot grasp." Cited on p. 173 n. 51.

80 *Monol.* LXIV (I. 75.1-3): "I think that it ought to be sufficient for anyone who is investigating an incomprehensible matter if by his reasoning he attains to the knowledge that this most definitely is, even if he cannot penetrate with his understanding to a knowledge of how it is." Cf. *ibid.* (I. 75.11f.): ". . . a higher consideration comprehends rationally that this is incomprehensible." Cf. also *Cur Deus homo?* I.1(II. 47.8-11): Many seek understanding, "not so that they may attain faith through reason, but so that they may be delighted by the understanding and contemplation of those things which they believe, and so that, as far as they can, they may be 'always ready to satisfy anyone who asks them for the reason of their hope.' "

81 *Monol.* LXIV (I. 75.3-6).

without reason. For although they therefore seek reason because they do not believe, and we because we certainly do believe, nevertheless what we both seek is one and the same.[82]

What is this "one and the same"? It is a unity much closer and more fruitful than the unity of past harvest and forthcoming sowing in a grain of wheat, which is at once the fruit of an ear that has just been reaped and the seed that is about to germinate in a cultivated field. It seems to us that there is only one way to understand this unitary "one and the same" without incoherence. This is to discern it in the light of the revelation that progressively takes possession of the universe, which in its entirety is revealable and in its entirety is destined for the revelation of the Son of God, because in its entirety it was created in Christ and toward Christ. Because Christ is first, faith is first and revelation is first. It is this faith and revelation which provoke the movement of reflection that blossoms in love, and which complete it. Faith does not seek reason in order to find in the latter some force or light that is lacking in it. No, just as a form unites itself with and assumes matter only in order to "vanquish" matter by communicating its own unity to it,[83] so faith brings reason into submission only in order to complete it; it assumes reason only in order to communicate to reason its own divine unity, its own divine light of understanding.

The most faithful and forceful expression of this control over the entire universe by the divine revelation is the Eucharist: The bread of our *agape* is assimilated by us into the flesh of our body; the Bread of life assimilates us into the very life of God.[84]

2. CONSEQUENCES

Paul Vignaux recovers both the true meaning of St. Anselm's argument and the truth itself when he writes,

When we wish to think of God in an absolute way, according to his own dignity, we move toward a logical dynamism so radical that the object of the proof is also the means for the proof. *De se per seipsum probat*: What

[82] *Cur Deus homo?* I.3 (II. 50.16-20). Italics added.

[83] This account of form and matter is from St. Thomas, *Summa contra Gentiles* II.68.

[84] This is inversely evoked by a liturgical formula: not "Take care of the Body of Christ" (a formula found in certain liturgical prayers), but "May the Body of our Lord Jesus Christ take care of your soul," which is a faithful echo of the "Let it be done to me" (not of the "Let me do"!) spoken by Mary, the servant of the Lord (Luke 1:38).

he proves about himself he proves by means of himself. The achievement of the *Proslogion* is to have converted the Augustinian consciousness of absolute divine grandeur into a dialectical principle such as this.[85]

And this author concludes: "In the order of thought, a real presence appears. By means of the proof, the believer attains understanding."[86]

The "real presence" which Vignaux discovers does not differ from the "irresistible force" of which Gilson speaks. It is the presence and the force of Christ at work in the world. And therefore, if we seek the origin of Thomist reflection in St. Anselm's "contemplative and apostolic dialogue" with the fool, to be precise we will not discover the *whence* of St. Thomas' thought, but the *from whom* and *to whom*.

To make such a discovery is to become aware of an appeal, and to begin already to respond to that appeal. For the source from which St. Thomas' reflection has its "genesis in St. Anselm" has not dried up. The continuation of its gushing forth, however, depends on our living insertion into the Church.

The *initiative* for the dialogue with the fool is not my responsibility. I cannot choose my speech partner. It is not a matter of suspending the prohibition of the *Index* in order to read the philosophy that captivates *me* and that *I* would like to evangelize—that, say, of Karl Marx or Schopenhauer. It is a matter of practicing, even in the study of philosophy, the demand for *full* scientific rigor and for the *genuine* understanding of others. Quite simply it is a matter of being faithful to the grace of the present moment, as has been too briefly emphasized in a preceding note. In order to move toward other men, there is no need to leave the monastic cloister, or to leave the wider, but still limited, field of "the Christian action of a layman." *There is only need to go to Christ*, and to be at the disposal of his control, which will lead me toward men because through me it will extend to the entire universe and will gather the whole of creation into him who *is* the Revelation, the Light of life.

Yet by the same fact this radical surrender of oneself to Christ, this unique concern for fidelity to the Church and to the living tradition of Christian reflection will be only a façade if, under the pretext of not yielding to curiosity or of not claiming or usurping the initiative, we slip away from fidelity by separating ourselves in prayer or study from the fool, who bears the suffering face of Christ even more than the financially poor.

85 Vignaux, *op. cit.*, French p. 40, English p. 43.
86 *Ibid.*, French p. 43, English pp. 46f.

In the monastery's faithfully guarded cloister and in its solicitude for the *opus Dei*, as in the work of inner reflection in the educational program of a seminary or theological college, and as in the silent library of a Catholic institute—in all these situations the condition *sine qua non* for an authentic contemplation and for its purity of attention to God, the condition *sine qua non* for an authentic theological *science* and for the "fullness" of its rigor, or rather of its scientific vigor, is the beginning of the conversion of a person who is not yet wise, in other words, the beginning of the fool's faith in the Lord.

If theology (like philosophy) too often vegetates and then dries up, is it not because too often teachers and students, little concerned to love all men and to lead them to the joy of their communion, do not fully open themselves to the love which comes from God and without which God cannot be known, since God is love?

We believe that in St. Anselm's dialogue with the fool we have discovered the genesis of Thomistic reflection in St. Anselm. Yet is this not a silent but ardent call to enter courageously and actively into "the hope of glory" of the Church today?[87] This call is proclaimed in a magnificent text from the First Vatican Council. For when we ask about the original intention from which the meditation of Anselm and his monks proceeds *in necessary collaboration with the fool*, is this not that divine *invitation* which is the soul of the Church and of its living witness?

By this it happens that the Church, as a sign set up among the nations, *both* invites to itself those who have not yet believed, *and* makes its sons more certain that the faith which they possess rests on the firmest of foundations. Indeed, effective aid comes to this testimony from supernatural virtue.[88]

Is not the grace of this "effective aid" precisely that of the dialogue accepted and pursued in all its exigencies by the believing community with all those who do not yet believe? And does not this grace urge the clergy and all Christian intellectuals, all those who are concerned for the irrefragable witness of the Church and of its testimony, to a common examination of consciousness, in the light of a humble loyalty, in a joy avid with hope and in the energy of this very grace?

[87] Col. 1:27f.: ". . . which is Christ in you, the hope of glory. Him we proclaim, warning every man and teaching every man in all wisdom, that we may present every man mature in Christ."

[88] Denzinger and Rahner, *Enchiridion Symbolorum*, No. 1794. Chapter III of Session III of the Council.

VIII

Anselm Stolz

Anselm's Theology in the Proslogion[1]

INTEREST in Anselm's *Proslogion* has remained alive over the centuries. Since Gaunilo's time philosophers as well as theologians have worked on it, especially on the "proof of God's existence" in Chapters II-IV.[2]

Karl Barth has recently come to an understanding of this "problematical Anselm" in a very suggestive study.[3] He is not satisfied either with the traditional view that finds in Anselm an ontological argument or with the various other interpretations. His resolution of the problem rests on two presuppositions: first, that before everything else Anselm's proof must be understood in connection with his peculiar theological program; and secondly, that an exegesis of the early chapters of the *Proslogion* must take into account Anselm's controversy with his first critic, Gaunilo, and must investigate the meaning of each word with this in mind.[4]

This approach leads Barth to the following conclusion: There is no trace of an ontological argument to be found in Anselm. Anselm always speaks as a theologian, and the rule of faith is his constant presupposition. "On the assumption that this is true—that God exists, that God is the highest being, that he is one being in three persons, that he became man, etc.—Anselm discusses the question *in what way* this is true; and when he asks and is asked about this 'in what way' with regard to one or another of the articles of the faith, he answers on the basis of the presupposed truth of all the other

[1] Anselm Stolz, "Zur Theologie Anselms im Proslogion," in *Catholica. Vierteljahrschrift für Kontroverstheologie* (Paderborn), II (1933), pp. 1-24, transl. by Arthur C. McGill.

[2] A good survey of these investigations is given by Woestyne, *Cursus philosophicus* (1925), vol. II, pp. 708ff.

[3] Karl Barth, *Anselm.*

[4] *Ibid.*, Preface, German p. vii, English p. 8.

articles."[5] In the case of the proof for God's existence, the believed presupposition is the Name of God. (God is "that than which nothing greater can be conceived.") From this Name the believed existence of God should "be recognized and demonstrated, that is, should be understood as something which must be thought."[6] From this Name it follows that the being which we call God "cannot possibly be thought of as only existing in thought."[7] This is how essentially *theological* work is done.

The highest significance must be attached to Barth's method. Since the "proof of God's existence" is a piece of genuine and proper theology, it therefore must be understood in the context of Anselm's theologizing. "Whatever attitude people may take to the interpretation which I have secured by taking this road, at least I hope to have it acknowledged that this road is in fact the correct one."[8] Barth, however, will not and cannot secure this acknowledgment completely. For why does he consider only Anselm's *general* theological program? Must Anselm's method be the same in all his works? Perhaps the *Proslogion* has its own method, which alone guarantees a correct understanding of the uncertain opening chapters. Certainly the peculiar literary form of the *Proslogion* suggests this point. Anselm theologizes in prayer. This is distinctive, even in comparison with Anselm's other writings. Barth also, of course, refers repeatedly to this fact. But what meaning does this praying have? Is it based essentially on the progress of the theological speculation? Does it give the *Proslogion* a wholly unique character? Or is it simply a pious interruption of the theological reasoning? Does this touch on the deeper question of what Anselm really wanted in the *Proslogion*?

What is of preliminary interest, therefore, is the *special theology* of the *Proslogion*, its purpose, form, structure and method of demonstration. Then in this context we will also seek to understand the "proof of God's existence."

I

Anselm usually provides his works with a prefatory statement, where he expresses himself on the *purpose* and *literary form* of the

[5] *Ibid.*, German p. 63, English pp. 61f.
[6] *Ibid.*, German p. 82, English p. 78. See p. 124.
[7] *Ibid.*, German p. 103, English p. 94.
[8] *Ibid.*, Preface, German p. vii, English p. 9.

writing. For instance *Cur Deus homo?* is directed against the objections of the Jews, and is written in order to show that the Incarnation involves no contradictions.[9] To this end he purposefully chooses the dialogue form, "since those things which are investigated by question and response become clear and are thus more gratifying to many, and especially to those with slower minds."[10] The *Monologion* exhibits a different form corresponding to its special purpose. As its first title states (*Exemplum meditandi de ratione fidei*), it should be a model example of a meditation on the rationality of the faith. For this the dialogue form was obviously less appropriate. Anselm therefore chooses the form of thought reflecting in silence; the articles of the faith about God's nature and trinity are examined. The *Proslogion* grew out of the *Monologion*. As Anselm himself confesses, he struggled to find a single argumentation.[11] Nevertheless, the *Proslogion* is more than a resumé of the *Monologion*; the ideas are even expressed in another literary form. The difference between the two works is clearly set forth in the Preface of the *Proslogion*.[12]

The *Monologion*: "... a little work produced as an example of a meditation on the rationality of the faith, *in the person of someone who investigates what he does not know by silent reasoning with himself*."

The *Proslogion*: "Judging therefore that what I rejoiced to have found about this and certain other matters would, if written, be welcome to some readers, I have written the following little work, *in the person of someone striving to elevate his mind to the contemplation of God and seeking to understand what he believes*."

In the *Monologion* a silent meditation which should lead to understanding; in the *Proslogion* an effort of the soul to raise itself to a kind of vision of God. Within this effort, speculation is included. Anselm specifies the How of this quest for God: "seeking to understand what he believes." Thus, a general insight into the teachings of the faith is not at all intended. Instead, Anselm wants to *attain a vision of God*

9 See Plas, "Des hl. Anselms *Cur Deus homo?* auf den Boden der judisch-christlichen Polemik des Mittelalters," in *Divus Thomas* (Freiburg), 1929, pp. 446ff. and 1930, pp. 18ff.

10 *Cur Deus homo?* I.1 (II. 48.11-13). We also find this form in another of Anselm's works, the *De veritate*, Preface (I. 173. 2-4): "At various times in the past I have written three treatises pertaining to the study of sacred Scripture, which have this in common, that they are presented *through question and response*." Italics added.

11 *Prosl.* Preface (I. 93.5-13).

12 *Ibid.*, Preface (I. 93.2-4; 93.20-94.2). Italics added.

through an understanding of what the faith says about God. This explains the "seeking."[13] Insight into the dogmas about God should lead therefore to a vision of God. The *Proslogion* desires to pray for both. Accordingly, this is essentially a piece of mystical theology.[14]

This aim is also in accord with the title which Anselm gives to this work: *Proslogion.* At first the *Monologion* and the *Proslogion* were released to the world anonymously and without titles. Then Anselm wanted to give them brief headings, "which in some way might attract anyone who came upon them to read them." Therefore, he entitled the *Monologion* "An Example of a Meditation on the Rationality of the Faith," and the *Proslogion* "Faith Seeking Understanding."[15] By themselves both titles could signify the same thing: a meditation on the rationality of the faith. But in view of the peculiar purpose of the *Proslogion* we should see something more in the second title: a quest by faith for a vision of God. The difference between the two writings would then be expressed in the titles.[16] The first title *Proslogion* has regard only for the outer form: *Alloquium*, or ad-

[13] Anselm lets this be understood clearly enough in many places. *Prosl.* I (I. 100.12f., 15-18): "I acknowledge and I give thanks to you, O Lord, because you have created this image of yourself in me, so that I may be aware of you, may conceive of you and may love you. . . . *I do not endeavor to penetrate your sublimity, O Lord,* because in no way do I compare my understanding with that, but I desire *to understand to some degree your truth,* which my heart believes and loves." Also *Prosl.* XIV (I. 111. 8f.): "Have you found what you have sought, O my soul? *You sought God and you have found that he is the supreme good.*" Italics added. Anselm thus identifies the result of his quest for God with the result of his theological speculation.

[14] In his *Life of Anselm* (R. W. Southern ed., p. 31), Eadmer says of the *Prosl.*: "He composed a volume, very small in size but great with the weight of *the most subtle contemplation.*" Migne, *P.L.*, vol. 158. 63 D.

[15] *Prosl.* Preface (I. 94.2-7).

[16] Later, when Anselm adds his name to both works he calls one *Monologue on the Rationality of the Faith* (*Monoloquium de ratione fidei*) and the other *Address on the Rationality of the Faith* (*Alloquium de ratione fidei*). See *Epistle* 100 (III. 232.30-32). Apart from the distinction in form as monologue and address, no difference is evident in these titles. But perhaps precisely for that reason, Anselm later saw himself led to make a further alteration. He wrote to Archbishop Hugo of Lyons (*Epistle* 109, III. 242.7-15): "Therefore, I request that if you can recover the little books which I sent at the command of your holiness, after removing what is explained in the titles, namely 'on the Rationality of the Faith,' as something superfluous, you will call the one which I have named *Monoloquium, Monologion,* and will entitle the other, not *Alloquium,* but *Proslogion.* . . . For me, however, to explain why I ask that this change be made, provided only that it is made, is certainly not necessary, nor is it appropriate in this brief little note which I have written." See *Prosl.* Preface (I. 94.8-13). It is a pity that Anselm was unable to add his reason for this alteration.

dress.[17] The speaking subject is Anselm himself, not God.[18] The object is God and the soul, but chiefly God.[19] This corresponds to the purpose of the work: the ascent of the mind to God.

The first, programmatic chapter of the *Proslogion* completes what has been said in an important way. Strange to say, this is almost never considered by Anselm's interpreters. At best they see here a general introduction in elevated and poetic language. Even Barth grants it little attention, and takes it merely as a "long introductory invocation."[20] Actually, however, this chapter outlines the plan of the whole work, and the ideas which Anselm worked out here continually reappear in his writings.

"Arousing (*excitatio*) the mind to the contemplation of God,"[21] Anselm begins with an address to his soul. He calls it to composure and self-reflection. It should speak to God with its whole heart: "I seek your face, O Lord, your face do I seek" (Vulg. Ps. 26:8; A.V. Ps. 27:8). Then Anselm turns to God himself. Teach me where you are to be sought and where you are to be found. Where is that unapproachable light in which you dwell (I Tim. 6:16)? Where can I come to know you? Of all this I am ignorant.[22]

This leads to the lament over the painful loss that occurred through Adam's sin. He once possessed everything which we now desire and for which we must pray and exert ourselves.[23]

There then follows an initial reflection about this beginning: Anselm has withdrawn into the temple of his soul in order to find there consolation in God, but what he finds instead is frustration and sorrow.[24]

Again he turns to God in prayer and beseeches help; God alone

[17] *Prosl.*, Preface: "*Proslogion*, that is, address (*alloquium*)." (I. 94.13). The term *Proslogion* seems to be Anselm's creation. It has not been found in any Greek usage.

[18] In Latin religious usage, when it is a matter of communication between God and man and God is the speaking subject, the usual term is *alloquium*. For instance, Augustine *City of God* XVI, the title to Chapter 18: "Concerning God's Repeated *Alloquio* to Abraham."

[19] Eadmer, *op. cit.*, (R. W. Southern ed., p. 31): "Anselm composed a volume . . . which he called the *Proslogion*. For in this work, he addresses (*alloquitur*) either himself or God." Migne, *P.L.* vol. 158, 63D. While God is addressed in every chapter, Anselm turns to his soul only a few times.

[20] Barth, *op. cit.*, German p. 1, English p. 13.

[21] *Prosl.* Title of Chapter I (I. 97.3).

[22] *Ibid.*, I (I. 97.4-98.15).

[23] *Ibid.* (I. 98.16-99.7).

[24] *Ibid.* (I. 99.8-99.14): "I strove toward God, and I stumbled on myself. I sought peace in my privacy, and I found tribulation and grief in my inner depths."

can enable him to find him. The image of God in us is darkened by sin.[25] God must renew that image, must form it a new, for only then can the soul somewhat perceive that truth of God which the heart already embraces in faith and love.[26]

The reasoning of *Proslogion* II then immediately follows this introductory chapter: "O Lord, you who give insight to faith, give me. . . ." This means that in the first chapter we should be told precisely about what the next chapters will bring. In this connection there are three points of special significance.

1. Anselm writes his *Proslogion as a believing Christian.* Nothing is more absurd than to see a philosopher in the author of the *Proslogion.* As a philosopher, how would Anselm realize that God is not only his creator but also his redeemer? ("You have made me and remade me.")[27] How would he realize that Adam once possessed that knowledge of God to which he now wants to be elevated?[28] Or that we men are meant to be heirs of Adam's happiness?[29] Or that without God's help the soul cannot attain that happiness to which it is appointed by the creator?[30] Thus, Anselm stands wholly on the foundation of his Christian faith. That is why toward the end of the *Proslogion,* without any transition, he can introduce the dogma of God's tri-personality: In *Proslogion* XXII he had found the *summum bonum* and then immediately shows that this good is not only the Father, but also the Son and the Holy Spirit.[31] This is established explicitly for each Person. The Trinity of Persons is a presupposition; no trace of a "proof" is to be discovered. For Anselm the dogmas are not subject to discussion; his faith presumes them.

2. On the basis of this presumption, Anselm wants to pass *from faith into the vision of the ever-present God.* What does this mean for him? He wants to penetrate into the unapproachable light—God's dwelling place—and finally to attain that for which he was created:

[25] *Ibid.* (I. 100.12f.): "You have created in me this image of yourself, so that I may *be aware of you*, may *conceive of you* and may love you."

[26] *Ibid.* (I. 99.15-100.19).

[27] *Ibid.* (I. 98.13).

[28] *Ibid.* (I. 98.23): "He choked with satiety, we sigh with hunger."

[29] *Ibid.* (I. 98.25-99.1): "Why did he not guard for us, when he easily could have done so, that which we lack so desperately." See *Prosl.* XVIII (I. 114.3f.): "I fell before my mother conceived me."

[30] *Ibid.*, I (I. 100.14f.): Your image in my soul "cannot do that for which it was made, unless you renew and reform it."

[31] *Ibid.*, XXIII (I. 117.6f., 11f.): "This good is you, O God the Father; this good is your Word, that is, your Son. . . . This good is the one love common to you and your Son, that is, the Holy Spirit proceeding from both."

the vision of God.[32] In this life a direct gaze is not possible,[33] but only a perception "from afar, from the depths."[34] Once men were in fortunate possession of this good, but through his sin Adam flung it away from himself and us.[35] The manner of this vision of God is further explained in later chapters: Sin has dulled the faculties of our souls.[36] Our souls no more hear God, no more notice his fragrance, nor taste his savoriness nor feel him.[37] Thus, the vision of God which Anselm seeks is more accurately called an *experience* of God. In order to obtain this, Anselm withdraws into the inner chamber of his heart. Nothing should remain with him there except God alone and whatever can help him find God. Thus, at the very beginning of the *Proslogion* he already knows about God's dwelling in his heart, and therefore *a fortiori* about God's general existence. But he wants to be with God alone and then to seek his face.[38] This attitude toward God does not pertain only to "introductory invocation." How else could Anselm persist in his continuous address to God? Moreover, in the course of the *Proslogion* he comes back explicitly to the problem of the opening chapter. After completing a series of reasonings about God and his attributes (Chapters V-XIII), he poses the question: "O my soul, have you now found what you sought? You sought God, and you found that he is the highest being of all, than which a greater cannot be thought."[39] Here for the first time since the opening summons of the first chapter, the soul is again addressed to seek God. Reference to the introduction is unmistakable, especially since shortly after this, in Chapter XVIII, the same passage from Psalm 26 which appeared in the opening summons in the present tense (*quaero vultum tuum*) is now set in the perfect tense (*quaesivi vultum tuum*).[40]

32 *Ibid.*, I (I. 98.5f., 7, 14f.): "How shall I approach the unapproachable light? Who will lead me to it and bring me into it, that I may see you in it? . . . *I have never seen you*, O Lord my God, I do not know your face. . . . I was made to *see* you, and I have not yet done that for which I was made." Italics added. See *Prosl.* XIV.

33 *Ibid.*, XXVI (I. 121.6-9).

34 *Ibid.*, I (I. 100.8).

35 *Ibid.*, I (I. 98.20f., 22f.): "Man once ate the bread of angels . . . . Alas for the general weeping of men, for the universal anguish of the sons of Adam."

36 *Ibid.*, XVII (I. 113.14f.): "But the sinful senses of my soul have become stiffened, paralyzed and obstructed by their ancient listlessness."

37 *Ibid.*, XVII (I. 113.9-12): "For it gazes, and does not see your beauty. It listens, and does not hear your harmony. It tastes, and does not recognize your sweetness. It touches, and does not feel your softness."

38 *Ibid.*, I (I. 97.7-9): " 'Enter into the inner chamber' of your mind; shut out everything except God and what can help you in seeking him; 'close your door' and seek him. . . . Speak now to God, saying, 'I seek your face.' " (Matt. 6:6; Vulg. Ps. 26:8; A.V. Ps. 27:8.)

39 *Prosl.* XIV (I. 111.8f.).

40 *Ibid.*, XVIII (I. 114.9).

Before Anselm again takes up his search for God after this interruption, prayers like those in Chapter I come from his lips.[41] There always remains the same theme, the search for the ever-present God: "You are within me and around me, and yet I do not feel you!"[42] Accordingly, everything contained in the intervening chapters is subordinated to the purpose of an experience of God.

Anselm designates this striving for God as "seeking the face of God," "seeing him," "approaching," "eating the bread of angels," etc. Together with the experience of God there is given the joy of immortality.

Anselm explains how he plans to come to this experience of God in the celebrated programmatic statement of Chapter II: "O Lord, you who give understanding to faith, insofar as you know it to be beneficial, give to me so that *I may understand* that you are *just as we believe*, and that you are *what we believe*."[43] Anselm therefore *wants to advance toward God through the* intellectus fidei, *through an understanding of the dogmas about God.*

3. The experience of God should bring Anselm *joy*. In the opening chapter he says, as if by chance: "*I wanted to laugh*, out of the joy in my mind, but I am forced to scowl 'from the tumult in my heart.' *Joy was hoped for*, but behold, sighs have closed in around me."[44] Barth has referred to the fact that Anselm also seeks joy in the *intelligere*.[45] But for the *Proslogion* joy has a special meaning as the goal of the understanding. It shapes the conclusion of the seeking in the *Proslogion*: "For I have found a joy that is full, and more than full."[46] This joy results from knowledge, and is intensified with increasing knowledge. Nevertheless, the fullness of joy is in store for us only in the life to come.[47] The *Proslogion* closes with a hymn to joy and with an ardent prayer for joy:

O faithful God, I ask that I may receive, that my joy may be full. Meanwhile let my mind meditate on it and my tongue speak of it. Let my heart love

[41] *Ibid.*, XVIII (I. 114.10f., 12f.): "Redeem me from myself for you. . . . Let my soul recover its strength, and let it again strive toward you, O Lord, with its whole understanding."

[42] *Ibid.*, XVI (I. 113.4).

[43] *Ibid.*, II., (I. 101.3f.). Italics added.

[44] *Ibid.*, I (I. 99.12-14). Italics added.

[45] Barth, *op. cit.*, German pp. 4-13, English pp. 15-21.

[46] *Prosl.* XXVI (I. 120.25f.).

[47] *Ibid.*, XXVI (I. 121.16-18): "Let my knowledge of you advance in me here, and let it be made full there. Let my love of you increase here, and let it be full there, so that here my joy may be great in hope, and *there full in reality*." Italics added.

it and my mouth converse on it. Let my soul hunger for it, let my flesh thirst for it, and let my whole being desire it, until I enter into the joy of my Lord, who is God three and one and is blessed for ever and ever. Amen.[48]

The joy that results from understanding is so great that men cannot receive it into themselves, but rather men are received into it.[49] It comes from God, and we must pray that we may have a share in it.[50] Joy is the last thing of all. It gives finality and consummation to all things. It is the ultimate goal in all seeking for God.[51] The fact that the *Proslogion* concludes with the finding of this joy therefore means that Anselm *has actually attained his goal, has found the knowledge of God, the experience of God.* The hidden God reveals himself and thereby gives Anselm the joy which he seeks.[52]

II

We are now acquainted with the peculiar goal of the *Proslogion*; the Preface and the opening chapter leave no doubt standing on this matter. In conformity with this goal, then, Anselm chooses the literary form of an address to God. When we inquire about the *structure* of the *Proslogion*, we will discover *how Anselm actually executed his program.* In this way we will know the larger context which embraces the "proof for God's existence."

Barth divides the *Proslogion* into two very unequal parts. "Of the two parts in Anselm's *Proslogion* (Chapters II-IV and V-XXVI), the proof for the *existence* of God forms the disproportionately short first part. The second and larger part deals with the nature of God."[53]

This division of the *Proslogion*, however, is based on the same "optical illusion" on the basis of which the *Proslogion* sometimes carries the subtitle *De existentia Dei.* Would Anselm really have

[48] *Ibid.*, XXVI I. (121.21-122.2).

[49] *Ibid.*, XXVI (I. 121.3f.): "Therefore, that whole joy does not enter into the beatified, but the beatified wholly enter into that joy."

[50] *Ibid.*, XXVI (I. 121.18f.): "Through your Son you command, or rather counsel, us to pray, and you promise that we will receive so that our joy may be full."

[51] *Ibid.*, XXVI (I. 121.9f.): "They will rejoice as much as they will love; they will love as much as they will know."

[52] We should compare this meaning of joy in Anselm with the Philonic conception of joy. The latter "marks religious experience in its most perfect and purest form." (H. Windisch, *Die Frommigkeit Philos*, Leipzig 1909, p. 56.) On the affinity of the ideas of "joy" and "sober drunkenness," see H. Lewy, *Sobria ebrietas*, Griessen, 1929, pp. 34f., 118.

[53] Barth, *op. cit.*, German p. 1, English p. 13.

set together two such unequal parts? There is, of course, a reason for this division. Barth rests his position on the first sentence of Chapter II: "O Lord, insofar as you know it to be beneficial, give to me so that I may understand that you are just as we believe, and that you are that which we believe." So begins the exposition proper after the long opening invocation of *Proslogion* I. Barth finds confirmation for this outline in the Preface, when Anselm speaks of the "one argument" common to both parts which "proves that God truly exists (*vere est*) and that he is the highest good (*summum bonum*)."[54] Here also it is supposed that the whole structure of the *Proslogion* is being indicated.[55]

To be sure, once *Proslogion* I is eliminated, then only the first sentence of *Proslogion* II gives the program. But this division does not blend with the peculiar goal of the *Proslogion*. It sees in the work only a treatise on God's existence and nature. But the work is more, for it seeks an experience of the ever-present but hidden God. In such a program it would certainly be remarkable for a proof of God's existence to be the chief part. Even a "proof of God's nature," of which Barth speaks, does not altogether fit the matter.[56] The sentence about the "one argument for proving that God truly exists, etc." appears in the Preface of the *Proslogion*, of course. But this is not a statement of the program of the *Proslogion*. For Anselm expresses himself on this matter three sentences farther on: "Judging therefore that what I was delighted to have found would, if written down, please some readers, I have written the following little book *about this very thing* [i.e., about the one argument which he has found] *and also about certain other matters* [and therefore not solely about what that one argument contains]."[57] Barth's division therefore is untenable; the real structure of the *Proslogion* is to be understood only on the basis of *Proslogion* I.

The soul wants to experience God. To this end it strives for an insight into the articles of faith about God, about his existence and his nature. In that regard even the statement in *Proslogion* II—"that I may understand that you are, just as we believe, and that you are that which we believe"—is programmatic. But for the structure of the whole work it is more important, and even decisive, to determine

54 *Prosl.* Preface (I. 93.7f.).

55 Barth, *op. cit.*, German p. 1, English p. 13: "This *argumentum* must be identified, not with the proof developed in *Prosl.* II-IV, but with a technical element which Anselm uses in *both* parts of his work."

56 *Ibid.*

57 *Prosl.* Preface (I. 93.20-94.2). Italics added.

whether in the course of the *Proslogion* a progress is evident in "the effort to raise the mind to the contemplation of God."[58] This indeed is how this writing should be considered.

After the opening chapter the attempt to advance toward God through an understanding of the articles of faith begins with the sentence cited above. This attempt continues unbroken through Chapter XIII. But Chapter XIV again refers to the appointed goal.[59] Here Anselm gives a brief review of the understanding which has been secured up to this point. Then, wholly within the meaning of his original intention, he investigates why this *intelligere* has still not led to the *sentire* of God. The "unapproachable light," which was identified in Chapter I as the dwelling place of God, has indeed been found,[60] but the fact that the soul still does not experience God is due to the dulling of its faculties by sin.[61] Thus, the first effort to come to God leads again to sorrow and frustration, rather than to joy and exultation.[62] With renewed prayers for God's help,[63] the soul once more collects itself in order once more to elevate itself to God.[64] Here there obviously begins a second attempt, since the first only succeeded in reaching God's dwelling place but not God himself. This second attempt concludes with the understanding of the one supreme good in the tri-personal God.[65] Chapter XXIV interrupts the discussion with a summons to the soul to direct all its efforts to the understanding of this good.[66] In this understanding, then, the soul attains its joy, i.e., it has reached its goal.

58 *Ibid.*, Preface (I. 94.1).

59 *Ibid.*, XIV (I. 111.8): "O my soul, have you discovered what you have sought? *You have sought God,* and *you have discovered* that he is, etc." Italics added.

60 *Ibid.*, XVI (I. 112.20): "O Lord, this [which I have discovered] is truly the unapproachable light in which you dwell."

61 *Ibid.*, XVII (I. 113.14f.). This thought is similar to that expressed at the end of Chapter I (I. 100.13f.), where Anselm speaks of the image of God in us: "It has been so destroyed by the abrasion of vices, and so besmirched by the smoke of sins that it cannot do that for which it was made."

62 *Ibid.*, XVIII (I. 113.18-114.2): "Behold, again there is confusion; behold, again grief and mourning meet the one who seeks joy and gladness. My soul now hoped for satisfaction, and behold again it was overwhelmed with need. I now desired to feast, and behold I am all the more hungry. I tried to rise (*conabar assurgere*) to the light of God, and I fell back into my own darkness." Cf. Preface (I. 94.1): *conantis erigere.*

63 *Ibid.*, XVIII (I. 114.11f.): "Cleanse, heal, sharpen and enlighten the eye of my mind, so that it may gaze upon you."

64 *Ibid.* (I. 114.12-14): "Let my soul *again* collect its powers, and let it *again* direct itself to you, O Lord. *What are you, O Lord, what are you?*" Italics added.

65 *Ibid.*, XXII and XXIII.

66 *Ibid.*, XXIV (I. 117.25f.): "Now, O my soul, arouse and elevate your whole

Thus, the *Proslogion* contains a two-phase movement toward God. Each is initiated by an address and summons to the soul, as well as by a statement of the difficulties and a prayer for helping grace. This pattern causes the *Proslogion* to fall into two almost equally long sections: Chapters I-XIII and Chapters XIV-XXVI. The first part concerns itself with the treatment of the *argumentum* that "God is that than which nothing greater can be conceived." The second part does not eliminate this argument, but goes beyond it: God is no longer "that than which a greater cannot be conceived," but is now that which is "greater than can be conceived."[67] For that reason, God reigns in unapproachable light, and everything which our understanding grasps in him bit by bit actually exists in him unified and undivided.[68] Therefore, he is the one supreme good, the possession of which bestows joy.

The *Proslogion* is executed according to this plan. The description of the second part is not so interesting to us here. We are concerned about the meaning of the "proof of God's existence" in the early chapters. Therefore, we must analyze the first part more closely.

We can approach an understanding of this part from either of its two sides. That is, first from the Preface, where there are statements about the meaning of the *argumentum*, and then from Chapter XIV, which provides a brief but comprehensive summary of what has gone before. Because of the most varied interpretations of the alleged proof of God's existence, the analysis of the early chapters has become extremely difficult for us. For this reason, it is more expedient to take our first guideline from a noncontroversial section, that is, from the summary in Chapter XIV. It says there:

> You have sought God and you have discovered that he is the supreme good, than which nothing better can be conceived; that this good is life itself, light itself, wisdom itself, goodness itself, eternal beatitude itself and beatific eternity itself; and that this is everywhere and always.[69]

There is no reference here to discovering the existence of God. And yet Anselm undoubtedly wishes to indicate the content of the preceding chapters at least in their essential outline. If *Proslogion* II-IV

---

understanding, and conceive as far as you can the quality and the greatness of that good."

[67] *Ibid.*, XV.

[68] *Ibid.*, XVIII (I. 114.16-24), although again by means of an appeal to the "that than which nothing greater can be conceived" (I. 114.21f.).

[69] *Ibid.*, XIV (I. 111.8-11).

contains proof of God's existence as its major theme, why does it remain unmentioned here? Anselm specifies only three points as the result of his inquiries:

1. It is found that God is "that than which a greater cannot be conceived."
2. This "than which a greater, etc." is essentially light itself, life itself, etc.
3. It is omnipresent and eternal.

Does this division really correspond to the early chapters, or does it neglect something essential? The last two points certainly correspond to Chapters V-XIII. To be sure, the content of each individual chapter is not given, but the decisive point is mentioned. This section begins in Chapter V with the question: "Therefore, what are you, O Lord, than whom nothing greater can be conceived?" Thus, it is already presupposed that God is that than which a greater cannot be conceived; on the basis of this idea, it then becomes a question of his nature. In a general form the answer is: "You are just and truthful and blessed and *whatever else it is better to be than not to be*."[70] With this, all the attributes of God are demonstrated *in globo*. The following sections (Chapters VI-XI) resolve difficulties which arise against God's being sensitive, omnipotent, compassionate and impassible.[71] These chapters are therefore subordinate to the thesis of Chapter V. This also proves that the statement in Chapter XI is a summarizing conclusion: "Therefore, you are just as much sensitive, omnipotent, merciful and impassible as you are living, wise, good, blessed, eternal and whatever it is better to be than not to be."[72] Chapter XII then leads on to a further step: God's attributes constitute his nature; from himself he is life itself, wisdom itself, goodness itself, etc.[73] Chapter XIII then derives his omnipresence and eternity.

There can be no doubt, therefore, that Points 2 and 3 in the statement of contents from *Proslogion* XIV correctly summarize the preceding discussion. There remains only Point 1: "You have discovered that he is the supreme good than which nothing greater can be conceived." This must be a statement of the content of *Proslogion* II-IV. There can be no doubt that these chapters belong

70 *Ibid.*, V (I. 104.15f.). Italics added.
71 *Ibid.*, XI (I. 110.1-3).
72 *Ibid.*, XI (I. 110.1-3).
73 *Ibid.*, XII (I. 110.6f.): "Whatever you are, you are not through another but through yourself. Therefore, you are the very life by which you live, the very wisdom through which you are wise, etc."

together. The opening statement of *Proslogion* II prays for insight into the articles of faith, "so that I may understand that you are, just as we believe (*quia es, sicut credimus*) and that you are that which we believe (*et hoc es, quod credimus*)." These last words—"and that you are that which we believe"—refer to *Proslogion* V-XIII, for there, insight into God's nature is indeed secured. Accordingly, the first words must refer to *Proslogion* II-IV. But what do these words mean when translated? Barth renders them: "... give to me so that I may understand *dass du da bist, wie wir glauben*, that you exist, as we believe."[74] This would clearly establish the fact that Anselm is praying for the knowledge of God's existence. It would be more literal and undesigning to say: "that you are, as we believe." Barth consistently interprets the rest of *Proslogion* II as a theological proof of God's existence.

After this opening prayer for insight into the faith, Anselm continues: "And we certainly believe that you are something than which nothing greater can be conceived."[75] Therefore, we *can* give this meaning to the prayer for insight: Give to me so that I may understand that you are a being than which a greater cannot be conceived. And then at the end of *Proslogion* IV, when Anselm thanks God for that insight into the faith which he has been given, we *can* refer this to the same knowledge. The text would then mean: "I thank you, good Lord, I thank you that what I first believed through your grace [namely, that you are that than which a greater cannot be conceived], I now so understand through your illumination that, even if I did not wish to believe that you are [this], I would still be unable not to understand it."[76] Then Chapter V would follow with its question about the nature of that than which a greater cannot be conceived; at the same time the meaning of *Proslogion* XIV would be fully preserved: "You have discovered that he is the supreme good, than which nothing better can be conceived, etc." Therefore, on the basis of Chapter XIV, *Proslogion* II-IV would seem to be only a matter of proving that God (whose

[74] Barth, *op. cit.*, German p. 111, English p. 101.

[75] Schmitt's reference to *De doctrina Christiana* I.7 is surely justified. The idea also occurs in ancient philosophy. Seneca, *Naturalium quaestionum* I. Preface, 8: "What men have long sought for is at last taught to them: They begin to know God. What is God? The universal mind. What is God? The whole which you see and the whole which you do not see. So, if God alone is everything and if his work holds sway both inside and outside of everything, then his magnitude *than which nothing greater can be conceived* is at last represented to men." Italics added.

[76] *Prosl.* IV (I. 104.5-7).

existence is fully assured throughout) is really that than which nothing greater can be conceived.[77]

Yet with this, the content of *Proslogion* II-IV has not yet been correctly presented. For the phrases, "that I may understand that you are," and "even if I did not wish to believe that you are" point too directly to the fact that in some way Anselm is speaking of God's existence. Moreover, *Proslogion* II speaks emphatically of "being in the understanding" and "being in reality," which means intellectual and real existence. The Preface also announces openly that something real about God's existence will be proved. Anselm there reports of his long search for the "one argument," the meaning and importance of which are emphasized: "I began to seek if one argument could be securely discovered, which would be sufficient by itself for proving *that God truly is*, and that he is the supreme good . . . and whatever else we believe concerning the divine substance."[78] Thus, he wishes to prove something about God's existence, as we grasp it in faith: "that he truly is (*vere esse*)." *Proslogion* III returns to this phrase *vere esse*. There it is connected *every time* with the fact that God "cannot be conceived not to exist"; and *in this sense*, on the basis of the formula "that than which a greater cannot be conceived," the phrase is proved to characterize God. From this two things result.

1. *Vere esse* does not mean "real existence," in the sense that other things outside God have real existence. Rather, it designates a very definite kind of real being, which we experience through faith from God. It denotes an existence of such reality that it cannot ever be conceived as not existing. When Barth sees two different meanings in the *vere esse* (existence in general and existence in the special sense just explained),[79] his sole ground for this is the fact that he sees in *Proslogion* II and III two distinct sequences of thought —a presupposition which also must be explicitly refuted later.

2. *Proslogion* II-IV contains a *two-fold* proof. The first is that God truly is, for he is just as faith teaches us; the other is that God really is "that than which nothing greater can be conceived." That both proofs must be in the controversial chapters is to be concluded from the Preface and the summary in Chapter XIV. Nothing more.

77 In *Prosl.* III this is also proved in the following way: "If some mind could conceive of something better than you, the creature would rise above and would judge his Creator, which would be completely absurd." (I. 103.4-6.)

78 *Ibid.*, Preface (I. 93.5-10). Italics added.

79 Barth, *op. cit.*, German pp. 111, English p. 101.

Nothing is said about the existence of God in general, but only about the special form of his existence, and the justification for applying formula "that than which a greater cannot be conceived" to God.

Up to this point the two texts—"give to me that I may understand that you are" and "if I did not wish to believe that you are"—have been interpreted *only* on the ground of the conclusions drawn from Chapter XIV. This interpretation was intentionally offered only in the form of a *possibility*. Now, after we have considered the statement in the Preface, we will be able to understand both of these texts about the being and indeed the special existence of God. This effort is now to be made.

III

The purpose and structure of the *Proslogion* do not allow us to conclude that the opening chapters contain in some sense a proof of God's existence. Rather, the opposite is more nearly the case. But this still has not been decisively proved. In order to do this, we ought not to dwell on the surrounding texts, but must investigate the demonstration of Chapters II-IV, in just that word-by-word fashion which Barth has undertaken. We should then discover whether Anselm, while on the way toward an understanding of God's special existence and of the article of faith that God is that than which a greater cannot be conceived, has not also developed a proof of God's general existence. This possibility should now be eliminated. Caution, however, is necessary. If we ask whether a proof is present, we must be able to distinguish proofs as such. The first thing, then, is *to characterize the kind of demonstration which is proper to the Proslogion.*

If the *Proslogion* is indeed a mystical writing which should lead to a vision of God, it nevertheless has the intention, like the *Monologion*, of carrying out theological speculative work. In contrast to the *Monologion*, however, it is not done in silent reflection ("investigating what he does not know by reasoning silently with himself"), but in the form of an address to God ("trying to elevate his mind to the contemplation of God," by means of an *alloquium*).[80] Therefore, if in the *Proslogion* Anselm changes over from intellectual reasoning

[80] *Prosl.* Preface (I. 93.3f., 94.1, 13).

to addresses to God, this is no interruption of his theological reasoning, no mere decoration which could just as well be eliminated. The address is rather the necessary goal of every "proof," through which he "seeks to understand what he believes."[81] Every proof either must be conducted in the form of an address to God or must at least conclude in such an address. Otherwise, the literary form of *Alloquium* would not be continually observed. Therefore, if Anselm changes over from intellectual reasoning to addresses to God, this is a sign that a particular process of reasoning is concluded, and that it is now being used for the contemplation of God. Conversely, before the *allocutio* begins, we should under no circumstances consider one of Anselm's demonstrations to be finished; his reasoning cannot yet be completed.

Anselm consistently holds fast to this form of address in his *Proslogion.* In this regard, Chapters V-XI, where the nature of God is deduced by means of the celebrated *argumentum*, are especially instructive. In this section we can distinguish two ways in which the form of address is related to the reasoning.

1. Sometimes, as in Chapter VIII, the address to God is observed throughout the whole speculative deduction.[82]

2. At other times, Anselm uses a three-step procedure: A. The problem is posed in the form of an address to God. B. There then follows such an analysis of ideas as is required to resolve the question which has been posed. This analysis is conducted in the form of silent reasoning. C. After this highly developed analysis, the form of address is taken up again; thus, the result secured by the reasoning is fully used for the contemplation of God. Therefore, the proof, which of course has God in view, comes to its conclusion the moment that the address to God begins, or, more exactly, in that address itself.[83]

[81] *Ibid.*, (I. 94.1f.).

[82] *Ibid.*, VIII (I. 106.5-14): "But how are you both compassionate and impassible at the same time? . . . Therefore, how are you compassionate and ont compassionate, O Lord, unless it is that you are compassionate from our point of view (*secundem nos*) but not from your own? And so you are according to our experience, but not according to your own. Even when you look upon us wretched ones, we feel the effect of compassion, but you do not feel the effect. Therefore, you are compassionate in that you save the wretched and spare those who sin against you; and you are not compassionate in that you feel no compassion for this wretchedness."

[83] See, for instance, *Prosl.* VI (I. 104.21-105.6), after the general introduction to Chapters VI-XI: "(A) If only bodies are sensitive, since the senses envelop a

In the course of the *Proslogion*, whenever Anselm abandons his address to God, he always takes it up again at the conclusion of his reasoning. He cannot do otherwise, if he wishes to remain true to the literary form of address which he has chosen. Therefore, we should not pull out the passages of the *Proslogion* which are not presented in the form of an address to God and treat them as independent sequences of reasoning. After we come upon a "therefore," we ought not to suspend our attention while an address to God is being taken up. Otherwise, we will cut ourselves off from the meaning of the *Proslogion*. Such a separation would only be justified if it could be expressly proved that Anselm meant to abandon his literary form.

With these considerations the final assumption is given for a correct understanding of *Proslogion* II-IV. The second kind of demonstration is to be found here. The address to God is interrupted, and the analysis of the idea "that than which a greater cannot be conceived" is inserted.

The opening sentences of *Proslogion* II are in the form of address:

Therefore, O Lord, who give insight to faith, give to me . . . that I may understand that you are, as we believe (*quia es, sicut credimus*), and that you are that which we believe.[84] And we certainly believe that you are something than which a greater cannot be conceived.

At this point the form of address is abandoned. It reappears again in the middle of *Proslogion* III:

---

body and are in a body, in what way can you be sensitive, since you are not a body but are the supreme spirit which is better than a body?

"(B) But if being sensitive is only understanding or for the sake of understanding—for he who is sensitive understands according to the proper functions of his senses, so that he understands colors through his vision and flavors through his taste—therefore whatever understands in some way is not inappropriately said to be sensitive in some way.

"(C) Therefore, O Lord, although you are not a body, nevertheless you are genuinely sensitive in the way that you supremely understand everything, although not in the way that an animal understands through his body."

Here the three-step procedure is very conspicuous.

84 The words "that you are (*quia es*), just as we believe" refer to the Preface (I. 93.7-9): a single *argumentum* to demonstrate "that God truly is (*quia deus vere est*) . . . and whatever else we believe about the divine substance." Barth's translation of this phrase (*op. cit.*, German p. 111, English p. 101)—"that you exist (*da bist*), as we believe"—immediately inserts the question of God's existence into the text. Anselm, however, prays for insight that God's way of being is as faith teaches us, namely, is *vere esse*.

And this is you, our Lord and God.[85] You are so real, my Lord and God, that you cannot ever be conceived not to exist.[86]

And with good reason.[87] For if a mind could conceive of something greater than you, then the creature would rise above the Creator and would judge the Creator, which would be completely absurd.[88]

There then follow some considerations in the form of address about the divine way of being, which has been discovered, and about its difference from what is creaturely. After resolving the difficulty posed by Psalm 13 : 1 Vulgate (14 : 1 A.V.) about "the fool who says in his heart, 'There is no God,'" there follows a prayer of thanksgiving for the insight of faith which has been bestowed;

I thank you, good Lord, I thank you, for what I hitherto believed by your grace I now see so clearly by virtue of your illumination that, even if I I wanted not to believe in your being, I would still be unable not to understand it.[89]

The two passages in the form of address—at the beginning of Chapter II and at the end of Chapter III—must correspond to one another. A two-fold article of faith appears in both. At the beginning of *Proslogion* II there is prayer for insight into God's being, as we believe it to be; at the same time there is presented as an article of faith that God is a being than which a greater cannot be conceived. *Proslogion* III attains insight into the absolutely real being of God (God cannot be conceived not to exist), and at the same time understands the justification for God's name as that than which a greater cannot be conceived. Therefore, the form is scrupulously preserved; at the same time the claim made earlier that *Proslogion* II-IV involves a *double* proof is confirmed.

85 "And *this* is you, our Lord and God," namely that than which a greater cannot be conceived, as is clear from the immediate context. Thus, the connection is made with *Prosl.* II: "We believe that you are something than which nothing greater can be conceived." Hence, the third part of the demonstration begins here, referring back to the initial posing of the problem.

86 Here the analysis of the idea "that than which a greater cannot be conceived" is applied to God, with the result not only that existence belongs to such a being, but that this being cannot be conceived without existence.

87 Referring to *both* of the previous statements, of which the second is only an elucidation of the first.

88 In this way Anselm advances to an *intelligere* that God is that than which a greater cannot be conceived, and at the same time that he is (truly, most truly), just as we believe.

89 This sentence is therefore to be understood as pertaining to insight into God's particular way of being, of which alone Anselm speaks.

The section which lies between the two addresses must be considered in the light of the Anselmian schema of proof. Actually there is offered here nothing but an analysis of the idea "that than which a greater cannot be conceived." It begins with the question whether existence does not belong to such a being ("whether some such nature does not exist");[90] the subject is "that than which a greater cannot be conceived." This question is answered with a double "therefore"—one at the end of *Proslogion* II and the other in the middle of *Proslogion* III, just before the form of address reappears.

According to the first conclusion: "Therefore, 'something than which a greater cannot be conceived' undoubtedly exists (*existit*) in knowledge *and* in objectivity."[91]

According to the second conclusion: "Therefore, 'something than which a greater cannot be conceived' possesses existence in such perfect measure that it cannot even be *conceived* not to exist."[92]

In both conclusions there is reference only to "that than which a greater cannot be conceived." God is not the subject. This "that than which a greater, etc." is according to the first conclusion not a mere mental entity, and according to the second is unthinkable as not existing. Hence, it possesses real being in the highest measure.

The statement in the form of address introduces God as subject for the first time; he possesses this real being, for he is indeed a being than which a greater cannot be conceived.

The error in the interpretation of Karl Barth and of all those who speak of an Anselmian proof for God's existence lies in the fact that with the conclusion of Chapter II ("Therefore, something than which a greater cannot be conceived undoubtedly exists both in the understanding and in reality") they consider the proof which should say something about God as closed. In Barth's words, "from the impossibility of God existing in the understanding alone the conclusion is drawn about his existence *both* in the understanding

[90] *Prosl.* II (I. 101.5f.).

[91] *Ibid.*, (I. 102.2f.). Italics added. Barth quite correctly translates the sentence in this way (*op. cit.*, German p. 144, English p. 127). And as Barth observes (German p. 145, English pp. 127f.), the sentence does not conclude with the existence of a that than which a greater cannot be conceived, for "in spite of the fact that *existit* opens this sentence, the emphasis *can* lie, not on this *existit*, which in itself is ambiguous, but only on its explication—'both *in* the understanding *and in* reality'—through which the *existit* first becomes unambiguous in the sense of the desired result."

[92] *Prosl.* III (I. 103.1f.). Italics added.

and in reality."[93] What justifies Barth in making God the subject of this statement? For Anselm it is always a matter only of a *talis natura*, only of a "something (*aliquid*)" than which nothing greater can be conceived. Only concerning *this* is it proved that this must be more than a merely mental entity. The next chapter—*Proslogion* III—begins with the assertion: "This (*quod*) so truly is (*sic vere est*) that it cannot be conceived not to be." Here also, evidently, the subject is not God but the "that than which a greater cannot be conceived." Also the relative pronoun (*quod*) clearly means that a new sequence of thought is not begun, but that the old is being continued. In any case the demonstrative form of the *Proslogion* prohibits any interruptions. Why, then, the separation into two proofs?[94] Anselm clearly indicates the point when God becomes the subject: "And this is you, O Lord our God [namely the one than which a greater cannot be conceived]. Therefore, you are so truly that you cannot be conceived not to be."[95] Prior to this, only the fact a "that than which, etc." entails objective and necessary existence was explained in a connected chain of reasoning.

According to what has just been said, Anselm's sequence of thought may be summarized perhaps in this way:

From God we believe that existence in reality belongs to him, and that he is a being than which a greater cannot be conceived.

A being than which a greater cannot be conceived entails (logically) objective and necessary existence, existence in truth.

If God is a being than which a greater cannot be conceived, then necessary being, that is, being in the fullest truth (*verissime esse*), belongs to him.

God is indeed a being than which a greater cannot be conceived, because otherwise the creature could raise himself above the creator.

Such is the way in which Anselm attains insight into the revealed proposition that has hitherto been only believed.

Nowhere in the *Proslogion* has Anselm fashioned an argument "for God's existence in general, in the limited sense in which things different from God also exist."[96] There is no trace of a proof of God's existence. We can only find such a thing in Anselm's deduction if we pay no attention to the kind of demonstration in the *Proslogion*,

93 Barth, *op. cit.*, German p. 146, English p. 128.
94 Discussion of the meaning of the division into chapters will be found below.
95 *Prosl.* III (I. 103.3f.).
96 Barth, *op. cit.*, German p. 139, English p. 123.

and in addition import into the text a change of subject that has no basis.

IV

A difficulty against the above interpretation seems to arise from the *division of the Proslogion into chapters.* If *Proslogion* II and III are to be considered as a connected thought-structure, then why their separation into two chapters with different titles? Should we not say that *Proslogion* II—with its own title ("That God Truly Is") and its own conclusion ("Therefore, there undoubtedly exists, etc.")—only wants to prove the general existence of God, and Chapter III the special manner of God's being?

In the last analysis, the division into chapters is the most cogent ground for Barth and his predecessors. It allows them to assume that *Proslogion* II is meant to be taken for itself alone. In that case we can certainly find there a philosophical proof of God's existence, or at least a theological proof in Barth's sense.

Therefore, the chapter titles are worth a more exacting study. There is first that of Chapter II: "That God Truly Is (*vere sit*)." Judging strictly according to this title, we should expect to find at the end of the chapter the conclusion, "Therefore, God truly is," or even, "Therefore, you truly are, O Lord." Barth sees a conclusion of this kind expressed in the final sentence of *Proslogion* II. In fact, however, at that point God is not the subject of discussion, and the language is not about "true being." "True being" is not found at all in the entire reasoning of *Proslogion* II. It first appears in Chapter III; and there also it is applied to God for the first time. Therefore, this chapter title can hardly be intended for the thesis that is proved in *Proslogion* II; it is rather intended for the thesis of the following chapter.[97]

The title of *Proslogion* III ("That it Cannot be Conceived Not to Be") also has its misfortune. It does not at all fit into the train of thought. Barth's very wordy translation of the final sentence in *Proslogion* II and the sentences immediately following make this clear:

97 Barth's observations (*ibid.*, German p. 102 n. 2, English p. 94 n. 2) about "the first possible meaning of the title of *Proslogion* II" lack any textual basis. He translates this title, "That God Exists in Truth" (*ibid.*, German p. 110, English p. 100). In that connection it should be noticed that in the context of the *Proslogion* the phrase *vere esse* never has the general meaning of "to exist."

Therefore, "something than which a greater cannot be conceived" undoubtedly exists in knowledge *and* in objective reality.

3: "That He cannot be conceived not to exist." This positively exists so fully in truth that it also cannot even be conceived not to exist.[98]

In the first sentence the subject is "that than which a greater cannot be conceived." In the title which follows the subject is God, without his actually being named. There follows a relative pronoun referring to the subject of the final sentence in Chapter II. The title, then, directly interrupts the flow of thought. This fact remains, however one handles the Anselmian "proof of God's existence"; it is not the postulate of some interpretation. Barth, however, gives no thought to this in his "scrupulous exegesis that investigates every word."[99]

A radical solution to this problem would be to eliminate the titles as not genuine. However, "the findings of source-criticism support the hypothesis that even the chapter titles in the *Proslogion* came from Anselm himself."[100] In any case, no outer ground for doubting their genuineness has been offered. Two points should be noticed about the titles

First, the oldest manuscripts, which go back to Anselm's time, have a list of chapters with numbers at the beginning. In the text itself, however, the beginning of each chapter is indicated by the respective number being put in the margin; the repetition of the titles in the text is not original.[101] This explains the possibility of Chapter III's opening with a relative pronoun.

Secondly, we should not assume that the chapter titles are *theses* which are meant to be proved in the corresponding chapters. Then they would turn into real mischief-makers, and in interpreting the text of the *Proslogion* we would come into conflict with several titles. Such would be the case, for instance, of Chapter XVII, where the title—"That in God There is Harmony, Fragrance, Sweetness, Softness and Beauty in His Ineffable Manner"—does not fully correspond with the contents. For the proof of this assertion plays an unimportant role in the chapter; the main point is rather the complaint that the soul, dulled by sin, no longer perceives God's attributes. Therefore, we ought to see in the titles only statements which set off one important thought but not the entire content. An

[98] *Ibid.*, German pp. 144 and 150, English pp. 127 and 132.

[99] *Ibid.*, German p. vii, English p. 8.

[100] *Ibid.*, German p. 110, English p. 100.

[101] A communication by letter from Father Francis S. Schmitt.

absolutely programmatic meaning does not belong to them. An unprejudiced consideration of the text leads to this conclusion.

If the titles are not theses, then, there is no need to be troubled over the fact that the title of *Proslogion* II does not correspond very precisely to the content of that chapter. It states the main theme only, the development of which *begins* here. Furthermore, the new title of Chapter III does not mean that the theme stated in the title to Chapter II has already been completed; it only indicates that a new and important step in the investigation is being taken; the special form of existence of the "that than which a greater cannot be conceived" is introduced.

Thus, the last assumption of the Barthian interpretation is overturned. He considers the title "That God Truly Is" to be the thesis which *Proslogion* II means to prove, and for that reason finds this thesis proved in the concluding "therefore" of the chapter.[102] But if we break free from this assumption and consider the peculiar argumentation in the *Proslogion*, then it becomes clear that Anselm never thinks there of proving God's existence; he only wishes to deduce God's special way of being and so to take the first step to that end which the whole *Proslogion* seeks: the knowledge of the articles of faith about God and the immediate experience of God.

Many things must still be done for a complete realization of this interpretation. The problem of the fool and the controversy between Anselm and Gaunilo require a separate treatment. The theological ideas of the *Proslogion* must be pursued further. There remains to be investigated why Anselm wanted to attain to a vision and a mystical experience through a penetration into the dogmas about God's being and essence. The nature of Anselmian piety must be clarified here. Later it must be determined whether the *Proslogion* is original, or whether Anselm followed the example of some model, at least in the manner of his procedure. Yet the indications given above about the theology of the *Proslogion* and its structure and method will already have done enough in showing that *Proslogion* II-IV is to be trusted neither as philosophy nor as pure theology, but as a piece of mystical theology, in which we can find a proof for God's existence only if we forcibly separate parts of the work that belong together and place them by themselves outside their context.

[102] Barth, *op. cit.*, German p. 111, English p. 101.

PART II

The Argument in Recent Philosophy

PART

II

The Argument in Recent Philosophy

IX

John Hick

Introduction

This Introduction is designed for the users of this book who are not already familiar with the philosophical issues raised by the ontological argument, or with the history of the subject during the modern period of philosophy, which is generally regarded as beginning with the work of René Descartes in the seventeenth century. Any attempted contribution from the present writer to the still continuing discussion is reserved for the essay at the end of the volume.

Anselm's Argument: First Form

The story begins with Anselm and returns in its most recent phase (see pp. 301f.) to Anselm. The form of theistic proof or argument which has generally been discussed under the name of the ontological argument originates in Anselm's *Proslogion*, Chapter II. Anselm begins with the concept of God as "that than which no more perfect[1] can be conceived." Even the biblical "Fool" who says in his heart, "There is no God,"[2] possesses the idea of God, and the question is therefore whether that than which no more perfect can be conceived exists only in the mind (*in intellectu*) or both in the mind and in reality (*in intellectu et in re*). Anselm reasons

[1] Anselm usually says *maior*, greater; but it is clear that by "greater" he means "more perfect," and sometimes (e.g., *Proslogion* XIV and XVIII) he uses *melius*, "better."

[2] Psalms 14:1 and 53:1.

that that being than which no more perfect can be conceived *must* exist in reality, since if it existed only in the mind it would by this very fact be less than that than which no more perfect can be conceived. For we should then be able to conceive of something else yet more perfect—more perfect in that it exists in reality as well as in the mind. In that case we should have the impossible contradiction that there could be something more perfect than that than which no more perfect can be conceived! Hence, "that than which no more perfect can be conceived" must, and does, exist in reality.

DESCARTES:

At the close of the medieval period, René Descartes (1596-1650) restated the ontological argument in the form in which it has for the most part been discussed in the modern period.

Descartes' ontological argument starts from the definition of God as "a supremely perfect being" (*un être souverainement parfait*). This is not Anselm's definition, but nevertheless Descartes' argument is essentially the same as Anselm's in *Proslogion* II described above. For Descartes claims that, "It is certain that I no less find the idea of God, that is to say, the idea of a supremely perfect Being, in me, than that of any [geometrical] figure or [arithmetical] number whatever it is; and I do not know any less clearly and distinctly that an [actual and] eternal existence pertains to this nature than I know that all which I am able to demonstrate of some figure or number truly pertains to the nature of this figure and number . . ." For "existence can no more be separated from the essence [or definition] of God than can its having three angles equal to two right angles be separated from the essence of a [rectilinear] triangle, or the idea of a mountain from the idea of a valley; and so there is not any less repugnance to our conceiving a God (that is, a Being supremely perfect) to whom existence is lacking (that is to say, to whom a certain perfection is lacking), than to conceive of a mountain which has no valley."[3]

Descartes is thus explicitly treating existence as an attribute—an attribute which a supremely perfect being must have, since

[3] *Meditations*, V. Haldane and Ross, *The Philosophical Works of Descartes*, I (Cambridge: 1911), pp. 180-181.

without it any being would be less than perfect. Descartes himself presents his argument as turning upon this view of existence as a "perfection." He says that "whenever it happens that I think of a first and sovereign Being, and, so to speak, derive the idea of Him from the storehouse of my mind, it is necessary that I should attribute to Him every sort of perfection. . . . And this necessity suffices to make me conclude (after having recognized that existence is a perfection) that this first and sovereign Being really exists. . . ."[4]

The doctrine that existence is a predicable attribute enables Descartes to meet the objection that the various internal elements of the concept of God cannot guarantee that there is a real Being corresponding to this concept—or, in other words, that a Being such as we are obliged to conceive in this way actually exists. Descartes states and answers the objection as follows:

> But although I cannot really conceive of a God without existence any more than a mountain without a valley, still from the fact that I conceive of a mountain with a valley, it does not follow that there is such a mountain in the world; similarly, although I conceive of God as possessing existence, it would seem that it does not follow that there is a God which exists. . . . But a sophism is concealed in this objection; for from the fact that I cannot conceive a mountain without a valley, it does not follow that there is any mountain or any valley in existence, but only that the mountain and the valley, whether they exist or do not exist, cannot in any way be separated one from the other. While from the fact that I cannot conceive God without existence, it follows that existence is inseparable from Him, and hence that He really exists. . . [5]

Thus, given that existence is rightly regarded as an attribute which a particular kind of being may have or lack, and which a supremely perfect being must have, Descartes is able effectively to defend his ontological argument. However it is precisely the assumption that existence is an attribute or predicate that has been decisively questioned in the next phase of the discussions. Descartes' contemporary, Pierre Gassendi (1592-1655), urged that existence is something more fundamental than an attribute, since it is that apart from which there can be no attributes: "Existence is a perfection neither in God nor in anything else; it is rather that in the absence of which there is no perfection. This must be so if, indeed, that which does not exist has neither perfection nor imperfection, and that which exists and has various perfections, does not have its existence as a

[4] *Ibid.*, p. 182. [5] *Ibid.*, p. 181.

particular perfection and as one of the number of its perfections, but as that by means of which the thing itself equally with its perfections is in existence, and without which neither can be said to possess perfections, nor can perfections be said to be possessed by it. Hence, neither is existence held to exist in a thing in the way that perfections do, nor if the thing lacks existence is it said to be imperfect (or deprived of a perfection), so much as to be nothing."[6]

KANT:

This challenge to a fundamental presupposition of the Cartesian proof was more fully developed by Immanuel Kant (1724-1804) in his famous critique of the ontological argument, a critique which on account of its great force and clarity has ever since tended to dominate the discussion of the matter.[7]

Kant makes two main points. The first grants that there is an analytic or necessary connection between the idea of God and the idea of existence, such that it would be contradictory to affirm the former without the latter: A "God" who does not exist would not be God. But, says Kant, "if we reject subject ['God'] and predicate ['exists'] alike, there is no contradiction; for nothing is then left that can be contradicted. To posit a triangle, and yet to reject its three angles, is self-contradictory; but there is no contradiction in rejecting the triangle together with its three angles. The same holds true of the concept of an absolutely necessary being. If its existence is rejected, we reject the thing with all its predicates; and no question of contradiction can then arise."[8]

This argument already contains implicitly the view that existence is not a "real predicate," i.e., cannot properly appear as part of the definition of a specific kind of being. This contention is made explicit in Kant's second main point, that the function of the word "exists" is not to add a new element to a concept but to posit, or affirm, a reality corresponding to the concept. Says Kant:

"*Being*" is obviously not a real predicate; that is, it is not a concept of

[6] Haldane and Ross, *op. cit.*, II, p. 186.

[7] Between Gassendi and Kant the Scottish philosopher David Hume had made the same point in his *Treatise of Human Nature* (1739), Book I, Part III, sect. vii.

[8] B 622-623. (Kemp Smith's translation.)

something which could be added to the concept of a thing. It is merely the positing of a thing, or of certain determinations, as existing in themselves. Logically, it is merely the copula of a judgement. The proposition, "God is omnipotent," contains two concepts, each of which has its object—God and omnipotence. The small word "is" adds no new predicate, but only serves to posit the predicate *in its relation* to the subject. If, now, we take the subject (God) with all its predicates (among which is omnipotence), and say "God is," or "There is a God," we attach no new predicate to the concept of God, but only posit the subject itself with all its predicates, and indeed posit it as being an *object* that stands in relation to my *concept*.[9]

RUSSELL:

This second point has been definitively formulated in the present century by Bertrand Russell in the well-known analysis of the word "exists" which arises from his theory of descriptions.[10] This shows that the question "Does x exist?" does not imply that in some prior sense the x of which we speak is, or subsists, or has being; and from this it follows that the assertion that x exists is not an attribution to a subsisting x of the further characteristic of existence. It is rather the assertion, with regard to a certain description (or name as standing for a description) that this description has a referent. Thus, "horses exist" has the logical structure: "There are x's such that 'x is a horse' is sometimes true." This analysis exorcizes the puzzle which has tended since the time of Plato to haunt negative existential propositions. "Unicorns do not exist" does not entail that unicorns must first in some mysterious sense *be* in order that we may then say of them that they do not exist; it means simply that "there are no x's such that 'x is a unicorn' is true." And "God exists" means, "there is one (and only one) x such that 'x is omnipotent, etc.' is true." This Russellian analysis makes it clear that the logical structure of propositions asserting existence is such that they cannot be true by definition, nor therefore by a priori necessity.

[9] B 626-627.

[10] *Principia Mathematica*, I (Cambridge, 1910), Introduction, ch. 1, and Part I, Section B, p. 14; "The Philosophy of Logical Atomism," 1918, V and VI, in *Logic and Knowledge*, ed. by R. C. Marsh (London, 1956); *Introduction to Mathematical Philosophy*, (London; 1920), ch. 16; *History of Western Philosophy* (London, 1946), pp. 859-860.

In effect Russell qualifies Kant's teaching that existence is not a real predicate, for he treats existence as a property, although only of propositional functions; and other logicians have argued that "exists" is a predicate, but a redundant one.[11] Further, some aspects of Kant's argument against the view that existence is a real predicate have been criticized (e.g., in the paper reprinted here by Jerome Shaffer);[12] but the criticisms that have been made do not affect Kant's central contention that the question whether a concept, even with "existence" as a component, applies to anything outside our minds, cannot be settled a priori. As Shaffer says, " 'Particulars exist,' when asserted tautologically, is used to make a claim about the meaning of the word 'particulars' and therefore cannot be used to make a claim about the extension of the term. Similarly, if someone uses the sentence, 'God exists,' tautologically, he tells us only that being an existent is a logical requirement for being God. If, on the other hand, someone asserts, 'God exists,' nontautologically, then he claims that the term 'God' has extension, applies to some existent. In the case of the Ontological Argument the only valid conclusion is an intensional statement about the meaning of the concept of God."[13]

Again, in qualification of the general statement that existence is not a predicate, various kinds of sentences have been offered in which it seems more natural to regard "exists" as a predicate than to insist that it is not, e.g.:

(1) "This (apparent) table exists (i.e., it is real rather than hallucinatory).[14]

(2) "President Johnson exists (i.e., is now alive), but President Lincoln does not."[15]

However, these special uses do not support the ontological argument. For God is not there asserted to exist as a real in distinction from a hallucinatory material object, nor as a living in distinction from a deceased man. The basic Kantian and Russellian thesis stands that

[11] G. Nakhnikian and W. Salmon, " 'Exists' as a Predicate" in *The Philosophical Review*, LXVI, 4 (October 1957).

[12] See also William Alston, "The Ontological Argument Revisited," in *The Philosophical Review*, LXIX, 4 (October 1960).

[13] Pp. 242-243.

[14] Cf. G. E. Moore, "Is Existence a Predicate?" in *Philosophical Papers*, pp. 124-126.

[15] Cf. P. Geach, "Form and Existence," in *Proceedings of the Aristotelian Society*, 1954-1955, pp. 262-268.

it is not possible so to form the concept of *x*, or so to define the term *x*, as to guarantee a priori that an *x* exists in the world outside our minds.

Thus, the general outcome of the kind of discussion represented here by the papers of Russell, Ryle and Shaffer has been to confirm Kant's central criticism of the Cartesian ontological argument, namely that one cannot deduce real existence from a concept, while at the same time suggesting caution concerning the over-simple formula that "Existence is not a predicate" into which Kant's critique has sometimes been compressed.

The Hegelian Use of the Argument

As a separate development, claiming to be immune to the Kantian type of criticism, G. W. F. Hegel (1770-1831) restated the ontological argument in a manner radically different from that of Anselm (either first or second form) and Descartes. Hegel's own discussions of the ontological argument[16] are brief and leave room for varying interpretations. The basic thought, however, of all Hegelian and Idealist uses of the argument is that God, conceived as the Absolute or the Whole, is presupposed in all rational thinking. To think rationally is by implication to affirm the existence of God, and the ontological argument simply brings explicitly to our attention this necessity of our thought.

It may be useful at this point to quote from the treatment of the argument by a leading Hegelian philosopher writing at the end of the nineteenth century, when Hegelian Idealism was still in its heyday. Edward Caird speaks of "the general truth, that the consciousness of God is not separable from but presupposed in the consciousness of self," and continues:

> And it leads to a new view of the ontological argument. The thought of God ceases to be regarded as simply one among many other thoughts we *may* have, and becomes the idea of the unity which is presupposed in all our consciousness of the particular existence either of ourselves or of anything else, an idea which in some form or other we *must* have. The

[16] *Lectures on the Philosophy of Religion*, Appendix: "Proof of the Existence of God"; *Encyclopedia, Logic*, para. 51; *Lectures on the History of Philosophy*, Part II, Section II.

argument, therefore, according to this interpretation of it, is not from an idea viewed as a subjective state of the individual mind to an object corresponding to it; but rather the idea of God, by its priority to all distinction of objectivity and subjectivity, is to be regarded as at once the principle of being and of knowledge, and therefore at once objective and subjective. For, if we know all things, and especially the subject as opposed to the object, and the object as opposed to the subject, by the differentiation of a presupposed unity, it becomes absurd to treat this presupposed unity as itself a special phase of the subject. This, no doubt alters the form of the argument—as an argument from an idea in our minds to something out of our minds, an argument presupposing the absoluteness of the very distinction which by means of the idea of God it seeks to reduce to something relative, and therefore makes the conclusion the direct negation of of the premises. Rather, we are now bound to say, the division of subject and object, as a division in our consciousness, is possible only on the presupposition of a unity which is beyond the division and which manifests itself in it.[17]

Thus, according to Caird, "to say *that* God *is*, is to say that there is a principle of unity without relation to which we cannot finally comprehend anything."[18] R. G. Collingwood's version of the argument,[19] and that of Professor E. E. Harris (reprinted below) offered in the course of his defense of Collingwood, fall within this same tradition; and some of the philosophical hazards to which a Hegelian ontological argument is exposed are very clearly pointed out in the two papers by Professor Ryle which are also reprinted below.

The line of thought which is here termed Hegelian can be traced back beyond the German Idealists to embrace such mystics as Meister Eckhart and then back through Anselm to Augustine, and farther back through Neoplatonism to its source in Plato himself. A distinguished contemporary representative of this tradition, Paul Tillich, says, "The Augustinian tradition can rightly be called mystical, if mysticism is defined as the experience of the identity of subject and object in relation to Being itself . . . . On this basis the ontological argument for the existence of God must be understood. It is neither an argument, nor does it deal with the existence of God, although it has often been expressed in this form. It is rather the

[17] Edward Caird, "Anselm's Argument for the Being of God," in *The Journal of Theological Studies*, I, 1 (October 1899), p. 31.

[18] *Ibid.*, p. 35.

[19] R. G. Collingwood, *Philosophical Method* (Oxford; 1933), Ch. VI, Sec. 2.

rational description of the relation of our mind to Being as such. Our mind implies *principia per se nota* which have immediate evidence whenever they are noticed: the transcendentalia, *esse, verum, bonum.* They constitute the Absolute in which the difference between knowing and known is not actual. This Absolute as the principle of Being has absolute certainty. It is a necessary thought because it is the presupposition of all thought."[20]

There are affinities between the Hegelian use of the ontological argument and that found in recent French "reflexive" philosophy, on which an article is included below. Members of this movement identify philosophy with the mind's reflexive consideration of itself while in the process of thinking. They discover by this method that the human consciousness has a dynamism which aspires to the universal and absolute. It is constantly reaching for a good beyond what it already enjoys and for a truth beyond what it already knows. Through Blondel's reflexive study of our self-consciousness, they find that this dynamism is present in every individual mental act. In other words, according to this school, the human mind is informed by the idea of the perfection which is God. They do not consider this an idea in the sense of a mental representation of something "out there." In their view the absolute stands rather as the origin of the mind's inner activity, and is responsible for the fact that the mind always reaches not only toward, but also beyond, the objective data that actually confront it. For reflexive philosophy the idea of God is simply the mind's awareness that its inner life is grounded in the absolute; and one of the chief concerns of the reflexive philosophers has been to justify this movement from thought, as we know it within ourselves, to the affirmation of the absolute, as the hidden principle of our thought.

In the ontological argument they find this justification. For the argument makes explicit the peculiar relation between my acts of thinking and the idea of God which works in me and which moves me to perform these acts. Since this "idea" designates the source of my every thought, it is the idea of that which my mind cannot place over against itself, cannot represent to itself, cannot surpass and therefore cannot question or deny. The proof simply argues that the idea of God cannot arise from some act of my thinking and so have the possibility of being untrue, since it is the

[20] Paul Tillich, "The Two Types of Philosophy of Religion," in *Theology of Culture* (New York: 1959), pp. 14-15.

ground within me of all my acts of thinking. In other words, it is impossible for human thinking to deny the reality of that which is its inner source.

Anselm's Argument: Second Form

Karl Barth, in his famous study of Anselm, pointed out that the argument in *Proslogion* III and in Anselm's reply to Gaunilo is either a different argument, or at least a different form or phase of the argument, from that in *Proslogion* II. The distinction between the two pieces of reasoning has since been emphasized by Charles Hartshorne and Norman Malcolm, who both contend that while the former argument is invalid, essentially for the reason stated by Kant, the latter is valid. As a result of the work of these men, it can no longer be overlooked (as it has been in so much of the literature) that there are two significantly different forms of the Anselmic argument, of which the second is the more subtle and perhaps the more persuasive.

The difference between the two forms of the argument hinges upon the notion of necessary existence. The proof in its first form claims that the most perfect conceivable being must have the attribute of *existence*; and in the second form, that such a being must have the attribute of *necessary existence.*

The newly emphasized "second form" of the argument raises difficult and complex philosophical issues which cannot be treated in this Introduction. The rediscovery of this second form represents the "growing edge" of the subject today, and the reader will find a fairly full, although still inconclusive, coverage of it in the last section of the present volume.

A. Is Existence a Predicate?

X

BERTRAND RUSSELL

General Propositions and Existence*

I AM going to speak today about general propositions and existence. The two subjects really belong together; they are the same topic, although it might not have seemed so at the first glance. The propositions and facts that I have been talking about hitherto have all been such as involved perfectly definite particulars, or relations, or qualities, or things of that sort, never involved the sort of indefinite things one alludes to by such words as "all," "some," "a," "any," and it is propositions and facts of that sort that I am coming on to today.

Really all the propositions of the sort that I mean to talk of today collect themselves into two groups—the first that are about "all," and the second that are about "some." These two sorts belong together; they are each other's negations. If you say, for instance, "All men are mortal," that is the negative of "Some men are not mortal." In regard to general propositions, the distinction of affirmative and negative is arbitrary. Whether you are going to regard the propositions about "all" as the affirmative ones and the propositions about "some" as the negative ones, or vice versa, is purely a matter of taste. For example, if I say "I met no one as I came along," that, on the face of it, you would think is a negative proposition. Of course, that is really a proposition about "all," i.e., "All men are among

* From "The Philosophy of Logical Atomism" (1918), Section V. Bertrand Russell, *Logic and Knowledge*, ed. by Robert Charles Marsh (London: George Allen and Unwin, Ltd., 1956), pp. 228-234. Reprinted with permission.

those whom I did not meet." If, on the other hand, I say "I met a man as I came along," that would strike you as affirmative, whereas it is the negative of "All men are among those I did not meet as I came along." If you consider such propositions as "All men are mortal" and "Some men are not mortal," you might say it was more natural to take the general propositions as the affirmative and the existence-propositions as the negative, but, simply because it is quite arbitrary which one is to choose, it is better to forget these words and to speak only of general propositions and propositions asserting existence. All general propositions deny the existence of something or other. If you say "All men are mortal," that denies the existence of an immortal man, and so on.

I want to say emphatically that general propositions are to be interpreted as not involving existence. When I say, for instance, "All Greeks are men," I do not want you to suppose that that implies that there are Greeks. It is to be considered emphatically as not implying that. That would have to be added as a separate proposition. If you want to interpret it in that sense, you will have to add the further statement "and there are Greeks." That is for purposes of practical convenience. If you include the fact that there are Greeks, you are rolling two propositions into one, and it causes unnecessary confusion in your logic, because the sorts of propositions that you want are those that do assert the existence of something and general propositions which do not assert existence. If it happened that there were no Greeks, both the proposition that "All Greeks are men" and the proposition that "No Greeks are men" would be true. The proposition "No Greeks are men" is, of course, the proposition "All Greeks are not-men." Both propositions will be true simultaneously if it happens that there are no Greeks. All statements about all the members of a class that has no members are true, because the contradictory of any general statement does assert existence and is therefore false in this case. This notion, of course, of general propositions not involving existence is one which is not in the traditional doctrine of the syllogism. In the traditional doctrine of the syllogism, it was assumed that when you have such a statement as "All Greeks are men," that implies that there are Greeks, and this produced fallacies. For instance, "All chimeras are animals, and all chimeras breathe flame, therefore, some animals breathe flame." This is a syllogism in Darapti, but that mood of the syllogism is fallacious, as this instance shows. That was a point, by the way, which had a certain historical interest, because it impeded Leibnitz in his attempts to construct a mathematical logic. He was always engaged in trying to construct such a mathematical logic as we have now, or rather such a one as Boole constructed, and he was always failing because of his respect for Aristotle. Whenever he invented a really good system, as he did several times, it always brought out that such moods as Darapti are fallacious. If you say "All *A* is *B* and all *A* is *C*, therefore, some *B* is *C*"—if you say this you incur a fallacy, but he could not bring himself to believe that it was fallacious, so he began again. That shows you that you should not have too much respect for distinguished men.[1]

Now when you come to ask what really is asserted in a general proposition, such as "All Greeks are men," for instance, you find that what is asserted is the truth of all values of what I call a propositional function. A *propositional function* is simply *any expression containing an undetermined constituent, or several undetermined constituents, and becoming a proposition as soon as the undetermined constituents are determined.* If I say, "*x* is a man" or "*n* is a number," that is a propositional function; so is any formula of algebra, say $(x+y)(x-y) = x^2-y^2$. A propositional function is nothing, but, like most of the things one wants to talk about in logic, it does not lose its importance through that fact. The only thing really that you can do with a propositional function is to assert either that it is always true, or that it is sometimes true, or that it is never true. If you take:

If *x* is a man, *x* is mortal,

that is always true (just as much when *x* is not a man as when *x* is a man); if you take:

x is a man,

that is sometimes true; if you take:

x is a unicorn,

that is never true.

One may call a propositional function

necessary, when it is always true;
possible, when it is sometimes true;
impossible, when it is never true.

[1] Cf. Couturat, *La logique de Leibniz.*

Much false philosophy has arisen out of confusing propositional functions and propositions. There is a great deal in ordinary traditional philosophy which consists simply in attributing to propositions the predicates which only apply to propositional functions, and, still worse, sometimes in attributing to individuals predicates which merely apply to propositional functions. This case of *necessary, possible, impossible* is a case in point. In all traditional philosophy there comes a heading of "modality," which discusses *necessary, possible* and *impossible* as properties of propositions, whereas in fact they are properties of propositional functions. Propositions are only true or false.

If you take "x is x," that is a propositional function which is true whatever x may be, i.e., a necessary propositional function. If you take "x is a man," that is a possible one. If you take "x is a unicorn," that is an impossible one.

Propositions can only be true or false, but propositional functions have these three possibilities. It is important, I think, to realize that the whole doctrine of modality only applies to propositional functions, not to propositions.

Propositional functions are involved in ordinary language in a great many cases where one does not usually realize them. In such a statement as "I met a man," you can understand my statement perfectly well without knowing whom I met, and the actual person is not a constituent of the proposition. You are really asserting there that a certain propositional function is sometimes true, namely the propositional function "I met x and x is human." There is at least one value of x for which that is true, and that therefore is a possible propositional function. Whenever you get such words as "a," "some," "all," "every," it is always a mark of the presence of a propositional function, so that these things are not, so to speak, remote or recondite: They are obvious and familiar.

A propositional function comes in again in such a statement as "Socrates is mortal," because "to be mortal" means "to die at some time or other." You mean there is a time at which Socrates dies, and that again involves a propositional function, namely, that t is a time, and Socrates dies at t is possible. If you say "Socrates is immortal," that also will involve a propositional function. That means that "If t is any time whatever, Socrates is alive at time t," if we take immortality as involving existence throughout the whole of the past as well as throughout the whole of the future. But if we take immortality as only involving existence throughout the whole of the future, the interpretation of "Socrates is immortal" becomes more complete, viz, "There is a time *t*, such that if t^1 is any time later than *t*, Socrates is alive at t^1." Thus, when you come to write out properly what one means by a great many ordinary statements, it turns out a little complicated. "Socrates is mortal" and "Socrates is immortal" are not each other's contradictories, because they both imply that Socrates exists in time; otherwise he would not be either mortal or immortal. One says, "There is a time at which he dies," and the other says, "Whatever time you take, he is alive at that time," whereas the contradictory of "Socrates is mortal" would be true if there is not a time at which he lives.

An undetermined constituent in a propositional function is called a variable.

EXISTENCE

When you take any propositional function and assert of it that it is possible, that it is sometimes true, that gives you the fundamental meaning of "existence." You may express it by saying that there is at least one value of *x* for which that propositional function is true. Take "*x* is a man." There is at least one value of *x* for which this is true. That is what one means by saying that "There are men," or that "Men exist." Existence is essentially a property of a propositional function. It means that that propositional function is true in at least one instance. If you say "There are unicorns," that will mean that "There is an *x*, such that *x* is a unicorn." That is written in phrasing which is unduly approximated to ordinary language, but the proper way to put it would be "(*x* is a unicorn) is possible." We have got to have some idea that we do not define, and one takes the idea of "always true," or of "sometimes true," as one's undefined idea in this matter, and then you can define the other one as the negative of that. In some ways it is better to take them both as undefined, for reasons which I shall not go into at present. It will be out of this notion of *sometimes*, which is the same as the notion of *possible*, that we get the notion of existence. To say that unicorns exist is simply to say that "(*x* is a unicorn) is possible".

It is perfectly clear that when you say "Unicorns exist," you are not saying anything that would apply to any unicorns there might happen to be, because as a matter of fact there are not any, and therefore, if what you say had any application to the actual individuals, it could not possibly be significant unless it were true. You can consider the proposition "Unicorns exist" and can see that it is false. It is not nonsense. Of course, if the proposition went through the general conception of the unicorn to the individual, it could not be even significant unless there were unicorns. Therefore, when you say "Unicorns exist," you are not saying anything about any individual things, and the same applies when you say "Men exist." If you say that "Men exist, and Socrates is a man, therefore, Socrates exists," that is exactly the same sort of fallacy as it would be if you said "Men are numerous, Socrates is a man, therefore, Socrates is numerous," because existence is a predicate of a propositional function, or derivatively of a class. When you say of a propositional function that it is numerous, you will mean that there are several values of x that will satisfy it, that there are more than one; or, if you like to take "numerous" in a larger sense, more than ten, more than twenty, or whatever number you think fitting. If x, y and z all satisfy a propositional function, you may say that that proposition is numerous, but x, y and z severally are not numerous. Exactly the same applies to existence, that is to say that the actual things that there are in the world do not exist, or, at least, that is putting it too strongly, because that is utter nonsense. To say that they do not exist is strictly nonsense, but to say that they do exist is also strictly nonsense.

It is of propositional functions that you can assert or deny existence. You must not run away with the idea that this entails consequences that it does not entail. If I say "The things that there are in the world exist", that is a perfectly correct statement, because I am there saying something about a certain class of things; I say it in the same sense in which I say "Men exist." But I must not go on to "This is a thing in the world, and therefore, this exists." It is there that the fallacy comes in, and it is simply, as you see, a fallacy of transferring to the individual that satisfies a propositional function a predicate which only applies to a propositional function. You can see this in various ways. For instance, you sometimes know the truth of an existence-proposition without knowing any instance of it. You know that there are people in Timbuctoo, but I doubt if any of you could give me an instance of one. Therefore, you clearly can know existence-propositions without knowing any individual that makes them true. Existence-propositions do not say anything about the actual individual but only about the class or function.

It is exceedingly difficult to make this point clear as long as one adheres to ordinary language, because ordinary language is rooted in a certain feeling about logic, a certain feeling that our primeval ancestors had, and as long as you keep to ordinary language, you find it very difficult to get away from the bias which is imposed upon you by language. When I say, e.g., "There is an x such that x is a man," that is not the sort of phrase one would like to use. "There is an x" is meaningless. What is "an x" anyhow? There is not such a thing. The only way you can really state it correctly is by inventing a new language *ad hoc*, and making the statement apply straight off to "x is a man," as when one says "(x is a man) is possible," or invent a special symbol for the statement that "x is a man" is sometimes true.

I have dwelt on this point because it really is of very fundamental importance. I shall come back to existence in my next lecture: existence as it applies to descriptions, which is a slightly more complicated case than I am discussing here. I think an almost unbelievable amount of false philosophy has arisen through not realizing what "existence" means.

XI

JEROME SHAFFER

Existence, Predication and the Ontological Argument*

HUME said, "There is no being . . . whose nonexistence implies a contradiction,"[1] and Kant said, "The predicate of existence can . . . be rejected without contradiction."[2] In making these claims, Hume and Kant intended to bring out a peculiarity in assertions of existence, for they both would admit that assertions that something was (or was not) for example, round might turn out to be self-contradictory, whereas assertions that something exists (or does not exist) could never turn out to be self-contradictory. Now if this is a genuine peculiarity of assertions of existence, then it follows that any proof that something exists because its nonexistence implies a contradiction will be invalid.

A famous example of an argument which purports to prove the existence of something by showing that its nonexistence implies a contradiction is the Ontological Argument, which purports to show that it follows from a particular concept of God that such a being exists, and therefore that the assertion of the nonexistence of God is self-contradictory. Most philosophers have agreed with Hume and Kant that the Ontological Argument is invalid, although it has recently been defended.[3] My own view is that the argument is basically unsound, but I find the standard criticisms totally unconvincing. In

* From *Mind*, Vol. LXXI, N.S., No. 283, July 1962. Reprinted with permission.

[1] *Dialogues Concerning Natural Religion*, Part IX.

[2] *Critique of Pure Reason*, transl. by Norman Kemp Smith (Macmillan, 1953), p. 504.

[3] Norman Malcolm, "Anselm's Ontological Arguments," Ch. XVI in the present volume.

this paper I shall show what I take to be the faults in the standard criticisms and then go on to show what I take to be the proper criticism of the argument.

The many versions of the Ontological Argument have in common the following feature: a definition of "God" is given from which, by the use of certain premises, the conclusion, "God exists," is deduced. The Ontological Argument has frequently been attacked by casting doubt upon the acceptability of these premises. I wish to avoid such controversies. I am interested in the move from a definition to an existential statement. Therefore, I shall use an argument which brings attention to bear just on that move. This will be the specimen under discussion:

> Let the expression, "God" mean "an almighty being who exists and is eternal." Therefore, "God is an almighty being who exists and is eternal" is true by definition, and that entails "God exists."

This argument purports to demonstrate that "God exists" is a tautology, true by definition. It is not necessary to show that the expression "God" really does mean what it is here defined to mean, for the definition is purely stipulative. But given that meaning, it is argued, anyone who denies that God, in the sense laid down, exists has contradicted himself. Only the laws of logic are required to show that he has contradicted himself.

The following short objections to this argument will not do. (1) The question is begged from the start by using a proper name, "God." No, for "God" is not used here as a logically proper name. I have simply introduced an expression into discourse, an expression which is, grammatically, a proper noun. (2) Even if we grant the conclusion "God exists," that does not imply that there is a God or that something is a God. Why not? In ordinary discourse the expressions are used interchangeably in most contexts. It must be shown, if it is true, that the implication does not hold here. (3) Tautologies only tell us about our use of language, about the meanings of our terms, not about what actually is the case. This objection begs the question. Proponents of the argument claim that there is a tautology which tells us about what actually is the case, namely that God exists. (4) But then with suitable definitions we could "prove" the existence of a number of things which we know perfectly well do not exist. No, for the things we know not to exist would necessarily be different from the things picked out by our definitions. (5) The argument involves a *non sequitur*, for the premise is about a *word* but the conclusion is about something different, a *thing*. No, the definition of the word allows us to prove, by substitution, that the conclusion is a tautology.

The traditional attack on the Ontological Argument consists in trying to show that the definition is inadmissible because it is ill-formed. Kant argued that definitions can consist only of strings of predicates, and since "exists" is not a predicate it cannot be a part of the definition. Others have argued that "exists" is a purely formal element, present in any definition of a thing, and therefore could not be used to show that some particular thing exists as opposed to anything else. I shall, in Part I, discuss these arguments in detail and show that none of them succeeds in establishing any impropriety in the definition of "God" I have proposed. In Part II, I shall show that the argument, although formally correct, does not do what the religious expect it to do. The agnostic will still be able to raise his doubt, and the atheist will still be able to affirm his disbelief, no contradiction arising in either case, even if each accepts the specimen argument under consideration.

I

" 'EXISTS' IS NOT A PREDICATE"

The Ontological Argument purports to show that God must exist because the condition that He exists is a part of the definition of the kind of thing He is. Kant argued that it could not be the case that existence was a defining feature of God or of anything else, because "exists" is not, as he put it (p. 504), a "real" or "determining" predicate (he admitted that, grammatically, "exists" is a predicate).

What is a "real" predicate? Kant defines it as something "which is added to the concept of the subject and enlarges it" (*ibid.*). This is a most unfortunate definition for Kant to use, however, since it leads to contradiction with another important doctrine of his, that *existential propositions are always synthetic* (*ibid.*). Synthetic judgments are those which "add to the concept of the subject a predicate which has not been in anywise thought in it" (p. 48), and if existential judgments are always synthetic, then "exists" must be a predicate which adds to the concept of the subject, in short, a "real" predicate as defined above. But even without the difficulties this definition of "real" predicate raises within the Kantian system, it is not a very helpful definition, for it represents predicating something of a subject as *revising the concept* of the subject (by enlarging that concept), something only philosophers of a Reconstructionist bent do very often. But I shall say more of Kant's misrepresentation of predication below.

What argument does Kant give for holding that "exists" is not a "real" predicate, that is, not a predicate which adds something to the concept of the subject? He argues that if "exists" were a real predicate, then in asserting that something exists, we would be altering our concept of that something, thereby ending up with a different concept from the one we started with. Since we now have a new and different concept, we will have failed to assert existence of the original subject. Thus, if "exists" were a predicate, "we could not, therefore, say that the exact object of my concept exists" (p. 505). But since we obviously can say that, we cannot be adding anything to the concept of the subject when we say that the subject exists, and therefore "exists" cannot be a real predicate.

It is astonishing that this argument has stood up for so long and is still commended by philosophers, *e.g.*, by Malcolm (p. 304 below). For the argument, if sound, shows that nothing could be a real predicate. Suppose I wish to say that something is red, where "red" is intended as a real predicate. In asserting that the thing is red, I would be adding to my concept of the thing, and hence would be unable to say that the object as originally conceived is red, that "the exact object of my concept" is red. The argument which shows that "exists" is not a "real" predicate also shows that nothing could be one.

The difficulty here lies in an incomplete picture of predication. Kant seems to think that when I say that so-and-so is such-and-such, I must be doing one of two things: Either I am extracting the concept of such-and-such from the concept of so-and-so (an analytic judgment) or else I am revising my concept of so-and-so by adding to it the concept of such-and-such (a synthetic judgment). Now which of these two things am I doing when I say that so-and-so exists? Noticing that existential propositions are often justified by an appeal to experience (p. 506), Kant decides that they cannot be cases of extracting the concept of existence from the concept of the subject. So they must be cases of revising concepts; thus, "all existential propositions are synthetic." But this really will not do either, since to revise one's concept of the subject is simply to change the subject of the proposition. Hence, in other places Kant concludes that "exists" is not a predicate at all. Kant's vacillation here comes from an overly narrow account of predication. To say that so-and-so is such-and-such is sometimes neither to analyze the concept of so-and-so nor to revise it, but, to put it roughly, to say something about the object conceived of. This use of language is obviously not peculiar to existential propositions. The sentence "Crows are black" may be used to express a proposition not about the concept of crows but about crows, and when so used would create as much difficulty for Kant, given his account of predication, as "Crows exist." There may well be important differences between ". . . are black" and ". . . exist," but Kant fails to bring them out by this line of argument.

Philosophers have tried to express what they took to be the truth in Kant's claim that "exists" is not a real predicate without appeal to that obscure notion of a real predicate. For example, Malcolm restates Kant's argument in this way:

> Suppose that two royal councillors, A and B, were asked to draw up separately descriptions of the most perfect chancellor they could conceive, and that the descriptions they produced were identical except that A included existence in his list of attributes of a perfect chancellor and B did not. (I do not mean that B put nonexistence in his list.) One and the same person could satisfy both descriptions. More to the point, any person who satisfied A's description would *necessarily* satisfy B's description and vice versa (p. 304 below).

While Malcolm admits that this is not a "rigorous" argument, and "leave(s) the matter at the more or less intuitive level," he thinks it does show that "exists" is very different in character from the expressions which go to make up a description or list of attributes of something. But I cannot see how it goes to show that at all. For it seems to me false that any person who satisfies B's description necessarily satisfies A's. Could not a nonexistent person, say Merlin, satisfy B's description but not A's? It cannot be said that Merlin fails to satisfy B's description (B might have had Merlin in mind when he drew up the list), unless the notion of *satisfying a description* is such that only real things, existent beings, can be said to satisfy a description. But if one uses this rather technical notion, the argument loses its intuitive appeal.

SUBJECT-PREDICATE STATEMENTS AS REALLY HYPOTHETICALS

Some philosophers have attempted to bring out the special feature of "exists" which debars it from appearing in a definition in the following way. It we take "Crows are black" as a typical affirmative subject-predicate statement and "Crows are not black" as a typical negative one, then they would claim that the affirmative statement is equivalent to the hypothetical, "If there exists anything which is a crow, then that thing is black," and the negative statement is equivalent to the hypothetical, "If there exists anything which is a crow, then that thing is not black." Now if we hold that existential statements are of the same form then "Crows exist" would be equivalent to "If there exists anything which is a crow, then that thing exists," and "Crows do not exist" would be equivalent to "If there exists anything which is a crow, then that thing does not exist." But the former hypothetical is a tautology whereas "Crows exist" obviously is not a tautology, and the latter hypothetical is not readily intelligible whereas "Crows do not exist" is perfectly clear. Therefore, it is most implausible to claim that existential statements are of the same form as the typical subject predicate statements, that is, implausible to construe "exists" as a predicate.

I do not find this argument very compelling. It is a mistake to think that the hypothetical expresses the meaning of the typical subject-predicate statement. Notice that the hypothetical must be put in the form, "If *there exists* anything which is . . . ." If we allow the antecedent clause to range over nonexistent as well as existent things, then the hypothetical, "If anything is . . . , then it exists," is not tautological and the hypothetical, "If anything is . . . , then it does not exist," is perfectly clear. And therefore the main reason for saying they cannot be equivalent to categorical existential statements has disappeared. But if we take the antecedent in the strong existential sense, then the claim that such hypotheticals express the meaning of subject-predicate statements breaks down. Consider the following subject-predicate statement: "Unicorns are proper subject-matter for mythologists." It is not equivalent to "If there exists anything which is a unicorn, then that thing is proper subject matter for mythologists," for the former is true but the latter is false. On the other hand, "Unicorns are proper subject matter for zoologists" is false but "If there exists anything which is a unicorn, then it is proper subject matter for zoologists" is true. And these are not just odd cases. There are many other things which it would be true to say of unicorns, if they existed, *e.g.*, that they would obey the laws of physics, be sought after by zoos, be mentioned in books which describe the species of animals, etc., but which are not true of them since they do not exist; and there would be many things which it would be false to say of them if they existed but which are not false since they do not exist. So the purported equivalence of subject-predicate statements to hypotheticals does not hold. The reason is evident enough. If a thing exists, then given the way the world is, it will have certain features and lack others, so to say something about a thing is not the same as to say what the thing would be like if it existed. Of course, a thing keeps its defining characteristics whether it exists or not, so analytic subject-predicate statements will entail analytic hypotheticals, but in general the equivalence does not hold. Nor does it hold if we understand the hypothetical as that of material implication, for "Unicorns do not have horns" is false but the parallel hypothetical, "If there exists anything which is a unicorn, then it does not have a horn," is true if taken materially, which shows that they cannot be equivalent.

Since it is a popular view that subject-predicate statements are equivalent to hypotheticals, it is important to see how someone might come to such a view. One way would be through the Kantian restriction of subject-predicate statements to statements about the *concept* of the subject. If this were correct, then the kind of counter-example I used, where the thing referred to by the concept turns out, given the nature of the world, to have some feature could not arise. All subject-predicate statements would be tautologous, either by analysis of the concept of the subject or by revision of the concept of the subject, and in this limited case the equivalence would hold.

But there is a line of argument more plausible to the modern mind which would yield the same result. Suppose one thought that for a series of words to express a meaningful subject-predicate statement, the grammatical subject must refer to some existent or set of existents. Then there would be no difference between attributing a property to a thing and attributing a property to the thing if it exists. Again my counter-examples could not arise. And philosophers have held such a view. Ryle once said:

How can we make propositions about Mr. Pickwick or sea-serpents, given that they do not exist? We cannot. For a proposition is only about something when something in fact answers to the designation in it. And nothing answers to the pseudo-designation "Mr. Pickwick" or "those sea-serpents."[4]

And Broad holds, "*Dragons do not exist* . . . cannot be about dragons; for there will be no such things as dragons for it to be about."[5] Since such propositions are not meaningless, they must be about something, however, and philosophers of this persuasion have offered various candidates for the subject of statements about nonexistents, urging that they are really about beliefs, books, paintings, propositional functions, properties, inscriptions, or storytellers.

I do not see why statements cannot be made about nonexistents. We can dream about them, think about them, and describe them, just as we can wait for them, hope to have them and look for them. We can mention them, allude to or direct attention to them and make reference to them. One thing we cannot do, of course, is to *point* to them, and someone who thinks of mentioning, alluding or referring as a substitute for pointing will be puzzled as to how we can point to what does not exist. But if we have not fallen prey to this overly narrow conception of what it is to mention something, then we will not be puzzled about how we can mention something nonexistent.

The most modest proposal along this line is that of Strawson, who abandoned his earlier position that the use of a referring expression in cases where the object referred to is nonexistent is "a spurious use"[6] in which we either "pretend to refer, in make-believe or in fiction, or mistakenly think we are referring when we are not referring to anything" (p. 40). His modified view is that the "primary" use of referring expressions occurs when the speaker believes the expression to refer to some existent, but that such expressions may be used to "refer in secondary ways, as in make-believe or in fiction."[7] But I take it that Strawson would still wish to say that un-

[4] G. Ryle, "Imaginary Objects," in *Aristotelian Society*, Supplementary Volume XII, 1933, p. 27.

[5] C. D. Broad, *Religion, Philosophy, and Psychical Research* (New York, 1953), p. 182.

[6] P. F. Strawson, "On Referring," reprinted in *Essays in Conceptual Analysis*, ed. by A. Flew (London, 1956), p. 35.

[7] *Ibid.*, footnote (added to original article), p. 40. See also Strawson's "A Reply to Mr. Sellars," in *Philosophical Review*, 1954, p, 229.

less we refer to an existent we do not succeed in expressing a subject-predicate "statement," that is, an assertion which admits of truth or falsity. And if he is right about this, then it becomes more plausible to claim that subject-predicate statements are equivalent to hypotheticals. (I do not wish to suggest that Strawson would claim they are equivalent.)

But here again it seems perfectly obvious to me that statements which are true or false can be made about nonexistent things. After all, unicorns do have horns, giants are two-legged, and Mr. Pickwick is a most benevolent gentleman. Nor am I engaging in make-believe or storytelling when I assert these things. My grounds for such assertions are quite different from my grounds for claiming that my neighbor is a most benevolent gentleman, but that does not detract from the truth of such assertions.

To summarize, the claim that subject-predicate statements are equivalent to hypotheticals fails, although perhaps a case could be made for their equivalence with hypotheticals in those cases in which the grammatical subject refers to some existent or set of existents. If so, we might introduce a technical sense of "subject-predicate statement" for those statements which are translatable in the way that "Crows are black" is translatable into "If anything exists which is a crow, then that thing is black." For reasons which differ in each case, none of the following would be subject-predicate statements: "Crows are plentiful," "Crows scatter during storms," "Crows vary greatly," "Crows change over the centuries," and "Crows live in our barns." "Crows exist" would not be a subject-predicate statement either, since the requirement that the subject must refer to some existent would yield the result that if it were a subject-predicate statement, it would have to be true.[8] No wonder it would only come to the trivial "If anything exists which is a crow, then it exists," if construed as a subject-predicate statement in the technical sense we have given that term. But none of the peculiarities of "exists" which are brought out by saying that it cannot be an element in a subject-predicate statement, in the sense specified, go to indicate any impropriety in framing a definition in which "exists" appears, such as the definition of "God" given above.

[8] *Cf.* P. F. Strawson, *Introduction to Logical Theory* (London, 1952), pp. 190-191.

"EXISTS" AS A UNIVERSAL PREDICATE

When faced with the claim that if "exists" is taken as a predicate, positive existential assertions become tautological and negative existential assertions not readily intelligible, most philosophers have decided that "exists" cannot be taken as a predicate. But some have boldly accepted the consequence that "exists" is a trivial predicate, predicable of everything conceivable. Hence, the Ontological Argument becomes harmless, for "exists" is a necessary predicate not only of God but of everything conceivable. As recent supporters of this view have put it:

Every conception involves the predicate "exists." Thus, not only God's essence but every essence implies existence.[9]

And Hume suggested a doctrine very much like this when he said:

To reflect on any thing simply, and to reflect on it as existent, are nothing different from each other. That idea, when conjoined with the idea of any object, makes no addition to it. Whatever we conceive, we conceive to be existent.[10]

Thus, attributions of existence to anything I conceive become tautological, and denials of existence not readily intelligible.

Now whatever the intrinsic merits of this view, it is a most embarrassing one for Hume to hold. For he also wishes to maintain that "whatever we conceive as existent, we can also conceive as nonexistent,"[11] and thus that "the nonexistence of any being is as clear and distinct an idea as its existence."[12] Since Hume uses "conceive to be existent" and "conceive as existent" interchangeably,[13] these two doctrines are flatly contradictory, for the first implies that whatever we conceive we *cannot* conceive as nonexistent and the second states that whatever we conceive we *can* conceive as nonexistent. Nor can we save Hume by interpreting the second to mean

[9] G. Nakhnikian and W. Salmon, " 'Exists' as a Predicate," in *Philosophical Review*, 1957, p. 541.

[10] David Hume, *A Treatise of Human Nature*, ed. by L. A. Selby-Bigge (Oxford, 1888), p. 66.

[11] David Hume, *Dialogues Concerning Natural Religion*, Part IX.

[12] David Hume, *Enquiries Concerning the Human Understanding*, ed. by L. A. Selby-Bigge (Oxford, 1902), p. 164.

[13] Hume, *op. cit.*, *Treatise*, pp. 66-67.

that whatever we can conceive we can believe to be nonexistent, for if I cannot conceive of a thing except as existent, then surely I cannot believe in its nonexistence.

Perhaps Hume was writing carelessly when he said that "whatever we conceive, we conceive to be existent," and expressed his real thoughts more precisely when he said, "whatever the mind clearly conceives includes the idea of possible existence."[14] But if he did seriously hold the first view, there are many ways in which he might have come to it. The reason he does give,

> Since we never remember any idea or impression without attributing existence to it, the idea of existence . . . must be the very same with the idea of the perception or object,[15]

confuses the existence of the conception with the existence of what is conceived, the *realitas formalis* of the idea with its *realitas objectiva*. But he might have argued, in line with his notion of ideas as pictures, that we cannot form the picture of a thing as nonexistent, and therefore cannot conceive such a thing. Also, his attack on the abstract idea of existence as distinguishable and separable from the ideas of particular objects[16] and his connected claim that in making judgments that something exists we only entertain the idea of the thing in an especially lively and forceful way[17] lead him to say that the idea of existence cannot be something over and beyond the things we conceive, and therefore would incline him to say that whatever we conceive, we conceive to be existent.

Such a doctrine leaves most unclear what negative existential judgments could be, and yet it is obviously most important to be able to give such judgments sense. At one point, when Hume concerns himself with negative existential judgments, he abandons this doctrine, interpreting them as judgments in which the idea of the object is conjoined with the idea of nonexistence,[18] although in another place he flatly rejects such an interpretation without giving what he takes to be the correct account.[19] As far as I can see, the contradiction here was one which Hume was never able to eliminate.[20] Nor, as far as I can see, is it possible to reconcile the two. If the

[14] *Ibid.*, p. 32.
[15] *Ibid.*, p. 66.
[16] *Ibid.*, p. 623.
[17] *Ibid.*, p. 86 and *passim.*
[18] *Ibid.*, p. 15.
[19] *Ibid.*, p. 96, footnote.
[20] J. A. Passmore, in his illuminating book, *Hume's Intentions* (Cambridge, 1952), diagnoses the difficulties which appear here as arising from Hume's attempts to produce "a logic in which the only links are psychological" (p. 27).

definition of a substantive must include the notion that the thing exists (which is what I take Hume's doctrine to mean), then that the thing exists follows from the definition and is necessarily the case. To deny that the thing exists is to contradict oneself just as certainly as to deny that the thing possesses any other defining characteristic is to contradict oneself. And if all our conceptions of things include existence as necessary properties of the things, then no denials of existence will make sense.

Hume was mistaken in thinking that whatever we conceive of we must conceive to be existent. For suppose it is a necessary feature of a chimera that it be not only a she-monster of a particular sort but an imaginary she-monster. Then it would be a necessary statement that chimeras do not exist; anyone who held that chimeras exist would contradict himself. Could one conceive of a chimera? I do not see why not. But one would be conceiving of it as nonexistent.

I do not wish to suggest that philosophers were mistaken in thinking that "exists" is in many ways different from grammatically similar expressions, for it obviously is. To take Hume's point, for example, if I wish to picture an animal, it will make a difference whether I picture it as yellow; but one cannot make the same kind of sense out of speaking of picturing it as existent or nonexistent. It does not follow from this that whatever I picture, I picture as existing, but Hume is certainly right in thinking that I cannot represent the existence or nonexistence of the thing by adding to my picture in an exactly parallel way to the way in which I represent the yellowness or nonyellowness of the thing by adding to the picture. It requires some special convention to indicate that what is pictured is pictured as, say, imaginary. (Comic-strip creators have special conventions for showing this, for example, by encircling it and linking it by a stream of small circles to someone's head to show that he is just imagining it.) To make this point is to bring out a difference between "exists" and predicates like "is yellow." Further differences between "exists" and other predicates are brought out in the arguments for the slogan, " 'Exists' is not a predicate." What must be shown, however, is that these differences bear relevantly on the issue whether existential statements can be true by definition. I have been concerned to argue, in this section, that no differences have been noted which rule out existential statements which are true by definition.

II

Until further arguments are offered, it seems reasonable to hold that there is nothing logically improper in so defining the expression "God," that "God exists" is a tautology and "God does not exist" self-contradictory. In fact, it seems to me that the definition I have given expresses a concept of God (i.e., as necessarily existing) which many people actually accept (just as it is a common conception of Satan that he merely happens to exist). I wish to show in this section that this concept of God can give no support to the religious. I shall argue that no matter what its content, this concept of God is still simply a concept. What must be shown, and what cannot be shown just by an analysis of the concept, is that there actually exists something which answers to the concept. Even if we have here the concept of an object which necessarily exists, a further question remains whether any existent meets the specifications of the concept. The difficulty lies in showing that this further question makes sense, for I have admitted that "God exists" is a necessary statement, analytically true, and therefore it looks as if there could be no further question. But that is an illusion. It must, however, be dispelled.

As a first step, I wish to point out that the concept of God is hardly unique in its capacity to generate a tautological existential statement. For one thing, we could invent new tautologies. Suppose we introduce the word "particular" to mean "object which exists" and the word "nonentity" to mean "object which does not exist." Then to bring out the difference between these two words, we might properly say, tautologically, "Particulars exist and nonentities do not exist." Nor, for another thing, do we have to invent such words, for we already have many words with existential notions included in their meanings. The following sentences all have tautological uses: "Existents exist," "Fictitious objects do not exist," "Members of extinct species existed once but no longer exist," "Hallucinatory objects do not exist," "Historical persons have at some time existed." I do not suggest that these sentences can never be used in non-tautological ways, but I do suggest that they may be used tautologically in those circumstances in which we wish to emphasize that such concepts include as a necessary feature, as a defining element, notions of existence or nonexistence.

As a preliminary to seeing what these tautological existential claims come to, let us examine the relation between expressions of the form, "A's exist," and of the form, "There are A's." Take the tautology, "Fictitious objects do not exist." One might think that "Fictitious objects do not exist" means the same as "There are no fictitious objects." But a moment's thought will show that this is incorrect, for although the former is true, the latter is false. There are fictitious objects, many of them—Alice's looking glass, Jack's beanstalk, Wittgenstein's beetle, to mention only a few. So "Fictitious objects do not exist" does not mean the same as "There are no fictitious objects." Similarly, "Particulars exist" does not mean the same as "There are particulars." In general, given a tautology of the form, "A's exist," we cannot deduce from it, "There are A's," nor from a tautology of the form, "A's do not exist," can we deduce "There are no A's." And specifically, given the tautology, "God exists," we cannot deduce from it, "There is a God." The statement, "God necessarily exists, but there is no God," is *not* self-contradictory.

As it stands, the situation is most paradoxical. For in many of its ordinary uses, "A's exist" is equivalent to "There are A's." If I raise a question about the existence of pearls as large as my fist, it usually does not matter whether you say, "Yes, such pearls exist," or "Yes, there are such pearls." So if there is a way of saying that certain things exist which does not mean that there are such things, then this must be explained.

Now I have misinterpreted the situation somewhat. I have spoken as if it were important whether we used the form "A's exist" rather than "There are A's." But this is not the case. "There are A's" is perhaps more resistant to being treated as a tautology, but it is still possible to frame tautologies of the form, "There are A's." "There is what there is" and "There are what there are," are tautologies, and one could imagine situations in which one might say them in this tautological way. If I define "particulars" as "whatever entities there really are," then "There are particulars" is a tautology, namely, "There are whatever entities there really are." And if I define "a God" as "whatever divine being there is," then "There is a God" is tautological too. So there is nothing distinctive about the forms "A's exist" or "There are A's." They both function in very similar ways. But we do have both forms of expression, and that is most convenient. For it allows us to formulate a further existential question, using the alternative form, when we are presented with a tautological existential assertion. Thus, if someone says, tautologically,

"There are particulars" (i.e., there are whatever objects there are), we can avoid the danger of formal contradiction in asking, "I grant that there are particulars, but do particulars *exist*?"

What I am claiming is that if we are given a tautological existential assertion like "Particulars exist" or "God exists," the existential question is not settled. Just as the tautology, "Fictitious objects do not exist," leaves open the question whether there are fictitious objects, so the tautology, "God exists," leaves open the question whether there is a God. But what is this further question? How paradoxical it seems to deny that "once one has grasped Anselm's proof of the necessary existence of a being a greater than which cannot be conceived, no question remains as to whether it exists or not."[21]

It is tempting to try to resolve the paradox in accordance with Aristotle's principle that "there are several senses in which a thing may be said to 'be'." Then to say that fictitious objects do not exist would be to say that fictitious objects lacked, say, spatio-temporal existence, whereas to say that there are fictitious objects would be to say that they had some other kind of existence—hence no contradiction, since in a sense fictitious objects exist and in a sense they do not. But appeals to the systematic ambiguity of "exists" will not work in all cases, for we may deny that there are A's in precisely the same sense of "be" that we claim tautologically that A's exist. For example, it will be tautologically true that particulars exist in precisely the same sense of "exist,' say, temporal existence, that it might be true that there are no particulars.

A more promising line of argument consists in showing that a tautological existential claim is quite different from a nontautological existential claim. How are we to explain the difference? Suppose we say that a tautological existential assertion consists in attributing to the subject a special property, the property of necessary existence. We could explain this property by saying, *à la* Malcolm, that a being which has this property is such that it is senseless to speak of its non-existence or of its coming into existence or going out of existence or of the existence of anything else as a condition of its existence (pp. 307f.). Now this account will not do. First, the attempt to explain the necessity of the statement by postulating a special property commits us to an infinite regress of properties, for presumably this special property might not be one which a being just happens to have but one which it necessarily has and which it is senseless to speak of its not having, and thus by similar reasoning we are led to necessary

[21] Malcolm, p. 312

necessary-existence, etc. And it is most unclear what these properties could be or how we could distinguish them. But, secondly, it is not clear what this property of necessary existence is, if this is any more than a way of saying that the existential proposition is necessary. Am I making anything clearer when I say that squares, which are necessarily four-sided, have the special property of *necessary four-sidedness*? A defining property is not a special kind of property. So the tautological character of the existential assertions I have been discussing cannot be explained by postulating a special predicate, necessary existence. Their tautological character arises from nothing but the definition we have stipulated for the subject term. But then we are still left with our puzzle: How is it possible to say that A's necessarily exist but there may be no A's?

I wish to consider one further attempt to remove the paradox, one suggested by some remarks by Carnap on a somewhat different issue:

> If someone wishes to speak in his language about new kinds of entities, he has to introduce a system of new ways of speaking, subject to new rules; we shall call this procedure the construction of a *framework* for the new entities in question. And now we must distinguish two kinds of questions of existence: first, questions . . . *within* the *framework*; we call them *internal questions*; and second, questions concerning the existence or reality *of the framework itself*, called *external questions*.[22]

Carnap goes on to explain that "external questions" concern nothing but "whether or not to accept and use the forms of expression for the framework in question," a purely practical question to be answered in terms of expediency and fruitfulness (p. 23). To apply this distinction to our paradox, given the basic definitions and rules of a particular religious language it will be a necessary statement that God exists (although not, perhaps, a necessary statement that the Devil exists), but we may ask the further question, Is there a God? meaning, Is this language a useful one?

Now, waiving objections we may have about the vagueness of talking of the "fruitfulness" of a set of expressions, it still remains the case that "Are there any A's?" will not always be identical with asking if the language is fruitful, for it may be very fruitful to talk of perfect pendulums, frictionless pulleys, the ideal society, Euclidean points, and the economic man, even if it is perfectly clear that there do not exist such things. So the question whether there are such

[22] R. Carnap, "Empiricism, Semantics, and Ontology," *Revue Internationale de Philosophie*, §11, January 1950, pp. 21-22.

things cannot be identical with the question whether it is in some sense fruitful to use expressions which refer to them; a fiction or *façon de parler* may turn out to be useful and fruitful.

What lies at the heart of the puzzle about the Ontological Argument is the fact that our concepts have two quite different aspects, marked by the familiar philosophical distinction of intension and extension. A word like "horse" has a particular meaning and is logically connected with other words like "animal"; its corresponding concept, the concept of a horse, has a particular content and is connected with other concepts like the concept of an animal. It is this intensional feature of words and their corresponding concepts which makes certain assertions like "A horse is an animal" tautological. But words and concepts are also applicable to things. It turns out to be the case that there have existed, do now exist, and will exist entities such that it is true of each of them that it is a horse, true of each of them that the concept of a horse applies to it. And this fact we may express by saying that the word "horse" or the concept of a horse has extension. In making assertions about the extension of a concept, there are typical forms of expression which we use: ". . . exist," ". . . are nonexistent," "There are . . . ," "There are no . . . ," ". . . are plentiful," ". . . are scarce," ". . . are extinct," ". . . are mythological," " . . . are found in Africa," etc. That such expressions are typically used in assertions about the extension (or lack thereof) of particular concepts is what is correctly brought out in the slogan, " 'Exists' is not a predicate." But the typical use is not the only use. Since any statement, with suitable definition, can be true by virtue of the meanings of the terms, sentences with existential expressions can be used to express tautological statements. The very same sentence which is typically used to make a claim about the extension of the concept may instead be used to make a claim about the intension of the concept. We cannot tell by the form of the expression how the expression is being used. "Particulars exist," when asserted tautologically, is used to make a claim about the *meaning* of the word "particulars" and therefore cannot be used to make a claim about the extension of the term. Similarly, if someone uses the sentence, "God exists," tautologically, he tells us only that being an existent is a logical requirement for being God. If, on the other hand, someone asserts, "God exists," nontautologically, then he claims that the term "God" has extension, applies to some existent. In the case of the Ontological Argument the only valid conclusion is an intensional statement about the meaning of the concept of God. *A fortiori* the conclusion cannot be about whether anything exists to which the concept applies. The *prima facie* plausibility of the Argument comes from the use of a sentence intensionally when the typical use of that sentence is extensional. In this way it conceals the illicit move from an intensional to an extensional statement.

It looked as if the familiar distinction between intension and extension stood in danger of breaking down in the case of existential tautologies. But we have seen that this is not the case. For even when we have an existential tautology like "Particulars exist" or "God exists," it still remains an open question whether the concept of particulars or the concept of God has application, applies to any existent. What is settled at one level is not settled at another level. It is important to see that we can go on to settle the question at the other level, too, for we can *make* it a priori true that the concept has application. For example, let the expression "the concept of God" mean "a concept which has application and applies to a being such that . . . ." Then by definition the concept of God has application; the statement, "The concept of God has application," is now a tautology, given the definition. But nothing is gained by such a maneuver. We have given the expression "the concept of God" a meaning; we have framed a concept, namely the concept of the concept of God, and this concept makes certain statements tautologically true. Yet we can still raise the extensional question. Does this concept refer to any existent? At this level the extensional question would be whether there actually is a concept of God such that this concept has extension, and there is such a concept only if there actually is a God. So making the condition of having application or extension a necessary condition for being a concept of God still leaves open the question, concerning *that* concept, whether it has extension. Nothing has been settled except the meaning of a certain expression.

Why is it that extensional assertions cannot be tautological? Because they do not merely tell us what the requirements are for being an A but, starting with these requirements, tell us whether anything meets these requirements. Even if it is a conceptual requirement that the thing exist in order to be an instance of the concept, that in no way settles whether the requirement is met. And if we *make* it a tautology that the requirement is met, by framing a concept of a concept, then we are left with the open question whether the newly framed concept has extension. That is what is true in the thesis that no "existential" proposition can be analytic. But we must remember that an "existential" proposition can turn out to be an intensional proposition, and therefore tautological.

Since much of what I have claimed depends upon the legitimacy of the intension-extension distinction, I wish to consider, finally, two threats to this distinction. The first concerns the so-called *intensional object*. When I conceive of an object, think about it, describe it, make a painting of it, long for it, look for it and expect to find it, it may nevertheless be the case that the object does not exist, that the concept has no extension. But it is tempting to say that there must be something such that I conceive of it, think about it, describe it, etc., tempting to say that the object in some sense exists. And thus it is tempting to say that the mere fact that there is a concept of some object entails that the object in some sense exists. Well, even if one says that, it is obviously not the sense in which the religious usually wish to say that God exists nor the sense in which the atheist wishes to deny that God exists. They disagree about whether anything answers to that concept of an object, not about whether that concept is a concept of an object.

A second, and more troublesome, threat to the intension-extension distinction arises when we try to apply the distinction to certain concepts. We seem quite clear that the concept of a horse does have extension and that the concept of a unicorn does not have extension, and that these are contingent facts. But now suppose we ask whether the concept of a number has extension. If we hold that the concept ultimately has as its extension things in the world, then it still remains a contingent fact that the concept has extension. But suppose we are inclined to say that the concept has extension simply because, as we all know, there are (infinitely) many numbers. Surely it is not a contingent fact that there are (infinitely) many numbers. So if this fact leads us to say that the concept of a number has extension, then it will be a necessary proposition that the concept of a number has extension and, given the concept of a number, we can say a priori that the concept applies to (infinitely) many things.

What makes this case puzzling is that we have no idea what would count as establishing that the concept of a number has extension or that it does not have extension. We can investigate whether the concept of a number is a legitimate one, clear and self-consistent; we can note its logical connection with other mathematical concepts; and we can frame propositions which state these connections, even propositions like "There exists a number which is even and prime." But what would count as showing that the concept, over and above its intensional content, has extension as well? Where would one look for traces, signs, evidences, intimations or testimonies of the existence of numbers? Would we not say of someone who did think such a search sensible that he had misconceived the nature of numbers? Nothing would count as showing that the concept of numbers had extension over and above its intensional content, and this is to say that the notion of extension does not apply here. The most that could be said is that numbers are *in*tensional objects.

The same thing must be said for the existence of God. The most that the Ontological Argument establishes is the intensional object, God, even if this intensional object has the attribute of existence as an intensional feature. To establish that the concept of God has extension requires adducing some additional argument to show that over and above its intensional features, over and above the content of the concept (or the meaning of the word "God"), the concept of God has extension as well. This additional argument will of necessity have to be an a posteriori argument to the effect that certain evidences make it reasonable to think that some actual existent answers to the concept. We are thus led to the result that the Ontological Argument of itself alone cannot show the existence of God, in the sense in which the concept is shown to have extension. And this is just as the religious wish it to be. They do not conceive of God as something whose being expresses itself entirely in the concepts and propositions of a language game. They conceive of Him as something which has effects on the world and can in some way be experienced. Here is a crucial respect in which His status is meant to be different from that of the numbers. The concept of God is a concept which *might* have extension. But some further argument is required to show whether it does or not.

Concepts are like nets. What they catch depends in part upon how we construct them and in part upon what is outside the net. Suppose I produce a net for catching fish one-millionth of an inch long. Of such a net we are entitled to say, "This net catches fish one-millionth of an inch long," and what shows that this statement is true is nothing but the construction of the net. Does the net catch anything? It catches fish one-millionth of an inch long. Still, a question remains. Shall we ever find such fish in our net? For those who hunger for such fish, the existence of the net does not in any way show that what they hunger for shall be given unto them.

B. The Hegelian Use of the Argument

XII

GILBERT RYLE

Mr. Collingwood and the Ontological Argument*

MR. COLLINGWOOD, in his interesting "*Essay on Philosophical Method,*" is embarking on a set of enquiries which are of obvious importance. His aim is to find out what philosophy is and what is the right way of proceeding in that activity. And his enterprise has a special momentary interest, for of recent years the discussion of these questions have been the monopoly of one or two schools of thought which are poles asunder from the point of view which Mr. Collingwood represents. For Mr. Collingwood is presumably to be classified, for what such labels are worth, as an Idealist, and it is high time that the questions which have been in the forefront of the debates of such thinkers as Russell, Moore, Broad, Wittgenstein, Carnap, Schlick, Stebbing, and again as the members of the school or schools of Husserl and Meinong, should be at least considered again in the quarters which protest (perhaps a little too much) allegiance to Plato, Kant (in his less Humean moods) and Hegel.

Now I think that Mr. Collingwood's general views are wrong; but I want only to discuss, and if possible to refute, certain theories which he expounds in his Chapter VI, which is entitled "Philosophy as Categorical Thinking." And I confess at once that I intend to be destructive only. That is, I do not propose to say that philosophical propositions are all or mostly of this or that logical form, but only to

* From *Mind*, Vol. XLIV, No. 174 (April 1935), pp. 137-151. Reprinted with permission.

show the mistakes which I believe Mr. Collingwood makes when he tries to show that philosophical propositions are (in a certain sense of the term) categorical. The question is of cardinal importance; for he holds that philosophical propositions are in a peculiarly close way connected with what exists; in a way, indeed, in which the empirical sciences are more remote from what exists than philosophy is. And a part of his theory is that philosophy can by the Ontological Argument establish the existence of a very important somewhat, and that philosophy in general aims at discovering—and no other sort of enquiry can discover—the nature of the somewhat. So that, if Mr. Collingwood is right, constructive metaphysics is the proper business of philosophy, and Hume and Kant were wrong insofar as they maintained that a priori arguments cannot establish particular matters of fact.

The chapter begins by elucidating the sense in which Mr. Collingwood and logicians generally declare that the propositions of geometry and arithmetic are "hypothetical," namely that although, in a sense, propositions may be "about" triangles or circles, yet there do not have to exist any triangles or circles for the propositions to be true. They only say, "if something had such and such properties, it would have such and such other properties"; and it is not said or implied that anything does so. At least, this is how I paraphrase Mr. Collingwood's own statement. He himself says, "In order to assert a proposition in mathematics, it is not necessary to believe that the subject of discourse has any actual existence. We say that every square has its diagonals equal; but to say this we need not think that we have any acquaintance with actual squares. . . . What is necessary is not to believe that a square anywhere or in any sense exists, but to suppose it. . . . In mathematics we frame a supposition and then see what follows from it. . . ." (pp. 117-118) And this seems unexceptionable.

He then argues that not indeed the whole but the body of empirical science consists of propositions which are hypothetical in the same sense. I think he slightly obscures his position here by failing to distinguish the *generality* of the propositions which profess to state "laws" from the innocent fictitiousness of certain sorts of scientific propositions which pretend to be about the "standard cases" of roses, e.g., or tuberculosis. But I do not think it matters to the argument. (The way in which "dogs are carnivorous" applies to Fido but does not depend for its truth on Fido's existing is different from the way in which "the typical schoolboy likes cricket" applies to

Tommy, but neither states nor implies that he exists.) Mr. Collingwood sees, of course, that empirical sciences must have propositions stating particular matters of fact among their premises, and that they may (as in the *Nautical Almanac*, I suppose) embody others in the application of laws to the world. And these will be categorical. But he asserts (I am not clear why) that the body of scientific knowledge "consists" of hypothetical propositions, and its categorical propositions are only "necessary or fortuitous accompaniments of it." (p. 121). But we need not quarrel over this, for it is clear that there are universal propositions in the findings of the empirical sciences and that these do differ in logical form from propositions asserting such particular matters of fact as that the patient's temperature has been this or that at such-and-such a time. Now Mr. Collingwood wants to show that none or few of the propositions of philosophy are hypothetical in the sense in which the propositions of mathematics and the universal propositions of empirical science are hypothetical; but on the contrary, that all or most philosophical propositions are categorical in the same sense (or anyhow an analogous sense) as the proposition about the patient's temperature was categorical.

But before we come to this I must, I fear, clarify one or two points in what I take to be Mr. Collingwood's use of the term "hypothetical." First of all, there are plenty of "if-then" propositions which do imply the existence of their subjects. "If Hitler lives for another year, he will be at loggerheads with Mussolini" cannot be true or false unless there exists a Hitler and a Mussolini. Mr. Collingwood is obviously referring to the universality of general propositions, rather than to their "if-then-ness"; he is affirming, that is, that philosophical propositions differ from the propositions of mathematics and the general propositions of empirical science in the fact that philosophical propositions directly refer to something which exists in a way in which the others fail to do this. He is not making what would be the quite different point that philosophers never or seldom say that from something's being the case something else would follow.

At least I think that this is all that his argument about mathematical propositions and the universal propositions of the empirical sciences can be intended to establish. Yet, in Section 4, where he appeals to the authority of Plato, Aristotle, Kant and Hegel, he does seem to confuse the two points. For in one breath he quotes Aristotle's definition of the subject matter of metaphysics as reality or being, Hegel's declaration that "the subject matter of philosophy is no mere thought and no mere abstraction but *die Sache selbst*," as well as Plato's assertion that dialectic demands for itself a nonhypothetical starting point, and Kant's dictum that "in a critique of pure reason anything in the nature of a hypothesis must be treated as contraband." But the Aristotle-Hegel point is quite different from the Plato-Kant point. Plato and Kant are saying that philosophy must not lay down propositions which depend for their truth upon premises not known to be true. Philosophy does not consist in deducing consequences from assumptions. And this, although true and important, is not the same thing as to say that philosophical propositions state or entail particular matters of fact, i.e., that they are "about" a designated entity. Some philosophers have, indeed, held that there are some general propositions which are known to be true a priori, and that philosophy starts from these. This theory (I do not think it is true) would secure what Plato and Kant are here demanding for philosophy without providing what Aristotle and Hegel require.

Let me try to restate the distinction between the two senses of "hypothetical proposition" which seem to be confused in Mr. Collingwood's treatment.

1. Primarily, Mr. Collingwood means by "hypothetical proposition" a general, indeed universal, proposition of the form "anything that is A is B" or "if anything is A, it is B" or "all A's are B." Such propositions do not depend for their truth on this or that thing being an A and thus do not "imply the existence of their subject terms."

2. But sometimes he means by "hypothetical proposition"a proposition which states that a certain consequent would follow if a certain protasis were true, when it is not known or said or implied that the protasis is true. The truth of the whole "if-then" is independent of the truth or falsity of the protasis taken as an independent proposition. That is how we can make deductions from a mere assumption.

But (*a*) in *this* sense a hypothetical proposition may well depend for its truth on the existence of its subject term: for it may, as we saw, be about Hitler or Julius Caesar, and so depend for its being true or false on there existing a Hitler or a Julius Caesar, although not, of course, on the protasis about Hitler, say, being true when taken as an independent proposition. The protasis of a hypothetical proposition may express the assumption that something not known to exist does exist; but it may equally well express the assumption that something known to exist has a character which it is not known to possess or the assumption that something known to exist does not exist. Not all assumptions are assumptions of the existence of a so-and-so.

And (*b*) the protasis of a *general* hypothetical proposition does not express the assumption that something of a certain description exists. "Anyone found trespassing will be prosecuted" is a general hypothetical. But the protasis cannot be taken by itself. It is nonsense to say "anyone is found trespassing." There is no such animal as "anyone."

Now, as Mr. Collingwood is concerned with such facts as that geometry is independent of the *existence* of squares, it is clear that his argument turns not on the general point that consequences can be deduced from protases which are assumed (i.e., not known to be true when taken as independent propositions), but on the special point that universal propositions do not depend for their truth on the existence of instances of the characters between which connection is asserted. For he is trying to prove not that philosophy requires self-evident premises, but that it is about something which can be known to exist, for which purpose he has to show that its propositions are not *general* hypotheticals.

In Section 5 Mr. Collingwood unfolds his main reason for thinking that philosophical propositions, or most of them, or the best of them, are not hypothetical but categorical. This we now see means that they refer to something which exists, or contain or rest on propositions which do so. And this must mean, to use language which is not Mr. Collingwood's, that philosophical propositions are or contain or rest on propositions embodying either at least one logically proper name or else at least one definite description which does in fact describe something. In short, every philosophical proposition is or contains or rests on a genuine singular proposition. (Although on p. 136 Mr. Collingwood distinguishes between the categorical singular judgments of history and the categorical universal [judgments] of philosophy. I cannot make head nor tail of this. After the labors Mr. Collingwood has taken to distinguish between (general) hypothetical propositions and categorical, it is upsetting to find that apparently after all some judgments may be universal and so (I suppose) expressible in purely general terms and yet categorical in the sense of referring to something actually existing. I fear that the principle of the overlap of Classes will be brought in to give us carte blanche to have it both ways when it suits our convenience!)

And his first argument for this conclusion is that the Ontological

Argument is valid, and is presupposed by all other philosophical arguments, or the best of them. He paraphrases the goal of Anselm's argument by saying that "thought, when it follows its own bent most completely and sets itself the task of thinking out the idea of an object that shall completely satisfy the demands of reason, may appear to be constucting a mere *ens rationis*, but in fact is never devoid of objective or ontological reference." (pp. 124-125.) (A caviler might want to know why the idea of an object *should* satisfy the demands of reason, or, more importantly, how reason can be dissatisfied with the idea of any object. And why should we suppose that it is in philosophy that thought is following its own bent most completely rather than in, say, astronomy or Antarctic exploration, in which we certainly discover things existing which we did not know of before?

Mr. Collingwood says, "Anselm's argument that in conceiving a perfect being we are conceiving a subject possessed of all positive predicates, including that of existence, so that to think of this is already to think of it as existing, is an argument open to objection on the logical ground that existence is not a predicate; but the substance of his thought survives all such objections. . . ." (p. 125.) But unfortunately this is precisely where I should have thought not only Hume and Kant but almost all recent logicians who have attended to the analysis of existential propositions would dig their heels in and say that the argument is an obvious fallacy *unless* existence is a "predicate"; and that existence is not a "predicate." We can see how implications obtain between "predicates," i.e., how *if* something is an A, it is B-ish. But how can the *existence* of an A or a B be implied? How can "something is an A" follow from the proposition "anything that is an A, is B-ish"? How can a particular matter of fact be deduced from a priori or nonempirical premises?

Mr. Collingwood rather cavalierly dismisses Kant's refutation of the Ontological Argument as merely a result of "that false subjectivism and consequent skepticism from which, in spite of heroic efforts, he never wholly freed himself. With Hegel's projection of subjective idealism, the Ontological Proof took its place once more among the accepted principles of modern philosophy, and it has never again been seriously criticized." (p. 126.) To my mind this dictum almost merits tears. One of the biggest advances in logic that has been made since Aristotle, namely Hume's and Kant's discovery that particular matters of fact cannot be the implicates of general propositions, and so cannot be demonstrated from a priori premises, is written off as a backsliding into an epistemological or psychological mistake, and all is to do again.

And we must swallow with regret the dismissal of the whole of the work in logic which can be loosely described as Russellian. Its criticisms, e.g., of the Ontological Argument, must not be accounted serious criticism—because, I suppose, it has rejected that very subject-predicate logic which made it verbally plausible to argue from "essence" to "existence." (Or perhaps, because it happens to use Greek letters for some of its symbols instead of the canonized *S*, *M* and *P*.)

But to continue. Mr. Collingwood, after showing that the Ontological Proof does not establish any particular *theological* truth, says "What it does prove is that essence involves existence, not always, but in one special case, the case of God in the metaphysical sense: the *Deus sive nature* of Spinoza, the Good of Plato, the Being of Aristotle: the object of metaphysical thought. But this means the object of philosophical thought in general; for metaphysics, even if it is regarded as only one among the philosophical sciences, is not unique in its objective reference or in its logical structure; all philosophical thought is of the same kind, and every philosophical science partakes of the nature of metaphysics, which is not a separate philosophical science but a special study of the existential aspect of that same subject matter whose aspect as truth is studied by logic and its aspect as goodness by ethics." (But what is an "existential aspect"? Is, after all, the existence of a thing just one among its other attributes or "predicates"?)

"Reflection on the history of the Ontological Proof thus offers us a view of philosophy as a form of thought in which essence and existence, however clearly distinguished, are conceived as inseparable. On this view, unlike mathematics or empirical science, philosophy stands committed to maintaining that its subject matter is no mere hypothesis, but something actually existing." (p. 127.)

But what is the cash value of this slogan "Essence involves existence"? First of all, "essence" is used only in relation; we speak of "the essence of . . ." or so and so is "essential to . . ." What sort of correlate is appropriate? We cannot speak (correctly) of the essence of this pipe or of Socrates, we can only speak (correctly) of the essence of some general character or description or "predicate." That is, we can say that it is part of the essence of Man, or of being a man, to be capable of inference. If *x* cannot infer then *x* is not a man.

There are cases, then, where we can correctly enough say that the essence of so-and-so involves so-and-so, namely where we can say that being of such and such a sort involves having such and such a property: or that if something has a certain character, it follows that it has such and such another.

Now there are some characters which are such that if anything has one of them, no other thing can have it; I think these are always complex, but for the present purpose that does not matter. "Being the President of the United States on August 19, 1934," is a character which, I think, belongs to one man and could not belong to two or more. "Being the oldest man now alive in Oxford" is another. We can call these, if we like, idiosyncratic or peculiar characters, or, if we prefer, call the phrases which symbolize them "definite" or "unique descriptions." (The word "the" is the customary English symbol for such nonsharable characters.) And in the case of these characters, too, we can say, although with a slight awkwardness, that being so-and-so is of the essence of having this or that idiosyncratic or peculiar character. It might, for example, be of the essence of being the senior member of a certain committee to be its chairman. But, of course, a definite description may not in fact apply to anyone, or a peculiar character need not characterize anyone. Oxford may have an exclusively feminine population and the United States may have no President. So even in this special class of cases "being *x* or being-the-*x* is essential to being-the-*y*" may be true, although nothing is the *x* or the *y*.

Now the Ontological Argument says that there is one case where a peculiar character *C* has as a part of its essence not, as elsewhere, a certain property *P*, but the fact-that-something-has-*C*.

It is part of the *analysis* of "perfectness" that something is perfect. Part of the meaning of this one definite description is that the description fits something. Which is surely a glaring fallacy. Let us attempt to make it glare even more vividly.

It is maintained that in one case "Essence involves existence." What is this notion of "involving"?

(1) Sometimes, perhaps, "involves" means what is nowadays often meant by "entails," namely the implication which holds between the having a certain specific character and the having the generic character of which the former is a species. Thus, being green entails or "involves" being colored, and being square entails or "involves" being shaped. But this is *not* the sense of "involves" in which the

Ontological Argument says that "Essence involves existence." For its champions would then have had to allow that the same argument would prove the existence of other things than God. But anyhow, as a question of history I doubt if any of them committed the absurdity of pretending that "existence" is the name of a generic attribute.

(2) Sometimes, "involves" is used to express whatever it is that natural laws formulate; for example, that a metal's being heated involves its expanding. But this sort of "involving" (if *pace* Hume, there is such a thing) is established only by induction. There is no contradiction in the negating of a natural law; whereas the Ontological Argument says that there is a contradiction in denying the existence of God or perfection.

(3) No; although I do not claim to have exhausted the various possible meanings of the word, the sense of "involves" required for the Ontological Argument is "includes" or "contains as a part or constituent." When I say that the essence of bicycles involves their having two wheels in tandem, I simply mean that the complex character of being a bicycle consists of the simpler characters *a*, *b* and *c*, and one of these simpler characters is that of having two wheels in tandem. So it is an analytic proposition to say that a bicycle has two wheels in tandem (unless it is a synthetic proposition about the English word "bicycle," as is the case with dictionary definitions). And as this is precisely what was claimed by the Ontological Argument, namely that it is a contradiction to deny (i.e., an analytic proposition to affirm) that God exists, it is clear that "involves" in "Essence involves existence" means precisely "contains as a part or constituent."

But the parts of a complex of characters are characters. So unless existence is a character or "predicate," it cannot be "involved" (in this sense) in the essence of a complex character. Certainly, "exists" is the grammatical predicate of heaps of English sentences; but it is precisely here that the fallacy of the Ontological Argument arises. For it assumes (what is false) that in every sentence which is of the noun-verb pattern or the noun-copula-adjective pattern, the noun is a genuine proper name and the verb or adjective ascribes a quality to the thing named by the grammatical subject. But even if Hume and Kant were too subjectivist for their treatment of existential propositions to be treated seriously, surely Russell's theory of descriptions and his consequential analysis of existential propositions as a species of general proposition has been before the philosophical public long enough for this ontological fallacy to merit immunity from any more exhumations.

Of course, there is a sense in which any character whatsoever involves existence. I mean that if it is true that something is green or square or north of London, that something must exist. What has a quality or stands in a relation or is of a kind *ipso facto* exists. (This is not a *significant* inference. But the object of the Ontological Argument was to show that there is one (peculiar) character of which we only know to start with that it *might* characterize something from the analysis of the constitution of which we could discover that it *does* characterize something.)

But although it would be a contradiction to say "this is a bicycle but it has not got two wheels in tandem" and nonsense to say "this is a bicycle but it does not exist," it is not a contradiction or nonsense to say "nothing has *deitas*."

There is then no way of arguing validity to the existence of something of a certain description from nonempirical premises, namely from premises about the characters the combination of which is symbolized by the description. There is no way of demonstrating a priori particular matters of fact. Inferences to the existence of something, if there are any, must be causal inferences and inferences from the existence of something else. Nor are there any "demands of reason" which can make us accept as proofs of existence combinations of propositions which contain an overt fallacy.

And if philosophy is or contains or rests on metaphysics and has no "subject matter" unless it has to do with a subject, the existence of which is established only in this way, then there is no such philosophical science as metaphysics and no such thing as philosophy. But, as I see no force in the argument that philosophy would have no subject matter unless it had access to a special entity, I do not find myself alarmed by this threat.

But this is not the end of the story. For in Section 7 Mr. Collingwood goes on to a new line of argument, which he appears to think is merely an expansion or continuation of the previous one. To state briefly his new point, he argues that logicians enunciate principles of logic in propositions which themselves exemplify those principles. So their propositions exist. So the essence of the principles of logic involves the existence of examples of them.

The argument is so extraordinary that I must quote the relevant passages *in extenso*. After maintaining that logic has thought for its subject matter and that it does not give a merely descriptive account of it, he says on page 129: "But neither is logic merely normative. A purely normative science would expound a norm or ideal of what its subject matter ought to be, but would commit itself to no assertion that this ideal was anywhere realized. If logic were a science of this kind, it would resemble the exact sciences; it would in fact be, or be closely related to, mathematics. The reason why it can never conform to that pattern is that whereas in geometry, for example, the subject matter is triangles, etc., and the body of the science consists of propositions about triangles, etc., in logic the subject matter is propositions, and the body of the science consists of propositions about propositions. In geometry the body of the science is heterogeneous with its subject matter; in logic they are homogeneous, and more than homogeneous, they are identical; for the propositions of which logic consists must conform to the rules which logic lays down, so that logic is actually about itself; not about itself exclusively, but at least incidentally about itself.

"It follows that logic cannot be in substance merely hypothetical. Geometry can afford to be indifferent to the existence of its subject matter; as long as it is free to suppose it, that is enough. But logic cannot share this indifference, because, by existing, it constitutes an actually existing subject matter to itself. Thus, when we say 'all squares have their diagonals equal,' we need not be either explicitly or implicitly asserting that any squares exist; but when we say 'all universal propositions distribute their subject,' we are not only discussing universal propositions, we are also enunciating a universal proposition; we are producing an actual instance of the thing under discussion, and cannot discuss it without doing so. Consequently, no such discussion can be indifferent to the existence of its own subject matter; in other words, the propositions which constitute the body of logic cannot ever be in substance hypothetical. A logician who lays it down that all universal propositions are merely hypothetical is showing a true insight into the nature of science, but he is undermining the very possibility of logic; for his assertion cannot be true consistently with the fact of his maintaining it.

"Similarly with inference. Logic not only discusses, it also contains reasoning; and if a logician could believe that no valid reasoning anywhere existed, he would merely be disbelieving his own logical theory. For logic has to provide not only a theory of its subject matter, but in the same breath a theory of itself; it is an essential part of its proper task that it should consider not only how other kinds of thought proceed, and on what principles, but how and on what principles logic proceeds. If it had only to consider other kinds of thought, it could afford to deal with its subject matter in a way either merely normative or merely descriptive; but toward itself it can only stand in an attitude that is both at once. It is obliged to produce, as constituent parts of itself, actual instances of thought which realize its own ideal of what thought should be.

"Logic, therefore, stands committed to the principle of the Ontological Proof. Its subject matter, namely thought, affords an instance of something which cannot be conceived except as actual, something whose essence involves existence."

I shall find it hard to condense within reasonable limits my objections to this argument. But my main objects are to show first that this argument has nothing to do with the Ontological Argument, and secondly that it has no tendency to establish the general conclusion that the propositions of logic are not hypothetical. But I have one or two subsidiary bones to pick with Mr. Collingwood as well.

The first of the subsidiary bones is this. Mr. Collingwood is at pains to show that a logician who *denies* the existence of any instances of logically regular thinking must be wrong because he himself is producing an instance of that which he denies to exist. Now this might, *per accidens*, be so (although a man might, if he troubled, deny the occurrence of genuine singular propositions without producing one, or argue against the occurrence of syllogisms in Disamis by syllogisms in Baroco). But it has no bearing on the point. For (general) hypothetical propositions do not *deny* the existence of their subjects, they only do not affirm or imply their existence. So a man who maintained that all the propositions of logic are (general) hypotheticals would not be denying the existence of anything. So his exposure as himself a producer of propositions would no more disconcert him than a lecturer on canine diseases would be disconcerted by hearing the bark of a dog.

The second subsidiary bone is to point out that when Mr. Collingwood argues that if logic were purely normative, "it would resemble the exact sciences: it would in fact either be, or be closely related to, mathematics," he does not seem to remember that this is precisely what is desired for logic by many logicians, past and present.

The third is this. It is not peculiar to logical propositions that they themselves (sometimes, not generally) belong to the subject matter which they discuss. The English grammarian writes grammatically about grammar; the educationist lectures instructively about lecturing instructively; the signaling instructor may signal instructions about signaling to his pupils; Horace writes his *Ars poetica* in poetry. Have *these* anything to do with the Ontological Argument?

I suppose Mr. Collingwood would reply that it is accidental if the principles of grammar or elocution or poetry are conveyed in vehicles which themselves exemplify those principles, but it is necessary that logicians' propositions should instantiate the principles which they themselves propound.

But even this seems to me not to be so. For, after all, one can talk about singular propositions in general propositions, negative propositions in affirmative ones, relational in attributive and attributive in relational propositions. One can reason about the syllogism in nonsyllogistic arguments and vice versa.

But let us suppose that sometimes logicians have to formulate logical principles or rules in propositions which are instances of them. Even so, the writer or reader might and usually would attend to what the propositions say without noticing that the propositions themselves were cases in point, just as he may study grammar without noticing that the grammarian is keeping the rules. And even if he noticed it, he might still not use the instances as illustrations. It is indeed difficult to attend, so to speak, twice at once to a given proposition, namely once to what it says and once to the fact that it exemplifies the rule that it states.

So when Mr. Collingwood says that "no such discussion" [as logic] "can be indifferent to the existence of its own subject matter," while it is not easy to see which of several things he means, it is easy to see that in all the possible meanings of the expression what he says is false.

(*a*) If he means that the reader of a logical textbook or the hearer of a logical lecture cannot understand the logical principles which are stated unless he uses the actual statements of them as illustrations, then this is false. For we very seldom find that this is the case, and when it is, we very seldom do use the statement as an illustration; and generally we do not require an illustration at all.

(*b*) If he means that logical principles cannot be stated save in propositions which exemplify them, then this is in general false.

How could, e.g., a singular proposition, tell us what a singular proposition is? And how will Mr. Collingwood state the principle of the syllogism in a syllogism?

(*c*) If he means that a given logical principle involves that a given logician should write or speak what he does write or speak about it, I challenge him to deduce from the principle of the syllogism the actual sentences which Mill or Russell propounds about it. The only thing of which we can say that it would of logical necessity be different from what it is, if a given proposition of Mill's or Russell's had been omitted or worded differently, is Mill's *System of Logic* or Russell's *Principia mathematica.* And they are books and not logical principles. If a sheep exists, its wool exists; and if Mill's Logic exists, its 365th proposition exists; but its existence is involved not by the truth of the principle which it states, but by the existence of the volume of which it is a part.

(*d*) But Mr. Collingwood avers that when a general proposition is propounded by a logician which happens to be *about* general propositions, then it is incidentally about itself. And this suggests (I hope I am wrong in discerning this suggestion) that it is part of the *meaning* of this proposition that it should exist: i.e., that the truth of what the proposition states depends upon and so implies that this proposition should be written or spoken as and when and where it is.

Now, of course, the word "about" is very ambiguous; but, in one sense of it, to say that a proposition is about itself is to commit the simplest of type fallacies. But anyhow, Mr. Collingwood's own argument only entitles him to use the term "about" in this other sense, namely that a proposition is "about" *x* when it applies to *x*. So "dogs are carnivorous" is "about" Fido in the sense that Fido is a dog and so is carnivorous. But we have long since accepted with Mr. Collingwood the view that (general) hypothetical propositions, while they may apply to this or that square or this or that case of tuberculosis, do not depend for their truth on this being a square or that being a case of tuberculosis. In the same way, then, if a logician's proposition is an instance of a logical principle of which it is the statement, the principle will apply to the proposition, but it will not imply its existence. (How *could* a perfectly general truth like a logical principle imply a particular spoken or printed occurrence?) But of course we only need to ask the simple question, How can we discover what propositions have been propounded by logicians? to see the position. For the answer is that we must read their books or hear their lectures, or infer from testimonies and traditions: that is, we can only discover this sort of fact empirically. We do not employ the Ontological Argument.

After all, Mr. Collingwood did say that there was only one case where essence involves existence, namely, where the essence of God, or the Good, or Being implied its existence. But here what is being hailed as necessarily existing is not God or the Good or Being but this and that remark of this and that logician. So that even if logicians could not help uttering logically regular propositions (which alas! they *can* help), this supposed necessitation would be something quite different from the supposed analytic necessity of existing which the Ontological Argument ascribes to God or the Good or Being. All that Mr. Collingwood's argument amounts to is that a man will be a bad logician unless he tells the truth and reasons validly or obeys the laws of logic which it is his professional business to expound. But there is, unfortunately, no logical contradiction in asserting that someone is a bad logician.

It is clear then that the fact that thousands of logicians' propositions exist or have existed has no tendency to show of what logical form the propositions of logic are or must be.

And it is clear, too, that the Ontological Argument is quite a different argument from this one of Mr. Collingwood's which tries to establish the categorical nature of the propositions of logic from the fact that some logical principles are exemplified in the propositions which are employed to formulate them.

I hope Mr. Collingwood will not find that my criticisms are vitiated by "subjective idealism."

XIII

E. E. Harris

Mr. Ryle and the Ontological Argument*

MR. GILBERT RYLE in his recent article[1] has treated a contention of Prof. Collingwood's as a challenge and has met it with a very closely reasoned criticism of the Ontological Argument, which seems to me to miss the essential point of Hegel's defense of the doctrine. In his eagerness to expose its formal defects, Mr. Ryle, not unlike Kant, has failed to see the philosophical truth underlying and inspiring the Ontological Argument and, at the same time, has overlooked the fact that Hegel was aware of the shortcomings of the Argument as well as its deeper truth. His criticism leaves Hegel's position untouched, and in consequence, Prof. Collingwood's contention (namely, that insofar as Hegel did and intended to reinstate the doctrine, his position still holds good) may stand—even in spite of Mr. Ryle's criticism.

Prof. Collingwood clearly was not much concerned to defend a doctrine which he considered to be in no need of a champion, so it is not with Mr. Ryle's particular criticism of him that I wish to deal. I shall concern myself simply with the position as Hegel left it, and if I do no more than repeat his view, it is because I think little else is necessary to show Mr. Ryle's shortcoming. Mr. Ryle's argument is, in effect, very like Kant's; and Hegel claims to refute Kant's. Yet I cannot see that Mr. Ryle has done anything special to meet Hegel's criticism of a view so like his own. I shall be content, therefore, although I may not succeed in throwing new light on the

* From *Mind*, Vol. XLV, N.S., No. 180 (October, 1936), pp. 474-480. Reprinted with permission.

[1] *Mind*, XLV, N.S., No. 180 (October, 1936), chap. XII.

matter, if I can at least show that the Hegelian view of the Ontological Argument is still intact.

Mr. Ryle's criticism may be summed up as follows: Existence is not and cannot be made a "predicate," and the Ontological Argument depends for its validity on just this illegitimate treatment of existence as if it were a "predicate." His own words are: "But unfortunately [for Mr. Collingwood] this is precisely where I should have thought not only Hume and Kant but almost all recent logicians who have attended to the analysis of existential propositions would dig their heels in and say that the argument is an obvious fallacy *unless* existence is a "predicate"; and that existence is not a "predicate." . . . How can particular matters of fact be deduced from a priori or nonempirical premises?"

What is meant by saying that existence is not a predicate is, I presume, that existence is not part of the character—the "what" (to use a Bradleian term)—of the subject which is asserted to exist. All the possible characters or "predicates" that can be attributed to it constitute its "what," but *that* it is is something beyond and, so to speak, external to its "what." I should be unwilling to agree that this is entirely and finally true, but so much may be admitted that to say, in bare abstraction, that x exists adds nothing to our conception of x. Hence, Hegel is led to remark, "if we look at the thought it holds, nothing can be more insignificant than being."[2] But if the denial that existence is a predicate comes to this, our conclusion should be not simply a refutation of the Ontological Argument but rather that the proof of God's bare existence is of no philosophical importance whatsoever, if only because of the extreme emptiness of the apparent predicate. Insofar as Mr. Ryle's view serves to suggest something of this sort, it is not without value.

But the matter may be regarded in a different light which reveals a deeper truth in the Ontological Argument and one which Mr. Ryle's criticism entirely overlooks. He protests that "matters of fact" cannot be deduced from "nonempirical premises." These he defines as "premises about the characteristics the combination of which is symbolized by the description"—of something whose existence (in this instance) is to be proved. But he does not say what he means by "matters of fact" nor does he tell us positively what sort of premises they could be deduced from. Presumably, these would be "empirical" premises. Now, premises "about the charac-

[2] *Encyclopaedie*, §51; Wallace's transl.

ters" of things are, I take it, such premises as arise out of classification of things according to their characters (e.g., propositions expressing the relation of species to genus), such as analyze the characters themselves, or state necessary connections between them. These are matters not given directly in sense perception. But what is presented in sense perception may, I suppose, be regarded as a "matter of fact," and propositions stating perceived facts will be "empirical" premises. I shall assume, therefore (I hope without doing violence to his view), that Mr. Ryle is prepared to admit as proper to a proof of existence the sort of premise which states a fact given in sense perception.

The question must then be raised: What is the nature of the evidence provided by sense perception for truths of fact? Let us consider an example. I am assured of the existence of this pen because I can feel it, see it, make marks on the paper with it which other people can see, and so forth. All these facts are the evidences of sense perception. None of them is simple, but I do not intend to discuss the nature of their complexity. What is important to notice is that the existence of the pen is not adequately proved by any one of them alone but can be proved only by all or a number of them taken together. An isolated perception can prove the existence of nothing, except a momentary state of consciousness. That I now seem to see a pen is not sufficient to justify my making the judgment "that this is a pen," for my visual sensations may be produced by curious effects of lighting or by anything that simply *looks like* a pen but is not one, or may even be imaginary. Nor would the judgment be justified by any number of different perceptions unless the bearing of each upon the fact to be proved reciprocally gave significance to and received it from all the rest. The fact of the existence of the pen is proved by the mutual corroboration of several perceptions which together provide a body of evidence. In the example taken, I can conclude from what I perceive to the existence of the pen because all my perceptions of it and of matters relative to it reveal to my mind a number of facts (that there is here something which feels smooth and hard, which appears black, which both looks and feels cylindrical, which I can handle and use, etc.). These facts form a system to complete which the fact of the pen's existence is necessary. The evidence is such that if it is accepted, the conclusion must follow. The further inquiry why it is necessary or how it is even possible to accept the evidence simply on the strength of sense perception would lead us into a discussion upon which I do not wish to embark in this article. I shall say only that I believe the answer is to be found in the fact that all judgments of perception are interpretations of what comes to us through sense in the light of the systematic conception of the world which we have built up in the course of our experience. This interpretative character gives value as evidence to what we perceive. Our experience of the world of things in space and time is the experience of an ordered world; of a world, that is, in which certain laws and principles are found to hold good (even before they come to be formulated abstractly in reflection). If this were not so, no valid reasoning from experienced "facts" to any other "matters of fact" would be at all possible, for all inference must rest on a system and the deduction of "matters of fact" rests on the systematic character of the experienced world. Accordingly, we may, on the basis of this system, reason from a set of facts (such as the body of evidence described above) to a conclusion which the nature of the evidence, on that basis, requires. We should say, in effect (if we made the argument explicit), "Things being what they are, I cannot, in the face of this evidence, deny that *x* exists."

The establishment of a fact, then, depends first on a body of evidence, and secondly on the ordered system of the experienced world. To prove the existence of a thing, we must show on sufficient evidence that the thing is a part of the system of things in space and time. The evidence is sufficient when to deny the conclusion to which it leads would disorganize the system. The necessity of the inference is due to the system, and lies ultimately in the impossibility of rejecting the system in its entirety.[3]

Here we have the crux of the matter, but before proceeding, certain points already reached must be emphasized:

(1) Mere sense perception cannot prove the existence of anything other than momentary states of consciousness.

(2) No judgment of perception by itself can prove a matter of fact; nor can any number of such judgments, except by demonstrating a body of evidence from which we can *infer* to the fact in question.

(3) This is true even when the matter to be proved is the existence of something at the time present to the senses.

Accordingly, we must conclude that, whether or not Mr. Ryle is justified in demanding "empirical" premises for deducing "matters

[3] Cf. Bosanquet, *Implication and Linear Inference*, Chap. I.

of fact," the essential element of the deduction (what has been called "the nerve of the inference"[4]) is not the so-called "empirical" character of the premises but the systematic character of the evidence which they contain.

To resume, however, the crux of the matter is that whatever doubts we may entertain about particular matters of fact, these doubts must be dispelled when they involve a challenge to the ordered character of the whole experienced world. The proof of any existence must stand, if it is to stand at all, upon that order, and there is no other means beyond the world as a whole of proving an existence which the evidences demonstrable within the experienced world disprove, or vice versa. When we are faced with the alternative, "this fact or nothing," we must choose "this fact" or commit intellectual suicide. In other words, whatever particular facts we may deny or doubt, what we cannot possibly deny or doubt is the whole world of fact, for upon it any denial must depend for its validity and any doubt for its justification.

Now those who believe that Hegel reinterpreted the Ontological Argument in a manner which put it beyond the reach of such attacks as that of Kant hold that our experience of finite things existing in space and time, although systematic enough for everyday purposes, reveals itself on reflection to be a very incomplete and imperfect system. Yet, they hold, it is one which, we find as we try to understand it, implies a wider and more perfect system. In fact, they go as far as to say that if the world of everyday experience is to be intelligible ultimately (i.e., philosophically), it must be regarded as a part, or an aspect or an appearance (according to the view taken) of an Absolute Whole of reality transcending the experience of finite things. This Absolute is to be identified with what the authors of the Ontological Argument call the most perfect being, and clearly to deny the existence of this Whole is a far more serious matter than to deny the existence of what is no more than a part of it, namely, the world of things in space and time. That, we saw, could not be denied, because the proof or denial of any and every finite existence must stand upon it. How much less, then, is it possible to deny the existence of that on which the intelligible reality of the whole world of finite existence depends.

This is the source of the Ontological Argument's truth and, in whatever form that Argument may be presented, this is what it

[4] *Ibid.*

ought to mean. If "God" means the most complete and perfect being, He (or It) must be identified with the absolute whole of Reality; and the existence of that whole our intellect demands as the logical condition of intelligibility of all our experience. The true meaning of the assertion that God's essence implies existence is that to be infinite and all-inclusive (the character or "essence" of God) is to be ultimate; on what is ultimate depends all existence and all proof of existence; therefore, there can be no denial of the existence of God, for there is nothing on which such denial could rest.

The Kantian criticism of the Ontological Argument, with which, as I understand him, Mr. Ryle wishes to associate his own, is that a demand of the intellect is no proof of existence, and we may not argue that because the intellect demands a complete system, therefore there is one. But this criticism breaks down in the face of what has gone before. No proof of existence is ever anything but the satisfaction of a demand of the intellect. We have seen that mere sense perception cannot prove matters of fact. Such proof requires, at least, the comprehension of sense data into a system from which we can infer to the existence in question. It is only by such inference that any existence can be unassailably established (even when the thing in question is present to our senses). Any such inference, to be valid, must satisfy the demands of the intellect, and the conclusion of such inference is no more nor less than what the intellect demands in the face of the evidence produced. If, then, our experience is such that, for it to have any recognizable character at all and be more than mere meaningless chaos, our intellect demands an absolutely whole system of reality, and if the satisfaction of this demand is the *sine qua non* of the validity of all arguments, including proofs of existence of finite things, then the absolutely complete system of reality must be.

On this view it follows, also, that we may not argue, as Mr. Ryle does, that because the proof of existence of a finite thing requires premises of a certain kind, therefore the proof of God's existence must require premises of the same kind. For any operation in thought upon any premises requires and must rest upon the existence of God in the manner explained. Apart from the Absolute, no proof or argument would be intelligible (let alone valid).

If, as is probable, Mr. Ryle would deny the truth of the Hegelian view of Reality, the onus is on him to show where it breaks down, but that is not the point at issue here. The point is that his argument that "matters of fact" cannot be deduced from "nonempirical" premises will not survive examination in this connection. Even if we overlook the fact that Mr. Ryle has done nothing to show whether, or why, the distinction of "empirical" from "nonempirical" is ultimate, and even if we assume that perceptual experience is all the one and not at all the other (questions not hitherto raised), it yet has to be proved by Mr. Ryle that to make any perceptual experience intelligible, it need not be interpreted in the light of the whole order of the experienced world and that in being further interpreted, it will not eventually come to be viewed as a part or an appearance of an Absolute Reality which transcends it; it yet had to be proved that "empirical" premises themselves are not, for the purposes of any proof, devoid of significance except as interpreted by reference to a systematic whole of reality. For if they are, we must still maintain that the existence of that whole is guaranteed by its very nature (or "essence") as the ultimate basis of all partial experiences.

Only if we conceive God under finite categories (as so many well-meaning religious people do) will Mr. Ryle's claim have any plausibility. If in attempting to prove God's existence, we were attempting to prove the existence of a finite being (whether or not we call Him finite), Mr. Ryle's condition for the validity of the argument might be admitted. In that case, clearly, His essence would not involve existence, for He would not be ultimate and we should have to argue from finite matters of fact. But the Absolute Whole is quite a different matter. The conception of the whole is a conception of something the reality of which cannot be doubted just because it is what it is—namely, that whole in which everything has its being. It is this truth that Hegel wished to indicate in his argument against Kant when he objected to the example of the *hundert Taler*, saying that in God "we have an object of another kind than any *hundert Taler* and unlike any one particular notion, representation or whatever else it may be called." And it is this truth which Mr. Ryle overlooks.

Moreover, it is here that we see what is at once the strength and the weakness of Mr. Ryle's position. The narrow sense of existence, that in which it applies to finite things in space and time, is not applicable to God (unless in a very special manner which we need not discuss here). So far is existence, in this sense, from being implied in God's essence that the contrary is rather the case. To quote Hegel again, "Existence is . . . a term too low for the Absolute

Idea, and unworthy of God." That should be clear from what has been said above, for if God is the whole, and existence means no more than a place in a limited and abstracted scheme within the whole (the spatio-temporal scheme), God clearly does not exist. God is not in existence so much as existence is in God.

Now when Mr. Ryle talks of the illegitimacy of deducing existence from "nonempirical" premises, when he says that it is not a predicate and cannot be proved a priori, he is referring to existence in just this narrow sense. And he is quite right, therefore, to deny that such existence can be proved to belong to God. The sort of demonstration that can prove the existence of finite things, namely, reasoning from "particular matters of fact," cannot be applied to God, for God is not a particular nor is Its existence a "matter of fact" (in the sense that the existence of this pen is one). God possesses reality of another order.

But this again is just the strength of the Ontological Argument—that it is not an attempt to prove from "particular matters of fact" that God has existence like finite things, and the weakness of Mr. Ryle's position is his complaint that the Ontological Argument is not such an attempt. Presumably, had the argument proceeded from "empirical" premises, Mr. Ryle would have made no objection to its method, whether or not he would have had much hope for its success. But the older philosophers were wiser than to attempt such a proof. They knew very well that God was not to be treated in the same way as finite things, and it is for that very reason, because God is infinite, that we cannot regard the idea of God (or, as Hegel would say, simply "The Idea") as something merely "subjective" lacking objective reality. Mr. Ryle's complaint, therefore, does not touch the Ontological Argument any more than Kant's did, and it leaves the whole matter in just that position which justified Prof. Collingwood's attitude.

XIV

GILBERT RYLE

Back to the Ontological Argument*

I AM glad that Mr. Harris challenges my attempted refutation of the Ontological Argument. It is a very important question about the nature of philosophical theories, whether philosophical arguments can establish the existence of anything. So it is encouraging to find someone who both believes in that possibility and produces arguments for it.

1. I have no objection to the suggestion that the argument which I tried to show to be fallacious is not identical with the argument which Hegel, and perhaps also Prof. Collingwood, champions. It is always possible that unsympathy may cause a critic to fail to read between the lines a doctrine which is clearly discerned to be there by more sympathetic spirits. And I have no desire to thrash out here hermeneutic questions, or adduce literary evidence that anyone does champion the Ontological Arguments (as I represented it).

2. The interesting question is whether the "deeper truth" in the Ontological Argument, which Mr. Harris thinks that I failed to discern, is a different argument from the one which I criticized, and if so, whether it is valid.

Now, as Mr. Harris formulates this argument, it certainly is different in one very important respect from what I called "the Ontological Argument." And it is at first sight a much better argument. For it is a variant of the Cosmological Argument or the argument *a contingentia mundi*. It argues from the fact that our world of ordinary or finite experience is of a certain character. And this

* From *Mind*, Vol. XLVI, N.S., No. 181 (January, 1937), pp. 53-57. Reprinted with permission.

is certainly intended to be or to contain an empirical existence-proposition. "We experience a world of such and such a sort" is an empirical or a posteriori premise to his argument.

And as this is precisely what I demanded for any argument of which the conclusion is to be an existence-proposition, I might stop here, just expressing my contentment that Hegel and Mr. Harris do admit by implication that arguments to existence from a priori premises are invalid.

3. Certainly, arguments for the existence of fountain pens or remote planets or for the occurrence of past events have very complex premises, and may be described as resting upon certain systematic conceptions or notions of system. But this does not make those premises nonempirical. The demands of mutual corroboration of perceptions must be satisfied, but they cannot be satisfied or unsatisfied unless perceptions occur. And of course such arguments can never constitute rigorous proofs. The pen's existence is never logically necessary, whatever empirical premises we employ. (Any scientist can be baffled by a conjuror—for a time.)

However, we should be foolish not to accept the conclusions of hosts of such arguments. And if the argument for the Absolute is really of the same logical pattern, and if the premises have the required empirical content plus systematic interlocking, we shall be foolish not to accept the conclusion that God or the Absolute exists. But is the doctrine really just a well-established hypothesis of Natural Science? Do the Fellows of the Royal Society support the views of Hegel in the same way as they vouch for spiral nebulae? Obviously they do not. So obviously the argument for the Absolute is not just a well-attested scientific hypothesis adduced to explain phenomena. What, then, is the difference?

4. The difference is that the Cosmological Argument is not a scientist's argument but a philosophical argument. And, as Kant saw, it presupposes the Ontological Argument (in the form in which I tried to refute it). True, it covers its tracks by reassuringly introducing an empirical premise about the whole world of fact or the world of finite experience. But this enters into the argument only in this way, that there is now alleged to be a contradiction not just in the denial of the existence of the Absolute but in the conjunction of this denial with the affirmation of the existence of our world of fact. The existence of our world of fact logically implies the existence of the Absolute. For the former is a part, or an aspect or an appearance of

the latter. (Incidentally, is it not high time that we were told which? For the alleged implication is different according to the relation adopted. On a matter of such importance we ought not to be left to pay our money and take our choice.) However, there are perfectly valid arguments of the various proposed forms.

(*a*) "Here is the grin of a Cheshire Cat" certainly entails that a Cheshire cat exists of which the grin is an aspect.

(*b*) "Here is the tail of a cat" certainly entails that there is or has been a cat of which the tail is or was a part.

(*c*) "Here is the smell of a cat" certainly entails that there is or was a cat of which the smell is or was an appearance. In each case the conclusion is certain—if the premise is known to be true. And we can know empirically that a grin is a cat's grin, a tail a cat's tail, and a smell a cat's smell. But, of course, a similar grin, tail or smell might belong to quite a different animal. How do we, or Mr. Harris, know that our world is an aspect, part or appearance of something else? From the *Proceedings of the Royal Society* or from philosophical considerations? Empirically or a priori?

Apparently from philosophical considerations. And I want to show that these considerations are hollow unless the Ontological Argument is valid. But I must in fairness say that my interpretation of what these considerations are is largely conjectural. For I have got to read between the lines of Mr. Harris' contribution. The nerve of the argument lies in the significance of the adjective "intelligible." A certain conclusion must be accepted because without it the world of fact is philosophically unintelligible. But Mr. Harris does not tell us what it is for something to be unintelligible or intelligible.

He does not mean, I think, by "unintelligible" "not yet subsumed under a causal law." Else his paper would have been a defence of the methods of Newton, and not of an argument of Hegel. Moreover, he uses the phrase "philosophically intelligible."

I surmise that what he means is this. The existence of something or the occurrence of something is philosophically unintelligible when its existence or occurrence is a brute empirical fact, and not logically necessary, i.e., when the denial of it involves no contradiction. And the existence of something is philosophically intelligible when the assertion of it is the assertion of an analytic proposition or of a consequence analytically following from an analytic proposition. And this is the principle of the argument from Essence to existence, namely that there is something, the denial of the existence of which involves a contradiction.

Against this I shall only repeat the conclusion of my original argument; namely, that existence-propositions are synthetic, and never logically necessary. So no existence-proposition is philosophically intelligible, if this is what it means to call something philosophically intelligible. But this does not imply that there is anything philosophically puzzling about the existence or occurrence of things and events in Nature, unless everything is puzzling which philosophers cannot demonstrate.

Now let us suppose that Mr. Harris means something different from this by his phrase "philosophically intelligible." No matter what it is, it will have to be consistent with the admission that no existence-proposition can be logically necessary or demonstrable from a priori premises or such that its denial involves a contradiction.

So there will be no possibility of demonstrating that our world of fact could not exist unless there exists something else of which it is an aspect, part or appearance, unless we know empirically that our world of fact is an aspect of something, a part of something or an appearance of something. What sort of knowledge would this be?

I will not quarrel with the, to me, suspect noun of assemblage "the world," except to say that I am not clear what it is supposed to be a totality of, or how, if it is a totality, it can be described as "incomplete."

Let us suppose that we are agreed as to what is denoted by "our world of fact" or "the world of finite experience," and concentrate on the question of how we might discover empirically that it is an aspect, part or appearance of something else.

(*a*) "*x* is an aspect of *y*" is often true, e.g., "that is the grin of a Cheshire Cat." But that there exists something which both grins and has such other properties as to rank as a cat of a certain sort is a complex synthetic proposition. There is no deducing these other properties from this one of grinning. Nor is there, strictly, an entailment between an occurrence of grinning and the existence of a grinner. Both are ways of expressing the single fact that something is grinning.

If it makes sense and is true to say that our world of fact is an aspect, then we are acquainted with the aspected something in being acquainted with the world. There is no place for an argument from the one to the other. Or if the argument was from that aspect which is our world to some other aspects, then the inference would not be logically necessary.

(*b*) "*x* is a part of *y*" is often true. But it is always a synthetic proposition. We have only inductive grounds for supposing that whenever things like cats' tails exist, there are also things like cats that they are attached to. So it is a synthetic proposition to say that our world belongs to something else as part to whole. Its denial would contain no contradiction.

(*c*) "*x* is an appearance of *y*" is often true. But here, too, either the appearance is an abstraction from the thing appearing, in which case there is no inference from the existence of the one to that of the other. For only one existence is given. Or the inference is from one appearance to other appearances, properties, parts, etc., of the thing appearing, in which case the inference is not better than probable, and must rest on inductive grounds.

So the argument from intelligibility proves nothing, unless "intelligible" means "logically necessary." The Cosomological Argument, then, if it is a philosophers' argument, embodies the principle of the old Ontological Argument, that there can be a logically necessary existence-proposition. And, as this is false, the Cosmological Argument is invalid. There can be no proof from a priori premises that there exists something of which the world of finite experience is an aspect, part or appearance.

Nor will the argument be bettered by the substitution which Mr. Harris recommends, of some notion of being or being real in place of that of existing. For, apart from the suggestion which I am sure Mr. Harris did not intend to convey, that "existing," "being" and "being real" signify different species of one (generic) attribute—the very error from which the old Ontological Argument drew its plausibility and its fallaciousness—the arguments for the being or the being real of something of a certain description are of the same logical pattern as those for the existence of something. Indeed, I am at a loss to see any but a verbal difference between them.

Mr. Harris must show that there is a contradiction in "our world is not an aspect, part or appearance of anything else" or else that there are good empirical reasons for supposing that our world is an aspect, part or appearance of something else. And if he accepts the former task, he must face the question: Can an existence-proposition be logically necessary?

I very much hope that Mr. Harris will face this question. It is to me rather shocking that there should exist a large school of thought which treats as a well-established principle a doctrine which has been for a century and a half accused of formal fallaciousness. There may be an answer to the accusation—but it ought to be divulged, in order that it may be tested.

To summarize: A philosophical argument for the existence or reality of something must be of one of two forms.

(1) Either it argues that there is a contradiction in the denial of the existence or reality of such a thing, which is the Ontological Argument proper.

(2) Or it argues that something is empirically known to exist but that it is logically impossible for anything to exist unless either its existence is logically necessary or its existence logically implies that something else exists of logical necessity.

Neither holds water if "there exists a so-and-so" is a synthetic proposition or one the negation of which contains no contradiction and so is logically possible.

XV

AIMÉ FOREST

St. Anselm's Argument in Reflexive Philosophy[1]

THE most remarkable character of contemporary thought is the development of a reflexive philosophy. It appears in very diverse forms, but in all its movements it pursues the same aim. It wishes to make us see what is purely spiritual in us, and by its own efforts to work gradually back to the source of our activity. It is especially noteworthy that several of these movements lead us to the teaching of St. Anselm. They wish to recover the meaning and value of the argument of the *Proslogion*; they give us a renewed understanding of it. Such encounters enable us to discern certain affinities of an intellectual order, and the study of these can be very valuable. With the thought of St. Anselm and of those who mean to continue his inspiration today, we can clarify the one by means of the other.

Reflection is the turning back of thought upon itself. It does not adopt a purely projective, outgoing attitude, submitting itself to the solicitations which come to it from things. The reflexive experience involves a duality that is difficult to surmount; it appears to be privative on the one hand, and possessive on the other. It can be considered as a rupture, a breaking off of the dynamic thrust of life. It can appear as "the sickness of the consciousness." It allows us, on the contrary, to be assured of what is present in us, and there-

1 *Spicilegium Beccense* (Paris: J. Vrin, 1959), pp. 273-294, transl. with permission by Arthur C. McGill. In English the word "reflection" usually designates the fact that an object throws back the lights or sounds which fall upon it. The term, however, is also associated with any situation where something turns back and acts upon itself, in the fashion of a "reflexive" verb. This essay is concerned solely with the second meaning, and not with the first. The word "reflection" is therefore the noun form of the adjective "reflexive," not of the verb "to reflect."

fore to experience in a more lucid fashion; in it, we become fully spiritual for the first time. Reflection undoubtedly opposes life when it is unfaithful to its valid purpose. But when it conforms to its true requirements, it is not a ruptured existence but a capacity for recovering the self. It accompanies every movement of consciousness, so that the mind can enter within itself. It allows us to identify ourselves with what we are, not through a direct intuition of our being, but through the assurance of the rectitude of our action. It reaches an *inner* dynamic, and thus surpasses the simple recognition of what is given to our experience. It rests on a fundamental activity present in each of our particular acts and distinctive of consciousness itself. It allows a reaffirmation of the self. It gives us access to a new life beyond our immediate and given being, a life penetrated with clarity.

The aim of reflexive philosophy, however, is not simply to lead us back to what is inside us. It also intends to be a manifestation of the absolute. It usually proceeds from the realization that interiority cannot be thought except in its relation with universality. This relation is constitutive of our being, understood in its spiritual sense; without this relation we would discern only reality as given to us, but not that openness to reality and values by which we have access to ourselves. In affirming what pertains peculiarly to us, we surpass what is limited in us. By this orientation, this surpassing, we enter into the order of spirit. What is primary in us is our relationship to the universal. Consequently, our activity participates in the values toward which it tends and which come to be written into it. Reflection on this form of our action allows us to discern a determinative principle which conditions our action and which cannot be reduced simply to a movement of our thought. We affirm this principle under the mode of a presence that sustains our intellectual processes and that thus becomes interior to us in its effects, although not in its source. We cannot embrace it in any representation, if we understand it in the sense of something that determines us; but neither can we deny the absolute, since without it there would be no progress for thought. In this way we form a properly reflexive certainty. We perceive this in a light which thought can attain—or, better, can form from within—solely by the effort of turning back upon itself. Reflection understood in this way becomes "the most elevated kind of knowledge that we have," according to the expression of Lachelier. It surpasses the thought of the given, and, without reaching the state of intuition, it affirms what is at the source of our interior being. It realizes that task by which Lachelier defined metaphysics: "a flowing back of light into its source."

Reflection intends to make manifest the wholly internal relation of act and absolute. It is the movement of thought which Ravaisson explained in these words: "From the interior and central point of view of reflection, the soul does not discern only itself, but also, at its foundation, the absolute from which it emanates."[2] Reflexive philosophy understood in this way consists of very diverse forms. A very important part of the history of present-day thought is the history of this difficult philosophic aim, of this intention which is mixed with great uncertainty. Among these doctrines we can give particular attention to those which are inspired by St. Anselm. Reflexive philosophy wishes to show what there is legitimate in his aim, by recovering this spiritual message in it.

* * *

The ontological argument has been explained several times by Maurice Blondel. It appears as an essential moment in the development of his thought. It represents a return to an ancient teaching, but at the same time it is an original elaboration. Blondel insists on this recovery of doctrinal tradition in a philosophy which nevertheless has its distinctive characteristics. "The ontological argument is going to take on a new meaning and vigor."[3]

The force of this proof comes first of all from the fact that it is not isolated. In order to understand it properly, we must envisage it in its relation to those proofs which, under other forms, express the movement of thought toward the absolute. Thus, one can consider a sequence of diverse proofs; they give support to each other, as it were, and are valuable only in their synthetic unity. Blondel does not mean to say that, properly speaking, there is only one proof of God's existence which people express in different ways. He recognizes that each chain of reasoning has its own significance and value. He rather wishes to show that the first proofs are preparations for and announcements of those which finally complete them. It is indeed remarkable that thought recognizes its fundamental intention when it comes to establish the ontological proof. Kant was the one who established that the proofs for God's existence

[2] Ravaisson, *Rapport sur la philosophie contemporaine en France*, p. 271.
[3] M. Blondel, *L'Action* (1893), p. 348.

derived all their genuine significance from the ontological argument. But the error which he discovered in it is characteristic of the whole movement of rational theology, where we can only see a transcendental illusion. Blondel rediscovers this intimate connection between all the proofs which Kant brought to light, but in the ontological proof he sees the completed form of a thought which is capable of being raised to the absolute. He wants to establish what is valuable in this proof, not what is exclusive in it. What he finds is that it manifests, better than any other proof, what is implied by the relation of immanence and transcendence, which is the constant object of the Blondelian meditation. This proof enables us to see in the movement of spiritual immanence the divine presence, not in its being, to be sure, but in its act, sustaining our spiritual vitality from within. God is a mystery of presence. Each of the proofs thus expresses under a partial form a truth which finally lays bare the supreme effort of thought.

The proof from contingency intends to make us see the one necessary being. Blondel recovers the classic form of this proof. He shows that if contingency is the condition of some being, so that it does not account for itself by itself, we are led, step by step, to perceive in this contingent being a relation to being by itself, a dependence on the absolute at its very center. He, however, insists on one of the characteristics of this proof which in his view constitutes its whole force. The absolute should not be affirmed as having only the character of exteriority; contingent being must manifest its presence at the same time as its transcendence. Necessary being not only stands outside contingency as an exterior term. It is a reality which sustains it and gives it being. This thought is completely classical. Blondel seeks to justify it by showing the meeting point of the truth of being and the dynamism of the consciousness which affirms it. To this end he comes to express the ontological argument in these memorable phrases: "Instead of depending on the fiction of a necessary ideal, it depends on the necessity of the real itself. It is not necessary to maintain that our acts are nothing and that phenomena are entirely empty. In what he does, in the life of his senses, in his acts and his pleasures, man experiences at once a strange poverty and a more astonishing fullness."[4]

The teleological argument means to conclude, not simply in the necessity of wisdom, but in its absoluteness. Above all it considers

[4] *Ibid.*, p. 343.

exemplary causality. It causes us to recognize in ourselves and in things a wisdom which of itself is by nature productive of imitations and reflections, and which therefore, in order to be itself, calls for the perfection of a model. In this way, the proof does not lead us to see an absent cause, but rather a presence, conceived under the rather original form of exemplarity rather than efficacy.

The ontological argument does not elevate us to the affirmation of necessity or wisdom, but to that of perfection. It completes a movement of thought which is anterior to it. In what is definitive in it, it expresses a truth which the other proofs also announce: The divine presence is manifested within our thought, if we consider it as a particular form of action. Blondel reflects on this idea of perfection; He wants to show its living reality, its active presence in us. Perfection, he writes:

> is for us less something seen than a life. It does not result from a speculation; it is tied to every movement of thought and action. It is not an abstraction from which we could only draw another abstraction, but an act which brings forth action. It is not an ideal from which we claim to extract the real, but a real in which the ideal is to be found. Therefore, it is not necessary to seek in it for that which would allow us to raise an objection against it, that is, for a reality distinct from the ideal itself.[5]

We can see the value which Blondel intends above all to establish. It is that of a divine presence at the root of our action, constitutive of the intellectual dynamism which shows itself in the affirmation of God's existence. God is actually recognized from within the thought which proceeds toward him, as the infinite that is present in the idea of the infinite. The value of the ontological proof is that it enables us to attain to a truth that is not only reasoned but is also manifested internally, to a presence about which we can say in all strictness that "it is more internal to us than our own interior." The force of this proof comes from the fact that it allows us to establish the truth toward which the preceding intellectual steps have been moving. It is like a recovery and a completion. It carries higher an intellectual dynamism that moves toward the possession of that truth which the ontological argument reveals in its fullness.

Blondel's analysis does not bear simply on the place of the ontological argument in the movement of thought. He intends to make us understand its genuine meaning and to establish its value. The essential idea is that this proof "is for us less something seen

[5] *Ibid.*, p. 348.

than a life." It does not proceed from an abstraction, from which we could only draw an equally abstract conclusion. The idea itself is an act. It does not lead back to a reality of the notional order, which is alien to being and the thought of which still leaves us confined within the limits of the purely mental. The idea of God, we can say, is not present in us in a static, but in a dynamic, fashion. It is not received in us and merely recognized "in the treasure house of my spirit," according to the Cartesian expression. It is active, the principle of the intellectual dynamism in which its true nature is expressed. Blondel is less concerned with the idea apprehended notionally than with the concrete and living thought recognized reflexively.

This interpretation of the idea of perfection fits in with the general spirit of his philosophy. Thought is itself action, if one understands the latter as spiritual activity grasped in its very source and exercise. Action is the synthesis of knowing, willing and being—the integral spiritual experience. Thought is envisaged as an act, but this view has the danger of being perverted and of causing us to misunderstand what is original in our intellectual experience. Thought is not an initiative which is in danger of being purely subjective and therefore perhaps irrational. The distinctive mark of thought is that in its exercise it itself is penetrated with light; clarity characterizes not only the object of knowledge but also the vitality which excites it. Thought is an act, but grasped in its relation to the light which it receives and which directs it. One can thus distinguish two elements in thought, the noetic and the pneumatic. The noetic is the objective aspect of thought; the pneumatic is the life of thought in which the idea is only a moment. To want to reduce our intellectual experience to one or the other of these elements is the opposite error of that made by notionalism or idealism. We must apprehend the act and the idea in their relationship, placing ourselves at the point of view of thinking thought. In this sense we can say that the thought of God is a life, and that the idea of God is an act. For in order to see our intellectual dynamism properly, we consider it in terms of what it has concretely, when it is moved by this idea.

The difficult problem that confronts philosophic reflection is to justify the passage from thought, as we know it within ourselves, to the affirmation of the absolute. Blondel's original idea is that in order to manifest the connection between these, we must proceed from the action within thought itself. Thought "bears on everything; and that is why the unquestionable presence and the constraining proof of Being proceeds from it and from it alone."[6] When understood in this way, action has the advantage of enabling us to perceive not only what we are, but also what is at our very origin, that without which we would not be. We seek to equate ourselves with ourselves, but the idea of God which is present in us creates a distance between us and ourselves which we cannot leap over simply by considering what is our own. In the very depths of the act in which we become conscious of what we are, we recognize an interior beyond, since this is constitutive of the dynamism of our souls.

> I am not equal to myself, because I am not equal to it [this "beyond" which lies within me]. It is not the obscure face of my thought, or the invisible reverse side of my consciousness and action, as if I should see it only as something within me, and as if its whole reality consists only of the idea which I have of it. I am led to conceive of it only because I am led by necessity to recognize what I lack, even in what I do: the absolute identity of the real and ideal, of power and wisdom, of being and perfection—this is what must be, in order for me to be what I am. The thinking of this and the willing of this—without which there would be neither thinking nor willing in me, and which at the same time neither my thought nor will can understand—such are the interdependent terms of the mystery which imposes itself on my consciousness.[7]

In order to understand the ontological argument, it is still necessary to recognize in what sense it is not a view of Being. We do not perceive God himself. We cannot grasp this interiority of perfection within existence as it is in itself, so that then it would be the absolute truth of God and would give to the proof the meaning of a revelation of the divine mystery, not for faith but for knowledge. There are some who expect the ontological argument to do this, but Blondel expresses their demand in such a way that he repudiates it. "The Trinity is the ontological argument transferred into the absolute. That is where this proof is not a proof but the very truth itself and the life of being."[8] We apprehend God in ourselves and not in himself. The necessity which works here is that of logical affirmation, not that of an essence unveiled before us. In no way can the argument lead us to what the ontologists call "the certainty of simple vision." Blondel's interpretation has its meaning in opposition to this ontological direction of thought.

[6] *Ibid.*, p. 350. [7] *Ibid.*, p. 347. [8] *Ibid.*, p. 349.

The remarks in *L'Action* and in certain other passages certainly realize Blondel's intention to give the ontological argument "a new meaning and vigor."[9] In fact, he interprets it in the very spirit of the philosophy of action. It is in the practical life that this argument finds its basis. It is the reflexive coming-to-consciousness of what is present in us and yet distinct from us, since the perfection which we must affirm is recognized in its causality at the very foundation of our thought. Blondel expresses the spirit of his thought in saying that the proof which he develops is "a necessary consent"; he even speaks of a docility of the spirit, an assent of thought as preliminary to the consent of the will. The spirit of Blondelism is the movement from a sincerity that forms reflection to a consent that expresses it. When understood in this way, reflexive philosophy leads us to use the light which it finds within us to resolve the problem of our destiny, which is to know whether we can "will infinitely without willing the infinite." The ontological argument establishes a certainty in us which makes us ready for such an act of will. The originality of this step is well expressed in the statement

> The problem is to know, not whether this one necessary being is the abstract term of an argument, but whether it can re-enter as a living truth into the development of deliberate action.[10]

* * *

Jacques Paliard pursues the study of the ontological argument in the spirit of Blondel's thought. This is especially a philosophy of destiny. It means to discover the meaning of our life, to resolve the problem of action, and to find in it the principle of an intelligibility which is capable of bearing on both being and thought. Reflection on transcendence allows us to recognize in the spirit a motion, an inner solicitation, a constituent presence beyond that which appears to us as given in the analysis of our experience. Paliard's philosophical inquiry is the same as Blondel's, but does not bear on exactly the same object. Blondel considers action, and seeks to find out how our action can be equal to its own vitality. He recognizes a lack in everything that we do. Because there is this beyond in every-

[9] See especially M. Blondel, *La Pensée* (1934), vol. I, pp. 189-193; and *L'Être et les êtres* (1935), pp. 163, 169.

[10] M. Blondel, letter to Paul Archambault, dated February 23, 1928, cited by B. Romeyer, *La philosophie religieuse de Maurice Blondel*, p. 51.

thing that is willed, our action is prevented from falling back into nothingness. But this goal of our attention, although capable of moving our purposes, can only be thought of as not being that which has been willed already.

Paliard focuses all his attention on a different problem, that of self-consciousness. This is the essential question of modern philosophy. Descartes defined thought in terms of consciousness, or interior apperception. Yet it is remarkable that philosophical inquiry asks about this interiority, which is the character of thought itself, and which therefore makes thought participate in values which are difficult for it to grasp. Paliard reflects on consciousness rather than on action. He thus poses a problem that is more spiritual than practical, more metaphysical than moral. The original idea which he brings to light is that of a spiritual dialectic. Our consciousness is a progress; we must understand it, not as a becoming like that of nature, but as a genesis by which the spirit itself seeks to conquer itself and realize its essence. The spirit is present to itself rather than given to itself; it catches hold of itself in its inner dynamism. The progress of consciousness consists in surmounting an interior duality, which in essence is that of thought and life. To itself the soul is not all clarity, and the light which we have to throw upon things and ourselves does not entirely unite with existence. Our originative experience is this duality, this interior distance, in which the principle of the spiritual dialectic must be seen. This duality is close to, and yet distinct from, that which Blondel envisages between the will willing and the will willed. Paliard seeks to resolve the problem posed by the structure of consciousness. The ontological argument brings us to the solution of this problem, by leading us to recognize a hidden presence in which we participate and which becomes the principle of all our spiritual processes.[11]

Paliard seeks to determine with great rigor what ought to be the method which leads us to affirm the existence of God from the study of thought alone. This is the reflexive method, the effort of

[11] Paliard has often explained and commented on St. Anselm's argument. The principal passages are the following: *Intuition et réflexion* (1925), pp. 194-200; "La Conscience de soi et l'idée de Dieu," in *Études philosophique* (1943); "Prière et dialectique," in *Dieu vivant* (1946), No. 6; "Sur un aspect de la structure conscientielle," in the *Actes du Congrès de Bruxelles* (Louvain, 1947); *Maurice Blondel, ou le dépassement chrétien*, pp. 115, 152-162; *La pensée et la vie*, pp. 252-257. One will find an excellent analysis of these passages in Pierre Masset, *La Dialectique de la conscience chez Jacques Paliard*, pp. 187-207.

thought itself to grasp itself, by entering into a possession of itself which goes beyond consideration of the content given to it. Reflection so understood is a recovery of the self; it presumes a moment of arrest, it is a distinct regression from the outward, prospective attitude. We must grasp the originality of a recuperative reflection. To understand it properly, we should envisage a duality in our intellectual experience: the dynamism of the soul toward the truth on the one hand, and the effort to penetrate the soul's movement with clarity on the other. In taking this view, Paliard recognizes that he is distinguishing himself from Maurice Blondel. "He separates the spiritual from the intellectual less than I do."[12] The ontological argument can only be understood in terms of this distinction and this connection. Paliard presents this in a profound analysis of the *Proslogion* which he offers as a meditation rather than as a commentary.

> What we intend to recover is this rhythm, where invocation and argumentation do not cease from alternating with and stimulating each other. The beauty of Anselm's work lies in this union between the movement of the soul and the demands of the intellect, which both together pursue the quest for their well-being. There is here a profound bond which, in our view, merits reflection.[13]

Reflection is this noëtic moment. We had better distinguish it from the moment of aspiration, if it is true that by itself to understand is not to love. In Anselm, the attitude of rigorous thought is especially apparent in his *Reply* to the objections of the fool, for there "inspiration is obliged momentarily to suspend its fervor, to reflect upon itself, and to be concerned with itself."[14] The distinction thus established, however, prepares the way for an original form of connection; it is that of alternation, or rhythm. The proof is developed in this movement of recovery and progression, between "times of fervor and times of subtle argumentation." Intellection and aspiration thus sustain each other; in this form of reciprocity and what we could call circular causality, the spiritual life appears as an advancing movement. It is still the fact that reflection ought to carry the weight of the proof. The latter is undoubtedly the expression of a spiritual movement, but the dynamism here must reflect upon itself. It is in this reflexive act of consciousness that we can

[12] J. Paliard, *Maurice Blondel, ou le dépassement chrétien*, p. 31.
[13] J. Paliard, "Prière et dialectique," in *Dieu vivant* (1946), No. 6, p. 54.
[14] *Ibid.*, p. 56.

see what is universal in a movement which yet remains that of a singular experience. This spiritual movement is capable of a truth which is written within it and which must be perceived intellectually. In another way, reflection on the development of the proof should allow us to pass beyond what is in danger of remaining subjective in the affirmation of God. It makes us go back to the foundation of our thought; it shows it present and acting in us. It permits us to establish a connection, and in that very way also a difference, between individual thought and absolute thought. By itself the self-consciousness of aspiration would not have that force which only belongs to critical thought. It would show what is an indefinite movement in us, without delivering an actual infinite to us. The ontological argument supposes our recognition of the special value of reflection. It is this reflection which establishes the connection and which also establishes the distance in the study of the soul's relations with God.

The reflexive method gives its meaning to the ontological argument. This argument consists in discerning, in the affirmation of God, the interiority of existence within thought. It must be understood, not as a passage, but as a perception. It is not a movement of thought which would lead us from the logical to the real. We do not proceed from the analysis of an idea present in the mind, which enables us to grasp within it the necessity of existence. The idea of God is in no way comparable to the idea of the blessed islands; for it allows us to affirm the infinite in such a way that our spirit cannot embrace it, circumscribe it, or in this sense possess it internally. The argument is not a passage from essence to existence which presupposes some kind of vision of God, some kind of recognition of what is characteristic to God. The idea of God from which the proof issues is not abstract but reflexive. It is the idea of the unsurpassable. We form it by becoming conscious of the impossibility of grasping the infinite in any of our mental representations, although the infinite is nevertheless the object of our thought. When reflection seeks to penetrate this process with clarity, under the motion of the idea of God, it recognizes the poverty and grandeur of thought. It is this impossibility for thought wholly to take possession of itself which obliges it to recognize an interior transcendence within itself. It cannot entirely appropriate to itself that which is nevertheless given to it as the goal of its dynamism, and which is in this sense present in it. It recognizes that its power to produce the idea of the unsurpassable does not come from itself. At bottom thought is not from itself, through some creative spontaneity out of which all its own content arises. Consequently, the ontological argument allows us to resist "the tempting sumptuousness" of idealism. Thought does not entirely explain itself in terms of its own becoming. From the thought of the infinite alone, without any other consideration being added, reflection draws out the affirmation of that which is outside ourselves and in being, the principle without which our thought would not be.

Such, we believe, is the essential significance of the argument, which does not at all consist in passing from the logical to the real, but in grasping at the very heart of an intellectual experience the reality which conditions it and which it means to reflect. You would not affirm me, it could be said, if you did not already possess me.[15]

In the ontological argument reflection manifests its true nature and value. It has the power to go beyond interior observation, to grasp as present and active in us what is not entirely given, since it is at the foundation of thought. In this way we understand that the ontological argument is a perception and not a passage. To be sure, in a certain way it must involve a passage, since it leads us from our subjective thought to the absolute of thought. But the connection between these is made manifest and recognized internally, not by observation but by reflection. The distinctive characteristic of the argument is that it causes us to see a reflexive implication. We do not have to take this implication in the logical sense of dependence, but in the spiritual sense of envelopment. It allows us to affirm what is present and requisite in that which is given to us, what is enveloping rather than enveloped. Implication is an original form of relationship, which ought not to be expressed solely in terms of exteriority. One can say that it reveals the necessity of a passage in what still remains an object of a reflexive perception. When understood in this way, the ontological argument seems to to be a response to the problem which the study of self-consciousness poses. It seeks to bring us, not to that which is given to the consciousness, but to that which is the foundation of consciousness. It is therefore to be distinguished from those proofs which proceed from the consideration of an interior fact. We should not say simply that we have a desire for the infinite, and that we could be raised from the fact of this desire to the affirmation of the infinite. This desire for the infinite is what we *are*, rather than what we have. The

[15] *Ibid.*, p. 57.

idea of God is not somehow situated inside us, but it gives us our being. Reflection is that analysis which makes us perceive the infinite in the idea of the infinite. Paliard, it seems, expresses his whole thought when he says that St. Anselm's argument should be called metaphysical rather than ontological.[16] It does not enable us to see what is being in itself, but what is metaphysical in us. It shows us that a thirst for and a relation to the absolute are essential in self-consciousness.

Jacques Paliard's meditation leads him to affirm a transcendence in reflection. He wants to recognize its grandeur and weakness. In our experience reflection is the purely noetic moment, but the truth which it affirms is not given in a vision; it is not "an entrance into being." It designates God, rather than giving us an understanding of him. The idea which we form is "the word of faith." But the progress of faith is to go beyond the single, if not evident, certainty which faith gives. Living faith is a spiritual experience, of the "God perceptible to the heart." Reflection is thus extended and completed in aspiration. Then the soul attains to the possession of the truth which it affirms. The history of the religious consciousness is the history of this alternation between argumentation and aspiration, where "falling on one's knees is a symbol for reflection."[17] The spiritual life is this elevation to God in prayer and charity. It is not a vision, even though it unites us in a thoroughly intimate way with the absolute which reflection can only designate. It allows us to recognize the absolute, and to experience it internally. The soul itself seeks to realize itself. This new life is the concentration of the soul in God, above and beyond its dispersion in that which is thought apart from God. "We must participate in love in order to be ourselves." Such is the final truth that rescues philosophy from subjective consciousness. We must take this relation in its full sense. "The soul does not aspire to love because it exists, but it exists because it aspires to love." It itself affirms itself, not within the limits of its poverty, but through that which permits it to return to its own

[16] "The meaning of the argument is precisely such that we prefer to call it metaphysical rather than ontological. For we envisage this argument, not *in abstracto*, as a passage from the possible to the real, but in the concrete reality of the movement of consciousness. Reflection cannot reflect on this reflection, which is exhausted in trying to master all its realizations without projecting it into the Being that we are, not." ("Sur un aspect de la structure conscientielle," in *Actes du Congrès de Bruxelles*, p. 39.)

[17] Paliard, *op. cit.*, "Prière et dialectique," p. 61.

foundation and become more and more interior to itself. Jacques Paliard's profound idea is that the mystical life is itself the concrete expression of the ontological argument.

* * * * * *

In the whole development of his thought Louis Lavelle intends to make us see the value of reflection. He never ceases to show the richness and force of this experience; he wants to set aside the suspicions which often rise against it. We do not have to consider it only as something impoverishing but in its full meaning as something enriching. To be sure, reflection turns us away from that which is given to us in an immediate fashion, from that which is imposed upon us without any criticism. We cease to see things in their diversity, or to experience an ever-changing flow of feelings, before a spectacle which would be limited only to a feigned, or apparent, reality. Yet in reflection we have recourse to an essential activity which is most often forgotten or endangered—spiritual freedom. Reflection is not an absolute beginning, but a recovery of the self. It leads us to find again what is originative and fundamental in us. This experience is accompanied by a purification of the self, the me. It enables us to recover, not one activity among others, but that activity which corresponds to our whole spiritual needs.

Lavelle's most original idea is the connection which he establishes between reflection and wisdom. We do not have to think of wisdom as the simple and perhaps very old-fashioned ideal of moderation and inner stability. It is the value found in the depths of our recovery of ourselves. There we have the experience, not of that which is merely given, but of that which gives itself to itself, of that which becomes in this sense interior. But this process is always in danger of being stopped, and this presence of being obscured. Reflection enables us to catch hold of that which threatens to enslave us. It enables us to recover the primitive activity of the me in its essential integrity. It has value because the wisdom that it forms strongly attracts us. This connection between reflection and wisdom becomes the source of the truths and values which are accessible to us. Reflection is a new life; it is also creative of a new world. Indeed, the values which constitute it find their source in the spirit itself, in its reconquered purity. Its value is like a re-creation of things, a re-creation which transforms what is given to us into spiritual meanings; it is the world taken into ourselves. Wisdom becomes the spiritual understanding of being. It is the foundation of a new being above and beyond appearances, of a being which the spirit recognizes and can justify. Philosophic thought is the coming to consciousness of this relation between reflection and wisdom. In this way we can say that metaphysics is the science of spiritual intimacy.

By placing ourselves in this perspective, we can see the connection between the reflexive act and the creative act. There is an opposition here which seems definitive, but which we surmount in the spiritual life. The idea of creation is that of invention or establishment. In and with the very difficulty of this idea, it causes us to envisage a contribution of being. Reflexive experience, on the contrary, is a regression. We should note, however, that reflection is a recovery of the self; it is not a stoppage but a new dynamism; it enables us to regain an activity that is itself superior. Reflection so understood gives us the highest idea of the absolute; creation of the self by the self, even with the incompleteness that marks it, leads us to think of creation in the absolute sense. By restoring us to spiritual experience, reflection allows us to form the idea of an act which is always interior to itself. It is by means of the reflexive categories that we can think of the absolute. The truths that we attain in these two very different orders of relative and absolute creation do not remain completely separated. It is the idea of participation which allows us to see their relation. We understand this form of relationship when we take it in its dynamic, and not in its static, sense. It is not simply an incorporation into some totality, but is a dynamic cooperation. Thus, participation leads us back to interiority and causes us to experience even from within our own activity that which transcends us. It allows us to possess and make our own what is given to us from outside. "It is this apparent contradiction of an activity indivisibly exercised and received that constitutes the essence of participation."[18] Participation is the interval which separates us from absolute being, but which we are nevertheless able to dominate. This relationship is actually clarified when we take it in its fully spiritual sense. The absolute is recognized as invitation, or even as support, and the subject as consent. The significance of this relationship is lost to us when our own activity collapses, when we are placed in the plane of nature and instinct. A purer kind of consciousness helps us to understand how we can "trace our path in the gift of being." When carried to its completion, reflection somehow becomes

[18] L. Lavelle, *De l'acte*, p. 338.

the experience of the absolute. The affirmation of God is primarily due to reflection on human freedom.

It is noteworthy that Lavelle is not content with the analysis of metaphysical experience understood in this way. He offers us an elaborate proof for the existence of God and takes up the ontological argument. In whatever way we understand this argument, it consists in seeing the interiority of thought and existence. However, it should not be reduced to establishing a necessary connection between concepts. For the idea of God from which the argument proceeds is not, properly speaking, representative of an existent reality distinct from it. It is a reflexive and not a representative idea. It does not designate, as a concept does, some reality that it would keep distinct from itself. The idea of God is always that of the infinite; it must be understood as the infinite of effectiveness, perceived at the end of a reflexive analysis. When the idea of being is understood in its relation to action, it has by itself a concrete character. It is "the only idea which cannot be reduced to a simple concept."[19] By proceeding from the idea of God, we can affirm God's existence without passing from the logical to the real. The argument will consist in passing "from the idea-object to the idea-source."[20]

Lavelle gives two very different statements of this intellectual process. According to the first, the idea of God envelops existence because it is the cause of it, according to the doctrine of God as *causa sui*. The me finds itself capable of giving being to itself in a participative kind of way, by taking to itself and making its own that which is given to it. The me participates in being by creating its own being, that is, by activity. It thus proceeds to the idea of an infinite causality by which God exists. It is necessary to understand this causality in the way in which Descartes wished, not as an efficient causality of essence over existence, which would imply a duality in God, but as "a quasi-efficient cause," the reason for which is taken from the infinity of the divine power.

If we speak at the level of God, the ontological argument is the *cogito*, just as the *cogito* is the ontological argument at the level of man; in the one case and the other, it is the spiritual activity which we attain insofar as that activity is *causa sui*, in God with his absolute creative efficacy, and in us under its limited form, as the conversation of a possibility into an actuality.[21]

[19] L. Lavelle, *De l'être*, p. 222. [20] *Ibid.*, p. 239.

[21] L. Lavelle, *De l'âme humaine*, p. 102.

We can consider the proof in a second way. The idea-source is now no longer understood in terms of the causality which it exercises within God, but in terms of the way it constitutes our thought. It is at the source of ourselves. We recognize the existence of God solely by considering the idea of him, when we understand that this presence in us is not our work, and that in this affirmation we are unable to deny what causes us to think.

There can hardly be a passage in the argument; for the idea of God is already the being of God. How would it be otherwise, if it is true that this idea cannot be contained in thought, but that rather my thought is contained in it, since it limits my thought.[22]

Whatever may be the form in terms of which we view the ontological argument, that argument has its point of departure in the *cogito*. In fact, it is by reflection upon our action that we form the idea of God and recognize that characteristic which allows it to envelop all existence. The idea of God is reflexive, not representative; it expresses the coming-to-consciousness of our action. But it cannot be formed in a reflection which leads us to wisdom. This recovery of ourselves is the experience of spiritual participation. It is a completely intimate relationship of activity and passivity. It allows us to make our own and to experience internally only what is given to us and recognized at the foundation of ourselves. We must acknowledge a passivity proper to the spirit; it does not consist in submitting from without but in appropriating from within and consenting. This experience allows us to form the idea of God, or better, to discover it in ourselves and to recognize its value. The ontological proof is based upon the *cogito*, if one sees it in its pure, completed form.

True knowledge is a union with total being, that is, a confluence of perfect activity and perfect passivity.[23]

* * * * * *

We find a remarkable interpretation of St. Anselm's argument in the philosophy of Ferdinand Alquié. He shows with particular clarity that the weight of the proof is carried by reflection, and not by representation. The truth which we can attain is a translation of our spiritual experience grasped reflexively. The return of the spirit upon itself discloses its fundamental activity and allows us to recognize its significance; this revelation of what is within us, or better, of what is

[22] L. Lavelle, *Introduction à l'ontologie*, p. 22.

[23] L. Lavelle, *La Conscience de soi*, p. 136.

at the foundation of our consciousness, becomes of itself the affirmation of God's existence. Alquié's effort is to recover what is pure and authentic in the life of the spirit. Through his studies of the history of philosophy, he seeks an essential value that is present, although perhaps hidden, in the movement of ideas: the purity of metaphysics. In its classic sense this is the recognition of the primacy of being. We must understand it as a knowledge of the self and of the self's essential relation to being. The ontological argument appears in the very depths of this knowledge.

We can distinguish several forms of our consciousness. The analysis of intellectual and emotional experience reveals the same truth, that of separation. In modern thought the opposition between knowing and being is made evident in very many ways and is constantly being emphasized. Descartes and Kant expressed this same idea, that we can know only in a condition of separation. This is not in any way a consequence which the mind is unable to avoid; this is the very foundation of its movements. We must recognize "the separation by which the consciousness becomes intellectual."[24] The object of representation is constituted by this division. In fact, the subject must be opposed to the object in order to think it. Objective knowledge separates us from being. Such is the Kantian idea of a constructive knowledge that knows itself only in its opposition to intuition, which it is not. In attaining its fulfillment, this knowledge does not hurl itself against a limit which it cannot surmount; from within itself it recognizes the finitude which is at the very source of its progress. Thought is therefore the consciousness of a lost unity. To be sure, this idea is difficult to grasp, namely that our certainty about being is given in the construction of the object, in the sense that this is a situation related to the being which the object is not. To understand thought properly, we must keep this idea in mind. The analysis of the affective consciousness can lead us to the same truth. This experience comprises our subjective reactions, the satisfaction which the me feels for itself. The affective life is incapable of truly uniting us with another being. It is only a project which by itself it cannot justify and the reason for which always collapses at some point.

The metaphysical consciousness is formed through the analysis of our intellectual and affective processes. Nevertheless, it is an original attitude, like a new life, involving a self-recovery that is purer and that is able to restore us to what is originative and fundamental.

[24] F. Alquié, *La Nostalgie de l'Être*, p. 98.

This consciousness transcends the simple experience of separation, in that it causes us to understand the whole meaning of our separation. It is the affirmation of our essential relation to being. It unites certainty about being with consent for its absence. Consequently, we can say that the metaphysical consciousness transcends this separation, without building a bridge over it by means of some intellectual process. It is "a fundamental experience, a nonconceptual presence of being to consciousness, common to philosophers and all men."[25] It is a situation, a placing of the object in relation to being and values, but in what for us is already a way toward tranquility. Metaphysical consciousness is this return to the self made completely lucid. It understands separation as a sign of our relation to being; it knows how to read, in all its incompleteness, the message which all language about it brings to us.

This act of reflexive consciousness is the fulcrum of the ontological argument. It therefore appears to us as a metaphysical disclosure. It is not a forward movement of thought, which seeks to attain a new certainty deductively. It is a return to a certainty already possessed internally. If we understood the argument as a passage, then this philosophic reflection would soon show its bankruptcy. As long as it proceeded from the analysis of an idea, it could only establish an existence within this idea and marked by the same subjectivity. Instead, the argument means to show the truth to which the consciousness witnesses when it sees itself moving beyond its objects toward being. The affirmation of God's existence is therefore given to us in a state of attentiveness, in a return to what is disclosed internally. The ontological argument consists in naming the presence which becomes manifest when the mind is aware of returning to itself. Although the discernment of this truth seems natural and easy, it remains hidden for a long time, for it rests upon the difficult experience of reflection. It does not consist simply in setting out from a representation which we want to investigate more fully. The idea which it involves is not simply in us. We could say rather that we are by it, and that it constitutes us.

> Man does not have the idea of God. He is the idea of God, the sign of God, and in this world the witness that the object is not reality.[26]

The idea of God is originative in us; it is consciousness itself.

[25] *Ibid.*, p. 148.
[26] F. Alquié, *La Découverte métaphysique de l'homme chez Descartes*, p. 236.

Consequently, one can say that the ontological argument reveals man rather than God. It establishes a truth which we do not see by itself, but which we read internally, in the difficult and ceaseless effort to hold the spirit's attention upon itself.

Philosophical reflection, however, cannot confine itself to the simple manifestation of what is disclosed internally. Descartes said that it is "almost the same thing to conceive of God and to conceive that He exists."[27] On this basis he notes the necessity for a rational argument. Alquié intends to show the force of this argument. Reflexive philosophy always consists in recognizing the limits and dynamism, the poverty and grandeur in thought. This opposition is the starting point for the proof which Alquié proposes. In the affirmation of God's existence, thought is not able to see itself creating what it does not embrace in any of its representations. A single reflection on the idea of God is sufficient to show that thought does not wholly arise from itself. Alquié takes this reasoning as the essential thing. He shows that thought discovers its limits, and in this way comes to the point of going beyond itself, for it recognizes that it does not have the power to deny the infinite. But he gives this proof a renovated form by insisting on an opposition of immense importance, that between "ideas" and "presences." The characteristic of an idea is that we can delimit it; it is in us in such a way that in principle nothing can prevent us from saying that we are its author. A presence, on the contrary, is not objective, if by this term we understand the character of that which lends itself to being determined. The ontological argument is the discovery of the absolute; it is necessary to affirm its existence because of the discovery that a presence cannot be reduced to the objectivity of ideas. By reflecting upon an interior presence, the spirit sees its limits and at the same time recognizes what sustains its vitality. It does not have the ability to deny what it cannot dominate.

The eternal quarrels over the ontological argument seem therefore to result from the fact that men do not pay sufficient attention to the difference between ideas properly speaking—ideas which are contained in the mind, which are limited, which can be embraced and comprehended by the mind, and which therefore can be placed in doubt and denied—and metaphysical ideas which we prefer to call presences, and which the mind cannot deny since it does not contain them.[28]

[27] Descartes, Letter to Mersenne, dated July 1641.

[28] Alquié, *op. cit.*, *La Découverte métaphysique*, p. 229.

Alquié's analysis enables us to see the significance of the reflexive proof. It is an effort to recover the purity of the philosophic consciousness, and to bring this experience to its fruition. The proof so understood is wholly opposed to that which idealism offers us. This philosophy claims to establish us within being itself. It is the origin of panlogism and absolute rationalism, with their pretensions to demonstrate being a priori, in terms of essence alone. Reflexive philosophy intends to see the necessity for affirming God's existence in the human consciousness. It is the only way to return to what is original and fundamental in us. We might say that it results from the dialectic of the *cogito*. It shows how each person returns to himself in his affirmation of being. In interpreting this reflexive philosophy, Alquié's thought presents great originality. It has its starting point in critical philosophy; it proceeds from a meditation on Kantian philosophy, and preserves the lessons which that teaches us. Separation is the truth of self-consciousness. Yet reflection can overcome this separation without denying it. The philosophical consciousness becomes that of transcendence. When it rises up to the affirmation of God's existence, reflexive philosophy is always the passage from an inner sincerity to a consent. In Alquié's the latter takes the form of a confession of Being. Perhaps we should take this experience in a religious sense, or at least consider it as the fastening point for a philosophy of religion. Alquié's thought is the movement from Kant to St. Anselm, from critical philosophy to spiritual philosophy.[29]

* * * * * *

We can recognize the unity of this philosophical movement that restores St. Anselm's argument. It is a different interpretation of the proof than what we find in classical philosophy. The common task pursued by the contemporary thinkers is not to analyze a representation but to grasp what can be called a reflexive implication.

[29] The direction of thought just indicated is to be found in a number of contemporary philosophers. Here are some bibliographical leads to guide research. The origins of this tradition should be found in P. Gratry, *De la connaissance de Dieu*, Vol. I, p. 340; Vol. 2, p. 64. Reference should also be made to Jean Guitton, "Note sur l'argument ontologique et sur la critique que Kant en a faite," in *Travaux du premier Congrès des Societés de philosophie de langue française*, pp. 23-29; J. Lachelier, "Notes sur le pari de Pascal," in his *Oeuvres*, Vol. II, pp. 37-65; R. Le Senne, *Introduction a la philosophie*, pp. 393f.; H. de Lubac, *Sur les chemins de Dieu*, pp. 96-98; J. Marias, "San Anselmo y el insensato," in his *Obras*, Vol. V, p. 5; J. Moreau, "Dieu dans la philosophie classique," in *Giornate di metafisica*, 1958, pp. 285-295; and M.-F. Sciacca, *L'Existence de Dieu*, pp. 173-182.

In this sense Maurice Blondel could say that the reflexive analysis was a renovated ontological argument.[30] This direction of thought is entirely different from that followed by idealism and ontologism. It is not a passage from the possible to the real, such as one finds in Hamelin and before him in Hegel. Moreover, it is not a matter of establishing the identification of God with being-in-general, as the ontologists mean to do after the fashion of Malebranche. These philosophic movements tend toward the extreme of placing us inside the truth of God, of transposing us to the source of being.

Reflexive philosophy completely abandons this kind of pretension. It proceeds from what might be called a more human expectation, which nevertheless has a great boldness that must be recognized. It is guided by the single concern to recover in its integrity the dynamism which is within us, and to express in its fullness the truth thus recovered. The purpose of this philosophy is really to place us in the order of the spirit. It considers what is spiritual in us, in the axiological, rather than ontological, sense of this word. The characteristics through which the life of the spirit is expressed are delicacy and subtlety, in opposition to heaviness—in the same way that we can oppose "sluggishness and vivacity." These characteristics represent the victorious unity of what has been dispersed in us, the elevation that rules in us over everything that is in constant danger of falling back. We are able to have an experience of self-communion which delivers us from the temptation of a splintered life.

This act of self-consciousness leads us to the proof for God's existence, for the idea of God is itself the highest action in us, so that the analysis of this idea enables us to perceive the dynamism which it sustains. Reflection is not confined solely to the description of what is interior to us. It allows us to reascend to the source of our spiritual life. It thus comes to manifest a presence. When understood in this way, the proof for God's existence is the passage from the reflexive idea to the originating idea. The idea which is discovered in the spirit's self-transcendence is the basis for an affirmation of existence, because it conditions our mental representations and cannot remain purely subjective. Such a proof is in no danger of "floating in a vacuum."[31] Ultimately, however, and solely through the consideration of spiritual interiority, this reflexive proof does con-

[30] Cited by B. Romeyer, *La philosophie religieuse de Maurice Blondel*, p. 51.

[31] Contrasting the ontological argument with the different ways of causality, Étienne Gilson writes: "St. Anselm, on the contrary, makes no reference to these, and that is why his argument gives every philosopher the impression of floating in

sist in recognizing the evidence of causality, and does approach the reasoning that proceeds by an analysis of contingency. In moving from a consideration of the idea of God, it intends to see, not merely what we have, but rather what we are, and to disclose our essential dependence. According to the penetrating remark of Jacques Paliard, "reflection grasps both the connection and the distance."

The history of Anselm's argument is that of the restorations and criticisms of it. It appears in ever-new forms, and never ceases to exercise a very strong attraction over thought. Its difficulties are often evident, but philosophic speculation seeks to overcome them by presenting a renovated interpretation. In this intellectual tradition reflexive philosophy has a very rich significance. However, to understand it properly, we must not only examine it in itself, but also ask to what extent it is faithful to St. Anselm's own thought. Here, it seems, we are led to very different conclusions, according to whether we consider Anselm's method or his doctrine.

The originality of the *Proslogion* lies above all perhaps in its method. The much emphasized harmony of thought and life here takes on a very original meaning. In the establishment of his proof, St. Anselm relies on the double experience of the self-reflection of thought on the one hand, and its truthfulness—or "rectitude"—on the other. Self-reflection is taken in its spiritual sense. This is not simply the passage from the outside to the inside, but also from dispersion to unity. "Enter into the chamber of your heart." That is the essential lesson which Anselm gives us, and it is when we follow it that we gain access to the highest truth. We grasp it in the calm of our spirit, in our effort to gather the self together within itself.

> Rise now, weak man! Flee from your occupations for a moment; hide yourself for a little from your tumultuous thoughts; cast aside your overwhelming cares and neglect your laborious tasks. Abandon yourself ever so little to God and rest for a little in him. Enter into the chamber of your heart. Exclude everything but God and what can help you to seek him. Then, having closed the door, seek him.[32]

This is not only an initial attitude; it should be constantly revived and should accompany every moment of the quest. St. Anselm reminds us of the necessity for this when he wants to make us perceive new truths.

---

a vacuum." From "Sens et nature de l'argument de S. Anselme," in *Archives d'histoire doctrinale et littéraire du moyen-âge*, 1934, p. 18.

[32] St. Anselm, *Prosl.* I (I. 97.4-9).

Let my soul recover its strength, and with all its understanding let it move toward you again, O Lord.[33]

Self-reflection is like the insertion of the spiritual into the intellectual. It is completed in meditation. St. Anselm recognizes this characteristic of it in the *Monologion*: "an example of meditating on the *ratio* of faith."[34] He does not use this same expression to describe the *Proslogion*, but he suggests the same idea. He says that it is a movement toward contemplation.[35] The process which he describes is always an intellectual effort, an ascent which is completed in contemplation. One might say that the *Proslogion* is a contemplative meditation. It prompts us to seek the truth within ourselves, because self-reflection forms the truth in us, by rendering it present to the soul. This spiritual movement, in its properly intellectual aspect, always remains that of monastic experience. Without misunderstanding what is distinctive in it, we are justified in comparing it with the kind of reflection that is envisaged by contemporary philosophy.

If one considers the reasoning which St. Anselm offers us by itself, we note that it is an appeal to the rectitude of thought. The proof consists in establishing the bond between *esse in intellectu* and *esse in re*, in showing it to be the truth. Consequently, the proof depends on the idea of truth that St. Anselm develops. This he defines in terms of rectitude. True thought is that which articulates what it should. Truth is above all a rightness, which can be affirmed just as much of the will as of thought. We might view the rectitude of thought as that condition where it is conformed to the essence which it affirms. Such is the most classic interpretation of this idea. We should note, however, that Anselm does not confine himself only to this consideration. He appeals to the rectitude of thought in action, of thinking thought. Rectitude consists not only in the perception of an essence, but also in the presence of the spirit to itself. St. Anselm wishes to formulate the thinking which is understood in this way, and to make it bear the weight of his proof. This is what is especially apparent in his criticism of the fool. This consists in his showing that the fool cannot truly think what he has nevertheless said in his heart.[36] He has taken only a notional, and not a real, point of view. The fool is not actually present to that which he thinks;

[33] *Ibid.*, XVIII. (I. 114.12f.).

[34] *Ibid.*, Preface (I. 93.2f.).

[35] "... in the person of one who strives to lift his mind to the contemplation of God, and seeks to understand what he believes." *Ibid.*, (I. 93.21-94.2).

[36] *Ibid.*, IV.

he does not carry his thought through to its conclusion. He lacks that rectitude of thought which renders it equal to itself, and faithful to its own requirements when it takes possession of itself in the affirmation that it forms. St. Anselm wishes to bring forth in the faithful this kind of thought, in its concrete and completed form. This is what is shown in one aspect of his reply to Gaunilo. The latter maintains that the idea of God does not have even the *esse in intellectu.* St. Anselm answers that Gaunilo's misunderstanding arises from the absence of thought from itself. "That this is false I appeal to your faith and your conscience, as well as to my forceful argument."[37] It is significant that Anselm appeals to the consciousness at the same time as to faith. In this way he wishes to show that real thought is that which consents to itself, and in this actual experience grasps its own richness and power. Consequently, we might say that the *Proslogion* is a constant meditation on the rectitude of thought. It thus defines a spiritual method, the principles of which have happily been recovered by contemporary thinkers.

One will still hesitate to acknowledge an accord between reflexive philosophy and St. Anselm's teachings. We cannot say that these extremely original endeavors hold to the letter of the argument in the *Proslogion*. St. Anselm, it seems, disengages the principles of a reflexive philosophy. But in his case this method only leads him to secure a better grasp on that necessity of existence which is contained in the idea of the divine essence. The argument keeps showing that "if only God can be thought, then he necessarily exists."[38] It finds its foundation in a metaphysics of essence.[39] The reflexive proof has a quite different meaning. It seeks to discover, not what is manifest analytically in the connection from essence to existence, but what is manifest causally, in the recognition of the originating idea, the source for the life of thought. To be sure, we can recover the principles of this reflexive form of the argument in St. Anselm. But we should recognize that in his thought this is only an uncompleted and roughly sketched idea, an intellectual outline rather than a system. The reflexive proof wants to show, in the duality of its grandeur and limits, what is at once the measure and rule of thought. "I suffer," Jacques Paliard says, "from this grandeur which condi-

37 *Reply* I (I. 130.16). 38 *Ibid.* (I. 131.5f.).

39 "In a philosophy where existence is a function of essence, it is indeed the modality of the divine Being which is the ground for the necessity of his existence." Étienne Gilson, *Le Thomisme*, p. 75.

tions me and makes me know my narrowness." Perhaps St. Anselm suggests this interpretation. He does bring this duality to light. The soul sees itself before God. It is "darkened by its own smallness and overpowered by your immensity."[40] This is a restatement of the Augustinian idea: The spirit is too narrow to contain itself. It could lead St. Anselm to discover the divine presence by reflection on this experience. But this is not the way that he actually follows. His reasoning rests expressly on the analysis of what can be affirmed through the consideration of essence alone. We can therefore say that the reflexive proof is authorized by St. Anselm, rather than in agreement with him.

The interpretation of the *Proslogion* offered to us today has great philosophic importance. When we see it in terms of the development of contemporary philosophy, it confronts us with a fundamental option. We can distinguish two directions for thought. One establishes the principle of what we can call the constituting consciousness; the other intends to show that at the foundation of ourselves we are a praying consciousness. In the first case, philosophy is oriented toward idealism; it finally comes to discover in the constructive me the absolute which realizes itself in us. In the other case, philosophy shows that the self-transcendence of the spirit is the sign of an interior transcendent. In relation to that which is at its foundation, the consciousness discovers itself to be essentially an act of prayer. Philosophic thought is the effort to perceive this primitive activity within us. It comes to recognize in the prayer of the spirit the prayer which is the spirit. It is enveloped in Christian faith and prayer, but not absorbed by them. The ontological argument is completed with the understanding of this last point.

We may recall that at the end of his life Husserl was assessing the difficulties and possible failure of his religious philosophy. He said that his mistake had been to want to seek God without God. That is the temptation of idealism. More than any other experience, the Anselmian kind of self-reflection is able to deliver us from it. The experience of the spirit, in the depths of its return to itself, is an invocation in which the originating truth comes to show itself. The rectitude of thought is completed in an attitude of consent. St. Anselm's meditation supports the effort of present-day philosophy. The latter is faithful to his inspiration, and discovers the fulfillment of reflexive philosophy in spiritual philosophy.

[40] *Prosl.* XIV; in the Schmitt ed., Vol. I, p. 112.4-5.

C. The Second Form of the Argument

XVI

NORMAN MALCOLM

Anselm's Ontological Arguments*

I BELIEVE that in Anselm's *Proslogion* and *Responsio editoris* there are two different pieces of reasoning which he did not distinguish from each other, and that a good deal of light may be shed on the philosophical problem of "the ontological argument" if we do distinguish them. In Chapter II of the *Proslogion*[1] Anselm says that we believe that God is *something a greater than which cannot be conceived*. (The Latin is *aliquid quo nihil maius cogitari possit*. Anselm sometimes uses the alternative expressions *aliquid quo maius nihil cogitari potest*, *id quo maius cogitari nequit*, *aliquid quo maius cogitari non valet*.) Even the fool of the Psalm who says in his heart that there is no God, when he hears this very thing that Anselm says, namely, "something a greater than which cannot be conceived," understands what he hears, and what he understands is in his understanding although he does not understand that it exists.

Apparently Anselm regards it as tautological to say that whatever is understood is in the understanding (*quidquid intelligitur in intellectu est*): he uses *intelligitur* and *in intellectu est* as interchange-

* From *The Philosophical Review*, Vo.. LXIX, No. 1 (January 1960), pp. 41-62. Reprinted with permission.

[1] I have consulted the Latin text of the *Proslogion*, of *Gaunilonis pro insipiente*, and of the *Responsio editoris*, in S. Anselmi, *Opera omnia*, ed. by F. S. Schmitt (Secovii, 1938), Vol. I. With numerous modifications, I have used the English transl. by S. N. Deane: *St. Anselm* (LaSalle, Illinois, 1948).

able locutions. The same holds for another formula of his: Whatever is thought is in thought (*quidquid cogitatur in cogitatione est*).[2]

Of course, many things may exist in the understanding that do not exist in reality; for example, elves. Now, says Anselm, something a greater than which cannot be conceived exists in the understanding. But it cannot exist *only* in the understanding, for to exist in reality is greater. Therefore, that thing a greater than which cannot be conceived cannot exist only in the understanding, for then a greater thing could be conceived: namely, one that exists both in the understanding and in reality.[3]

Here I have a question. It is not clear to me whether Anselm means that (a) existence in reality by itself is greater than existence in the understanding; or that (b) existence in reality and existence in the understanding together are greater than existence in the understanding alone. Certainly he accepts (b). But he might also accept (a), as Descartes apparently does in *Meditation III* when he suggests that the mode of being by which a thing is "objectively in the understanding" is *imperfect*.[4] Of course, Anselm might accept both (a) and (b). He might hold that in general something is greater if it has both of these "modes of existence" than if it has either one alone, but also that existence in reality is a more perfect mode of existence than existence in the understanding.

In any case, Anselm holds that something is greater if it exists both in the understanding and in reality than if it exists merely in the understanding. An equivalent way of putting this interesting proposition, in a more current terminology, is: Something is greater if it is both conceived of and exists than if it is merely conceived of. Anselm's reasoning can be expressed as follows: *id quo maius cogitari nequit* cannot be merely conceived of and not exist, for then it would not be *id quo maius cogitari nequit*. The doctrine that something is greater if it exists in addition to being conceived of, than if it is only conceived of, could be called the doctrine that *existence is a perfection*. Descartes maintained, in so many words, that existence is a

[2] See *Proslogion* I and *Responsio* II.

[3] Anselm's actual words are: *Et certe id quo maius cogitari nequit, non potest esse in solo intellectu. Si enim vel in solo intellectu est, potest cogitari esse et in re, quod maius est. Si ergo id quo maius cogitari non potest, est in solo intellectu: id ipsum quo maius cogitari non potest, est quo maius cogitari potest. Sed certe hoc esse non potest. Proslogion* II.

[4] Haldane and Ross, *The Philosophical Works of Descartes*, 2 vols. (Cambridge, 1931), I, p. 163.

perfection,[5] and presumably he was holding Anselm's doctrine, although he does not, in *Meditation V* or elsewhere, argue in the way that Anselm does in *Proslogion* II.

When Anselm says, "And certainly, that than which nothing greater can be conceived cannot exist merely in the understanding. For suppose it exists merely in the understanding, then it can be conceived to exist in reality, which is greater,"[6] he is claiming that if I conceived of a being of great excellence, that being would be *greater* (more excellent, more perfect) if it existed than if it did not exist. His supposition that "it exists merely in the understanding" is the supposition that it is conceived of but does not exist. Anselm repeated this claim in his reply to the criticism of the monk Gaunilo, Speaking of the being a greater than which cannot be conceived, he says:

> I have said that if it exists merely in the understanding, it can be conceived to exist in reality, which is greater. Therefore, if it exists merely in the understanding obviously the very being a greater than which cannot be conceived, is one a greater than which can be conceived. What, I ask, can follow better than that? For if it exists merely in the understanding, can it not be conceived to exist in reality? And if it can be so conceived, does not he who conceives of this conceive of a thing greater than it, if it does exist merely in the understanding? Can anything follow better than this: that if a being a greater than which cannot be conceived exists merely in the understanding, it is something a greater than which can be conceived? What could be plainer?[7]

He is implying, in the first sentence, that if I conceive of something which does not exist then it is possible for it to exist, and *it will be greater if it exists than if it does not exist*.

The doctrine that existence is a perfection is remarkably queer. It makes sense and is true to say that my future house will be a better one if it is insulated than if it is not insulated; but what could it mean to say that it will be a better house if it exists than if it does not? My future child will be a better man if he is honest than if he is not; but who would understand the saying that he will be a better man if he exists than if he does not? Or who understands the saying that if God exists he is more perfect than if he does not exist? One might say, with some intelligibility, that it would be better (for one-

5 *Ibid.*, p. 182.

6 *Proslogion* II; Deane, p. 8.

7 *Responsio* II; Deane, pp. 157-158.

self or for mankind) if God exists than if he does not—but that is a different matter.

A king might desire that his next chancellor should have knowledge, wit, and resolution; but it is ludicrous to add that the king's desire is to have a chancellor who exists. Suppose that two royal councillors, A and B, were asked to draw up separately descriptions of the most perfect chancellor they could conceive, and that the descriptions they produced were identical except that A included existence in his list of attributes of a perfect chancellor and B did not. (I do not mean that B put nonexistence in his list.) One and the same person could satisfy both descriptions. More to the point, any person who satisfied A's description would *necessarily* satisfy B's description and vice versa! This is to say that A and B did not produce descriptions that differed in any way but rather one and the same description of necessary and desirable qualities in a chancellor. A only made a show of putting down a desirable quality that B had failed to include.

I believe I am merely restating an observation that Kant made in attacking the notion that "existence" or "being" is a "real predicate." He says:

> By whatever and by however many predicates we may think a thing—even if we completely determine it—we do not make the least addition to the thing when we further declare that this thing *is*. Otherwise, it would not be exactly the same thing that exists, but something more than we had thought in the concept; and we could not, therefore, say that the exact object of my concept exists.[8]

Anselm's ontological proof of *Proslogion* II is fallacious because it rests on the false doctrine that existence is a perfection (and therefore that "existence" is a "real predicate"). It would be desirable to have a rigorous refutation of the doctrine, but I have not been able to provide one. I am compelled to leave the matter at the more or less intuitive level of Kant's observation. In any case, I believe that the doctrine does not belong to Anselm's other formulation of the ontological argument. It is worth noting that Gassendi anticipated Kant's criticism when he said, against Descartes:

> Existence is a perfection neither in God nor in anything else; it is rather that in the absence of which there is no perfection. . . . Hence

[8] *The Critique of Pure Reason*, transl. by Norman Kemp Smith (London, 1929), p. 505.

neither is existence held to exist in a thing in the way that perfections do, nor if the thing lacks existence is it said to be imperfect (or deprived of a perfection), so much as to be nothing.[9]

II

I take up now the consideration of the second ontological proof, which Anselm presents in the very next chapter of the *Proslogion*. (There is no evidence that he thought of himself as offering two different proofs.) Speaking of the being a greater than which cannot be conceived, he says:

And it so truly exists that it cannot be conceived not to exist. For it is possible to conceive of a being which cannot be conceived not to exist; and this is greater than one which can be conceived not to exist. Hence, if that, than which nothing greater can be conceived, can be conceived not to exist, it is not that than which nothing greater can be conceived. But this is a contradiction. So truly, therefore, is there something than which nothing greater can be conceived, that it cannot even be conceived not to exist.

And this being Thou art, O Lord, or our God.[10]

Anselm is saying two things: first, that a being whose nonexistence is logically impossible is "greater" than a being whose nonexistence is logically possible (and therefore that a being a greater than which cannot be conceived must be one whose nonexistence is logically impossible); second, that *God* is a being than which a greater cannot be conceived.

In regard to the second of these assertions, there certainly is *a* use of the word "God," and I think far the more common use, in accordance with which the statements "God is the greatest of all beings," "God is the most perfect being," "God is the supreme being," are *logically* necessary truths, in the same sense that the statement "A square has four sides" is a logically necessary truth. If there is a man named "Jones" who is the tallest man in the world, the statement "Jones is the tallest man in the world" is merely true and is not a logically necessary truth. It is a virtue of Anselm's unusual phrase, "a being a greater than which cannot be conceived,"[11]

[9] Haldane and Ross, *op. cit.*, II, p. 186. [10] *Proslogion* III; Deane, pp. 8-9.

[11] Professor Robert Calhoun has pointed out to me that a similar locution had

to make it explicit that the sentence "God is the greatest of all beings" expresses a logically necessary truth and not a mere matter of fact such as the one we imagined about Jones.

With regard to Anselm's first assertion (namely, that a being whose nonexistence is logically impossible is greater than a being whose nonexistence is logically possible) perhaps the most puzzling thing about it is the use of the word "greater." It appears to mean exactly the same as "superior," "more excellent," "more perfect." This equivalence by itself is of no help to us, however, since the latter expressions would be equally puzzling here. What is required is some explanation of their use.

We do think of *knowledge*, say, as an excellence, a good thing. If A has more knowledge of algebra than B, we express this in common language by saying that A has a *better* knowledge of algebra than B, or that A's knowledge of algebra is *superior* to B's, whereas we should not say that B has a better or superior *ignorance* of algebra than A. We do say "greater ignorance," but here the word "greater" is used purely quantitatively.

Previously I rejected *existence* as a perfection. Anselm is maintaining in the remarks last quoted, not that existence is a perfection, but that *the logical impossibility of nonexistence is a perfection.* In other words, *necessary existence* is a perfection. His first ontological proof uses the principle that a thing is greater if it exists than if it does not exist. His second proof employs the different principle that a thing is greater if it necessarily exists than if it does not necessarily exist.

Some remarks about the notion of *dependence* may help to make this latter principle intelligible. Many things depend for their existence on other things and events. My house was built by a carpenter: its coming into existence was dependent on a certain creative activity. Its continued existence is dependent on many things: that a tree does not crush it, that it is not consumed by fire, and so on. If we reflect on the common meaning of the word "God" (no matter how vague and confused this is), we realize that it is incompatible with this meaning that God's existence should *depend* on anything. Whether we believe in him or not, we must admit that the "almighty and everlasting God" (as several ancient prayers begin), the "Maker of

---

been used by Augustine. In *De moribus Manichaeorum* (Bk. II, ch. xi, sec. 24), he says that God is a being *quo esse aut cogitari melius nihil possit* (*Patrologiae Patrum Latinorum*, ed. by J. P. Migne, Paris, 1841-1845, vol. 32: *Augustinus*, Vol. I).

heaven and earth, and of all things visible and invisible" (as is said in the Nicene Creed), cannot be thought of as being brought into existence by anything or as depending for his continued existence on anything. To conceive of anything as dependent upon something else for its existence is to conceive of it as a lesser being than God.

If a housewife has a set of extremely fragile dishes, then as dishes they are *inferior* to those of another set like them in all respects except that they are *not* fragile. Those of the first set are *dependent* for their continued existence on gentle handling; those of the second set are not. There is a definite connection in common language between the notions of dependency and inferiority, and independence and superiority. To say that something which was dependent on nothing whatever was superior to ("greater than") anything that was dependent in any way upon anything is quite in keeping with the everyday use of the terms "superior" and "greater." Correlative with the notions of dependence and independence are the notions of *limited* and *unlimited.* An engine requires fuel, and this is a limitation. It is the same thing to say that an engine's operation is *dependent* on as that it is *limited* by its fuel supply. An engine that could accomplish the same work in the same time and was in other respects satisfactory, but did not require fuel, would be a *superior* engine.

God is usually conceived of as an *unlimited* being. He is conceived of as a being who *could not* be limited, that is, as an absolutely unlimited being. This is no less than to conceive of him as *something a greater than which cannot be conceived.* If God is conceived to be an absolutely unlimited being he must be conceived to be unlimited in regard to his existence as well as his operation. In this conception it will not make sense to say that he depends on anything for coming into or continuing in existence. Nor, as Spinoza observed, will it make sense to say that something could *prevent* him from existing.[12] Lack of moisture can prevent trees from existing in a certain region of the earth. But it would be contrary to the concept of God as an unlimited being to suppose that anything other than God himself could prevent him from existing, and it would be self-contradictory to suppose that he himself could do it.

Some may be inclined to object that although nothing could prevent God's existence, still it might just *happen* that he did not exist. And if he did exist, that too would be by chance. I think, however, that from the supposition that it could happen that God

[12] *Ethics*, pt. I, prop. 11.

did not exist it would follow that, if he existed, he would have mere duration and not eternity. It would make sense to ask, "How long has he existed?", "Will he still exist next week?", "He was in existence yesterday but how about today?", and so on. It seems absurd to make God the subject of such questions. According to our ordinary conception of him, he is an eternal being. And eternity does not mean endless duration, as Spinoza noted. To ascribe eternity to something is to exclude as senseless all sentences that imply that it has duration. If a thing has duration, then it would be merely a *contingent* fact, if it was a fact, that its duration was endless. The moon could have endless duration but not eternity. If something has endless duration it will *make sense* (although it will be false) to say that it will cease to exist, and it will make sense (although it will be false) to say that something will *cause* it to cease to exist. A being with endless duration is not, therefore, an absolutely unlimited being. That God is conceived to be eternal follows from the fact that he is conceived to be an absolutely unlimited being.

I have been trying to expand the argument of *Proslogion* III. In *Responsio* I Anselm adds the following acute point: If you can conceive of a certain thing and this thing does not exist, then if it *were* to exist, its nonexistence would be *possible*. It follows, I believe, that if thc thing were to exist, it would depend on other things both for coming into and continuing in existence, and also that it would have duration and not eternity. Therefore, it would not be, either in reality or in conception, an unlimited being, *aliquid quo nihil maius cogitari possit*.

Anselm states his argument as follows:

> If it [the thing a greater than which cannot be conceived] can be conceived at all, it must exist. For no one who denies or doubts the existence of a being greater than which is inconceivable, denies or doubts that if it did exist, its nonexistence, either in reality or in the understanding, would be impossible. For otherwise it would not be a being a greater than which cannot be conceived. But as to whatever can be conceived but does not exist: If it were to exist, its nonexistence either in reality or in the understanding would be possible. Therefore, if a being a greater than which cannot be conceived, can even be conceived, it must exist.[13]

What Anselm has proved is that the notion of contingent existence or of contingent nonexistence cannot have any application to God.

[13] *Responsio* I; Deane, pp. 154-155.

His existence must either be logically necessary or logically impossible. The only intelligible way of rejecting Anselm's claim that God's existence is necessary is to maintain that the concept of God, as a being a greater than which cannot be conceived, is self-contradictory or nonsensical.[14] Supposing that this is false, Anselm is right to deduce God's necessary existence from his characterization of him as a being a greater than which cannot be conceived.

Let me summarize the proof. If God, a being a greater than which cannot be conceived, does not exist, then he cannot *come* into existence. For if he did, he would either have been *caused* to come into existence or have *happened* to come into existence, and in either case he would be a limited being, which by our conception of him he is not. Since he cannot come into existence, if he does not exist, his existence is impossible. If he does exist, he cannot have come into existence (for the reasons given), nor can he cease to exist, for nothing could cause him to cease to exist nor could it just happen that he ceased to exist. So if God exists, his existence is necessary. Thus, God's existence is either impossible or necessary. It can be the former only if the concept of such a being is self-contradictory or in some way logically absurd. Assuming that this is not so, it follows that he necessarily exists.

It may be helpful to express ourselves in the following way: to say, not that *omnipotence* is a property of God, but rather that *necessary omnipotence* is; and to say, not that omniscience is a property of God, but rather that *necessary omniscience* is. We have criteria for determining that a man knows this and that and can do this and that, and for determining that one man has greater knowledge and abilities in a certain subject than another. We could think of various tests to give them. But there is nothing we should wish to describe, seriously and literally, as "testing" God's knowledge and powers. That God is omniscient and omnipotent has not been determined by the application of criteria: rather these are require-

[14] Gaunilo attacked Anselm's argument on this very point. He would not concede that a being a greater than which cannot be conceived existed in his understanding (*Gaunilonis pro insipiente*, secs. 4 and 5; Deane, pp. 148-150). Anselm's reply is: "I call on your faith and conscience to attest that this is most false" (*Responsio* I; Deane, p. 154). Gaunilo's faith and conscience will attest that it is false that "God is not a being a greater than which is inconceivable," and false that "He is not understood (*intelligitur*) or conceived (*cogitatur*)" (*ibid.*). Descartes also remarks that one would go to "strange extremes" who denied that we understand the words "*that thing which is the most perfect that we can conceive;* for that is what all men call God" (Haldane and Ross, II, p. 129).

ments of our conception of him. They are internal properties of the concept, although they are also rightly said to be properties of God. *Necessary existence* is a property of God in the *same sense* that *necessary omnipotence* and *necessary omniscience* are his properties. And we are not to think that "God necessarily exists" means that it follows necessarily from something that God exists *contingently*. The a priori proposition "God necessarily exists" entails the proposition "God exists," if and only if the latter also is understood as an a priori proposition: in which case the two propositions are equivalent. In this sense Anselm's proof is a proof of God's existence.

Descartes was somewhat hazy on the question of whether existence is a property of things that exist, but at the same time he saw clearly enough that *necessary existence* is a property of God. Both points are illustrated in his reply to Gassendi's remark, which I quoted above:

> I do not see to what class of reality you wish to assign existence, nor do I see why it may not be said to be a property as well as omnipotence, taking the word property as equivalent to any attribute or anything which can be predicated of a thing, as in the present case it should be by all means regarded. Nay, necessary existence in the case of God is also a true property in the strictest sense of the word, because it belongs to Him and forms part of His essence alone.[15]

Elsewhere he speaks of "the necessity of existence" as being "that crown of perfections without which we cannot comprehend God."[16] He is emphatic on the point that necessary existence applies solely to "an absolutely perfect Being."[17]

III

I wish to consider now a part of Kant's criticism of the ontological argument which I believe to be wrong. He says:

> If, in an identical proposition, I reject the predicate while retaining the subject, contradiction results; and I therefore say that the former belongs necessarily to the latter. But if we reject subject and predicate alike, there is no contradiction; for nothing is then left that can be contradicted. To posit a triangle, and yet to reject its three angles, is self-contradictory; but

[15] Haldane and Ross, *op. cit.*, II, p. 228.
[16] *Ibid.*, I, p. 445.
[17] E.g., *ibid.*, Principle 15, p. 225.

there is no contradiction in rejecting the triangle together with its three angles. The same holds true of the concept of an absolutely necessary being. If its existence is rejected, we reject the thing itself with all its predicates; and no question of contradiction can then arise. There is nothing outside it that would then be contradicted, since the necessity of the thing is not supposed to be derived from anything external; nor is there anything internal that would be contradicted, since in rejecting the thing itself we have at the same time rejected all its internal properties. "God is omnipotent" is a necessary judgment. The omnipotence cannot be rejected if we posit a Deity, that is, an infinite being; for the two concepts are identical. But if we say, "There is no God," neither the omnipotence nor any other of its predicates is given; they are one and all rejected together with the subject, and there is therefore not the least contradiction in such a judgment.[18]

To these remarks the reply is that when the concept of God is correctly understood, one sees that one cannot "reject the subject." "There is no God" is seen to be a necessarily false statement. Anselm's demonstration proves that the proposition "God exists" has the same a priori footing as the proposition "God is omnipotent."

Many present-day philosophers, in agreement with Kant, declare that existence is not a property and think that this overthrows the ontological argument. Although it is an error to regard existence as a property of things that have contingent existence, it does not follow that it is an error to regard necessary existence as a property of God. A recent writer says, against Anselm, that a proof of God's existence "based on the necessities of thought" is "universally regarded as fallacious: it is not thought possible to build bridges between mere abstractions and concrete existence."[19] But this way of putting the matter obscures the distinction we need to make. Does "concrete existence" mean contingent existence? Then to build bridges between concrete existence and mere abstractions would be like inferring the existence of an island from the concept of a perfect island, which both Anselm and Descartes regarded as absurd. What Anselm did was to give a demonstration that the proposition "God necessarily exists" is entailed by the proposition "God is a being a greater than which cannot be conceived" (which is equivalent to "God is an absolutely un-

[18] *Ibid.*, p. 502.

[19] J. N. Findlay, "Can God's Existence Be Disproved?", in *New Essays in Philosophical Theology*, ed. by A. N. Flew and A. MacIntyre (London, 1955), p. 47.

limited being"). Kant declares that when "I think a being as the supreme reality, without any defect, the question still remains whether it exists or not."[20] But once one has grasped Anselm's proof of the necessary existence of a being a greater than which cannot be conceived, no question remains as to whether it exists or not, just as Euclid's demonstration of the existence of an infinity of prime numbers leaves no question on that issue.

Kant says that "every reasonable person" must admit that "all existential propositions are synthetic."[21] Part of the perplexity one has about the ontological argument is in deciding whether the proposition "God necessarily exists" is or is not an "existential proposition." But let us look around. Is the Euclidean theorem in number theory, "There exists an infinite number of prime numbers," an "existential proposition"? Do we not want to say that *in some sense* it asserts the existence of something? Cannot we say, with equal justification, that the proposition "God necessarily exists" asserts the existence of something, *in some sense*? What we need to understand, in each case, is the particular sense of the assertion. Neither proposition has the same sort of sense as do the propositions, "A low-pressure area exists over the Great Lakes," "There still exists some possibility that he will survive," "The pain continues to exist in his abdomen." One good way of seeing the difference in sense of these various propositions is to see the variously different ways in which they are proved or supported. It is wrong to think that all assertions of existence have the same kind of meaning. There are as many kinds of existential propositions as there are kinds of subjects of discourse.

Closely related to Kant's view that all existential propositions are "synthetic" is the contemporary dogma that all existential propositions are contingent. Prof. Gilbert Ryle tells us that "Any assertion of the existence of something, like any assertion of the occurrence of something, can be denied without logical absurdity."[22] "All existential statements are contingent," says Mr. I. M. Crombie.[23] Prof. J. J. C. Smart remarks that "Existence is not a property" and then goes on to assert that "There can never be any *logical contradiction* in denying that God exists."[24] He declares that "The concept of a logically necessary being is a self-contradictory concept, like the

[20] Haldane and Ross, *op. cit.*, pp. 505-506.

[21] *Ibid.*, p. 504.

[22] *The Nature of Metaphysics*, ed. by D. F. Pears (New York, 1957), p. 150.

[23] *New Essays in Philosophical Theology*, p. 114.

[24] *Ibid.*, p. 34.

concept of a round square. . . . No existential proposition can be logically necessary," he maintains, "for the truth of a logically necessary proposition depends only on our symbolism, or to put the same thing in another way, on the relationship of concepts" (p. 38). Professor K. E. M. Baier says, "It is no longer seriously in dispute that the notion of a logically necessary being is self-contradictory. Whatever can be conceived of as existing can equally be conceived of as not existing."[25] This is a repetition of Hume's assertion, "Whatever we conceive as existent, we can also conceive as nonexistent. There is no being, therefore, whose nonexistence implies a contradiction."[26]

Prof. J. N. Findlay ingeniously constructs an ontological *dis*proof of God's existence, based on a "modern" view of the nature of "necessity in propositions": the view, namely, that necessity in propositions "merely reflects our use of words, the arbitrary conventions of our language."[27] Findlay undertakes to characterize what he calls "religious attitude," and here there is a striking agreement between his observations and some of the things I have said in expounding Anselm's proof. Religious attitude, he says, presumes *superiority* in its object and superiority so great that the worshiper is in comparison as nothing. Religious attitude finds it "anomalous to worship anything *limited* in any thinkable manner. . . . And hence we are led on irresistibly to demand that our religious object should have an *unsurpassable* supremacy along all avenues, that it should tower *infinitely* above all other objects" (p. 51). We cannot help feeling that "the worthy object of our worship can never be a thing that merely *happens* to exist, nor one on which all other objects merely *happen* to depend. The true object of religious reverence must not be one, merely, to which no *actual* independent realities stand opposed: It must be one to which such opposition is totally *inconceivable*. . . . And not only must the existence of *other* things be unthinkable without him, but his own nonexistence must be wholly unthinkable in any circumstances" (p. 52). And now, says Findlay, when we add up these various requirements, what they entail is "not only that there is no God, but that the Divine Existence is either senseless or impossible" (p. 54). For on the one hand, "if God is to satisfy religious claims and

[25] *The Meaning of Life*, Inaugural Lecture, Canberra University College (Canberra, 1957), p. 8.

[26] *Dialogues Concerning Natural Religion*, pt. IX.

[27] Findlay, *op. cit.*, p. 54.

needs, he must be a being in every way inescapable, One whose existence and whose possession of certain excellences we cannot possibly conceive away." On the other hand, "modern views make it self-evidently absurd (if they do not make it ungrammatical) to speak of such a Being and attribute existence to him. It was indeed an ill day for Anselm when he hit upon his famous proof. For on that day he not only laid bare something that is of the essence of an adequate religious object, but also something that entails its necessary nonexistence" (p. 55).

Now I am inclined to hold the "modern" view that logically necessary truth "merely reflects our use of words" (although I do not believe that the conventions of language are always *arbitrary*). But I confess that I am unable to see how that view is supposed to lead to the conclusion that "the Divine existence is either senselesss or impossible." Findlay does not explain how this result comes about. Surely he cannot mean that this view entails that nothing can have necessary properties: for this would imply that mathematics is "senseless or impossible," which no one wants to hold. Trying to fill in the argument that is missing from his article, the most plausible conjecture I can make is the following: Findlay thinks that the view that logical necessity "reflects the use of words" implies, not that nothing has necessary properties, but that *existence* cannot be a necessary property of anything. That is to say, every proposition of the form "*x* exists," including the proposition "God exists," must be *contingent*.[28] At the same time, our concept of God requires that his existence be *necessary*, that is, that "God exists" be a necessary truth. Therefore, the modern view of necessity proves that what the concept of God requires *cannot* be fulfilled. It proves that God *cannot* exist.

The correct reply is that the view that logical necessity merely reflects the use of words cannot possibly have the implication that every existential proposition must be contingent. That view requires us to *look at* the use of words and not manufacture a priori theses about it. In the Ninetieth Psalm it is said: "Before the mountains were brought forth, or ever Thou hadst formed the earth and the world, even from everlasting to everlasting, Thou art God." Here

[28] The other philosophers I have just cited may be led to this opinion by the same thinking. Smart, for example, says that "the truth of a logically necessary proposition depends only on our symbolism, or to put the same thing in another way, on the relationship of concepts" (*supra*). This is very similar to saying that it "reflects our use of words."

is expressed the idea of the necessary existence and eternity of God, an idea that is essential to the Jewish and Christian religions. In those complex systems of thought, those "languages-games," God has the status of a necessary being. Who can doubt that? Here we must say with Wittgenstein, "This language-game is played!"[29] I believe we may rightly take the existence of those religious systems of thought in which God figures as a necessary being to be a disproof of the dogma, affirmed by Hume and others, that no existential proposition can be necessary.

Another way of criticizing the ontological argument is the following. "Granted that the concept of necessary existence follows from the concept of a being a greater than which cannot be conceived, this amounts to no more than granting the a priori truth of the *conditional* proposition, 'If such a being exists then it necessarily exists.' This proposition, however, does not entail the *existence* of *anything*, and one can deny its antecedent without contradiction." Kant, for example, compares the proposition (or "judgment," as he calls it) "A triangle has three angles" with the proposition "God is a necessary being." He allows that the former is "absolutely necessary" and goes on to say:

> The absolute necessity of the judgment is only a conditional necessity of the thing, or of the predicate in the judgment. The above proposition does not declare that three angles are absolutely necessary, but that, under the condition that there is a triangle (that is, that a triangle is given), three angles will necessarily be found in it.[30]

He is saying, quite correctly, that the proposition about triangles is equivalent to the conditional proposition, "If a triangle exists, it has three angles itself." He then makes the comment that there is no contradiction "in rejecting the triangle together with its three angles." He proceeds to draw the alleged parallel: "The same holds true of the concept of an absolutely necessary being. If its existence is rejected, we reject the thing itself with all its predicates; and no question of contradiction can then arise."[31] The priest Caterus made the same objection to Descartes when he said:

> Though it be conceded that an entity of the highest perfection implies its existence by its very name, yet it does not follow that that very existence is

[29] *Philosophical Investigations* (New York, 1953), sec. 654.

[30] *Op. cit.*, pp. 501-502.

[31] *Ibid.*, p. 502.

anything actual in the real world, but merely that the concept of existence is inseparably united with the concept of highest being. Hence, you cannot infer that the existence of God is anything actual, unless you assume that that highest being actually exists; for then it will actually contain all its perfections, together with this perfection of real existence.[32]

I think that Caterus, Kant and numerous other philosophers have been mistaken in supposing that the proposition "God is a necessary being" (or "God necessarily exists") is equivalent to the conditional proposition "If God exists, then he necessarily exists."[33] For how do they want the antecedent clause, "*If* God exists" to be understood? Clearly they want it to imply that it is *possible* that God does *not* exist.[34] The whole point of Kant's analysis is to try to show that it is possible to "reject the subject." Let us make this implication explicit in the conditional proposition so that it reads: "If God exists (and it is possible that he does not), then he necessarily exists." But now it is apparent, I think, that these philosophers have arrived at a self-contradictory position. I do not mean that this conditional proposi-

[32] Haldane and Ross, *op. cit.*, II, p. 7.

[33] I have heard it said by more than one person in discussion that Kant's view was that it is really a misuse of language to speak of a "necessary being," on the ground that necessity is properly predicated only of propositions (judgments), not of *things*. This is not a correct account of Kant. (See his discussion of "The Postulates of Empirical Thought in General," *op. cit.*, pp. 239-256, esp. p. 239 and pp. 247-248.) But if he had held this, as perhaps the above philosophers think he should have, then presumably his view would not have been that the pseudo-proposition "God is a necessary being" is equivalent to the conditional "If God exists, then he necessarily exists." Rather, his view would have been that the genuine proposition " 'God exists' is necessarily true" is equivalent to the conditional "If God exists, then he exists" (*not* "If God exists, then he *necessarily* exists," which would be an illegitimate formulation, on the view imaginatively attributed to Kant).

"If God exists, then he exists" is a foolish tautology which says nothing different from the tautology "If a new earth satellite exists, then it exists." If "If God exists, then he exists" were a correct analysis of " 'God exists' is necessarily true," then "If a new earth satellite exists, then it exists" would be a correct analysis of " 'A new earth satellite exists' is necessarily true." If the *analysans* is necessarily true, then the *analysandum* must be necessarily true, provided the analysis is correct. If this proposed Kantian analysis of " 'God exists' is necessarily true" were correct, we should be presented with the consequence that not only is it necessarily true that God exists, but also it is necessarily true that a new earth satellite exists: which is absurd.

[34] When summarizing Anselm's proof (in part II, *supra*) I said: "If God exists, he necessarily exists." But there I was merely stating an entailment. "If God exists" did not have the implication that it is possible he does not exist. And of course I was not regarding the conditional as *equivalent* to "God necessarily exists."

tion, taken alone, is self-contradictory. Their position is self-contradictory in the following way. On the one hand, they agree that the proposition "God necessarily exists" is an a priori truth; Kant implies that it is "absolutely necessary" and Caterus says that God's existence is implied by his very name. On the other hand, they think that it is correct to analyze this proposition in such a way that it will entail the proposition "It is possible that God does not exist." But so far from its being the case that the proposition "God necessarily exists" entails the proposition "It is possible that God does not exist," it is rather the case that they are *incompatible* with one another! Can anything be clearer than that the conjunction "God necessarily exists, but it is possible that he does not exist" is self-contradictory? Is it not just as plainly self-contradictory as the conjunction "A square necessarily has four sides, but it is possible for a square not to have four sides"? In short, this familiar criticism of the ontological argument is self-contradictory, because it accepts *both* of two incompatible propositions.[35]

One conclusion we may draw from our examination of this criticism is that (contrary to Kant) there is a lack of symmetry, in an important respect, between the propositions "A triangle has three angles" and "God has necessary existence," although both are a priori. The former can be expressed in the conditional assertion "If a triangle exists (and it is possible that none does), it has three angles." The latter cannot be expressed in the corresponding conditional assertion without contradiction.

IV

I turn to the question of whether the idea of a being a greater than which cannot be conceived is self-contradictory. Here Leibnitz made a contribution to the discussion of the ontological argument. He remarked that the argument of Anselm and Descartes

> is not a paralogism, but it is an imperfect demonstration, which assumes something that must still be proved in order to render it mathematically

[35] This fallacious criticism of Anselm is implied in the following remarks by Gilson: "To show that the affirmation of necessary existence is analytically implied in the idea of God, would be . . . to show that God is necessary if he exists, but would not prove that he does exist" (E. Gilson, *The Spirit of Medieval Philosophy*, New York, 1940, p. 62).

evident; that is, it is tacitly assumed that this idea of the all-great or all-perfect being is possible, and implies no contradiction. And it is already something that by this remark it is proved that, assuming that God is possible, he exists, which is the privilege of divinity alone.[36]

Leibnitz undertook to give a proof that God is possible. He defined a *perfection* as a simple, positive quality in the highest degree.[37] He argued that since perfections are *simple* qualities, they must be compatible with one another. Therefore, the concept of a being possessing all perfections is consistent.

I will not review his argument because I do not find his definition of a perfection intelligible. For one thing, it assumes that certain qualities or attributes are "positive" in their intrinsic nature, and others "negative" or "privative," and I have not been able clearly to understand that. For another thing, it assumes that some qualities are intrinsically simple. I believe that Wittgenstein has shown in the *Investigations* that nothing is *intrinsically* simple, but that whatever has the status of a simple, an indefinable, in one system of concepts, may have the status of a complex thing, a definable thing, in another system of concepts.

I do not know how to demonstrate that the concept of God—that is, of a being a greater than which cannot be conceived—is not self-contradictory. But I do not think that it is legitimate to demand such a demonstration. I also do not know how to demonstrate that either the concept of a material thing or the concept of *seeing* a material thing is not self-contradictory, and philosophers have argued that both of them are. With respect to any particular reasoning that is offered for holding that the concept of seeing a material thing, for example, is self-contradictory, one may try to show the invalidity of the reasoning and thus free the concept from the charge of being self-contradictory *on that ground.* But I do not understand what it would mean to demonstrate *in general*, and not in respect to any particular reasoning, that the concept is not self-contradictory. So it is with the concept of God. I should think there is no more of a presumption that it is self-contradictory than is the concept of seeing a material thing. Both concepts have a place in the thinking and the lives of human beings.

But even if one allows that Anselm's phrase may be free of self-

[36] *New Essays Concerning the Human Understanding*, Bk. IV, ch. 10; ed. by A. G. Langley (LaSalle, Illinois, 1949), p. 504.

[37] See *ibid.*, Appendix X, p. 714.

contradiction, one wants to know how it can have any *meaning* for anyone. Why is it that human beings have even *formed* the concept of an infinite being, a being a greater than which cannot be conceived? This is a legitimate and important question. I am sure there cannot be a deep understanding of that concept without an understanding of the phenomena of human life that give rise to it. To give an account of the latter is beyond my ability. I wish, however, to make one suggestion (which should not be understood as autobiographical).

There is the phenomenon of feeling guilt for something that one has done or thought or felt or for a disposition that one has. One wants to be free of this guilt. But sometimes the guilt is felt to be so great that one is sure that nothing one could do oneself, nor any forgiveness by another human being, would remove it. One feels a guilt that is beyond all measure, a guilt "a greater than which cannot be conceived." Paradoxically, it would seem, one nevertheless has an intense desire to have this incomparable guilt removed. One requires a forgiveness that is beyond all measure, a forgiveness "a greater than which cannot be conceived." Out of such a storm in the soul, I am suggesting, there arises the conception of a forgiving mercy that is limitless, beyond all measure. This is one important feature of the Jewish and Christian conception of God.

I wish to relate this thought to a remark made by Kierkegaard, who was speaking about belief in Christianity but whose remark may have a wider application. He says:

> There is only one proof of the truth of Christianity and that, quite rightly, is from the emotions, when the dread of sin and a heavy conscience torture a man into crossing the narrow line between despair bordering upon madness—and Christendom.[38]

One may think it absurd for a human being to feel a guilt of such magnitude, and even more absurd that, if he feels it, he should *desire* its removal. I have nothing to say about that. It may also be absurd for people to fall in love, but they do it. I wish only to say that there *is* that human phenomenon of an unbearably heavy conscience and that it is importantly connected with the genesis of the concept of God, that is, with the formation of the "grammar" of the word "God." I am sure that this concept is related to human experience in other ways. If one had the acuteness and depth to perceive these

[38] *The Journals*, transl. by A. Dru (Oxford, 1938), sec. 926.

connections, one could grasp the *sense* of the concept. When we encounter this concept as a problem in philosophy, we do not consider the human phenomena that lie behind it. It is not surprising that many philosophers believe that the idea of a necessary being is an arbitrary and absurd construction.

What is the relation of Anselm's ontological argument to religious belief? This is a difficult question. I can imagine an atheist going through the argument, becoming convinced of its validity, acutely defending it against objections, yet remaining an atheist. The only effect it could have on the fool of the Psalm would be that he stopped saying in his heart "There is no God," because he would now realize that this is something he cannot meaningfully say or think. It is hardly to be expected that a demonstrative argument should, in addition, produce in him a living faith. Surely there is a level at which one can view the argument as a piece of logic, following the deductive moves but not being touched religiously. I think so. But even at this level the argument may not be without religious value, for it may help to remove some philosophical scruples that stand in the way of faith. At a deeper level, I suspect that the argument can be thoroughly understood only by one who has a view of that human "form of life" that gives rise to the idea of an infinitely great being, who views it from the *inside*, not just from the outside, and who has, therefore, at least some inclination to *partake* in that religious form of life. This inclination in Kierkegaard's words is "from the emotions." This inclination can hardly be an *effect* of Anselm's argument, but is rather presupposed in the fullest understanding of it. It would be unreasonable to require that the recognition of Anselm's demonstration as valid must produce a conversion.

XVII

CHARLES HARTSHORNE

What did Anselm Discover?[1]

ANSELM'S problem, in his famous Ontological Proof, was metaphysical, and metaphysical problems all fit together into a single problem. On the highly abstract level of metaphysics there can be but one truth, which philosophers are trying to express in various necessarily imperfect ways. To be really clear, then, about what is right and what is wrong with Anselm, or his critics, is nothing less than to have an adequate metaphysics. Anselm's question is merely more central than most; it takes us at once close to the heart of the whole business. Hence, the demands upon the student's understanding are magnified.

Anselm made two principal attempts to formulate his insight. The first alone is usually cited, whether by critics or defenders. This extraordinarily poor scholarship, in which great scholars have indulged, is a melancholy instance of human fallibility. The first of the two formulations (*Proslogion* II) is now generally admitted to be a failure. But the second formulation (*Proslogion* III) is very different, and logically irreducible to the first and—although Anselm seems somewhat unclear himself about this—independent of it. Hence, to refute the first is not to refute the second. The latter is also much more cogent. Yet even Aquinas (as well as Kant) refuted only the first, although elsewhere he does expound the second. Nearly all the world has taken him to have refuted the Proof as such. This matter is too important for such carelessness to be permissible.

[1] This is a version, expanded by Professor Hartshorne, of his paper with the same title published in the *Union Seminary Quarterly Review*, XVII (1962), pp. 213-222.

Here is a crude paraphrase of the first or weaker formula: Existence is good, hence the best conceivable thing must have it, and hence must exist. (Existence here means *extra mentem*, as more than a mere object of our thought.) Objection: existence is not a property which a thing may have or lack, for without existence there is nothing either to have or to lack properties. An idea or definition attributes properties hypothetically, it says what a thing of a certain sort must be like *if* there exists such a thing. Hence, existence is not one of the properties in question. This famous objection is generally attributed to Kant; but it was first lucidly stated by Gassendi. Moreover, Descartes replied to it, and therefore in effect to Kant. (Historians have not told us this striking fact.) Descartes' reply amounted to a retreat from the weaker Anselmian formula to the stronger, which we shall now consider.

This second or stronger version is: To exist necessarily is better than to exist contingently; hence the greatest conceivable being can exist only necessarily. Moreover, whatever could be necessary is necessary ("reduction principle" of modal logic); hence to say that God does not exist necessarily is to say that he could not do so, and since he also could not exist contingently, it is to say that he could not exist at all. (Thus, theism reduces to positivism, denial even of the possibility of God.) Anselm assumes that the idea of God's existence is at least free from absurdity, does not represent an impossibility. He takes "the fool" to concede this much. Gaunilo urges the contrary, or positivistic, position, to which Anselm objects both on grounds of faith and also on rational or metaphysical grounds. At this point, however, his reasoning is not very convincing to present-day philosophers. We shall see that the greatest weakness of Anselm's system is precisely in his way of interpreting his formula, "such that none greater can be conceived." But in any case, the reduction of atheism to positivism stands and is a permanent contribution to both theology and philosophy. The only logically admissible way to reject theism is to reject the very idea of God as either contradictory or empty of significance.

The axiom that noncontingent existence is superior is stated by Anselm within a page of the statement of his first argument. Hence, it is hard to excuse its almost total ignoring in the literature. The "reduction principle" appealed to above is not made entirely explicit in Anselm, but is rather obviously implied in a number of passages. It is not accepted by all modal logicians, but is well defended by some of them, most recently by the Kneales in their great work on *The Development of Logic*. I believe the principle is entirely sound, in any such context as Anselm's.

Compare the following:

(A) For any x and y, x exists (not merely in the mind) and y does not, implies, x is greater than y.
(B) For any x and y, x exists noncontingently and y exists contingently implies, x is greater than y.

The principle of the first proof (A), involves two grand paradoxes. The first is, it seems a truism that any entity is an entity, hence a nonexistent y (or one only thought of) is meaningless. A conceived property or kind of thing may be nonexistent (or merely thought of), that is, unillustrated in any actuality (other than the thought thinking it), but since mere thought lacks a principle of individuation (at least as far as ordinary properties are concerned), to say that a certain individual exists only in the mind is to say that there is no such individual, in the mind or anywhere else. The second paradox is, if we define a property, and then ask if something having the property exists, we assume that the property in question is fixed and will not change according to whether the answer is yes or no. The notion that a property gets better by being exhibited in real individual existence is incoherent, since it is then not *that* property which is exhibited. Kant makes much of this point. It is these paradoxes which led to the saying that existence is not a predicate.

The second proof (B) involves neither of these paradoxes. First, the comparison is not between an individual entity which exists and one which does not, but between two entities both of which are conceived as existent, but in modally diverse fashions. Secondly, no property is supposed to alter according as it is or is not existentialized; for in the case of x the nonexistential status is by definition excluded as impossible (the meaning of "exists noncontingently") and does not enter into the comparison at all; while in the case of the y, its property or kind could perfectly well be the same if there were no y to illustrate it, this being what is meant by "contingently." Since the two paradoxes are precisely those which figure centrally in the classical refutations (Gassendi, Hume, Kant and Russell), it is obvious that the two Anselmian arguments differ in the very respects relevant to the classical criticisms. Nor do these criticisms take (B) into account.

The glaring difference between (A) and (B) is that in the latter, but not in the former, modal ideas enter constitutively. Over and over again Anselm employs modal expressions ("cannot be conceived," "can be conceived") as integral to the distinction he is making. I submit that all criticisms which proceed on a nonmodal level are patently guilty of the *ignoratio elenchi*. But this is a large part of the literature.

What is meant in (B) by "noncontingently," or, as Anselm put it, "so truly that thou canst not be conceived not to exist"? According to many philosophers, modal concepts must mean either what is compatible (or incompatible) with natural laws, or with logical laws. The impossibility of the divine nonexistence cannot refer to natural law; for then God's security of existence would depend upon his own decree, since the theistic view of a natural law is that it issues from a free fiat of deity. Is the impossibility a mere question of logical law? But logical laws are not ordinarily supposed to refer in any way to the existence of deity. What is required here is a theory of modality which is neither a mere question of law, nor of logical rules alone. But just such a theory is implicit in the very idea of God as unsurpassably excellent. This theory (which can only be crudely stated here) is that the basic referent of "possible" is to the divine capacity to create and enjoy creatures. This capacity is neither a law of nature nor a mere rule of logic, but the presupposition of any existence and of any law, meaning or truth whatever. *What God could not possess could not be*, and since he could not possess his own nonexistence, this could not be, and the notion of it is nonsense. Here the ontological impossibility appears as also a logical one, but because the concept of God and its logical content is put into the equation. We cannot consistently conceive God as worshipfully supreme and yet not the ground of all possibility and meaning. I believe that no less than this is implied in the concept of "Creator of all things, visible and invisible."

It has been objected to the second Anselmian argument that since "necessity of existence" includes "existence," if the former is a predicate, so is the latter (were it not, it could not be connoted by the predicate "greatest conceivable"); so do we not come back, after all, to the principle of the first or nonmodal argument, that existence is a predicate? No, I reply, we do not. There is a seldom-noticed ambiguity in the dictum "Existence is not a property."

(1) It may mean, in no possible case is existence a property.

According to this, there is an absolute rule *forbidding* it to be a property. But this begs the question, for even the second form of the Proof leads to the conclusion that *in the one divine case* existence is a property. That it is not a property with ordinary things does not prove that it cannot be so with God. This has to be shown; it is not enough to assert it. After all, God is by definition a radically exceptional being, exalted above all others, actual or conceivable. Only so can he deserve worship, that is, *unconditional* respect or love. Perhaps this exceptional status affects even the fashion in which "existence" can apply to God.[2]

(2) "Existence is not a property" may merely mean, "it need not be one, there is no rule *requiring* it to be in every case." Accordingly, it may (as a unique exception?) be a divine property, deducible from the definition of divinity.

To relax the rule forbidding existence to be a property does not, however, suffice to validate the proof. For exceptions to a rule can be proved, or made intelligible, only if there is some higher rule which they do come under. All reasoning is from rules. If thinking about God violates all rules, then it is not thinking in the logical sense at all, and there can be no talk of proof.

So far we have two proposed rules:

Existence is never a predicate.
Existence is always a predicate.

The first rule begs the question against the argument, the second begs it in favor of the argument. The second rule, in addition, is invalid. Existence is not ordinarily a part of the connotation of a definition.

Modality of Existence

Any logician can see that the two rules are contraries, not contradictories, in that both may be false. Perhaps, although existence is

[2] Tillich's refusal to say of God that he exists is an emphatic, and even over-emphatic, way of dealing with the radically exceptional status of deity. I think there is as much reason to keep the word "existence" as the word "being" which he employs. Much that he says about this, and about the Ontological Proof and its history, is profound. I cannot here explain just where and why we do not quite agree in these matters. See his article "The Two Types of Philosophy of Religion," in *Union Seminary Quarterly Review*, I (1946), No. 4, pp. 3-14, reprinted in *Theology of Culture* (New York: Oxford University Press, 1959).

not normally a property, yet it is one in the supernormal case of deity. But if so, what is the higher rule, the one without exception, from which we deduce the exception to the lower rule? It is this: *Modality of existence is always a property* and is always deducible from the definition of a thing. By modality I mean the kind of existence appropriate to a definition, whether contingent, necessary or impossible existence.

(1) With the modality termed *contingency*, existence and nonexistence are equally conceivable. This double conceivability follows from the definitions of all ordinary things. Thus, it is part of being human either to exist with the conceivable alternative of not having existed, or (like Mr. Micawber) to fail to exist with the conceivable alternative of having existed. We can always think of a state of affairs with, and another without, men, dollars, islands and so forth. In religious language, these are creatures which God might be pleased to create, and might also be pleased not to create. Or, if the religious language seems to beg the question, we can always imagine nature to have so developed that mankind had never existed, or so that some specified alternative sort of being had existed instead.

(2) With the modality of *impossibility*, existence is not (consistently) conceivable (example, round-square). This too is deducible from the definition. For if the definition is not consistent, then sooner or later deduction from it will elicit a contradiction.

(3) With the modality of *necessity*—if it be admitted there can be such a status—only the existence, but not the nonexistence, is conceivable. In this case existence must be affirmed, since its denial is contradictory. Anselm claimed to have discovered that we can tell from the definition of deity that the divine nonexistence is inconceivable. His chief (but not sole) reason was that the mere conceivability of nonexistence implies weakness, inferiority. This principle, which I call Anselm's Principle, is explicated in Chapter III of the *Proslogion*—subsequent to the most widely cited chapter—and reiterated many times in Chapters I, V and IX of the *Reply* to Gaunilo. These are the key passages, yet they are commonly ignored.

Were God to exist, yet his nonexistence to be conceivable, he would either exist by sheer chance or luck, or else owing to some cause. Either way, he would not be the best conceivable being, and hence would not be worthy of worship as God. He must then exist without conceivable alternative. If you say, "yes, supposing he exists at all," you unwittingly imply the conceivability of the very alternative you admit must be excluded. You forget that whether something is consistently conceivable or not cannot depend upon what happens to exist. If God's nonexistence *could* be inconceivable, it *must* be so. (This is the "reduction principle" referred to above.) Conceivability and its contradictory depend not on alterable relations of ideas to facts, but only on inherent and fixed relation of ideas to ideas. Yet critics of the argument often commit the absurdity of saying, "God's existence is necessary only upon condition that He exist." "Necessity," in the strict sense which alone is here in question, means, there can be no conditions which might be fulfilled and might be unfulfilled. God's existence can only be unconditioned. We assert it, or we ignore it; we cannot logically deny it.

There may seem to be the following difficulty. If necessary existence, existence incapable of an alternative possibility, is a property deducible from a definition, of what is it a property? If Anselm were to reply, of God, he might appear to beg the question, to assume that God is there to have the property. But the answer is, the definition, the idea of deity, is what is assumed to be there; and the necessity is that this definition, this idea, alone among ideas of an individual being, cannot fail to be realized in existence. For if it could fail, then it could not possibly succeed, since possible "success" here means the unconditional impossibility of failure. Thus, to suppose a possibility of the nonexistence of God is to assign deity to the status of round-squares and other impossible things.

But, some will ask, is this not the right status? Is not deity the idea of an impossibility? Anselm frankly assumed that even the atheist (the "fool") admits that there is a consistent idea of God. Apart from this assumption, the Proof might be like arguing from the definition, "necessarily existing round-square" to the existence of such a square, where the defined necessity of existence is canceled out by an equally obvious necessity of nonexistence. How does Anselm know that this is not what his Proof amounts to?

We may call this the positivistic attack upon the Proof. It is the intelligent attack. It was stated or implied by Gaunilo, and it is by far the best (although not the most cited) of his criticisms. Anselm's defense at this point was weak. But even so he had refuted "atheism," in the sense in which this consists in admitting the logical possibility of the divine existence while yet denying its reality. This is contradictory. Positivism, and theism taken as necessarily true: These exhaust the reasonable views. And the choice between them is no question of fact but of meaning, whether the definition of deity makes sense. God either could not, or he must, exist. How shall we decide which? To deal with this question we must go beyond the ontological argument, although not to consideration of facts, rather to further analysis of ideas or meanings. Anselm, replying at this point to Gaunilo, fell back upon faith: The believer, he thought, at least knows that his faith is not merely absurd. However, to combat unbelief in the positivistic form, some further argument is required, and a better one than Anselm had to offer (for he did outline such an argument). I do not wish on this occasion to present any anti-positivistic argument. Rather, I wish to explain why I think that Anselm's own idea of God was in truth absurd, so that for *this* idea positivism is actually valid.

Let us look at Anselm's definition: "that than which none greater or better can be conceived." Two meanings are possible here: none greater, except Himself in a greater state; or, none greater, even Himself. To be divine is at least to be unsurpassable *by another*, but is it also to be unsurpassable by self, incapable of growth? Anselm assumed this interpretation. He thought God was unsurpassable absolutely. But this leads to many difficulties. For instance, it makes it impossible for the world to have any value for God. He must be purely indifferent to the world, and to what happens in it. For otherwise the world could contribute value to God, and in this way he would surpass himself as He would be without the world, or with an inferior one.

There is another ambiguity in Anselm's view. God must, he rightly held, exist necessarily. But does it follow that everything about God is necessary? My existence tomorrow may be predicted with fair probability, but just what state of thought and feeling and sensation I shall be in cannot be deduced from the proposition that I shall exist tomorrow. So perhaps with God. That he exists necessarily means that in any possible case he exists and has, for instance, perfect knowledge of whatever world exists with him; but *what* world there is for him to know does not follow from his existence, or the perfection of his knowledge. For *whatever* the world may be, he will know it accurately and fully, and the accuracy and completeness of knowledge do not depend upon what there is to know. In contrast, the concrete content and character of the knowledge do depend upon what there is to know. It is one thing to know perfectly such and such a world, and (whatever theologians have said to the contrary) it is another thing to know perfectly a different world. Perfection is an abstract character; God's full or concrete quality is more than his bare existence.

Existence and Concrete Actuality

Here, I think, is the innermost reason for the opposition to Anselm's Proof. From an abstract definition it *seems* to derive a concrete actuality; for God is not supposed to be a mere abstraction. But the more concrete never follows from the less concrete. To this rule of logic not even God can be an exception, for the rule is self-evident. The concrete is richer than the abstract, and the more cannot follow by necessity from the less.

Let us call the concrete state of a thing its *actuality*. Then my proposition is, actuality is always *more* than bare existence. Existence is that the defined abstract nature is *somehow* concretely actualized; but *how* it is actualized, in what particular state, with what particular *content* not deducible from the abstract definition, constitutes the actuality. Of course, then, it would be contradictory to deduce this content by any proof.

Anselm, rightly contending that existence is deducible from the definition of God (assuming that the definition is conceivable), overlooked the immeasurable gulf between bare existence and actuality. Actuality can never be deduced, not even in the divine case.

The opponents of Anselm, on the other hand, rightly insisting upon the transcendence of actuality, were wrong in holding that bare existence is never deducible. To say this is merely to declare God impossible. For we understand that He *could* only exist by necessity of his nature, from the idea of which the existence must therefore be deducible. What the opponents should have said (but not one of them has) is that there are two steps to consider, one from essence to existence and the other from existence to actuality. The reduction of these two steps to one is the common fallacy of Anselm and his opponents. Even the step from essence to existence is, in the case of creatures, always a contingent one, a question of what the facts happen to be. But with God, as Anselm showed, no such existential contingency makes sense. His essence or nature must be actualized somehow, in some concrete state or other. But how it is actualized, the concrete state itself, cannot be deduced, for, being richer than any abstraction, it cannot be logically contained in any. Thus, there are two rules: (1) all creaturely existence, although not all existence, is contingent; and (2) all actuality, even that of the creator, is contingent. (What this really means is that God's total reality is a creature, not the mere creator.)

Noncompetitiveness of God

Why is the divine essence equivalent to existence? Because this is the most abstract individual nature there is, and because what is deduced is equally abstract, merely that the most abstract nature is somehow actualized, no matter how. The term "perfect" is as abstract as the term "imperfect"; but whereas there are innumerable possible kinds of imperfect individuals, there can be but *one* perfect individual. And so, although utterly abstract, the divine nature cannot be shared by several individuals. This shows that, among abstractions, it is in a class by itself. The same conclusion can be reached by other paths. (True, the divine *actuality* is not abstract, but neither is it what the argument should claim to prove.)

With ordinary abstractions, like "humanity," there can be indefinitely many individual cases. Whatever ones exist, various conceivable ones will thereby be prevented from existing. That a certain man is formed as an embryo prevents many otherwise possible embryos from being formed in that womb, or in any other. But God, by existing, interferes with no other individual in his class. There could be no other. More than that, his existence does not interfere with the existence of individuals of any class whatever. That God exists does not mean that this or that otherwise possible creature cannot exist. For God's power to have creatures is conceived as unlimited. Hence, any conceivable creature could coexist with God.

Thus, the existence of God is not a possibility *competing with other possibilities*. Such competitiveness is the very meaning of contingency. To say, "we might not have existed," is to say that something else might have existed instead. But nothing can exist instead of God. His role is not competitive. His is the only *noncompetitive* or completely abstract existential role, and hence the only one whose filling can be necessary.

We have seen that the divine actuality cannot be deducible, cannot be necessary for our knowledge. Can it be necessary at all? I hold that the divine actuality must be contingent, not only for us, but in itself. For concreteness must always be competitive, it must always exclude something else which would be equally concrete. Take the divine knowledge that this world exists. This excludes divine knowledge that some other world exists instead. God cannot know that this world and also some incompatible world both exist. Hence, the actuality of his knowledge must take sides between competing possibilities, and this means it must be contingent. That God exists and knows in a perfect way is deducible from his definition, but the content of this perfect knowledge is not. It can only be contingent.

Unsurpassability and Necessity

If God must have contingent qualities, then he must be able to surpass himself; for instance, by coming to know a greater world, one richer in beauty. He will not know the greater world more accurately, but it will be a more rewarding object of knowledge. So the two ambiguities which Anselm failed to notice, (1) that between unsurpassability by others, and unsurpassability by anyone, even by self, and (2) that between necessity of bare existence and necessity of concrete actuality as well, are both resolved in the same way, by denying the simple or absolute forms of unsurpassability and necessity and accepting the more complex or qualified forms. Thus, we have: unsurpassable, *except* by self; and necessary, except in concrete actuality. Is it surprising that the simplest view should be tried first? And is not the truth usually more subtle than our first crude guesses? I look upon classical metaphysics and theology, which Anselm well represented, as a long experiment with a suspiciously simple doctrine, that God is entirely or simply necessary, entirely or simply unsurpassable, immutable, independent, without parts, in *all* respects infinite, absolute, and eternally complete. God's bare *existence* is indeed entirely necessary, as well as unsurpassable, immutable, independent, and this is Anselm's glorious discovery; but God's full reality, his *actuality*, cannot be merely necessary, or merely unsurpassable, immutable, independent, without parts or complete once and for all.

In consequence, the world and our efforts can contribute value to the divine life, and thus religion makes sense. How could we serve God if his value were absolutely complete without us?

What is meant by saying that the nonexistence of God is inconceivable? Let us consider how we conceive nonexistence in general. "There are no elephants in the room" implies that we have or could have experiences we could *not* have if there were elephants. But what experience would be such that it could not occur if God existed? The experience of evil? If this shows that God does not exist, then, of course, it cannot be true that He does. But it shows this only on the assumption that the entire absence of evil is deducible from the presence of God. And one must first know that it makes sense to deduce, from the perfect freedom and goodness of God, that he must or even could create creatures not only imperfect in freedom but wholly without freedom, able to make no decisions except those duplicating what God decides for them. To me, this deduction seems entirely illogical. The supreme or perfect freedom neither could nor should result in mere puppets; and I do not believe that the idea of puppets can stand being absolutized without losing its meaning. The perfect freedom of deity should issue in lesser freedom of the creatures; and with such freedom, however slight, goes risk as well as opportunity. So I deny that the experience of evil implies the nonexistence of God. And what other experience could do so, if that of evil could not?

Let us now consider Gaunilo's undeservedly famous attempt to achieve a *reductio ad absurdum* against Anselm, an attempt which the saint rightly refused to take seriously. If greatest conceivable being must exist, why not greatest conceivable island? Of course the answer is obvious: "greatest conceivable island" has no clear meaning; moreover, an island *could not* exist necessarily, for it is competitive with other possibilities, such as the surrounding water's being at a high enough level to submerge the island. "Unsurpassable, necessary island" is nonsense. If "unsurpassable and necessary being" is also nonsense, then positivism is correct. But the nonsense could not be *for the same reason*, since "island" limits perfection while "being" does not. So the refutation is a failure. Could an "island" be the creator of all things?

Necessary Existence, not Necessary Actuality

What is the role of faith in the proof? It furnishes the question, and this question turns out to be self-answering, logical not factual. Put it this way: There are men of faith, and these, if they can understand their faith, will be the only ones who do understand it. The rest are either believers without understanding—or unbelievers also without understanding—of what it means to ask, does God exist? The unbelievers (if they are positivists) may excuse themselves on the ground that they doubt if *anyone* understands it, because, they suggest, the question has no intelligible meaning. But this and this alone is the issue. Someone fails to understand his attitude toward faith. Who is it?

All metaphysical questions are of this type: that error must be confusion. If the believer can be sure he is not confused, he is immune to attack. So is the unbeliever, in the like case. But can either be sure? That is the great question.

Anselm's own view of God *was*, I think, confused. One can see this on page after page. But his own definition, when its ambiguity is removed to allow for divine self-surpassing, can cure this confusion. Then his proof becomes very strong. But it is a proof of necessary *existence*, not of necessary actuality. We need a new type of theism to take this distinction into account. For several centuries this new theism has been emerging. Whitehead is one of its representatives. I am happy to be another.

XVIII

CHARLES HARTSHORNE

The Irreducibly Modal Structure of the Argument[1]

THE reader will have noticed the label "modal" in the title of this chapter. Had the proof been known as the Modal Argument, the chances of genuine inquiry would have been greater. Critics have generally discussed the problem as though it concerned a mere question of fact, of contingent existence versus contingent nonexistence. This is not a modal distinction in an unambiguous sense, inasmuch as the mode of contingency is the neutrality of a predicate as between existence and nonexistence, and the denial of such neutrality is the disjunction: necessarily existent or necessarily nonexistent (i.e., impossible). To squeeze this modal complexity into the mere dichotomy "existent versus nonexistent" is to fail to discuss what Anselm was talking about. He repeatedly expressed the principle that "contingently existing perfect thing" is contradictory in the same way as "nonexisting perfect thing." However, since what is not exemplified in truth is certainly not necessarily exemplified ($\sim p \rightarrow \sim Np$), and since what is not necessary could not be necessary ($\sim Np \rightarrow N \sim Np$), to exclude contingency (this exclusion being the main point of the Argument) is to exclude factual nonexistence as well as merely factual existence, leaving, as the only status which the idea of perfection can have (supposing it not meaningless or contradictory), that of necessary exemplification in reality; and it then, by the principle $Np \rightarrow p$, "the necessarily true is true," becomes contra-

[1] *The Logic of Perfection* (Lasalle; Open Court Publishing Co., 1962), Ch. 2, sect. VI, pp. 49-57. Reprinted with permission.

dictory to deny that perfection is exemplified. (Here, and throughout, we use the arrow sign for strict, not material, implication.)

Is it this subtle, beautifully logical reasoning that we meet in the numerous refutations? Rather, we find a gross simplification which amounts to the straw-man procedure.

The logical structure of the Anselmian argument, in its mature or "Second" form, may be partially formalized as follows:

"q" for "$(\exists x)Px$" There is a perfect being, or perfection exists
"N" for "it is necessary (logically true) that"
"$\sim$" for "it is not true that"
"v" for "or"
"$p \rightarrow q$" for "p strictly implies q" or "$N\sim(p \ \& \sim q)$"

1. $q \rightarrow Nq$	"Anselm's Principle": perfection could not exist contingently [hence, the assertion that it exists could not be contingently but only necessarily true[2]]
2. $Nq \vee \sim Nq$	Excluded Middle
3. $\sim Nq \rightarrow N\sim Nq$	Form of Becker's Postulate: modal status is always necessary
4. $Nq \vee N\sim Nq$	Inference from (2, 3)
5. $N\sim Nq \rightarrow N\sim q$	Inference from (1): the necessary falsity of the consequent implies that of the antecedent (Modal form of modus tollens)
6. $Nq \vee N\sim q$	Inference from (4, 5)
7. $\sim N\sim q$	Intuitive postulate (or conclusion from other theistic arguments): perfection is not impossible
8. Nq	Inference from (6, 7)
9. $Nq \rightarrow q$	Modal axiom
10 q	Inference from (8, 9)

Those who challenge the Argument should decide which of these ten items or inferential steps to question. Of course, one may reject one or more of the assumptions (1, 3, 7); but reject is one thing, refute or show to be a mere sophistry is another. To me at least, the assumptions are intuitively convincing, provided perfection is properly construed, a condition Anselm did not fulfill. Moreover, no absurd consequence seems derivable from them by valid reasoning.

Concerning (1). Note that we do not take as initial assumption

[2] Added at Prof. Hartshorne's request.

that $\sim q$ is directly contradictory, or that a nonexistent being must therefore be imperfect. Nonexistent subjects cannot be said to have predicates, even inconsistent ones. Rather, we reason that by virtue of (1) and certain principles of modal logic,

$$((\exists x)Px \ \& \sim N\ (\exists x)Px) \rightarrow \sim Px$$

and thus the antecedent is necessarily false, since it both asserts and by implication denies perfection, not of a supposed nonexistent but of a supposed contingently existent subject. Such a subject can very well have predicates, and indeed all ordinary subjects are precisely of this kind. Thus, we make contingency and its negation, not existence or nonexistence, the predicates with which the argument is concerned, in connection with the predicate perfection.

The postulate of logical possibility (7) is in my view the hardest to justify. One way of doing this is to employ one or more of the other theistic proofs, some forms of which demonstrate that perfection must be at least conceivable. Here, however, we encounter Kant's contention that the other proofs themselves need support from the ontological. Yet Kant's own analysis showed that what the other proofs need from the ontological is not really its conclusion (8 or 10), but only the exclusion of contingency from perfection (6), and this is a mere logical transformation of Anselm's Principle (1). Thus, there need be no vicious circle in employing all the proofs in mutual support. They are all complex, involving a number of assumptions and steps, and where one is weakest, another may be strongest. There need be no simple linear order, and indeed there is none, among them. Here too we must do our own thinking, and not expect Kant or Hume to have done it for us.

That modality with respect to existence is a predicate is assumed by the critics of the Argument themselves. For they hold, in effect, that to every predicate there is attached the status of contingency, i.e., its existence and nonexistence must alike be conceivable. Obviously, if "contingent" is a predicate, so is "noncontingent"; just as, if "perfect" is a predicate, so is "imperfect." This is then, as far as it goes, an answer to the crucial Logical-type Counterargument: Modality is (at least) as high in the type sequence as property! We shall see presently, however, that only neoclassical theism can consistently avail itself of this rebuttal.

It is to be noted that Anselm's Principle does not say that perfection would be imperfect if it were unexemplified, but that anything exemplifying it merely contingently (so that it could have been unexemplified) would be imperfect, and so would not exemplify it after all. Thus, the "homological mistake" is not committed [12th Counter-argument]. Moreover (and here too Anselm is subtler than most of his critics), "is necessarily exemplified" follows by Becker's Postulate from "could be necessarily exemplified," since –N–Np→ Np. This disposes of the [5th] Counter-argument, "Hypothetical Necessity Only."

Something should be said about the meaning of "necessity," symbolized by "N." As every logician knows, there are many interpretations of this symbol. In general, it means analytic or L-true, true by necessity of the meanings of the terms employed. This is the sense intended in the present essay. However, what is analytic in one language may, as Quine and others have sufficiently emphasized, not be so in another.[3] (Here, too, we see how absurd it is to suppose that the Ontological question is a simple one.) I cannot exhaust the modal subject here and now. But I must make clear the difference between merely conditional necessity and absolute necessity. As Von Wright has it, this last is the same as "necessity upon tautological conditions": not necessity assuming p, or necessity assuming not-p, but necessity, p or not-p. Since "p or not-p" must be true, it is meaningless to say, "q might be necessary but is not," when "necessary" is taken in the sense of "upon tautological conditions." This is the only sense at issue in connection with the ontological argument. The divine existence is by definition unconditioned, and its necessity can only be absolute, valid no matter what, or "given p or not-p." Thus, if God logically could be necessary, He must be, since no contingent condition can be relevant.

The technical difficulty with regard to the Argument is that the idea of God is apparently not a conception of formal logic. Hence, even if the idea implies the necessity of a corresponding object, so that the denial of such an object is contradictory, still the whole question seems to fall outside the basic rules of any language. However, the matter is not so simple. There ought to be a formal rule concerning the division between necessary and contingent statements, and as we shall see, by some reasonable criteria for this

3 Quine's conclusion that all truth is synthetic is fairly but powerfully criticized by A. Hofstadter in "The Myth of the Whole, a Consideration of Quine's View of Knowledge," *J. of Phil.*, LI (1954), pp. 397-417.

division, the statement "Divine Perfection exists" falls on the side of necessity. Moreover, there may well be an aspect of the idea of God which is formal in the logical sense. If, for instance, "deity" connotes, among other things, "the sole individual definable a priori" (distinguished a priori from all others, actual or possible), is this not a formal characterization? Or suppose it follows from the meaning of "God" that it can only refer to an individual "such that, given any statement about any other individual whatever, this statement can be translated without loss of meaning or truth into a statement about God." (Thus, for S *is* P we can always say *God knows that S is P*.) Of no other individual than God, I believe, could the quoted stipulation hold; yet it is a formal or logical stipulation. No special fact is mentioned, but only the ideas of individual, statement, and translatability or equivalence. No doubt some problems arise here, but I shall not attempt to deal with them now.

Carnap has proposed the notion of "meaning postulates," as a device for introducing analytic judgments, other than the merely logical, into a language.[4] The objection has been that apparently any scientific law could be turned into an a priori necessity by suitable meaning postulates, thus trivializing the procedure. However, as Bowman Clarke, in an unpublished thesis, has proposed, the trivialization may be avoided if we limit meaning postulates to ideas of metaphysical generality, ideas of unlimited range in space-time, and applicable to all grades of existence, low or high.[5] I think also that metaphysical universality is the same as the absence of exclusiveness [to be discussed in § IX] and that God (in his necessary essence only) is universal or nonexclusive, involved in all possible things. It may be that Carnap's proposal, qualified and developed in some such way, will solve the technical problem of reconciling the logical meaning of "necessary" with the ontological in the unique divine case.

One way to put the argument is this: Any language adequate to

4 See R. Carnap, *Meaning and Necessity*, 2d. ed. (Chicago: U. of Chicago Press, 1956), pp. 222-229; and R. M. Martin, *The Notion of Analytic Truth* (Philadelphia: U. of Pennsylvania Press, 1959), pp. 87-90.

5 See Carnap's somewhat analogous proposal in *Meaning and Necessity*, Sec. 21. Also my paper, "Existential Propositions and the Law of Categories," *Proceedings of the Tenth International Congress of Philosophy*, Amsterdam, August 11-18, 1948, ed. by E. W. Beth, H. J. Poss and J. H. A. Hollak, Fascicule I, pp. 342-344.

formulate the meaning of "perfect" in the theistic sense will make "perfection exists" analytic or L-true. Moreover, a language which does this will not thereby become inconsistent. This is more than can be said for a language making "perfect island exists" L-true (using "island" in anything like the dictionary sense). Since modal status is always necessary, mistakes in assigning such status can only lead to contradiction. Suppose for instance, we should speak of a "necessarily existent" island. Since the necessarily so is of course so, said island must exist. What is wrong? Simply that the notion of island is that of a contingent thing, resulting from causes whose operation is not infallible and everlasting. If an island could be necessary, anything could be so, and since the possibly necessary must be necessary ($\sim N \sim Np \rightarrow Np$), there would be no contingency or necessity in a significant sense. Thus, a language which required one to admit as a genuine concept "necessarily existing island" would be self-inconsistent. The "necessarily existing island" must exist, but also it must not and cannot exist. We can only start over again, by dismissing the alleged definition as ill-formed. If then the notion of "necessarily existing perfection" were likewise illegitimate, a contradiction would result from its use. If the contradiction can be exhibited, there is an end of the matter. But can it? If not, then the notion may be legitimate. And since religion seems to require the idea, there is some burden of proof on the negative. (In the foregoing I assume that we are not limited to classical theism as explication of "perfect," for if we were, then I would grant the charge of inconsistency without further ado.) To reason, "If the metaphysically perfect could be necessary, anything could be so," would be silly, as we shall see in more detail later. The metaphysically perfect is a radically exceptional case, on any analysis. "Perfect island" never did mean metaphysically perfect island, to any honest and careful thinker; for the phrase is too glaringly absurd. It never meant, *either* (classical theism) the exhaustion, through an island, of all possibility so far as positive or valuable, *or* (neoclassical theism) coincidence of actuality with the island's actuality and of possibility with the island's possibility. And if it did mean either of these things, then it meant nonsense. To be thus is not to be an island, but to be God.

The Cosmological Argument, not to be dealt with here, would perhaps show that any language adequate to formulate the universal categories, or to discuss the most general cosmological questions, would also make "perfection exists" L-true.

The foregoing meaning of N justifies the axioms that all modalities reduce to three: Np, N∼p, (∼Np & ∼N∼p); and that ∼N∼Np→ Np, and ∼Np→ N∼Np (*what could be* necessary is so, and what is not necessary could not be so). It must be understood that propositions are here identified by their meaning, not in some extrinsic way. As Church remarks, "the proposition occurring first on a certain page" may happen to be, in a certain language, a necessary proposition, but "it" might also have been a contingent proposition.[6] Clearly one is not in such cases dealing with the same proposition, as far as meaning is concerned. Some modal systems, at least, recognize the above axioms (Lewis, Prior, Carnap).

In systems of "strict implication," it has been termed a paradox that a necessary proposition is strictly implied by any proposition whatever. I agree with Lewis in not finding this paradoxical, at least if we consider only those cases which are free from empirical concepts. That "blue cheese contains microorganisms" (if this is part of what we mean by cheese) is only trivially a priori or necessary; for there might have been no such thing as cheese, or even any idea of such a thing. What is strictly a priori and purely necessary here is only some such principle as that the consequences of a defined term must be accepted if the term is accepted. This much more abstract proposition, or something like it, is, I believe, in a genuine sense implied by any proposition and any thought at all. I hold similarly that the validity of the Argument, if it be valid, can only mean that the existence of perfection is nontrivially necessary, an implicit or more or less hidden ingredient of any concept or any belief whatever. It follows that it must be highly abstract, highly general; and this consequence I accept and emphasize. We shall see that while this is therefore no threat to neoclassical, it is to classical, theism.

[6] A. Church, in his article in *Structure, Method and Meaning: Essays in Honor of Henry M. Sheffer*, ed. by P. Henle (New York: The Liberal Arts Press, 1951), pp. 22-23, footnote.

XIX

John Hick

A Critique of the "Second Argument"

I

The preceding three essays represent the most recent phase in the discussion of the ontological argument; and the purpose of the present essay is to continue the discussion by offering a critique of the form of ontological proof which has been independently formulated, on the basis of Anselm's *Proslogion* III, by Charles Hartshorne and Norman Malcolm.

The main contention of this critique will be that two importantly different concepts of necessary being are involved in the Malcolm-Hartshorne proof, and that the proof is vitiated by a shift in mid-course from one of these concepts to the other.

These two concepts of "necessary being" or "necessary existence" employ the quite distinct notions of logical necessity and ontological or factual necessity.

Consider first the notion of logical necessity, and its much discussed application by J. N. Findlay to the question of divine existence. In contemporary philosophical literature to say that a given proposition is logically true, or logically necessary, or analytic, is generally intended to signify that it is true by virtue of the meanings of the terms which compose it. Applying this usage in theology, to say that God has (logically) necessary being, or that his existence is (logically) necessary, would be to say that the meaning of "God" is such that the proposition "God exists" is a logical, analytic or a priori truth; or again that the proposition "God does not exist" is a self-contradiction, a statement of such a kind that it is logically impossible for it to be true. It is an implication of this contemporary empiricist view of logical necessity as analytic that an existential proposition (i.e., a value of the propositional function "*x* exists") cannot be logically necessary. On this view, the correct analysis of "*a* exists" is that the concept of *a* is instantiated; and the role of the word "exists" is to register this assertion. Such an analysis implies that existence cannot properly be included among the defining properties of *a*—except of course in the trivial sense that only existing entities can be instances of anything. Thus within the thought-world of modern empiricism the notion of logically necessary existence is not admissible, and cannot be employed as the foundation of a valid theistic argument.

This fact is used by J. N. Findlay in his much discussed article, "Can God's Existence Be Disproved?" (and often reprinted), as the foundation of a strict disproof of divine existence. Findlay puts the ontological argument into reverse by contending that the concept of a deity whose existence is logically necessary, so far from guaranteeing the existence of an entity corresponding to it, is such as to guarantee that nothing corresponds to it.

Findlay defines the concept of God as that of the adequate object of religious attitudes, a religious attitude being described as one in which we tend "to abase ourselves before some object, to defer to it wholly, to devote ourselves to it with unquestioning enthusiasm, to bend the knee before it, whether literally or metaphorically."[1] Such an attitude is rationally adopted only by one who believes that the object to which he thus relates himself as a worshiper has certain very remarkable characteristics. Findlay lists the most important of these characteristics. First, an adequate object of religious attitudes must be conceived as being infinitely superior to ourselves in value or worth. (Accordingly, Findlay refers to this object as "he" rather than as "it.") Second, he must be conceived as being unique: God must not merely be one of a class of beings of the same kind, but must stand in an asymmetrical relationship to all other objects as the source of whatever value they may have. Third, says Findlay, the adequate object of religious attitudes must be conceived as not merely happening to exist, but as existing necessarily; if he merely happened to exist, he would not be worthy of the full and unqualified

[1] *Mind*, Vol. 57, No. 226 (April, 1948), p. 177. Reprinted in Flew and Macintyre, eds., *New Essays in Philosophical Theology*, *op. cit.*, p. 49.

attitude of worship. And fourth, this being must be conceived as not merely happening to possess his various characteristics, but as possessing them in some necessary manner. For our present purpose we may conflate these two necessities, necessary existence and the necessary possession of properties, and treat them as one. It should be borne in mind throughout that in Findlay's argument "necessary" means "logically necessary."

It is the last two in his list of requirements that provide the ground for Findlay's ontological disproof of theism. "For if God is to satisfy religious claims and needs, he must be a being in every way inescapable, one whose existence and whose possession of certain excellencies we cannot possibly conceive away. And modern views make it self-evidently absurd (if they don't make it ungrammatical) to speak of such a Being and attribute existence to him."[2] For no propositions of the form "*x* exists" can be analytically true. Hence, Findlay argues, the concept of an adequate object of religious attitudes, involving as it does the notion of a necessarily existent being who possesses his characteristic in some necessary manner, is a self-contradictory concept. We can know a priori, from inspection of the idea itself, that there is and can be no such being.

We may distinguish in Findlay's argument a philosophical premise to the effect that no existential proposition can be an analytic truth, and a theological premise to the effect that an adequate object of religious worship must be such that it is logically necessary that he exists. Of these two premises, I suggest that the former should be accepted but the latter rejected. We must deny, that is to say, the theological doctrine that God must be conceived, if at all, in such a way that "God exists" is a logically necessary truth. We must deny this for precisely the same reason as Findlay, namely, that the demand that "God exists" should be a necessary truth is, like the demand that a circle should be square, not a proper demand at all but a misuse of language. Only, whereas Findlay concludes that the notion of an adequate object of religious attitudes is an absurdity, we should conclude that that of which the idea is an absurdity cannot be an adequate object of religious attitudes; it would on the contrary be an unqualifiedly inadequate object of worship.

Let us then ask the question, which seems highly appropriate at this point, as to how religious persons actually think of the Being

[2] *Ibid.*, p. 55.

whom they regard as the adequate object of their worship. What aspect of the Judeo-Christian experience of God lies behind the idea of necessary being?

The concept of God held by the biblical writers was based upon their experience of God as awesome power and holy will confronting them and drawing them into the sphere of his ongoing purpose. God was known as a dynamic will interacting with their own wills; a sheer given reality, as inescapably to be reckoned with as destructive storm and life-giving sunshine, the fixed contours of the land, or the hatred of their enemies and the friendship of their neighbors. God was not for them an inferred entity; he was an experienced reality. The biblical writers were (sometimes, although doubtless not at all times) as vividly conscious of being in God's presence as they were of living in a material environment. Their pages resound and vibrate with the sense of God's presence, as a building might resound and vibrate from the tread of some great being walking through it. They thought of this holy Presence as unique—as the maker and ruler of the universe, the sole rightful sovereign of men and angels, as eternal and infinite, and as the ultimate reality and determining power, in relation to whom his creatures have no standing except as the objects of his grace. But nowhere in the biblical thought about God is use made of the idea of logical necessity. The notion is quite foreign to the characteristically Hebraic and concrete utterances found in the Bible, and forms no part of the biblical concept or concepts of God.

But, it might be said, was it not to the Biblical writers inconceivable that God should not exist, or that he should cease to exist, or should lose his divine powers and attributes? Would it not be inconceivable to them that God might one day go out of existence, or cease to be good and become evil? And does not this attitude involve an implicit belief that God exists necessarily and possesses his divine characteristics in some necessary manner? The answer, I think, is that it was to the biblical writers psychologically inconceivable—as we say colloquially, unthinkable—that God might not exist, or that his nature might undergo change. They were so vividly conscious of God that they were unable to doubt his reality, and they relied so firmly upon his integrity and faithfulness that they could not contemplate his becoming other than they knew him to be. They would have allowed as a verbal concession only that there might possibly be no God; for they were convinced that they were at many times directly aware of his presence and of his dealings with them. But the question whether the nonexistence of God is *logically* inconceivable, or *logically* impossible, is a philosophical puzzle which could not be answered by the prophets and apostles out of their own firsthand religious experience. This does not of course represent any special limitation of the biblical figures. The logical concept of necessary being cannot be given in religious experience. It is a product—as Findlay argues, a malformed product—of reflection. A religious person's reply to the question, Is God's existence logically necessary? will be determined by his view of the nature of logical necessity; and this is not part of his religion but of his system of logic. The biblical writers do not display any view of the nature of logical necessity, and would doubtless have regarded the topic as of no religious significance. It cannot reasonably be claimed, then, that logically necessary existence was part of their conception of the adequate object of human worship.

Nevertheless, the biblical tradition, in its subsequent theological development, does contain an increasingly explicit understanding of God as necessary being. In this concept it is not logical but ontological or factual necessity that is attributed to the object of man's worship. More than one type of nonlogical necessity have been distinguished in philosophical literature. Kant, for example, speaks in the *Critique of Pure Reason* of "material necessity in existence (*die materiale Notwendigkeit im Dasein*) and not merely formal and logical necessity in the connection of concepts" (2d ed., p. 279), this material necessity being equivalent to what is sometimes termed causal necessity, i.e., participation in the universal causal system of nature. Kant also speaks in the same work of another kind of factual necessity when he treats of the three modal categories of possibility, existence and necessity. He derives the latter from the necessary or analytic proposition in formal logic; but its schema in time is the existence of an object throughout all time (2d ed., p. 184). This notion of necessary existence as existence throughout all time suggests the idea of a temporally unlimited Being, and this is an important part, although not the whole, of the concept of divine existence as ontologically necessary. The concept first appears in Anselm, in *Proslogion* III and especially in his *Reply* to Gaunilo. In *Proslogion* III, we read that "it is possible to conceive of a being which cannot be conceived not to exist." As most naturally understood by a twentieth-century philosopher, "a being which cannot be conceived not to exist" would be presumed to mean "a being whose nonexistence is logically inconceivable, i.e., logically impossible, or self-contradictory." However, when we turn to Anselm's *Reply* to Gaunilo, we find that he states explicitly what he means by the notion of beings which can and which cannot be conceived not to exist. "All those objects, and those alone," he says, "can be conceived not to exist, which have a beginning or end or composition of parts: also . . . whatever at any place or at any time does not exist as a whole. That being alone, on the other hand, cannot be conceived not to exist, in which any conception discovers neither beginning nor end nor composition of parts (*nec initium nec finem nec partium conjunctionem*), and which any conception finds always and everywhere as a whole".[3]

Here we have something quite different from the distinctively modern thought of "God exists" as a logically necessary truth. We have instead the essence of the contrasting notion of God as sheer, ultimate, unconditioned reality, without origin or end.

Thomas Aquinas also uses the term "necessary being" and uses it, I believe, in the sense of ontological or factual necessity. The conclusion of the Third Way argument is that "there must exist something the existence of which is necessary (*oportet aliquid esse necessarium in rebus*)."[4] In the preceding argument the mark of contingency is transiency or temporal finitude; and, by contrast, the mark of noncontingency, or of the necessary being of God, is existence without beginning or end—in other words, eternal being.

Another, and indeed more fundamental, aspect of the distinctively theological form of ontological or factual necessity is contributed by Anselm in the *Monologion*, where he draws the distinction between existence *a se* and existence *ab alio*. He says of God, "The supreme Substance, then, does not exist through any efficient agent, and does not derive existence from any matter, and was not aided in being brought into existence by any external causes. Nevertheless, it by no means exists through nothing, or derives existence from nothing; since, through itself and from itself, it is whatever it is" (*per seipsam et ex seipsa est quidquid est*). (Ch. 6.) Thus, aseity (*a se esse*) is central to the notion of the necessary being of God.

3 Ch. IV. Cf. Ch. I.

4 *Summa theologica*, Pt. I. Q. 2, Arg. 3. For support for the nonlogical interpretation of *necessarium* here see Peter Geach in *Three Philosophers*, by Anscombe and Geach (Oxford, 1961), pp. 114-115.

From God's aseity, or ontic independence, his eternity, indestructibility and incorruptibility can be seen to follow. A self-existent being must be eternal, i.e., without temporal limitation. For if he had begun to exist, or should cease to exist, he must have been caused to exist, or to cease to exist, by some power other than himself; and this would be inconsistent with his aseity. By the same token, he must be indestructible, for to say that he exists in total ontic independence is to say that there is and could be no reality able to constitute or to destroy him; and likewise he must be incorruptible, for otherwise his aseity would be qualified as regards its duration.

Again, to refer back to Findlay's discussion, it is meaningless to say of the self-existent being that he might not have existed or that he merely happens to exist. For what could it mean to say of the eternal, uncreated Creator of everything other than himself that he "merely happens to exist"? When we assert of a dependent and temporarily finite being, such as myself, that I only happen to exist, we mean that if such-and-such an event had occurred in the past, or if such-and-such another event had failed to occur, I should not now exist. But no such meaning can be given to the statement, "A self-existent being only happens to exist," or "might not have existed." There is no conceivable event such that if it had occurred, or failed to occur, a self-existent being would not have existed; for the concept of aseity is precisely the exclusion of such dependence. There is and could be nothing that would have prevented a self-existent being from coming to exist, for it is meaningless even to speak of a self-existent being as *coming* to exist.

What may properly be meant, then, by the statement that God is, or has, necessary rather than contingent being is that God *is*, without beginning or end, and without origin, cause or ground of any kind whatsoever. He *is*, as the ultimate, unconditioned, absolute, unlimited reality.

II

We have distinguished the following two concepts: (1) the logically necessary truth of a proposition, arising from the meaning of the terms employed in it; and (2) the factual necessity of a Being who exists eternally and *a se*. These two concepts are quite distinct; logical necessity is not a case of ontological necessity, nor vice versa. The necessary existence of an object, *x*, is defined as the existence of *x* without beginning or end and without dependence upon anything other than itself. The logically necessary truth of a proposition, *p*, on the other hand, reflects the circumstances that *p* is so formed as to be true by definition. It is, it seems to me, essential to keep this distinction clear. From the concept of God as ontologically necessary we can derive the analytic truth that if God exists, he exists eternally and *a se*, but we cannot deduce that it is a logically necessary truth that God exists, i.e., that the concept of an eternal Being who exists *a se* is instantiated in extramental reality. And yet this is precisely what Malcolm and Hartshorne try to do. They observe (rightly) that while "existence" is not a real predicate (i.e., cannot figure as an element in the concept of a kind of being), "necessary existence" in the ontological sense *is* a real predicate and can be a constituent element in the concept of deity. However, having established that ontological necessity (i.e., eternal existence *a se*) is a real predicate, they proceed as though what they had established is the quite different conclusion that logically necessary existence is a real predicate. From this point they have no difficulty in proceeding by "due process" to the conclusion that since God has logically necessary existence, he must and therefore does exist. The argument is, however, fatally disrupted by the illicit shift of meaning between logical and ontological necessity.

Basically, the same criticism applies to both Malcolm's and Hartshorne's versions of the ontological proof; but since the latter has so conveniently formalized his argument, I will expound the criticism first and more fully in relation to Hartshorne's formulation, which is as follows:*

1. $q \rightarrow Nq$	"Anselm's Principle": perfection could not exist contingently [hence the assertion that it exists could not be contingently but only necessarily true].†

* "q" for "$(\exists x)\, Px$" There is a perfect being, or perfection exists
"N" for "it is necessary (logically true) that"
"$\sim$" for "it is not true that"
"v" for "or"
"$p \rightarrow q$" for "p strictly implies q" or "$N\sim(p \,\&\, \sim q)$"

† The clause in square brackets does not appear in *The Logic of Perfection*, but is now added at Hartshorne's request.

2. $Nq \vee \sim Nq$	Excluded Middle
3. $\sim Nq \rightarrow N \sim Nq$	Form of Becker's Postulate: modal status is always necessary
4. $Nq \vee N \sim Nq$	Inference from (2, 3)
5. $N \sim Nq \rightarrow N \sim q$	Inference from (1): the necessary falsity of the consequent implies that of the antecedent (Modal form of modus tollens)
6. $Nq \vee N \sim q$	Inference from (4, 5)
7. $\sim N \sim q$	Intuitive postulate (or conclusion from other theistic arguments): perfection is not impossible
8. Nq	Inference from (6, 7)
9. $Nq \rightarrow q$	Modal axiom
10. q	Inference from (8, 9)

The key proposition in this argument is the first, $q \rightarrow Nq$, because at this point it is essential to decide whether N is to be understood as signifying logical or ontological necessity. Hartshorne himself is quite explicit that he is using exclusively the former. N, he says, "means analytic or L-true, true by necessity of the terms employed. This is the sense intended in the present essay" (p. 337 above). Concerning Hartshorne's argument, thus interpreted by himself, I wish to maintain:

(1) that when N is interpreted as signifying logical necessity, prop. 1 has no kind of self-evidence, and indeed does not conform to any propositional form recognized in standard logical theory;

(2) that in order to represent, as Hartshorne claims, Anselm's basic principle, N in prop. 1 must be interpreted as signifying ontological, rather than logical, necessity;

(3) that when N is so interpreted, prop. 1 constitutes an acceptable premise, and leads by valid steps to prop. 6;

(4) that in order to reach its conclusion in prop. 10, the argument, having established prop. 6 in terms of ontological necessity, must thenceforth proceed on the (false) assumption that prop. 6 has been established in terms of logical necessity; and that the proof is rendered invalid by this change of meaning of a key term in midcourse.

In support of these four theses I offer the following considerations:

(1) Prop. 1, interpreted in terms of logical necessity, asserts that a certain proposition, q, strictly implies another proposition which is a proposition about q, to the effect that q is a logically necessary truth. That a proposition should strictly imply another proposition, which

is a proposition about the first proposition, involves unformulated principles which form no part of accepted logical theory, and which require justifying considerations which Hartshorne has not supplied.

Further, to propose a logical transition from q to Nq, q being an existential proposition, is to reject one of the foundations of modern logic. Within the universe of discourse within which Hartshorne professes to be operating, and to the canons of which he appeals at other points in his argument, one cannot treat an existential proposition as a logically necessary truth. When Hartshorne insists that in the unique case of God the existential assertion is an exception to this rule, he has in mind, I believe, the *ontological* necessity (i.e., eternal aseity) which is part of the concept of God.

(2) In his explanatory gloss, Hartshorne describes his prop. 1 as "Anselm's Principle: perfection could not exist contingently [hence the assertion that it exists could not be contingently but only necessarily true]." Now it is, I think, as certain as a historical judgment can be that Anselm did not use the concept of logical necessity which Hartshorne is himself professedly using, in which N "means analytic or L-true, true by necessity of the terms employed" (p.337 above). For this is a distinctively modern understanding of necessity. Further, Anselm states explicitly what he means by "a being which cannot be conceived not to exist," and the kind of necessity which he there describes is not logical but ontological. I have already cited some of the key passages in Anselm's discussion, concluding with the sentence, "That being alone, on the other hand, cannot be conceived not to exist, in which any conception discovers neither beginning nor end nor composition of parts, and which any conception finds always and everywhere as a whole." Thus, in order for Hartshorne's prop. 1 to represent Anselm's principle, it must be interpreted in terms of ontological necessity: If Perfection exists, it exists eternally and *a se*.

(3) From the premise that "If Perfection exists, it exists eternally and *a se*" we can reach the further position, stated in Hartshorne's prop. 6, that the existence of Perfection is either (ontologically) necessary or (ontologically) impossible. For if an eternal and independent being exists, he cannot cease to exist, and his existence is thus ontologically necessary; while if such a being does not exist, he cannot come into existence, and his existence is thus ontologically impossible.

(4) However, from this disjunction, according to which the divine existence is (ontologically) either necessary or impossible, we cannot derive the conclusion that Perfection or God exists. What we can deduce is that if there is a God, he has ontologically necessary (i.e., eternal and self-existent) being. For the coming to exist and the ceasing to exist of an eternal Being are alike precluded; God exists either eternally or not at all. This is the maximum that can validly be derived from the concept of God as existing eternally and *a se*.

In order to proceed beyond this point to Hartshorne's conclusion that God exists (prop. 10), we have to make an illicit switch in the interpretation of N from ontological to logical necessity. Having established prop. 6 in terms of ontological necessity, we must now take it to have been established in terms of logical necessity: God's existence is either *logically* necessary or *logically* impossible. We can then argue, as Hartshorne does, that it has not been shown that the existence of God is logically impossible, and hence that it must be regarded as logically necessary. However, the argument is rendered invalid by the fact that prop. 6 has to be interpreted in terms of ontological necessity in relation to its supporting propositions, but in terms of logical necessity in relation to the propositions which are derived from it.

It should be emphasized at this point that I am not accusing Hartshorne of the fallacy of equivocation in his argument as he has himself presented it. He states explicitly that the proof is to be understood consistently in terms of logical necessity. What I am claiming is that, so interpreted, the argument does not even have an acceptable premise from which to begin. I note, however, that if the initial premise is interpreted in terms of ontological necessity, the first half of the argument becomes valid; and I suggest that it is this fact, aided by a dormant attention at this point to the distinction between the two concepts of necessity, that has led to the argument being regarded as cogent.

It must, however, be acknowledged that, while Hartshorne explicitly rests his proof upon the logical concept of necessity, he is well aware of the differing theological concept, and addresses himself to what he describes as "the technical problem of reconciling the logical meaning of 'necessary' with the ontological in the unique divine case" (p. 338). The phrase added in square brackets on p. 335 assumes that this has been accomplished. Hartshorne's suggestion is that this might be done by adapting Carnap's notion of meaning postulates,[5] these being promulgated within an artificially constructed language system thereby creating logical necessities within that language.

Hartshorne's suggestion is, apparently, that a meaning postulate might be formulated which would import the factual or ontological necessity which is part of the concept of God into an artificial theological language, with the result that in that language it will be L-true that God exists. The suggestion is, however, not further spelled out in Hartshorne's chapter. In particular, he does not formulate the meaning postulate on which he wishes to rely. It is, therefore, not easy to appraise his suggestion. But there are two features of Carnap's notion which seem to disqualify it for the use which Hartshorne proposes. (1) The Carnapian meaning postulates contain no existential quantifier. They do not assert existence, but only meaning equivalences. But the meaning postulate required for an ontological argument would presumably have to assert existence, and would thus diverge radically from the original Carnapian notion. (2) Meaning postulates perform a function within an artificial language; but Hartshorne's object is to make the ontological argument work within our natural language. No doubt it is possible to construct an artificial language for the purpose of proving the existence of God within it, or even such that the existence of God is axiomatic within it and does not need to be proved. But this would not affect the ontological argument propounded by Anselm in Latin and propounded by Hartshorne in English. If we cannot prove God's existence in English, it is not clear how we should be advantaged by being able to construct an artificial language in which we *can* prove it; for it would then only be proved to those who elect to use this special language.[6]

III

The other important recent treatment of the second form of the Argument is that of Norman Malcolm in his article, "Anselm's

[5] Rudolf Carnap, *Meaning and Necessity*, 2d ed., Supplement B.

[6] These two critical points were made by me in a review of *The Logic of Perfection* in *Theology Today*, July 1963, in which issue there is also a reply by Prof. Hartshorne including a brief defense of his use of Carnap's meaning postulates (pp. 282-283).

Ontological Arguments," reprinted in the present volume. This defends the ontological proof on the grounds which are essentially the same as those offered by Hartshorne and which are (as it seems to me) open to essentially the same criticism. Having already presented this criticism in relation to Hartshorne's version of the argument, the same point can now be applied more briefly to Malcom's no less significant and thought-provoking discussion.

Malcom summarizes the proof as follows: "If God, a being greater than which cannot be conceived, does not exist, then he cannot *come* into existence. For if he did, he would either have been *caused* to come into existence or have *happened* to come into existence, and in either case he would be a limited being, which by our conception of him he is not. Since he cannot come into existence, if he does not exist, his existence is impossible. If he does exist, he cannot have come into existence (for the reasons given), nor can he cease to exist, for nothing could cause him to cease to exist nor could it just happen that he ceased to exist. So if God exists, his existence is necessary." Thus far we have an admirable account of the ontological concept of necessary being. If an eternal and independent being does not exist, he cannot come into existence (for he would not then be eternal); and if such a being does exist, he cannot cease to exist (for, again, he would then not be eternal). His existence is thus either necessary or impossible. But, we must immediately ask, is this necessity, and is this impossibility, logical or ontological? The correct answer is I think complex, at least to the extent that it must contain the following propositions, in which "eternal being" is intended as short for "eternal being who exists *a se*":

(1) If there is an eternal being, his existence is ontologically necessary; but
(2) it is not logically necessary that there should be an ontologically necessary being.
(3) If there is no eternal being, it is not logically impossible that there should have been one; but
(4) it is logically impossible that there should now come to be one.

The bearing of these four propositions upon Malcolm's ontological proof is as follows. Whether there is an ontologically necessary being (i.e., a being who exists eternally and *a se*) is a question of fact, although of uniquely ultimate fact. Given this concept of an ontologically necessary being, it is a matter of logic that if there is such a being, his existence is necessary in the sense that he cannot cease to exist, and that if there is no such being, none can come to exist. This logical necessity and this logical impossibility are, however, dependent upon the hypotheses, respectively, that there is and that there is not an ontologically necessary being; apart from the hypotheses from which they follow they do not entail that there is or that there is not an eternal self-existent being.

Hence, there is no substance to the dilemma: The existence of God is either logically necessary or logically impossible. And yet this is the dilemma upon which Malcolm's argument rests. The passage quoted above continues: "Thus, God's existence is either impossible or necessary. It can be the former only if the concept of such a being is self-contradictory or in some way logically absurd. Assuming that it is not so, it follows that he necessarily exists." Here Malcolm is equating proposition (1), that the existence of an eternal being is either ontologically necessary or ontologically impossible, with proposition (2), that the existence of an ontologically necessary being is either logically necessary or logically impossible. The former (1) is validly derived from the concept of God as self-existent and eternal. The latter (2) receives its plausibility from its not being distinguished from (1).[7] Once attention is focused upon the distinction between them, the plausibility of (2) disappears and the argument which depends upon it likewise loses its force.

IV

To complete this critique we must return to the source of the second argument in Anselm himself. Perhaps his most subtle piece of reasoning in the passages expounding his second form of ontological

[7] This ambivalence between the notions of logical and factual necessity runs through Malcolm's article. He describes very clearly the idea of God as the factually necessary being. "If God is conceived to be absolutely unlimited being, he must be conceived to be unlimited in regard to his existence as well as his operation. In this conception it will not make sense to say that he depends on anything for coming into existence or continuing in existence. . . ." But he concludes, "What Anselm has proved is that the notion of contingent existence or of contingent nonexistence cannot have any application to God. His existence must be either logically necessary or logically impossible." Surely, however, what Anselm has shown is that God exists either as ontologically necessary being, or not at all. But he has not shown, because logic alone cannot show, that there is in fact an ontologically necessary being.

proof occurs in *Reply* I, and is formulated twice, in two successive paragraphs, the first of which is as follows: "If that being (than which no greater can be conceived) can even be conceived to be, it must exist in reality. For that than which a greater is inconceivable cannot be conceived except as without a beginning. But whatever can be conceived to exist, and does not exist, can be conceived to exist through a beginning. Hence, what can be conceived to exist, but does not exist, is not the being than which a greater cannot be conceived. Therefore, if such a being can be conceived to exist, necessarily it does exist."

This argument from not-having-a-beginning can be set out as follows:

(i) to be unsurpassably perfect is to be incapable-of-having-a-beginning;
(ii) to be nonexistent-but-capable-of-existing is not to be incapable-of-having-a-beginning; and
(iii) therefore to be unsurpassably perfect is not to be nonexistent-but-capable-of-existing.

What this argument proves is that God is not nonexistent-but-capable-of-existing, that is, that he is not contingently nonexistent. It does not however prove that he exists.

We can present the difficulty, again, in terms of the statement that "whatever can be conceived to exist, and does not exist, can be conceived to exist through a beginning" (and is therefore not the greatest conceivable being, which is by definition eternal). This is in general a sound rule; but there is an exception to it, and the exception is precisely the case in question. On the one hand, an eternal being can be conceived to exist; and on the other hand, we can conceive that there is no such being. But it does not follow that we can conceive an eternal being to have a beginning. On the contrary, the notion of such a being precludes the thought that it should come or have come to be (at a certain point in time). We can, nevertheless, conceive that the notion of an eternal being is unexemplified—providing we understand that if it is ever unexemplified, it must be eternally unexemplified.

In his next paragraph Anselm restates his argument: "Furthermore: if it can be conceived at all, it [a being than which no greater can be conceived] must exist. For no one who denies or doubts the existence of a being than which a greater is inconceivable, denies or doubts that if it does exist, its nonexistence, either in reality or in the understanding, would be impossible. For otherwise it would not be a being than which a greater cannot be conceived. But as to whatever can be conceived, and does not exist—if there were such a being, its nonexistence, either in reality or in the understanding, would be possible. Therefore, if a being than which a greater is inconceivable can even be conceived, it cannot be nonexistent." This is essentially the same argument, and it must be challenged at the same point. Anselm says, "But as to whatever can be conceived, but does not exist: If there were such a being, its nonexistence, either in reality or in the understanding, would be possible." But, once again, the notion of an eternal being constitutes an exception to this rule. Let us suppose that there is no eternal being. It does not now follow that if there *were* an eternal being, its nonexistence would be possible. For it is by definition impossible for an eternal being to cease to exist. If there were an eternal being, its nonexistence would in that case be impossible. Neverthertheless, it does not follow from this circumstance that there *is* an eternal being.

Let me put the criticism again in another way. We may paraphrase Anselm's argument as follows: Whatever does not exist but can be thought of as existing would, if it were to exist, be able to be thought of as not existing. But anything that can be thought of as not existing is not unsurpassably perfect. Therefore the unsurpassably perfect cannot not exist (i.e., cannot be such that if it were to exist it would be able to be thought of as not existing).

Or again, more briefly: Whatever does not exist, but might exist, would if it were to exist be a contingent thing. But a most-perfect-conceivable cannot be contingent. Therefore a most-perfect-conceivable cannot not-exist.

The argument can be set out as follows:

(i) every nonexistent-which-might-exist is a contingent;
(ii) no unsurpassably-perfect is a contingent;
(iii) therefore no unsurpassably-perfect is a nonexistent-which-might-exist; and
(iv) therefore every unsurpassably-perfect is other than a nonexistent-which-might-exist (i.e., is other than contingent).

Once again what is thus proved is that God is not a contingent being, or more precisely that he does not contingently not-exist. In being other than a nonexistent-which-might-exist, he *either* exists *or* is a nonexistent which could not exist (i.e., whose existence is impossible). But what is not proved is that he exists.

Selected Bibliography

I. General Histories of the Argument

BORRELLI, F. *L'Argomento ontologico nei grandi pensatori* (Naples: Conti, 1953).

CAPONE-BRAGA, G. "Varie forme dell' argomento ontologico," in *Sophia*, 2 (1934), 34-38.

ESSER, M. *Der ontologische Gottesbeweis unds eine Geschichte* (Bonn, 1905).

HARTT, J. N. *The Ontological Argument for the Existence of God* (unpublished dissertation, Yale University, 1940). This traces the argument through the history of Western thought.

HENRICH, D. *Der ontologische Gottesbeweis: sein Problem und seine Geschichte in der Neuzeit* (Tübingen: J. C. B. Mohr, 1960).

HERRLIN, O. *The Ontological Proof in Thomistic and Kantian Interpretation* (Uppsala: Lundequistska Bokhandeln, 1950; in the series Uppsala University Arsskrift, No. 9).

KOPPER, J. *Reflexion und Raisonnement im ontologischen Gottesbeweis* (Cologne, 1962).

RUNZE, A. *Der ontologische Gottesbeweis, kritische Darstellung seiner Geschichte seit Anselm bis auf die Gegenwart* (Halle, 1882).

II. The Argument in Anselm

A. TEXT AND ENGLISH TRANSLATION

ST. ANSELM *Opera omnia*, edited by Dom Francis de Sales Schmitt, 5 volumes (Edinburgh: Thomas Nelson, 1945-1951), Vol. 1, 101-104, 125-139. This critical edition has replaced the previous edition done by Gabriel Gerberon 1675; improved and enlarged 1721; reprinted by J. P. Migne, *Patrologia Latina*, 158 (1863), 227-229, 241-260.

ST. ANSELM *Proslogium: Monologium: an Appendix in Behalf of the Fool by Gaunilon; and Cur Deus homo?* translated by Sidney N. Deane (La Salle, Ill.: Open Court Publishing House, 1903; Rev. ed., *St. Anselm: Basic Writings*, 1962).

A Scholastic Miscellany: Anselm to Ockham, edited and translated by Eugene R. Fairweather (London: S.C.M. Press, and Philadelphia: Westminster Press, 1956). This contains the *Proslogion* and an extract from Anselm's reply to Gaunilo.

The Wisdom of Catholicism, edited and translated by A. C. Pegis (New York: Random House, 1949). This contains a translation of the *Proslogion.*

St. Anselm's "Proslogion" with "A Reply on Behalf of the Fool" by Gaunilo and "The Author's Reply to Gaunilo," translated with an introduction and philosophical commentary by M. J. Charlesworth (Oxford: The Clarendon Press, 1965).

The Ontological Argument from St. Anselm to Contemporary Philosophers, edited by Alvin Plantinga, with an introduction by Richard Taylor (Garden City, N.Y.: Doubleday, 1965).

B. ANSELM AND HIS ARGUMENT IN THE CONTEXT OF MEDIEVAL THOUGHT

FOREST, A., F. VON STEENBERGHEN and M. DE GANDILLAC *Le Mouvement doctrinale du XIe au XIVe siècle* (Paris: Bloud and Gay, 1951), 31-68.

GILSON, É. *History of Christian Philosophy in the Middle Ages* (New York: Random House, 1955), 128 ff.

——— *The Spirit of Mediaeval Philosophy*, translated by A. C. Downes (New York: Charles Scribner's Sons, 1936), Ch. 3.

GRABMANN, MARTIN *Geschichte der scholastischen Methode* (Freiburg im Breisgau: Herder, 1909) I, Part 5: "Anselm von Canterbury, der Vater der Scholastik."

GRUNWALD, G. "Geschichte der Gottesbeweise im Mittelalter, bis zum Ausgand der Hochscholastik," in *Beiträge zur Geschichte der Philosophie des Mittelalters*, 6, 3 (Münster: Aschendorffschen Verlagsbuchhandlung, 1907).

UEBERWEG, F. *Grundriss der Geschichte der Philosophie*, 2, reedited by B. Geyer (11th ed., Berlin: Mittler, 1928; 12th ed., Basel: Schwabe, 1951), 192-205, 698-708.

VIGNAUX, P. *Philosophy in the Middle Ages: An Introduction*, translated by E. C. Hall (New York: Meridian Press, 1959), 35-51. This is a translation of the 3rd ed. of *Philosophie au moyen âge* (Paris: Leclerc, 1958).

C. THE ARGUMENT IN RELATION TO ANSELM'S TOTAL THOUGHT

BARTH, KARL *Anselm: Fides quaerens intellectum*, translated by Ian Robertson (London: S.C.M. Press, and Richmond, Virginia: John Knox Press, 1960). This is a translation of the 2nd ed. of *Fides quaerens intellectum: Anselms Beweis der Existence Gottes im Zusammenhang seines theologischen Programms* (1st ed., Munich: Chr. Kaiser Verlag, 1931; 2nd ed., Zurich: Evangelischen Verlag, 1958).

Discussions of Barth's Study.

BOUILLARD, H. "La preuve de Dieu dans le *Proslogion* et son interprétation par Karl Barth," in *Spicilegium Beccense* (Paris: J. Vrin, 1959), 191-207.

CAPPUYNS, M. in *Bulletin de théologie ancienne et médiévale*, 2, No. 388.

HAENCHEN, E. "Anselm und Barth, zur Frage der Apologetik," in *Wort und Geist—Festgabe für Karl Heim* (Berlin, 1934), 181-205.

KUHLMANN, GERHARDT "Zu Karl Barths Anselmbuch," in *Zeitschrift für Theologie und Kirche*, Neuen Folge 13 (1932), 269-281.

SAMUEL, O. "Der ontologische Gottesbeweis bei Karl Barth, Immanuel Kant und Anselm von Canterbury," in *Theologische Blätter*, 14 (1935) 141-153.

SCHMITT, F. S. "Der ontologische Gottesbeweis Anselms," in *Theologische Revue*, 32 (1933), 217-223.

CAPPUYNS, M. "L'Argument de S. Anselme," in *Recherches de théologie ancienne et médiévale*, 6 (1934), 313-330.

DE VORGES, D. *Saint Anselme* (Paris: Felix Alcan, 1901), 267-319.

FILLIATRE, CHARLES *La Philosophie de Saint Anselme* (Paris: Libraire Felix Alcan, 1920).

GILSON, É. "Sens et nature de l'argument de Saint Anselme," in *Archives d'histoire doctrinale et littéraire du moyen age*, 9 (1934), 5-51. In correspondence with the editors (1963) M. Gilson writes that, as he now sees it, the discussion of the problem "should be carried out in a different spirit" than was done by him in this article.

KOLPING, ADOLF *Anselms Proslogion—Beweis der Existenz Gottes im Zussammenhang seines spekulativen Programms: Fides Quaerens Intellectum* (Bonn: Hanstein, 1939) in the series *Grenzfragen zwischen Theologie und Philosophie*, No. 8.

KOYRÉ, A. *L'Idée de Dieu dans la philosophie de S. Anselme* (Paris: J. Vrin, 1923).

D. THE SOURCE OF ANSELM'S ARGUMENT

AUDET, T. A. "Une source augustinienne de l'argument de S. Anselme," in *Étienne Gilson, philosophe de la Chrétienté. Rencontres*, 30 (1949), 105-142.

DRAESEKE, J. "Zu Anselms *Monologion* und *Proslogion*," in *Neue kirchliche Zeitschrift*, 11 (1900), 243-257.

——— "Zu Frage nach dem Einfluss des Johannes Scotus Eriugena," in *Zeitschrift für wissenschaftliche Theologie*, 50 (1907), 326 ff.

FAGGIOTTO, P. "La Fonte Platonica dell' argomento ontologico di Anselmo d'Aosta," in *Rivista di filosofia Neo-Scolastica*, 46 (1954), 495 ff.

JOHNSON, J. PRESCOTT "The Ontological Argument in Plato," in *The Personalist*, 44 (1963), 24-34.

MOREAU, J. "L'Argument ontologique dans le *Phédon*," in *Revue philosophique*, 137 (1947), 320-343.

VERGNES, J. "Les Sources de l'argument de Saint Anselme," in *Revue des sciences religieuses*, 4 (1924), 576-579.

E. SPECIAL STUDIES OF ANSELM'S ARGUMENT

ADLHOCH, B. "Der Gottesbeweis des Hl. Anselm," in *Philosophische Jahrbuch der Görres-Gesellschaft*, 8 (1895), 52-69, 372-389; 9 (1896), 280-297; 10 (1897), 261-274, 394-416; 16 (1903), 163-170, 300-309; 21 (1908), 288-292.

BECKAERT, A. "Une justification platonicienne de l'argument a priori," *Spicilegium Beccense* (Paris: J. Vrin, 1959), 185-190.

BERG, JAN "An Examination of the Ontological Proof," in *Theoria*, 27 (1961), 99-106.

BERGENTHAL, F. "Ist der 'Ontologische Gottesbeweis' Anselms von Canterbury ein Trugschluss?," in *Philosophische Jahrbuch*, 59 (1949), 155-168.

CAIRD, EDWARD "Anselm's Argument for the Being of God," in *The Journal of Theological Studies*, 1 (1899), 23-39.

DE BEAUPUY, C. "L'Argument de S. Anselm est a posteriori," in *Revue de philosophie*, 12 (1908), 120-133.

DONDEYNE, A. "De argumento S. Anselmi," in *Collationes Brugenses*, 30 (1930), 126-131.

EVDOKIMOV, PAUL "L'Aspect apophatique de l'argument de S. Anselme," in *Spicilegium Beccense* (Paris: J. Vrin, 1959), 233-258.

GRAVE, S. A. "The Ontological Argument of St. Anselm," in *Philosophy*, 27 (1952), 30-38.

HENRY, D. P. "The *Proslogion* Proofs," in *Philosophical Quarterly*, 5 (1955), 147-151.

MILLER, R. "The Ontological Argument in Anselm and Descartes," in *The Modern Schoolman*, 32 (1954-1955), 341-349. The companion article on Descartes is listed in Section IV below.

MIRANDA, E. B. "Las Provas Anselmianas da existência de Deus," in *Revista Portuguesa de Filosofia*, 1 (1945), 158-175.

MORETTI-COSTANZI, T. *L'Ascesi di coscienza e l'argomento di S. Anselmo* (Rome, 1951).

Revue de philosophie, 15 (1909), 593-766. This entire issue is devoted to Anselm's sources and doctrines. Relevant articles are:

LEPIDI, A. "La Preuve ontologique de l'existence de Dieu et S. Anselme," 655-664.

GEYSER, J. "La Demonstration *a priori* de l'existence de Dieu chez S. Anselme," 665-672.

ADLHOCH, B. "Anselme et Gaunilon," 673-691.

SAMUEL, O. *Ueber die Beweisbarkeit der Existenz Gottes. Konsequenzen des Anselmischen Beweisverfahrens* (Munich: Kaiser, 1936), in the series *Forschungen zur Geschichte und Lehre des Protestantismus*, Reihe 8, Band 3.

SMART, HUGH R. "Anselm's Ontological Argument: Rationalistic or Apologetic?" in *Review of Metaphysics*, 3 (1949), 161-166.

SPEDALIARI, F. "Anselmus an Gaunilo, seu de recta argumenti sancti doctoris interpretatione," in *Gregorianum*, 28 (1947), 55-77.

——— "De intrinseca argumenti S. Anselmi vi et natura," in *Gregorianum*, 29 (1948), 204-212.

STOLZ, A. " 'Vere esse' im *Proslogion* des Hl. Anselm," in *Scholastik*, 9 (1934), 400-409.

——— "Zur Theologie Anselms im *Proslogion*," in *Catholica* 2 (1933), 1-24.

WEBB, C. C. J. "Anselm's Ontological Argument for the Existence of God," in *Aristotelian Society Proceedings*, 3 (London, 1896), 25-43.

WIHLER, A. "L'Argomento del *Proslogion* di S. Anselmo per l'esistenza di Dio," in *La Scuola Cattolica*, 70 (1942), 441-449.

WOLZ, H. G. "Empirical Basis of Anselm's Arguments," in *Philosophical Review*, 60 (1951), 341-361.

——— "The Function of Faith in the Ontological Argument," in *Proceedings of the American Catholic Philosophical Association*, 25 (1951), 151-163.

F. STUDIES OF OTHER ASPECTS OF ANSELM'S THOUGHT RELEVANT TO THE ARGUMENT

BALTHASAR, N. "Idéalisme anselmien et réalisme thomiste," in *Annales de l'Institut Supérieur de Philosophie* (Louvain), 1 (1912), 431-467.

BAYERT, J. "The Concept of Mystery according to St. Anselm of Canterbury," in *Recherches de théologie ancienne et mediévale*, 9 (1937), 125-166.

BECKER, JOS. "Der Satz des Hl. Anselm: Credo ut intelligam, in seiner Bedeutung und Tragweite," in *Philosophische Jahrbuch*, 19 (1906), 115-127, 312-326.

BETZENDOERFER, W. "Glauben und Wissen bei Anselm von Canterbury," in *Zeitschrift für Kirchengeschichte*, (1929).

DAVIES, A. E. "The Problem of Truth and Existence as Treated by Anselm," in *Aristotelian Society Proceedings*, 20 (London, 1920), 167-190.

DE GHELLINCK, J. "Dialectique et dogme aux Xe-XIIe siècles," in *Festgabe Baeumker*, I, 79-99 (*Beiträge zur Geschichte der Philosophie des Mittelalters*, supplementary volume, Munster: Aschendorffsche Verlagsbuchhandlung, 1913).

DE VORGES, D. and GARDIER, J. "L'Objectivité de la connaissance intellectuelle (à propos de S. Anselme)," in *Revue de philosophie*, 2 (1901-1902), 243-251, 529-538.

FISCHER, J. "Die Erkenntnislehre Anselms von Canterbury," in *Beiträge zur Geschichte der Philosophie des Mittelalters*, 10, 3 (Munster: Aschendorffsche Verlagsbuchhandlung, 1911).

HAENSCHE, E. "Anselm, Glaube und Vernunft," in *Zeitschrift für Theologie und Kirche*, 48 (1951), 312-342.

HAYEN, A. "Saint Anselme et Saint Thomas. La vraie nature de la théologie et sa portée apostolique," in *Spicilegium Beccense* (Paris: J. Vrin, 1959), 45-85.

HENRY, D. P. "Was Anselm Really a Realist?" in *Ratio* (Dec., 1963).

JACQUIN, A. M. "Les 'rationes necessariae' de S. Anselme," in *Mélanges Mandonnet* (Paris: J. Vrin, 1930), 2, 67-78.

OTTAVIANO, C. "Questioni e Testi Medioevali. (1) Le 'rationes necessariae' in S. Anselmo," in *Sophia*, 1 (1933), 92-97.

PHELAN, P. *The Wisdom of St. Anselm* (Latrobe, Pa.: Archabbey Press, 1960).

SCHMIDT, M. A. "Quod maior sit quam cogitari possit (Anselm von Canterbury, *Proslogion*)," in *Theologische Zeitschrift*, 12 (1956), 337-346.

SOHNGEN, G. *Die Einheit der Theologie in Anselms Proslogion*, in *Die Einheit in der Theologie Gesammelte Abhandlungen, Aufsätze, Vortrage* (Munich: Karl Ziak, 1952), 24-62. Staatliche Akad., 1938).

——— "Die antik-christliche Wissenschaft und Weisheit in Anselms neuer germanische Denkform," *Wissenschaft und Weisheit*, 8 (1941), 14-23.

STOLZ, A. "Das *Proslogion* des Hl. Anselm," in *Revue Bénédictine*, 47 (1935), 331-347.

VIGNAUX, P. "Structure et sens du *Monologion*," in *Revue des sciences philosophiques et théologiques*, 31 (1947), 192-212.

III. The Argument in the Middle Ages after Anselm

CHATILLON, J. "De Guillaume d'Auxerre à S. Thomas d'Aquin: L'Argument de S. Anselme chez les premiers scolastiques du XIIIe siècle," in *Spicilegium Beccense* (Paris: J. Vrin, 1959), 209-231.

DANIELS, A. "Quellenbeiträge und Untersuchungen zur Geschichte der Gottesbeweise im XIII Jahrhundert," in *Beiträge zur Geschichte der Philosophie des Mittelalters*, 8, 1-2 (Münster: Aschendorffsche Verlagsbuchhandlung, 1909).

DYROFF, A. "Der Ontologische Gottesbeweis des Hl. Anselmus in der Scholastik," in *Probleme der Gotteserkenntnis* (Münster: Aschendorff, 1928), 79-115.

HISLOP, I. "St. Thomas and the Ontological Argument," in *Contemplations* (Oxford: Blackfriars, 1949), 32-38.

PASCHEN, O. *Der Ontologische Gottesbeweis in der Scholastik* (Aachen, 1903).

PAULUS, J. "Henri de Gand et l'argument ontologique," in *Archives d'histoire doctrinale et littéraire du moyen age* (1935-36), 265-323.

PUECH, P. L. M. "Duns Scot et l'argument de Saint Anselme," in *Nos Cahiers* 2 (Montreal, 1937), 183-199.

IV. The Argument from Descartes to Kant

APEL, W. *Spinozas Verhältnis zum ontologischen Beweis*, (Leipzig, 1911).

BOYER, C. "De forma Leibniziana argumenti ontologici," in *Angelicum*, 14 (1937), 302-310.

CARNES, R. D. "Descartes and the Ontological Argument," in *Philosophy and Phenomenological Research*, 24 (1964), 502-511.

CRAHAY, F. "L'Argument ontologique chez Descartes et Leibniz et la critique kantienne," in *Revue philosophique de Louvain*, 47 (1949), 458-468.

ENGEL, S. M. "Kant's 'Refutation' of the Ontological Argument," in *Philosophy and Phenomenological Research* 24 (1963), 20-35.

FIMIMCE, JOSEPH DE "Position anselmienne et démarche cartésienne," in *Spicilegium Beccense* (Paris, 1959).

FLIMONS, S. "Kant and the Proofs for the Existence of God," in *American Catholic Quarterly*, 48 (1923), 14-48.

GOUHIER, H. "La Preuve ontologique de Descartes," in *Revue internationale de philosophie*, 8 (1954), 295-303.

GUÉROULT, M. *Nouvelles réflexions sur la preuve ontologique de Descartes* (Paris, 1955).

KERN, W. "Über den ontologischen Gottesbeweis in der metaphysik des 17. Jahrhunderts," in *Scholastik* 39 (1964), 87-107.

KOCH, P. *Der Gottesbeweis bei Leibniz; Darlegung und Kritik* (Freiburg, 1926).

KOYRÉ, A. *Essai sur l'idée de Dieu et les preuves de son existence chez Descartes* (Paris, 1922), 174-193.

MESNARD, P. "Les Preuves cartésiennes de l'existence de Dieu dans les *Méditations Métaphysiques*," in *Cartesio* (Milan, 1937), 599-614.

MILLER, ROBERT "The Ontological Argument in St. Anselm and Descartes," in *The Modern Schoolman*, 33 (1955-56), 31-38. The companion article on Anselm is listed in Section II E above.

NINK, C. "Zum ontologischen Gottesbeweis bei Kant," in *Philosophia Perennis* (Festgabe J. Geyser), 1 (Regensburg, 1930), 309-321.

V. The Hegelian and Idealist Use of Argument

CAIRD, E. *Introduction to the Philosophy of Religion* (Glasgow, 1880), 153-159.

——— "Anselm's Argument for the Being of God," in *Journal of Theological Studies*, 1 (1899), 23-39.

COCK, ALBERT A. "The Ontological Argument for the Existence of God," in *Aristotelian Society Proceedings*, 18 (1918), 363-384.

COLLINGWOOD, R. G. *An Essay on Philosophical Method* (Oxford: Clarendon Press, 1933), 123-136.

HAMELIN, O. "Valeur de la preuve ontologique," in *Les études philosophiques*, 12 (1957), 144-150.

HARRIS, E. E. *Revelation Through Reason* (New Haven: Yale University Press, 1958), 53-63, 88-94.

HEGEL, G. W. F. *Vorlesungen über die Philosophie der Religion*, edited by P. Marheincke (Berlin, 1832), II, 466-483: Anhang: Beweise für das Dasein Gottes. English translation by E. B. Speirs and J. B. Sanderson, *Lectures on the Philosophy of Religion* (London: Kegan Paul, Trench, Trübner & Co. Ltd., 1895) III, 347-367.

——— *Vorlesungen über die Geschichte der Philosophie*, edited by K. L. Michalet (Berlin, 1836), III, 164-169. English translation by E. S. Haldane and F. H. Simson, *Lectures on the History of Philosophy* (London, 1896), III, 62-67.

HOCKING, WILLIAM ERNEST "On the Ontological Argument in Royce and Others," in *Contemporary Idealism in America*, edited by Clifford Barrett (New York: The Macmillan Co., 1932).

RYLE, G. "Mr. Collingwood and the Ontological Argument," in *Mind*, 44 (1935), 137-151.

Reply: E. E. Harris, "Mr. Collingwood and the Ontological Argument; Reply to G. Ryle," in *Mind*, 45 (1936), 474-480.

Rejoinder: G. Ryle, "Back to the Ontological Argument," in *Mind*, 46 (1937), 53-57.

SCHUZE, W. "Karl Marx und der ontologische Gottesbeweis," in *Theologische Zeitschrift*, 10 (1954).

TILLICH, PAUL "The Two Types of Philosophy of Religion," in *Theology of Culture* (New York: Oxford University Press, 1959).

VI. The Argument in Recent Continental Philosophy

ABRANCHES, CASSIANO "O Argumento Ontologico," in *Revista Portuguesa de Filosofia*, 1 (1945), 341-355.

ALQUIÉ, F. *La Découverte métaphysique de l'homme chez Descartes* (Paris: Presses Universitaires de France, 1950), 226-238.

BLONDEL, M. *L'Action* (Paris: Alcan, 1893 and 1950), 343-350.

——— *L'Être et les êtres* (Paris: Alcan, 1935), 159-170.

——— *La Pensée* 1st ed. (Paris: Alcan, 1934), 1, 176-199, 390-400. 4th ed. (Paris: Presses Universitaires de France, 1948), 1, 164-180, 325-334.

CALA ULLOA, G. "La vera prova ontologica dell' estistenza di Dio," in *Angelicum*, 27 (1950), 196-209.

——— "Il naufragio argumento ontologico," in *Angelicum*, 28 (1951), 55-74.

CAPONE-BRAGA, C. "Il valore dell' argomento ontologico: Dialogo," in *Logos* (1936), 169-179.

DOMÍNGUEZ BERRUETA, JEAN "El Argumento Ontologico," in *Verdad y Vida*, 1 (1943), 370-376.

FOREST, A. "L'Argument de S. Anselme dans la philosophie reflexive," in *Spicilegium Beccense* (Paris: J. Vrin, 1959), 273-294.

GIULIANI, S. "La Vera prova ontologica dell' esistenza di Dio," in *Sapienza*, 2 (1949), 177-202.

JASPERS, K. *Philosophie* (Berlin: Springer), 1st ed. (1932), 3, 200-204; 2nd ed. (1948) 847-850.

LAVELLE, L. *De l'acte* (Paris: Aubier, 1934 and 1946), 222ff.

——— *De l'âme humaine* (Paris: Aubier, 1951), 102ff.

LE SENNE, R. *Introduction à la philosophie* (Paris: Alcan, 1925), 292-302.

PALIARD, J. "La Conscience de soi et l'idée de Dieu," in *Études philosophiques*. (1943).

——— *Intuition et réflexion* (Paris: Alcan, 1925), 187-208.

——— "Prière et dialectique d'après le *Proslogion* de S. Anselme," in *Dieu vivant*, 6 (1946), 51-70.

SCIACCA, M. F. *L'Existence de Dieu*, translated from the Italian by R. Jolivet (Paris: Aubier, 1951), 173-182.

SPRINGER, J. L. *Argumentum Ontologicum* (Assen: Van Goricum, 1947). A study of the argument based on Karl Jaspers' philosophy.

VII. The Argument in Recent British and American Philosophy

ALSTON, WILLIAM "The Ontological Argument Revisited," in *Philosophical Review*, 69 (1960), 452-474.

ARMOUR, L. "The Ontological Argument and the Concept of Completeness and Selection," in *Review of Metaphysics*, 14 (1961), 280-291.

BALZ, A. G. "Concerning the Ontological Argument," in *Review of Metaphysics*, 7 (1953), 207-224.

COOK, A. A. "The Ontological Argument for the Existence of God," in *Aristotelian Society Proceedings* 18 (1917-1918), 363-384.

FINDLAY, J. N. "Can God's Existence be Disproved?", in *Mind*, 57 (1948), 176-183. Reprinted in the *New Essays in Philosophical Theology*, edited by Antony Flew and Alasdair MacIntyre (London: S.C.M. Press Ltd., 1958), 47-56.
Replies by: G. E. Hughes, *ibid.*, 56-67.
A. C. A. Rainer, *ibid.*, 67-71.
Rejoinder by: J. N. Findlay, *ibid.*, 71-75.

GRANT, C. K. "The Ontological Disproof of the Devil," in *Analysis*, 17 (1957), 71-72.
Discussion by:
Richman, R. J., "The Ontological Proof of the Devil," in *Philosophical Studies* (Minn.), 9 (1958), 63f.
Waldman, T., "A Comment on the Ontological Proof of the Devil," in *Philosophical Studies* (Minn.), 10 (1959), 49f.

GRAVE, S. A. "The Ontological Argument of St. Anselm," in *Philosophy*, 27 (1952), 30-38.

HARTSHORNE, CHARLES *Man's Vision of God and the Logic of Theism* (Chicago, 1941).

——— "Formal Validity and Real Significance of the Ontological Argument," in *Philosophical Review*, 53 (1944), 225-245.

Reply with rejoinder: W. Elton, "On Hartshorne's Formulation of the Ontological Argument," in *Philosophical Review*, 54 (1945), 63-65.

Second reply with rejoinder: "Professor Hartshorne's Syllogism," in *Philosophical Review*, 54 (1945), 506-508.

——— "Logic of the Ontological Argument," in *Journal of Philosophy*, 58 (1961), 471-473.

——— "What did Anselm Discover?" in *Union Seminary Quarterly Review*, 7 (1962), 213-222.

——— *The Logic of Perfection and Other Essays in Neoclassical Metaphysics* (La Salle, Ill.: The Open Court Publishing Co., 1962), Ch. 2.

Discussion by:

Cobb, J. B., Jr. " 'Perfection Exists': A Critique of Charles Hartshorne," in *Religion in Life*, 32 (1963), 294-304.

Fitch, Frederick, "The Perfection of Perfection," in *The Monist*, 47 (1963), 466-471. (Discussion of Hartshorne's *The Logic of Perfection.*)

Hartt, J. "The Logic of Perfection," in *The Review of Metaphysics*, 16 (1963), 749-769.

Discussion by: Nelson, J. O. "Modal Logic and the Ontological Proof for God's Existence," in *The Review of Metaphysics*, 17 (1963), 235-242.

Reply: Hartshorne, Charles, *The Review of Metaphysics*, 17 (1964), 608f.

"Rationale of the Ontological Proof," in *Theology Today*, 20 (1963).

Anselm's Discovery: A re-examination of the ontological proof of God's existence (La Salle, Ill., 1965).

Kiteley, M. "Existence and the Ontological Argument," in *Philosophy and Phenomenological Research*, 18 (1958), 533-535.

MALCOLM, NORMAN "Anselm's Ontological Arguments," in *Philosophical Review*, 69 (1960), 41-62.

Discussion by:

Philosophical Review, 70 (1961), 56-111.

Allen, R. E. "Ontological Argument," 56-66.

Abelson, R. "Not Necessarily," 67-84.

Penelhum, T. "On the Second Ontological Argument," 85-92.

Plantings, A. "Valid Ontological Argument," 93-101.

Henle, P. "Uses of the Ontological Argument," 102-109.
Matthews, G. B. "On Conceivability in Anselm and Malcolm," 110f.
Baumer, W. H. "Anselm, Truth and Necessary Being," *Philosophy*, 37 (1962), 257f.
Brown, T. P. "Professor Malcolm on 'Anselm's Ontological Arguments,'" in *Analysis*, 22 (1961), 12-14.
Coburn, R. C. "Professor Malcolm on God," in *The Australasian Journal of Philosophy*, 41 (1963), 143-162.
Hardin, C. L. "An Empirical Refutation of the Ontological Argument," in *Analysis*, 22 (1961), 10-12.
Rejoinder to C. L. Hardin: L. Resnick, "A Logical Refutation of Mr. Hardin's Argument," in *Analysis*, 22 (1962), 90f.
Huggett, W. J. "The Nonexistence of Ontological Arguments," in *The Philosophical Review*, 71 (1962), 377-379.
Yolton, John W. "Professor Malcolm on St. Anselm, Belief, and Existence," in *Philosophy*, 36 (1961), 367-370.
Zabech, F. "Ontological Argument and How and Why Some Speak of God," in *Philosophy and Phenomenological Research*, 22 (1961), 206-215.
Reply by Charles Hartshorne: "How Some Speak and Yet Do not Speak of God," *ibid.*, 23 (1962), 274-276.
Rejoinder: F. Zabech "Category-Mistake," *ibid.*, 23 (1962), 227f.

RESCHER, N. "The Ontological Proof Revisited," in *Australasian Journal of Philosophy*, 37 (1959), 138-148.
Discussion by:
Gunderson, Keith and Routley, Richard. "Mr. Rescher's Reformulation of the Ontological Proof," in *Australasian Journal of Philosophy*, 38 (1960), 246-252.

RICHARDSON, C. C. "The Strange Fascination of the Ontological Argument," in *Union Seminary Quarterly Review*, 18 (1962), 1-21.
Discussion by:
Charles Hartshorne, *ibid.*, 244f.
Joran Brkić, *ibid.*, 246-249.
Richard Comstock, *ibid.*, 250-255.

RUNYAN, MARY E. "The Relationship between Ontological and Cosmological Arguments," in *The Journal of Religion*, 43 (1963), 56-58.

SHAFFER, J. "Existence, Predication and the Ontological Argument," in *Mind*, 71 (1962), 307-325.

SHELDON, W. H. "Another Form of the Ontological Proof," in *Philosophical Review*, 32 (1923), 355-372.
Reply: H. R. Smart, *Philosophical Review*, 33 (1924), 73-82.

VIII. The Logic of "Exists"

BAIER, K. "Existence," in *Aristotelian Society Proceedings*, 61 (1960), 19-40.

CARTWRIGHT, R. L. "Negative Existentials," in *Journal of Philosophy*, 57 (1960), 629-639.

EBERSOLE, F. B. "Whether Existence Is a Predicate," in *Journal of Philosophy*, 60 (1963), 509-524.

GEACH, P. T. "On What There Is," in *Aristotelian Society Proceedings*, Suppl. 25 (1951), 125-136.

HANCOCK, ROGER; WALHOUT, DONALD; and KANE, WILLIAM H. "Problems and Perplexities," in *The Review of Metaphysics*, 15 (1961), 126-134.

HARRÉ, R. "A Note on Existence Propositions," in *Philosophical Review*, 65 (1956), 548-549.

HOCHBERG, H. "St Anselm's Ontological Argument and Russell's Theory of Descriptions," in *The New Scholasticism*, 33 (1959), 319-330.

HOERNLÉ, R. F. A. "Notes on the Treatment of 'Existence' in Recent Philosophical Literature," in *Aristotelian Society Proceedings*, 23 (1923), 19-38.

KITELEY, M. "Is Existence a Predicate?", in *Mind*, 73 (1964), 364-373.

KNEALE, W. "Is Existence a Predicate?", in *Aristotelian Society Proceedings*, Suppl. 15 (1936). Reprinted in *Readings in Philosophical Analysis*, edited by Herbert Feigl and Wilfrid Sellars (New York, 1949), 29-43.

LEONARD, H. S. "The Logic of Existence," in *Philosophical Studies* (Minn.), 7 (1957), 49-64.

MOORE, G. E. "Is Existence a Predicate?", in *Aristotelian Society Proceedings*, Suppl. 15 (1936). Reprinted in *Logic and Language*, edited by Antony Flew, 2 (Oxford, 1959), 82-94.

NAKHNIKIAN, G., and SALMON, W. C. "'Exists' as a Predicate," in *Philosophical Review*, 66 (1957), 535-542.

RESCHER, N. "A Ninth-Century Arabic Logician on: Is Existence a Predicate?", in *Journal of the History of Ideas*, 21 (1960), 428-430. Reviewed by E. A. Moody, *Journal of Symbolic Logic*, 25 (1960), 345-346.

——— "On the Logic of Existence and Denotation," in *The Philosophical Review*, 68 (1959), 157-180.

ROSS, J. F. "Logically Necessary Existential Statements," in *Journal of Philosophy*, 58 (1961), 253-262.

——— "Does 'X Is Possible' Ever Yield 'X Exists'?", in *Theoria*, 28 (1962), 173-195.

RUSSELL, BERTRAND "The Existential Import of Propositions," in *Mind*, 14 (1905), 398-401.

RUSSELL, BERTRAND "On Denoting" (1st pub. 1905), in *Readings in Philosophical Analysis*, edited by Herbert Feigl and Wilfred Sellars (New York, 1949), 103-115.

RUSSELL, BERTRAND, and WHITEHEAD, A. N. *Principia mathematica* I (Cambridge, 1910), Introduction, Ch. I and Part I, Section B, 14.

RUSSELL, BERTRAND "The Philosophy of Logical Atomism" (1918), in *Logic and Knowledge*, edited by Robert C. Marsh (London, 1956).

——— *Introduction to Mathematical Philosophy* (London, 1920), Ch. 16.

——— *History of Western Philosophy* (London, 1946), 859-860.

RYLE, GILBERT "Systematically Misleading Expressions," in *Aristotelian Society Proceedings*, 1931-1932. Reprinted in *Logic and Language*, edited by Antony Flew, I (London, 1951), 11-36.

STRAWSON, P. F. "On Referring," in *Mind*, 59 (1950). Reprinted in *Essays in Conceptual Analysis*, edited by Antony Flew (London, 1956), 21-52.

IX. The Concept of Necessary Being

ABRAHAM, W. E. "Is the Concept of Necessary Existence Self-Contradictory?" in *Inquiry*, 5 (1962), 143-157.

FRANKLIN, R. L. "Necessary Being," in *Australasian Journal of Philosophy*, 35 (1957), 97-100.

HICK, JOHN "God as Necessary Being," in *The Journal of Philosophy*, 57 (1960), 725-734.

——— "Necessary Being," in *Scottish Journal of Theology*, 14 (1961), 353-369.

HUTCHINGS, P. Æ. "Necessary Being," in *Australasian Journal of Philosophy*, 35 (1957), 201-206.

——— "Necessary Being and Some Types of Tautology," in *Philosophy*, 39 (1964), 1-17.

KENNY, ANTHONY "Necessary Being," in *Sophia*, I (1962), 1-8.

——— "God and Necessity," in *British Analytical Philosophy*, ed. by Bernard Williams and Alan Montefiore (London and New York, 1966), 131-151.

PENELHUM, T. "Divine Necessity," in *Mind*, 69 (1960), 175-186.

PUCCETTI, R. "The Concept of God," in *Philosophical Quarterly*, 14 (1964), 237-245.

ROSS, J. F. "God and Logical Necessity," in *Philosophical Quarterly*, 11 (1961), 22-27.
Comment by C. J. F. Williams, *ibid.*, 356-359.

Index of Topics

Index of Names